Praise for *Sea*

'Richard Girling calls the sea our ci
His story of its violation by oil poll   , over-fishing, climate-
change-driven erosion and our belief that we have the wisdom to
"manage" the marine environment is shocking. It's a story of
arrogance, ignorance and greed, and in Girling's electrifying prose
it becomes a parable of wilful matricide.'
Richard Mabey

'For centuries our sea, less our lands, was what characterized us
as a people. Now we fly over it, seek it less for work and play, and
fail to recognize that it is in crisis. Richard Girling's wonderfully
informed, hard-hitting and inspired account of what is happening
on our shoreline shatters this ignorance. *Sea Change* is a book
which seems to be energized by the ocean itself and one which
could bring us back – just in time – to face the gains and losses of
our coast.'
Ronald Blythe

'Anyone who cares about the coast should read this book – before
it is too late.'
Nicholas Crane

Richard Girling is a senior feature writer for the *Sunday Times Magazine*. He was named Specialist Writer of the Year in the UK Press Awards in 2002 and shortlisted for the same award in 2005 and 2006. He has been a consultant to the former Department of the Environment and the Department of Culture, Media and Sport, and author of campaigns for the Campaign to Protect Rural England (CPRE). He is currently a trustee of the Tree Council. Richard Girling lives and works in North Norfolk.

Also by Richard Girling
and available from Eden Project Books

RUBBISH! – Dirt on Our Hands and Crisis Ahead

SEA CHANGE

Britain's Coastal Catastrophe

Richard Girling

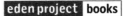

TRANSWORLD PUBLISHERS
61–63 Uxbridge Road, London W5 5SA
A Random House Group Company
www.rbooks.co.uk

First published in Great Britain in 2007 by Eden Project Books
an imprint of Transworld Publishers

This paperback edition published in 2008

A CIP catalogue record for this book
is available from the British Library.

ISBN 9781903919781

Addresses for Random House Group Ltd companies outside the UK
can be found at: www.randomhouse.co.uk
The Random House Group Ltd Reg. No. 954009

The Random House Group Limited supports The Forest Stewardship
Council (FSC), the leading international forest-certification organization. All our
titles that are printed on Greenpeace-approved FSC-certified paper carry the FSC logo.
Our paper procurement policy can be found at
www.rbooks.co.uk/environment

Typeset in Sabon by Falcon Oast Graphic Art Ltd.

Printed in the UK by CPI Cox & Wyman, Reading, RG1 8EX

2 4 6 8 10 9 7 5 3 1

For Caroline

Full fathom five thy father lies;
Of his bones are coral made:
Those are pearls that were his eyes:
Nothing of him that doth fade,
But doth suffer a sea-change
Into something rich and strange.
Sea-nymphs hourly ring his knell:
Ding-dong.
Hark! Now I hear them, – ding-dong, bell.

Shakespeare, *The Tempest*

Contents

Acknowledgements

Few books rely entirely on material purposefully gathered for them – this one certainly doesn't. Many people over the years helped unknowingly with the accumulation of facts and ideas that have somehow grown into what I hope may be a cogent pattern of thought. A complete list of contributors and consultees would have to include my long-dead grandparents, my parents, various Norfolk neighbours, men in pubs and writers of every period and style from Homer to the Parliamentary Counsel Office. To acknowledge every source from which I have drawn benefit – often without knowing that I was doing so – would require an application of memory-enhancing drugs and immunity to writer's cramp. I shall not attempt it.

To the many who did knowingly help, however, I extend the customary thanks for their generosity and assurances that mistakes are all my own work. For some of them, the only reward for their kindness will be to see me rudely disagree with them in print. To these few in particular, I offer apologies as well as thanks. I apologize also for the absence of source notes and bibliography, though readers will find the most important sources acknowledged in the text. In addition to those acknowledgements, I would like also to mention – and to recommend – two books in particular. Ian Friel's *Maritime History of Britain and Ireland* is a fine single-volume encapsulation of a very long and complex story. And *England's Sea Fisheries*, edited by David J. Starkey, Chris Reid and Neil Ashcroft, is an exemplary compilation of many authors' work that charts every movement of every fleet – indeed, it counts almost every fish - from the Middle Ages to the 21st century. I leant on it heavily in the historical section of

Chapter 4, and would like to acknowledge particularly my debt to the work of Evan Jones, David Butcher, Michael Haines and Chris Reid. For those with an obsessive interest in the UK fishing industry (and time to spare), I recommend Defra's national fishery statistics, published annually and available on its website.

Others I would like to thank are: Karen Bermingham; Alan Brampton; David Cheslin; Peter Cullum; Trevor Dixon; Ted Edwards; John Ford; Peter Frew; Malcolm Kerby; Norman Lamb MP; Heather Leggate; Jason Lowe; Philip Lymbury; Malcolm MacGarvin; David Oakes; Bruce Sandison; Jeremy Smart; Don Staniford; Andrew Traill; Debbie Walker; Richard Whitehouse; plus the media staffs of Defra, the Scottish Executive, Scottish Environment Protection Agency, HM Revenue and Customs, the Maritime and Coastguard Agency, RSPB, WWF and many others. Too often writers and journalists forget to acknowledge those who help us most.

I thank also Robin Morgan, editor of the *Sunday Times Magazine*, for encouraging me to write about so many of the subjects that would find their way into this book, and allowing the recycling here of an occasional paragraph or two. Thanks, too, to my editors, Mike Petty at the Eden Project and Susanna Wadeson at Transworld; to my ever-alert copy editor, Deborah Adams; and to my editor-in-chief, provider of ideas and inspiration, my wife, Caroline McGhie.

CHAPTER ONE

The Rim of Salt

There is sudden silence, a moment of terror so primal that the synapses are closed to all but animal instinct. In this green, cold absence of light, no words can form. Even if they could, they would not translate into sound. I do not scream until I am rescued.

Two young fathers have been pushing their sons back and forth on an airbed. The airbed, like so much in the post-war era, is khaki; the swimsuits, of fathers and sons alike, of saggy, navy wool. On the beach, where mothers sit in their summer cottons, the needles clack like Morse over the humdrum murmur of speech. The waves themselves are like ribbed knitting, hardly waves at all, no louder than licked ice-cream. One of the mothers comes down to paddle, skirt hitched, shoulders hunched over her red box Brownie. The label in the family album will say 'Point Clear, Essex, 1953'.

The seaside then was a kind of bliss. Take away the war, join together the cut ends of the Thirties and the Fifties, and nothing much had changed. 'Summer holidays' still meant a windy week on a stony English beach. Railway compartments still tempted travellers with muted prints of cliffs and coves. Bank holidays still saw mass migrations of small black cars – Fords, Morrises, Austins – and doughty, mackintoshed men piloting their families coastwards on motorbike and sidecar. In their Sunday suits they flew box kites, rode the dodgems and drove home again sticky with candyfloss and peppermint rock. Though the word 'charabanc' had fallen from use, its spirit was inextinguishable: Sunday school and works outings were little different from the one described by Laurie Lee in *Cider with Rosie*. Newspapers still promoted themselves with inky silhouettes of trilby-hatted mystery men who were paid to lurk in seaside towns and wait for readers to spot them. All you needed was a copy of the morning edition and the nerve to call out: 'You are Lobby Lud. I claim my five pounds.'

Point Clear is at St Osyth, on the Colne estuary in Essex. In 1953 it is a wooden shanty town of balconied chalets, many of them rented by the week. They have chemical lavatories, Calor gas rings and chancy plumbing, all with unforgettable smells. Children catch green shore crabs with lead-weighted lines at high tide; parents grub for cockles on the ebb. Mid-tide, there is the airbed. The young fathers, soldiers not long demobbed, become more energetic, propelling their seven-year-olds faster and faster until we are bucking over the wavelets like rodeo riders. The capsize is the most shocking thing that has ever happened to me. I cannot swim; I have never before immersed my head in water. The fathers are only waist-deep but I go down and down through the cabbage-green sea, disconnected from time and thought, sinking to cold infinity. More than fifty years later, it remains the closest thing to a near-death experience I can remember. The fathers panic too, plunging into the streaming water, groping for arms and legs. Long seconds pass before I am hoisted by an ankle, gulping with terror, to be wrapped in a towel and calmed with barley sugar on the beach.

You can't live in Britain and have no feeling for the sea. It is the amniotic fluid in which our civilization grew and was shaped. In sub-Freudian ways it lubricates our dreams and fires our imagination. In its presence we are mute spectators at a demonstration of unanswerable power – Cnut could have chosen no more potent a metaphor for the impotence of kings. The Atlantic and its inlets, the Channel and the Irish and North Seas, are the most powerful drivers of our economy, culture and politics. Our rim of salt has determined what we eat, how we use the land, how we relate to our neighbours, how and where we travel, even the thickness of our coats. Insulated by the Gulf Stream, our winters are 10 degrees warmer than Newfoundland's. The sea is what gives us our cherished landscape of oak and beechwoods. It's why we're so good at rain. It brought us the people – Romans, Vikings, Saxons, Normans – who filled our veins and shaped our culture, and kept out undesirables like Napoleon, Hitler and rabies.

Our national heroes – Nelson, Drake – have a nautical bias. The benchmark for commercial competence is the ability to run a whelk stall, and no town in the land escapes the odour of frying fish. We are, above all else, children of the ocean, never more than 72 miles from a coast. The family photographs are private extensions of the national psyche – hearts are of oak, horizons are blue, and Britannia rules the waves. If we had no other god we would probably worship it, for like a god it demands obedience, gratitude and fear.

My juvenile *memento mori* has left me with nothing worse than a lifelong determination to keep my head above water. But the North Sea earlier that same year had brought to eastern England a murderous devastation unparalleled in peacetime Britain. It will do the same again, and worse, for this most edgy and unpredictable of neighbours is growing more irascible. We have fouled it, plundered it, poisoned it, stripped it of fish and interfered with the climate. God-like it has given; and now, god-like, it will take away.

The international standard for the salinity of the sea is 35g of dissolved salts per litre of water, or 35 per cent. No surprise: the standard originates from Britain, though it was fixed not at one of our world-famous seaports – Plymouth, Dartmouth,

Portsmouth or Southampton – but in the landlocked county of Surrey, at the National Institute of Oceanography at Wormley. In all, more than 70 dissolved elements are traceable in seawater, but 99 per cent of the total is composed of just six – chloride, sodium, sulphate, magnesium, calcium and potassium. There is iron there, and manganese and gold, and plenty of other stuff too, but the concentrations are so weak that they are measurable only in parts per million. Salts get into the water in a number of different ways – from volcanic eruptions, chemical reactions between sea and rock, and the weathering of rocks into soils that wash into the water.

From this you would expect it to be getting saltier all the time, with marine life under pressure constantly to adapt, but strangely it isn't. The University of Saskatchewan is kind enough to make its geology class notes available on the internet, and from these I learn that, despite all the eruptions, leachings and grindings down, the chemical composition of the oceans, as deduced by geologists, has changed little over billions of years. Various mechanisms have been proposed to explain this. When an arm of the sea gets cut off from the ocean, the water may evaporate and leave the salts as a dry deposit. More is lost in sea spray blowing on to land, or by chemical interaction of seawater with sediment, or is absorbed into the skeletal frameworks of living organisms. Most importantly there is a constant circulation of seawater through the ocean crust that filters out magnesium and sulphate. Someone has worked out that the entire volume of all the world's oceans circulates in this way once every five or ten million years. This is fascinating in its way, but geology is not famous for sudden excitements and, as a science still in its infancy, it can't do much more than add a bit of labelling to what we already know. The sea is powerful, mysterious, salty, and very, very old.

Oceans have been washing the globe for 3,800 million years, chiselling the continents, alternately swallowing and regurgitating land, nibbling away at even the hardest rock. The process is constant but not always steady. Change may be too slow to measure in human time-spans; or it may be sudden and cataclysmic.

4

In June 1999, for example, Scarborough's four-star Holbeck Hall Hotel – grandiloquently timbered, gabled and lawned – collapsed like a fainting duchess when the South Cliff keeled away beneath. It made headlines, yet on England's volatile eastern flank it was just one more casualty on a very long list. Yorkshire's Holderness coast has fallen back by 32km (20 miles) in a million years, and 400m in 2,000. In the middle Stone Age, between 10,000 and 5,000 years ago when oceans of water were still locked in ice, much of what is now the North Sea was land roamed by hunters. For obvious reasons the volume of archaeological evidence is small, but enough stone tools – blades, scrapers, arrowheads – have been found under the water to show where and how they lived. Loss of land to the eastern sea is a *process*, not an event – a process that will influence our far-off descendants as much as it did our forebears. Drowned villages, whole medieval towns, lie on the seabed where – unless the government revises its policy on shoreline defence (see Chapter 2) – more will surely soon follow. The gradualness of the process does not preclude catastrophe. The loss of a church over a cliff edge is no less dramatic for being predictable; a great sea flood no less traumatic for being the cumulative effect of long-term change.

Such things are watermarked not only in our own culture, but on every continent on earth. More than 200 flood legends have been recorded, including most famously the Epic of Gilgamesh, the tale of a Sumerian king first written on clay tablets around 2000 BC. According to legend, a mortal, Utnapishtim, is warned by a god to build a great boat to protect 'all the living things of the earth'. There then occurs a flood so vast that even the gods are afraid. The parallels are obvious. Here, more familiarly, is Genesis VII, verse 23: 'And every living substance was destroyed which was upon the face of the ground, both man, and cattle, and the creeping things, and the fowl of the heaven; and they were destroyed from the earth: and Noah only remained alive, and they that were with him in the ark.'

Every child is taught the story. A wrathful God sends a flood that takes 150 days to abate. Every creature is drowned except Noah, his family and the animals, 'two of every sort', that he has driven on to the ark. Give or take a few biblical fundamentalists in Kansas, no one confuses this with the actual story of the planet. On the other hand, the dramatic extravagance of mythology does not preclude the possibility of an underlying truth, for there must be a reason why flood myths have flourished in so many different cultures around the world. Is it not likely that legends like these, written down centuries after the catastrophes they describe and embroidered by generations of storytellers, were based on real events? That dramatic licence and superstition set off a chain reaction in which local floods swelled into great inundations drowning entire worlds? By this interpretation, Noah's Flood is much easier to accept.

During the last few millennia of the Ice Age there was indeed a flood so great that anyone might have thought it stretched from one side of the earth to the other. The cause of it was melting ice, which had been gathering in freshwater lakes. One of these covered part of the land that now lies beneath the Black Sea. From a small pool, this had grown slowly into a huge oasis, surrounded by settlements and, crucially, lying some 500ft below the level of the Mediterranean. As ice went on melting, so seas went on rising. What happened next, 7,500 years ago, was so sudden, so cataclysmic and terrifying, that only one explanation was possible. The gods had looked down from their window in the sky, had not liked what they had seen and were in a rage. To get a notion of what might really have happened, look at a map of the Aegean Sea. You will see that in the north-east corner, taking a snip out of western Turkey, is a narrow inlet called the Sea of Marmara. At the time we are talking about, a narrow ridge of land separated this from the low-lying ground that contained the glacial lake. Higher and higher up this ridge crept the ice-fed waters of the sea. Heavier and heavier became the pressure on the land. Finally, with all the weight of the Mediterranean behind it, the Sea of Marmara burst through and drowned the country on the other side.

Ten cubic miles of seawater a day churned through the gap – the present-day Bosporus – raising the lake by six inches a day and flooding 60,000 square miles in less than a year. The sea, as it had now become, rose 500ft. Settlements in modern-day Turkey, Bulgaria, Moldova, Ukraine, Russia and Georgia disappeared beneath the waves and their people fled to the mountains. It is easy to imagine them making rafts or boats, even driving a few animals on to them; and so, in these simple acts of self-preservation, was born a legend. In the orthodox version, Noah lands on Mount Ararat, near the Armenian border in north-east Turkey, but this now seems improbable. If any family washed up anywhere, then a low hill far to the west is much more likely. But it doesn't matter. It's not the postcode that interests us but the power of the legend – a legend with too many factual overlaps to be explained by imagination alone. We are prompted to look not so much into our conscious minds as into our natures, into the primal sources of instinct and fear. The romantic view of the sea as something sublime, supernatural and exotic was not a poetic invention of the 18th century. Stories of sea monsters, devils and gods are even older than the languages in which they are expressed, and there is no more powerful a symbol of divine and eternal power. Christ didn't walk on air, remember. He walked on water.

The creation of the Black Sea is a classic example of a process that did more than any other to etch the outline of the known world. The writers of Genesis could have placed their mythical flood almost anywhere on the planet, including southern England. As the Ice Age dribbled to a close and the pulsating force of water replaced the slow grinding of ice, great rivers including the Rhine and the Thames (whose course had been shoved southward by the freeze) were pouring into a huge natural reservoir in what is now the southern North Sea. They were like taps filling a bath, held in by the wall of chalk – the so-called 'land bridge' –

that joined Dover to Cap Gris Nez. Had Noah been English or French, now would have been the time to get busy on the ark. The bridge was too weak to stand against the mounting sea. One hesitates to call 'catastrophic' an event that would contribute so decisively to the character and self-image of the country to the north, but it must have felt like the wrath of god. When the chalk fell, water burst into the valleys beyond, hurling huge boulders against what would become the cliffs of France. Had the story passed down through a scribe, his account of it would have had the authentic, apocalyptic ring of the Old Testament. As it is, we must depend on the deductive skills of geologists.

With its umbilicus from the motherland thus severed, the infant island set about defining itself. We took, as we continue to take, pride in our insular state. It is said of England's villages – falsely, in my opinion – that it takes newcomers 10, 20, even 25 years to earn the right of belonging. In the 20th and 21st centuries we have struggled with our historical selves, wrestling with new concepts of Britishness that have drawn new boundaries as fast as they have wiped away old ones. Our attitude to the natural world, where extreme views are not tested for political correctness, amounts almost to eco-fascism. In the case of trees, for example, our idea of what belongs in Britain verges on the biblical, as if nature had been handed down perfectly formed and was immutable. There is an almost Kansan resistance to change that will be tested – and tested far beyond its limit – as the climate warms, sea levels rise and species migrate.

To a purist, the word 'native' in this context has a precise and iron-clad meaning which, oddly, celebrates our apartness by pre-dating the Flood. A native British tree is one that colonized the land *after* the retreat of the ice but *before* separation from the continent. It is an arboreal aristocracy of just thirty-three species:

alder, ash, aspen, bay willow, beech, bird cherry, black poplar, box, common oak, crab apple, crack willow, downy birch, field maple, goat willow, hawthorn, hazel, holly, hornbeam, juniper, large-leaved lime, midland thorn, rowan, Scots pine, sessile oak, silver birch, small-leaved lime, strawberry tree, whitebeam, white willow, wild cherry, wild service tree, wych elm, yew.

Anything that crossed the water thereafter – common lime, elder, English elm, fir, holm oak, horse chestnut, larch, laurel, London plane, mulberry, sycamore, walnut, weeping willow – is a foreigner whose fate in conserved 'ancient' woodland is to be grubbed out like a weed. In the most literal way possible, the sea was the cut-off point. Our pride lay in being different, and the difference was fixed the moment the waters closed. In one way or another, in everything from lapdogs to the royal family, we have been obsessed with pedigree ever since. As each new wave of seaborne invaders – Romans, Angles, Saxons, Jutes, Vikings, Normans – broke across the shore, so we wove their bloodlines into a bizarre tapestry of breeding. By the 19th century it had all but driven us mad. Bearded ideologues believed they could classify the entire human population into historical breeds, like sheep. They spoke of the Old Black Breed, the Sussex, the Anglian, the Bronze Age Cumberland, the Neolithic Devon, the Teutonic-Black Breed Cross, the Inishmaan, the Brunet Welsh ... Some were dark and woolly; others fair and shorn. Some plump; some wiry. All were photographed for William Z. Ripley's anthropological field guide of 1900, *The Races of Europe*. Defined by a specific angle of brow, a roundness of head, a particular weight and stature, a length of nose, they gaze into the middle distance with the faraway, disinterested look of ruminants.

What the sea had brought us was snobbery. 'Native' Britons might be as old as the trees but, in the case of *Homo sapiens*, unlike *quercus* or *salix*, it was the latecomers who set the tone. 'The aristocracy,' said Ripley, then an assistant professor at the Massachusetts Institute of Technology, 'everywhere tends towards the blond and tall type, as we should expect.' The old British types, by contrast, tended to 'irregularity and ruggedness. The mouth is large, the upper lip broad, the cheek bones prominent.' Noses, too, were generally sizeable and 'not often very delicately formed'. A Victorian cleric, Bishop Whately, in his *Notes on Noses*, bluntly classified the British nasal standard as the 'anti-cogitative' type, as if the size of the snout were in inverse proportion to its owner's capacity to think. Most persistent of all, said Ripley, were the 'overhanging pent-house brows'.

This kind of stuff is unutterable now, but then it was as close to the scientific mainstream as the theory of gravity or movement of the planets. After Darwin, nothing lived that was not measured, classified and labelled, and this applied as much to dukes and swineherds as it did to orchids and finches. With calipers, rulers and weights, Victorian physicians and reverend gentlemen, gripped by the new science of 'anthropometry', toured the British Isles categorizing their fellow men with a zeal that stopped only just short of the specimen jar. The British Association for the Advancement of Science appointed an expert Anthropometric Committee, which in 1883 published a paper 'defining the facial characteristics of the races and principal crosses in the British Isles'.

After thousands of years of island living, we were still struggling with something very like tribalism. The human field guide was *Crania Britannica*, a vast, double-volume survey of skulls by the craniologists Joseph Barnard Davis and John Thurnam, for whom racial classification was not just a matter of physical differentiation but of psychological, intellectual and moral pedigree too. In this cranial caste system, the very lowest status was accorded to those who were suspected of having been here the longest; those whose earliest forebears may have walked here rather than sailed.

All too clearly we can see where this was leading. Supremacy, it was argued, belonged to the seafarers. In 1924, in *The Phoenician*

Origins of Britons, Scots and Anglo-Saxons, L. A. Waddell argued that 'civilisation properly so-called' began with the 'Aryanisation' of Britain in about 2800 BC, when, he believed, it was brought here by Phoenicians in the tin, bronze and amber trades. These great civilizers, he wrote, were 'Aryans in Speech, Script and Race – tall, fair, broad-browed and long-headed'. Ironically, in the light of what was to come, he dismissed the Germans as 'fair round-heads' and not 'Aryan' at all. The Germans, as would become all too horribly clear, had theories of their own. Hans F. K. Gunther, in *The Racial Elements of European History*, mourned the 'terrible contra-selection of the best blood' caused by the loss of officers in the First World War, and concluded that England had descended into a mongrelized pit of miscegenation. As a result, English skulls were growing shorter and rounder, less Nordic and less capacious. He quoted with approval a writer named Peters:

> The healthy English strain of the time of Dickens is no more. The old fair Anglo-Saxon population of 'Merry England' that worked on the land, and were the mainstay of Wellington's army and Nelson's ships, no longer exists. In its stead there is making its way more and more every year into the industrial towns a small, dark strain, in the midst of which the old aristocracy and the gentry stand out like isolated blond giants.

You can imagine what he had to say about 'the Jewish problem'. And so, in less than 50 years, the hobby-science of Victorian vicars brought us to Hitler and the greatest catastrophe of modern times. No longer could we speak innocently of 'race' and 'blood'. Racial history was not just politically incorrect; it was politically unthinkable. It was also, for the most part, just plain wrong. We are people enclosed by sea, across which our ancestors sailed at various times, from various points of origin and with varying degrees of bellicosity. But we are not tribespeople defined by our ancestry and bound by ancient bloodlines.

We have history in our veins. The sea did not just bring us here; it made us what we are.

Just before sunset, by a creek in North Norfolk, I watch a family canoeing homeward after a picnic. They have left it late and are silhouetted against the water, two lithe figures bending at the paddles, two more lolling in between. The falling tide has exposed acres of salty mud, forcing them seaward and doubling their journey to the quay. The murmur of their voices ('fish and chips', I hear) is drowned by the piccolo piping of wading birds. Behind them a long, low spit of shingle, home to terns and seals, merges with the dusk. Their bright beachwear and the pillar-box red of their plastic canoe are neutralized by the shadow so that nothing remains but their shape. It is an image as old as history. Fragile boat; infinite sea; frail humanity. From this distance it would look no different if the canoe were a dugout and its crew a Mesolithic family in furs.

No one can say when the first vessel braved a British sea but, whenever it was, the boat will have been a proto-canoe made from a hollowed tree. Its paddlers would have had no word for 'picnic', though food would not have been far from their minds. Like the modern family in its leisure-craft, they would have hugged the shore and been wary of pitting themselves against ocean swells. You don't get much freeboard with a log. The oldest surviving log-boat in Britain is a monster from the Iron Age, the so-called Hasholme Boat, currently being conserved at the Hull and East Riding Museum, which is 41ft long and was hewn from a single oak in around 300 BC. In terms of prehistoric time-spans, this is almost modern. An example from the Netherlands pushes the log-boat tradition in Northern Europe right back deep into the Mesolithic, to at least 7000 BC. Who knows what they thought was beyond the horizon? To me, whose courage is tested by an airbed, the idea of launching into the unknown is ungraspable.

Given the evidence of trade and culture, there is no reason to suppose that British Stone-Agers were any less intrepid than the Netherlanders. Archaeologists now believe Mesolithic people took to the sea in pursuit of fish (they certainly had sea-fish in their diets). Barry Cunliffe, Professor of European Archaeology at Oxford University, argues that people who hunted on land were likely also to have developed the habit of following the shoals at sea. If so, it looks like a pivotal point in the development of world communication. 'Both activities [hunting and fishing]', Cunliffe writes, 'required navigational skills and it could well be argued that it was in the Upper Palaeolithic-Mesolithic period that communities learned to use celestial phenomena to chart their courses.' He goes further. The extraordinary similarities in Mesolithic culture around Europe's Atlantic coasts, he reckons, are explicable only if we assume people travelled by sea.

By the time Julius Caesar arrived, the local shipbuilding tradition was well established. Log-boats were still popular, but other technologies were not only flourishing but already had long histories of their own. Hides had been stretched over wooden frames to make boats for at least five centuries (Pliny in the 1st century BC mentions such vessels being involved in the cross-Channel delivery of tin), and the earliest known planked boat in Britain dates to between 1890 and 1700 BC. We have a habit of underestimating the imagination and skill of our early ancestors, while puzzling over the enormity of their achievements. Like all manifestations of genius, it brings you up short and makes you wonder how rapid would have been the course of human progress if everyone had possessed brains and fingers like one's own. A Bronze Age boat found in the Humber estuary was over 43ft long, with a large, two-section keel and planked sides literally stitched together with twisted yew. The entire structure was internally braced; the seams caulked with moss and sealed with laths to protect the stitching and make them watertight. It is reckoned that 18 paddlers would have been able to drive it forward at up to six knots, carrying a total load, crew and cargo, of four-and-a-half tons. English modesty obliges us to confess that the workmanship was not up to the standard of, say, the ancient Egyptians, who had been building planked ships since at least 2600 BC, but modesty is a minor virtue, much overpraised. Think Bronze Age Britain. Think plank-built boat. Think maritime genius.

And so it went on. Subsequent refinements included oars, masts and sails, all of which appeared in northern Europe long after they were common in the Mediterranean. Caesar found a northern Atlantic confidently plied by nailed, plank-built square riggers heeling under the power of rawhide sails. The importance of markets was as well understood by the Roman Empire as it would be by Victoria's England or Bush's America. Early exports were based on tin, woollen cloth, leather and slaves. Wine and the Christian religion came in the other direction. As Vikings followed Saxons, Normans followed Vikings and sail turned to steam, the bones, sinews and organs of a maritime nation developed and went on growing. Trade meant wealth, and wealth meant power – a simple truth that has put wind in our sails, coal in our boilers, diesel in our tanks and muck on our beaches ever since. As we shall see in Chapter 7, the statistics of modern international trade and the ships that service it are almost meaninglessly vast, and our reliance on them total. Almost everything you use or consume – including the words and fabric of this book – will have depended for its existence on something imported. As we shall also see, this has opened us to a new kind of raider, subtler than the Vikings but no less predatory, whose ransom demand is rather more than Danegeld.

The greatest indignity for a country with so much salt in its blood is that, no matter how lustily we sing, there is no meaningful way in which, in commercial terms at least, Britannia now rules the waves. For more than a century, Britain's ocean liners dominated the North Atlantic and brought film-star glamour and sex appeal to the business of travelling between continents. In the Cunard Line's *Queen Mary* (launched 1934) and *Queen Elizabeth* (1938), John Brown & Co's Clydebank shipyard built two of the most iconic passenger vehicles in the entire history of travel. The liners themselves were superstars whose celebrity was more than equal to the royal personages whose names they bore, and simply to step aboard was to be granted membership of a global elite. Even ashore, the Cunard house style drove architectural high fashion – the new Odeon cinemas looked less like theatres than landlocked ocean queens. At sea, repeated attempts on the Blue Riband transatlantic record were the maritime equivalents of modern F1 motor racing, using speed to keep a brand name in the public eye. These intercontinental dashes were gloriously gung-ho, in a way that would make 21st-century finance directors reach for the oxygen. The fuel cost of each extra knot of speed was equivalent to the total cost of the first 20. The writing, however, if not actually on the wall was certainly in the sky. By the time the *Queen Mary* claimed the Blue Riband in 1938 with a 30-knot Atlantic crossing in three days, 21 hours and 48 minutes, she was already facing her aerial nemesis. Eleven years earlier, Charles Lindbergh's *Spirit of St Louis* had completed the trip in just 33 hours. The *Queen Mary* was withdrawn from service in 1967, and the *Queen Elizabeth* followed soon after.

It's very different now. Ocean liners still provide stately, dress-for-dinner holiday cruises for well-off middle-agers celebrating their retirements, but shipbuilding has gone the way of all other heavy industry in the UK. Working at only around 50 per cent capacity, it is more concerned now with repairs and conversions than it is with launching Atlantic record-breakers. There is utility in its output but little of the glamour that characterized its long reign as world market leader. According to the Shipbuilders and Shiprepairers Association, the primary market for British yards now is for fishing boats, dredgers, ferries, tugs, 'short sea mini-bulkers', gas and chemical carriers and other plain-faced daughters of toil. The direct workforce of 24,000 (plus 50,000 in support and supply industries) currently builds between 25 and 30 vessels a year, generating between £1.6m and £2.0bn. Like computers, televisions, trainers and jeans, the bulk of the deep-sea market has migrated to where labour is cheapest – to the Far East, and especially to South Korea, which has built its national economy on it. The one consolation is that it is not just the British industry that has suffered as the global economy has restructured itself over the last 30 years – the rest of Europe and the US have fared no better.

The sea impacts on our lives in more ways than we may realize. Our agrarian landscape, for example, in part is a legacy of the last war when German U-boats compelled us to raise our level of self-sufficiency. The vulnerability of merchant convoys to attack, and the food rationing that lasted well into peacetime, are sharp reminders – as if any were needed – of our reliance on seaborne trade, and the secure protection of a Royal Navy which, in the vanishingly improbable event of an invasion by sea, could be expected to honour the tradition of Nelson and Drake. (I recognize that this one passing reference does scant justice to the history of Britain as a naval power, but it is a subject that has been so exhaustively chronicled by so many historians that I have no urge to compete.)

Yet these are not the images that come to mind when most of us – I mean we landsmen – hear the word 'sea'. We see penny arcades, buckets and spades, jellyfish, sand, plodding donkeys and the pier. The English seaside is less a geographical feature than a cultural construct – a salty stew of eternal childhood and innocent old age, impervious to reality. It is in trying to reconnect adult perception with childhood memory that I find myself, on a sunlit February morning, on Platform 3 at Fenchurch Street Station in the City of London. Pilgrimage maybe is an overly portentous word to attach to a day at the seaside, but I can think of none better. I travel as a pilgrim should, alone.

The 10.30 to Shoeburyness is as near empty as makes no difference. Of the few who climb aboard, I am the only one going as far as Southend Central (or anywhere else much beyond Basildon). Last time I rode this line I was in short trousers and in the care of my maternal grandfather. The queen was still the radiant young Princess Elizabeth and school stopped once a year for Empire Day. Like any ordinary London family, and despite the fact that it's been 40 years since any of us actually paid it a visit, mine enjoys a historic relationship with Southend. My other grandfather earned his 15 minutes of fame there in the 1920s when, forgetting he couldn't swim, he jumped into the sea after a girl who had slipped from a jetty. He earned also the displeasure of my grandmother, for spoiling his suit.

Yes, *suit*. Even as late as the 1950s, men dressed for the seaside in their best blue three-piece, stiff collar and tie, watch-chain and trilby. Those who possessed two pairs of boots might nod to informality by wearing the brown. Since then, for reasons seen every summer at the airports, the British seaside has been written off more times than the English novel, and has just as often been reinvented. It is doing so again now, though each tweak scrapes off another layer of its identity. Ignore the decrepitude of Southend Central (the station has not grown old gracefully), and you could believe that you had indeed stepped off in Basildon.

The High Street – pedestrianized, brick-paved, bollarded – is a homogenized chunk of Anytown. Relics of the old, classically inspired grandeur survive on the upper floors, but street level is a mess of corporate liveries, indifferent to their context and lacking even the right kind of bad taste. Only the lozenge of sky at the seaward end, with its deep grey horizon, offers any clue as to place. It is not until you reach the Royal Hotel that you get the first hint of seaside style, the two-fingered salute of cheek against chic. A cut-price menu, and posters in the window offering live entertainment from ShitDisco.

It's not just Southend. Wherever land meets sea, the pressures are the same. The collapse of the fishing industry was balanced in part by tourism, which grew rapidly after the Holidays With Pay Act in 1938. (Ironically, both trends were driven by the railways. As their hunger for freight once encouraged overfishing, so now they brought the August hordes.) As it happened, there was little time for relaxation before beaches and piers were commandeered for very different purposes in the war, but the 1950s stirred themselves for a kind of last hurrah.

The coasts of England and Wales were crusted with resorts, each of which held the promise of escape, if not always of romance. The south coast offered Ramsgate, Hastings, Eastbourne, Brighton, Worthing, Bognor, Bournemouth, Torquay and Paignton. Round the toe end of Cornwall came Newquay; then Minehead, Weston-super-Mare and the Welsh fun-spots of Tenby, Aberystwyth, Barmouth, Bangor, Llandudno and Rhyl. The north-west had Southport, Blackpool, Morecambe. The long east coast, exposed and crumbling, was practically held together by its piers and promenades, all the way from Whitley Bay to Broadstairs. All claimed to be of unique character – sunniest, cheapest, healthiest, poshest – and to be either the pinnacle of good taste (Torquay) or fun-on-a-budget (Clacton). They fought for trade as fiercely as national tourist boards do now, and inspired some of the earliest examples of consumer journalism.

In August 1951 the *News of the World* sent its reporter 'in search of 20s worth of value for £1'. What with coach fares, sweets, fizzy drinks and ice-cream for the children (not even the *NoW* then had 'kids'), the arithmetic was shocking. 'Bless my soul,' said our man, 'we hadn't got to the seaside yet and I had spent £1 18s 5½d [approx £1.92].' By the end of the day, after pedal boats, speedboat ride, more ice-cream, a memorably awful lunch, paddle-steamer, deck chairs and a variety show on the pier, his expense account had been hit for £6 8s 4½d (£6.45). Even grossed up to its current equivalent of £137.13, this doesn't look obviously bad value for a family of four on a binge.

A quarter of a century later, in June 1975, domestic holidays still merited a two-page banner. *Don't let them diddle you by the seaside*, it urged. Round the coast went the paper's investigators again, jotting down the prices of roundabout rides, Pepsi-Cola, fish and chips, gin and tonic, jellied eels, buckets and spades, silly hats, admission to the pier, cups of tea. It's not so much the prices that suck you into the past (seven pieces of jellied eel at

Southend's Kursaal for 35p; gin and tonic at the Druid's Head, Brighton, for a penny less); it's the comparators themselves. Jellied eels! Halves of bitter! This was the year in which Queen's 'Bohemian Rhapsody' topped the charts, yet the seaside was stuck in the age of Gracie Fields, and Britain's biggest-selling newspaper was raging about watery eel and a 10p hike in the price of Kiss-me-Slowly hats. Even nostalgia was beginning to show its age. The early 1970s had been a late and cruelly deceptive boom time for the English resorts. Now, from the middle of the decade, they fell into steep decline.

Cheap-and-cheerful is the riskiest of all marketing ploys. Not only is fish-and-chip culture a bold call against the sophistication of 'abroad', but it's on a short, fast and direct route to end-of-the-line tawdriness. In targeting holidaymakers on lower and lower budgets, the resorts could no longer afford their own upkeep. Like every other sort of Victorian infrastructure, the ageing fabric of the seaside was finding it increasingly difficult to resist the ordinary depredations of daily life. This was nowhere more true, or more insidious in its progress, than in that proudest symbol of England-on-Sea, the pleasure pier. And no pier in the world has ever been more totemic than the object of my pilgrimage.

Southend.

Even now, you can see why people loved it. The line out of London tells its own story. There is a Hawksmoor spire or two as the train picks up speed east of Tower Bridge, and the metallic towers of Canary Wharf; but then comes West Ham and the heroic ugliness of the East End, its shallow sea of indigenous brick spiked with failed experiments in vertical living. Here and there you see a survivor, or perhaps a revivalist: net-curtained bay windows screening the kind of modest, wage-earning life that once found relief in a train ride along the estuary. London sprawls without a break deep into Essex, an octopus groping for the sea but finding only transport depots. Not until Benfleet do you feel confident of escape; and not until Leigh-on-Sea do your eyes meet the gleam of water. Then it's Chalkwell, whose station paddles its footings in the sea, Westcliff, and journey's end.

If you've not kept up with the architectural press, you're in for a surprise. From the High Street you emerge with shocking suddenness on to Pier Hill. Below, the world's longest pleasure pier begins its 1.34-mile journey out to sea. I find no connection with my childhood memory of it, and am surprised by its frailty. 'Regeneration' is a big word in seaside circles, and on Pier Hill we see what it means. The 'gateway' between High Street and sea has gone all glass and stainless steel, as if some design-conscious department store had spilled its guts out on to the grass. There are walkways, viewing platforms and a 'scenic lift' down to the Esplanade. Tucked into the slope, a fish-and-chip restaurant offers 'Colossal Cod'. It looks inviting, but I wonder if this is what the borough council meant when it predicted that this new 'open, fluid and attractive area' would 'encourage a cultural shift towards a "Café Society"'. It is one of the mantras of seaside redevelopers that a new sort of visitor is needed – the kind with an eye for architecture, landscape and heritage.

The new pier entrance, too, gleams with high-tech portentousness. You might be entering an urban multiplex, a university engineering faculty or a merchant bank. Whatever is the polar opposite of vulgar (cool, perhaps?), this is it. The contrast with its neighbour – the gloriously uncool Adventure Island fun park with its traditional rides and amusements – is beyond stark, a joke almost, as if the 19th and 21st centuries had entered an Odd Couple contest. In mid-February the amusements are laid up and silent, but still they tug at that thin little cord of childhood. I need a toffee apple.

The pier just makes me sad. Sad in the usual, nostalgia-laden way to have outgrown the capacity for wonder (do even children have that now?). Sad, too, after paying my 50p, to find myself alone on the mile-long walkway. But sad most of all for the pier itself. Few landmark structures can have suffered as much damage. The first to assault it was a barge in 1891, followed by a ketch (1898), a Thames Conservancy vessel (1908), a 'concrete vessel' (1921) and another barge (1933). In 1939 the pier itself became a kind of honorary vessel when it was commandeered by the Navy as HMS *Leigh*. By the time it returned to civilian use in 1945 it had dispatched 84,297 sailings in 3,367 convoys. The historic peak for visitors – more than 5m in 1949 – came shortly afterwards, when post-war belts were at their tightest. Thereafter the fortunes of the seaside would sink as fast as the nation's spending power grew. Oddly, visitors could often – and still do – look more like a liability than an asset. To local authorities who have to pay for the 'public realm' of clifftop shelters, sea walls, floral displays, lavatories and car parks, more visitors mean only more expense.

Southend Pier itself seemed jinxed. In 1959 the wooden pavilion at the landward end, a dance hall turned roller-skating rink, caught fire and marooned hundreds of people on the pier-head. No one doubted that the phoenix would rise again, but in what form? The answer was the most perfect emblem of the age. There would be no going back to roller-skating or to the dance-hall culture of yesteryear. People now were looking forward, not back, and forward meant surfing the wave of all things American. The future chewed gum and wore sneakers. The pier would have a bowling alley.

As ten-pins tumbled, so did profits. By 1970 the number of visitors had fallen to fewer than a million. In 1968, after ten years of loss for local ratepayers – £3m a year, it was said – there had been talk of a commercial takeover. In 1974 it was announced that the walkway needed rebuilding and the corporation seemed ready to abandon the thing altogether. The outcry could hardly have been louder if the councillors had abused the Queen Mother. John Betjeman wrote to *The Times*, London dockers signed a petition and the Shah of Persia was (probably falsely) rumoured to have lent £200m to a company that wanted to buy the pier and load it with hotels, conference centres, exhibition halls, theatres, casino and a North Sea ferry terminal. Faced with the concerted opposition of East End sentimentalists and connoisseurs of Victoriana, the corporation rediscovered its nerve and decided to spend another £3m on renovation. Its reward, yet again, was to be stung by fate.

On 29 June 1976, the amusement arcade, restaurant, bars and theatre dematerialized in a fireball. The calamity itself had a certain novelty value – 'disaster trips' to see the wreckage were a boost to business on the pier railway – but, though Southend Corporation voted to rebuild, councillors and ratepayers were soon muttering about the cost. It was all very well for Betjeman to bang on about the pier's 'national importance', but its loss-making habit was a local liability that looked incapable of getting anything but worse. Piece by piece, the British seaside was coming apart.

Other piers were in trouble too. Gone or going were Aberavon, Aldeburgh, Cowes, Douglas, Dover Promenade, Folkestone Victoria, Lee-on-Solent, Lytham, Minehead, Morecambe, New Brighton, Rhyl, St Leonards Palace, Scarborough North, Shanklin, Ventnor Royal Victoria, Walton-on-the-Naze . . . The National Piers Society now lists 36 losses in all, with the very loveliest of them – Brighton's wonderful West Pier – suffering pro-longed death agonies that are almost too harrowing to watch. No child, let alone teenager, in the late '70s would think wistfully of Clacton or Skegness. In the age of sangria and sex-in-the-sun, it would take more than ten-pin bowling to fill the vacuum left by the whelk stalls, halls of mirrors, donkey rides and Lobby Lud; more than a Bargain Break at Windy Villas to stem the flow to Palma, Ibiza and Corfu. As Donald McGill had always known, the English seaside stood for a kind of apple-cheeked innocence that was underlined, not challenged, by saucy innuendo. Young people did not want the *suggestion* of sex any more than they wanted the suggestion of sunshine. They wanted the real thing. If it was to survive into a new century, the seaside would have to find other ways to fill its beds.

And so it did. Cheap-and-cheerful plummeted through the

floors until it hit the deep sub-basement of cheap-and-cheerless. How the threshold of indignity alters! I remember at the age of five bringing outrage to an Eastbourne boarding house by clicking the dial on the lavatory from 'vacant' to 'engaged', thus condemning half a dozen old ladies to agony after their morning tea. Far greater offences to their gentility were now being threatened. Hotels, bed-and-breakfasts and seaside landlords, finding themselves starved of gentlefolk, turned their attention from quality to quantity – all too literally a policy of bums in beds. 'Costa del Dole' was the headline-writers' shorthand for what the seaside was now becoming. As MPs, councillors and chambers of commerce fulminated, so the Department of Social Security (DSS, as it then was) funded a seaward migration of job-seekers, single-parent families and others who, for one reason or another, had fallen through holes in the working economy. A latterday Dickens would have sketched human tragedy not through the Bridewell but through a Hastings bed-and-breakfast.

Unemployment at the seaside was suddenly the worst in the country, worse even than the wrecked industrial cities from which the newcomers – or 'scroungers' as the *Daily Mail* preferred to call them – had escaped. A few of the claimants obliged reporters by confirming how happy they were, whiling away their time at public expense swigging lager on the beach. MPs and hoteliers complained that visitors had to run a gauntlet of beggars, drunks, drug addicts and thieves, while the charity Crisis protested that homeless people in run-down hostels were being pressed into a new underclass of hidden homeless from which there was no way out. Brighton alone had 80 rough sleepers, and a population that ebbed and flowed with the tide. In Blackpool, the annual turnover in some primary school classes reached 100 per cent.

The collapse of the seaside felt like a ram-raid on the national shop window. Who could have believed that Ilfracombe, Clacton, Weymouth, Dover, Hastings, Great Yarmouth, the Isle of Wight – even palmy Torbay on the fabled 'English Riviera' – would hit the skids so hard that they would head the queue for economic aid?

The English Tourist Board, as it then was, struggled to extract its head from the sand. In August 1993 it published a report extolling the virtues (by which it meant market value) of nostalgia. To win the battle with Abroad, it suggested, we needed to go back to the beginning and start again. This would mean purging the sleaze, repairing historic buildings and basking in the restored elegance of Edwardian promenades. Who'd bother with the Bay of Naples when they could have Weston-super-Mare? A *Times* leader-writer, making merry with the board's 'platitudinous' recommendations, suggested that the appeal of Britain's beaches rested on a national characteristic even more fundamental than nostalgia – masochism.

Another year passed, and the *News of the World* yet again sent out its price-checkers. This time, however, it had no interest in afternoon cuppas or jellied eels. The rates being compared were those of Young Lady Chatterley, Lotta from Roedean and the Happy Hooker. 'One old man pays me to stand naked in a dust-bin while he throws cream cakes at me,' confided the Slave Mistress of Whitley Bay. Echoes of Regency and Edwardian England may have been there – echoes, too, of Naples – but they were not exactly what the tourist board had in mind. A year later it was the Conservative Party's turn to prescribe a solution. In a booklet, 'Tories for Tourism', it proposed that the government should concentrate its funding on a few 'premier division' resorts such as Bournemouth, Brighton, Torquay and Eastbourne, with the unavoidable corollary that basket cases such as Margate, Clacton, Skegness and Southend should resign themselves to life among the underclass. It did not catch on (the only copy I could trace was in the Bodleian Library). Southend's own Tory MP, Sir Teddy Taylor, reckoned the only thing to do with it was to 'chuck it off Southend pier'.

The pier itself, to the surprise of some and the delight of many, was still open. It had survived threats to sell or close it; had healed its wounds after a 645-ton sludge-boat chopped through it in August 1986; and in June 1995 had emerged from the smoke of yet another fire. Another chapter had closed. The blaze in 1959 had blown away the dance hall and armed the future with a bowling alley. Now it was bowling's turn for the ashes. Elsewhere the smarter resorts were promoting themselves less as holiday playgrounds than as commercial centres by the sea. Even the word 'resort' was starting to become unsayable. 'The visitor economy is now quite different,' said Peter Hampson, chief executive of the British Resorts Association. 'It includes anything that would create a need for someone to go somewhere. This is why we use the word "destination", not "resort".'

Among the most reliable seaside destination-users of course are the political parties, which fly to the coast each autumn with the regularity of homing geese. Thus it was at Bournemouth in 1999 that Labour delegates heard the chairman of the English Tourism Council tell them what they already knew – that too many bucket-and-spade resorts had failed to invest in new attractions and so had become ghettoes for the dispossessed. Eight months earlier, the Department of Culture, Media and Sport (DCMS) had said more or less the same thing. Significantly, in a 114-page report called *Tomorrow's Tourism*, it had managed precisely eight mentions of the word 'seaside', several of them squeezed into the same paragraph. Whatever the tourist boards hoped to sell, it was not whelks. By 2000, the traditional resorts had become too unsexy even for Radio One, which pulled the plug on its long-running seaside roadshow. The arts journal *Cultural Trends* reported in the same year that, with the exception of Cromer's indefatigable end-of-the-pier show, traditional seaside entertainments had died on their feet and popular entertainers were following their audiences to Spain. Even cinema – often seen by desperate local authorities as the answer to all ills – could not be guaranteed to deliver. The misbegotten Imax, opened on Bournemouth seafront in 2002 and closed in 2005, saddled the town not with an economic asset but with an architectural disfigurement that has cemented its place as one of the nation's most hated buildings.

SEA CHANGE

The more prescient resorts by now were entering a post-tourism phase in which middle-class visitors came to enjoy coastal landscape and heritage rather than old-fashioned kiss-me-quickery. Worthing announced its intention to 'reposition [itself] as an attractive town by the sea, on the edge of the Sussex Downs. It is no longer a seaside resort.' Other towns with less seductive hinterlands looked around for help. What they got, courtesy of New Labour, was the Resort Regeneration Task Force, whose 2001 report, *Sea Changes*, dispensed the same old truths that everyone had known for thirty years. Ancient infrastructure, lack of new investment, failure to 'evolve into a product that meets modern expectations of quality in entertainment experience, accommodation and service delivery . . .'

The language had changed, but not the message, so that what might have been urgency came across as fatalism. 'One thing is certain, however, procrastination and continued inactivity will . . . mean the demise of almost all resorts as they currently stand.' It was like telling a rough sleeper to pull up his socks. Not only had tourism lost the roof over its head, so had all the other industries – fishing, manufacturing, agriculture – on which coastal economies depended. A survey by Sheffield Hallam University in 2002 found that 35 of the 43 largest resorts in England and Wales had worse unemployment than their inland neighbours. Judged on the number of benefit claimants, Great Yarmouth had an unemployment rate of 10.3 per cent, against 2.9 per cent for Norfolk as a whole. This in itself was grim enough. But if you added the hidden unemployed – early retirees, non-claimants, people on government schemes, those diverted on to sickness-related rather than unemployment benefit – then the rate nearly doubled, to 20 per cent. Yarmouth was the worst, but not by much. Skegness on the same index scored 19.9 per cent, Newquay 17.4 per cent, Bridlington 17.0 per cent, Barry 15.7 per cent . . . Overall, only 15 of the 43 had rates lower than 10 per cent.

The message was underlined by the 'indices of multiple

deprivation' – the measurements of income, employment, health, education, housing, environment and crime which the government uses to assess the quality of people's lives. Many of the most deprived areas are exactly where you would expect them to be, in the seething bowels of the very inner cities – London, Liverpool, Manchester, Birmingham – from which factory workers once dreamed of escaping to the beaches. But many others are in the resorts themselves – Hastings, Yarmouth, Skegness, Torbay – where the elegant villas of the Edwardian seaside have crossed the Styx into a moribund netherworld of 'older housing stock' whose occupants have neither the will nor the means to banish the rats, never mind restore the architecture.

Even Blackpool is on the rack. It remains Britain's most dynamic and popular seaside resort, with tens of millions of pounds being pumped into regeneration schemes and the airport expanding to receive the anticipated hordes of businessmen and tourists. Much of the optimism, however, rested on the Northwest Development Agency's campaign to receive Tessa Jowell's gift to probity, prudence and uplift, the national supercasino. Betting on what it thought was a cert, Blackpool College was already running a Regional Gaming Academy to teach 'table game skills' and 'coin slot technology'. Alas, in January 2007 came the awful news – the Casino Advisory Panel had recommended the east side of Manchester as the national gambling headquarters, not Blackpool or its presumed closest rival the Millennium Dome. On the most recent index of deprivation, Blackpool is the 24th most deprived of England's 354 local authority areas. You wouldn't bet on its climbing the league table any too quickly.

Like the inner cities before them, the resorts are now plugged into a multiplicity of financial drip-feeds – Neighbourhood Renewal Funding, the Safer Stronger Community Fund, New Deal for Communities Partnerships, Neighbourhood Management Pathfinders, the Local Enterprise Growth Initiative, and so on. The regional development agencies, too, are squirting money into their neediest neighbourhoods, many of which are beside the sea. Supplicants have included run-down areas of Brighton, Southampton, Plymouth, Ilfracombe, Bournemouth, the Isle of Wight, Great Yarmouth, Hastings, Margate, Morecambe and Skegness. But none of these funds is for the sea-side alone. All are life-support systems for patients in intensive care, supplying basic needs rather than rolling out the carpet for tourists. As the British Resorts Association's Peter Hampson says: 'Nobody wants to regenerate coastal towns just as tourist destinations. They have to be made nice places to live and work before anyone would want to visit them.' This explains the almost manic preoccupation with house prices. A better class of resident brings a better class of business brings a better class of visitor. Reflecting on Urban Splash's £4m redevelopment of Morecambe's art deco classic, the Midland Hotel, Steven Broomhead of the Northwest Development Agency rejoices not so much in the rescue of an internationally important building as in the fact that 'property prices are rising in the vicinity'. There was excitement verging upon jubilation in 2005 when the Halifax reported average ten-year price increases in the 20 most popular seaside towns of between 224.7 and 311.5 per cent.

It is not easy to see where all this is leading; how far the aid will stretch; what will be the attitude of future governments; what will be the long-term effect on the property, business and tourism markets. As Paul Hudson, then chief executive of the South East England Development Agency (SEEDA), said to me early in 2006: 'You can't generalize. There is no common template. These towns all have different functions and they need to find the essential spark that makes them desirable.' The spark of course glows brightest where it is fanned with money. In the south-east, the principal beneficiary is Hastings, which, with its joined-at-the-hip sister, Bexhill, has had £38m of government money pumped into it as seedcorn from which the town hopes to harvest £400m in public and private investment over ten years. Hastings needs all the help it can get. Riddled with run-down, bottom-of-the-heap rented accommodation, with little or no employment in the town centre and with a cross-me-quick seafront carrying the busy A259 between Ashford and Brighton, it is officially the most deprived town in the south-east (27th on the national deprivation index for 2001; 38th in 2004). It needs jobs, homes, better education, a stable population, an architectural facelift, traffic management and a deep-cleaned environment. No town better exemplifies the discontinuity between the old and the new. Here in 1066 was laid the foundation of modern England. Here in 2006 – and not just in terms of the Norman castle – lay its ruin.

Hudson, who was to leave SEEDA to become chief planner in what was still the Office of the Deputy Prime Minister, echoed the conventional wisdom that resorts needed to 'reinvent themselves'. For much of the south coast, this means reversing the stream of day trippers from inward to out. 'Commuting will be the salvation of south-east resorts such as Margate and Hastings,' says Peter Hampson. The cross-Channel rail link will bring Folkestone within an hour of London, and the £8.6m redevelopment of Hastings railway station is not just serendipity. But it is all very well for Hudson to reflect that a regenerated Hastings will retain 'the vestiges of a resort function', or that Margate, brutalized as it is by time and neglect, 'is a breathtaking place potentially'. Their good fortune is to lie within the gravitational field of London and all the fast-buck expansion that John Prescott and his heirs are hell-bent on cramming into this most overcrowded corner of the country. It might not be pretty, but it will put bread on the table.

Places further afield will have a harder time of it. In England's most rural region, the south-west, more than 200 market and coastal towns are groping for economic lifelines to haul themselves into the future. Ilfracombe is typical. The biggest resort on the North Devon coast, it is as physically well endowed as any town could hope to be – the kind of England that expats dream about. From its historic harbour it rambles up through a cleft in one of Britain's most beautiful coastlines, with Exmoor as backdrop. In a checklist of ideal seaside ingredients it would tick every box. And yet it suffers in exactly the same way as its bigger, greyer and uglier cousins in the east. The Market and Coastal Towns Association, an independent offshoot of the South West Regional Development Agency, describes Ilfracombe in terms that could apply to any seaside town, anywhere. When the slump in domestic holidays came, it says, 'many of the main buildings became tired and derelict, unemployment figures soared and the town became a byword for decay'.

Frank Pearson, a retired Liverpudlian businessman who chairs the Ilfracombe Community Alliance, fills in the detail. The one-time jewel of the North Devon coast, he says, now contains the two most deprived wards in the whole of Devon, 'worse even than Plymouth'. The rot set in after the railway, which had once brought visitors from London, fell victim to the Beeching report. 'People looked for other business,' he says, and that meant exactly the same here as it did everywhere else – 'the bed-and-breakfast brigade on social security. It was a hell of a drain on the social fabric. The town went through the floor. It became really a vigilante town. People in the community would take pickaxes to other people in the community.' As regeneration initiatives went, it was on the wild side of unorthodox, but at least it was a start. The 'other people' driven out of town, he says, were the drug barons.

Here, as everywhere, the traditional beach holiday lies buried in the family photograph album. 'It's not bucket and spade now,' he says. 'It's Zimmer frame.' Even the blue-rinse coach tour is not delivering as it once did. 'People who take these holidays are either dying out or going to Spain.' So where do we look for scraps of hope? There is nothing on the scale of Hastings, but enough money is filtering in from government and the South West of England Regional Development Agency to at least stop 'moribund' from turning into 'dead'. The badly run-down '30s town hall is being refurbished – 'turning a very tawdry building into an iconic one', says Pearson – and a derelict redbrick Victorian pub, the White Hart on the harbourside, has meta-morphosed into 11 The Quay, an upmarket restaurant owned by the adoptive Devonian Damien Hirst. The local fishing fleet is doing seriously good business selling lobsters to the French. In June 2006 – for the first time in at least 30 years, Pearson thinks (the local tourist office says it's the first time ever) – the harbour played host to a cruise liner, and there is serious talk of a new ferry service across the Bristol Channel to Swansea. Oh, and Tesco is opening an edge-of-town supermarket.

This begs the thorniest question of all. Do 'regeneration' and 'character' sing the same tune? Bitter experience from towns all over the country tells us what happens when a big-league super-market hits the margins. The character of the place changes. Money that would have circulated within the local economy is siphoned off to distant shareholders. The High Street flaps and dies like a mackerel on a rock. 'I fear we may lose 30 per cent of our shops,' says Pearson.

Of course the larger resorts have all gone through this stage and are living with the consequences. Southend's is a classic example of a shopping centre that has swapped local distinctiveness for corporate identity. Its appeal to shoppers is not that it is distinct from everywhere else, but rather that it is the same. For those who cherish the unique character of each seaside town, this battle is now decisively lost. Yet other questions remain. English Heritage, guardian of our architectural integrity, worries that the character of the seaside – the 'essential spark' that the likes of Paul Hudson want to kindle – is being extinguished by the wrong kind of redevelopment. Seafront villas are coming down, making way for pseudo-vernacular blocks that replace the real thing with pastiche and turn the town into a simpering, fancy-dress parody of itself. The English seaside was once a test-bed for bold new ideas in architecture – Brighton Pavilion, the De La Warr Pavilion at Bexhill, Blackpool Tower, Taylor and Seddon's first bungalows at Margate in the 1880s, Stuart Ogilvy's garden-suburb-on-sea at Thorpeness, Clough Williams-Ellis's Portmeirion ... Even a modest resort like Cromer has the fantabulous Hotel de Paris, whose brickwork might have been piped through an icing funnel.

Not much of this happens now. Yes, Hove can look forward to

Frank Gehry's extravagant vision, like four gigantic squashed Daleks, in the redevelopment of its King Alfred leisure centre. If Blackpool does ever get its longed-for casino, then that, too, should be a landmark building that people will want to see. But Margate is not now to get its architectural white hope, the much-heralded, sail-shaped Turner art gallery. And in the general run of things new building at the seaside is no more inspiring than anywhere else. English Heritage meanwhile fights on to protect the best of the old. At Margate, for example, it is keeping a keen eye on the Dreamland amusement park, whose roller-coaster is the only one in Britain to be a listed building. In carrying out its task as official guardian of historic architecture, it has to fight not just decay, complacency and fatalism, but, from Tessa Jowell's DCMS, a degree of apathy to 'the historic environment sector' that is hard to distinguish from enmity.

Everywhere, the more insidious curse is the deadening back-wash of medium-rise mediocrity that drains the life out of every street it touches. If seaside towns are to suck fresh air into their lungs, then their future lies in exactly the same cradle as the past; in the elegant sweep of seafront villas and the hugger-mugger intimacy of lofts and cottages bunched against the wind. The old buildings need to be recognized as assets, not liabilities. Among the horrors lie a few modest triumphs. Yarmouth, once Britain's most important fishing port, was described by Charles Dickens as 'upon the whole, the finest place in the universe'; its quay lauded by Daniel Defoe as 'the finest quay in England and not inferior to Marseilles'. Its decline through the consecutive collapses of fishing and tourism has been awful to see; and yet, having been floored by serial misfortune, it offers a golden nugget of optimism and an example to fellow sufferers. A developer has been encouraged to convert William Pilkington's fine Royal Naval Hospital into flats. The old herring-curing works has become a museum. With aid from English Heritage, the Heritage Lottery Fund and government funding schemes, fishermen's cottages, shops and older commercial buildings are being restored. Such schemes are more than the sum of their parts. Just as a single derelict building can blight a street, or even a whole town, so a restored one can give it life. Conservation is not just a cosmetic facelift; it is a tool of economic revival. In Lytham St Anne's similarly, more than 40 shops have been restored on and around the seafront, with 5,000 square metres of office space, six business start-ups, 50 new jobs and 41 home improvements. It's hard to make such things sound glamorous. Harder still to over-state their importance.

A mile out on Southend Pier, the wind cutting across the Thames estuary ruts the sea and pierces my coat. The narrow-gauge rail-way comes to a sudden stop outside the pierhead station, blocked like the walkway by a contractor's fence. On the other side lies a blackened lamp-post, toppled like a pine in a forest fire. Beyond that are buckled rails, unidentifiable heaps of char improbably patrolled by a pair of oystercatchers, and the smudged outline of what had been the station, now framed in charcoal. Beyond that, the coke-coloured void of the pierhead itself. On 9 October 2005, fate returned to its favourite haunt. Along with the station, fire engulfed McGinty's pub, a restaurant, shops and lavatories. Bits of burned decking were offered for sale on eBay. Southend Borough Council insists the pierhead will be rebuilt, so the wheel of fortune will take at least one more spin. Piers are all about defiance, surviving the onslaughts of storm tides, rogue sea captains, arsonists and human habit. The signs are not all bad – Southwold has a new pier, Southport's has been successfully restored and Hastings's reopened. But I fear this pilgrimage will be my last. Turning landward, I step aboard the little train on which I shall be the only passenger. Behind me lies seaside past, burned at sea like a Viking chieftain. Ahead lies seaside future – the graded flank of Pier Hill, crowned with fortress Debenham's, gateway to anonymity.

Later, when I ask DCMS about its vision for the future, it offers a list of six selected 'Beacon Councils' – Birmingham, the Broads,

Greenwich, New Forest, South Hams and Tynedale – that it says demonstrate 'best practice' in sustainable tourism and self-promotion. Total number of traditional seaside resorts represented between them?

Zero.

CHAPTER TWO

The Monstrous Deep

Hartland Peninsula was once part of a mountain range as big as the Himalayas. A collision of continents and three million years of grinding attrition have marked it with all the scars and disfigurements of a geological war zone. Rock buckles like the armour of an ambushed tank; the cliffs are high, vertiginous and frightening; the Atlantic explodes upon reefs that swallow whole ships like canapés. Their rusting relics – boilers, deck-plates, entire hulls – lodge in its teeth like shreds of yesterday's lunch. A man who fell in here would be a strawberry pip in the maw of Leviathan.

Looking down, with the keening of buzzards above and behind me, the thud of the ocean ahead and below, I lose my grip on time. Hour, day, year, century – all swim together in an ocean of unchangingness. Inland, the grey stone hamlets and villages hunker down, as they have always done, in the necessary shelter of their valleys. More than half a century ago, in 1954, the great pioneer of landscape history, W. G. Hoskins, came here and fell under exactly the same spell as everyone else. 'One could,' he remarked in his book *Devon*, 'write a chapter about this wide, buzzard-haunted countryside, so remote and withdrawn from the villainies of the human race, far from railways and the lunacies of the modern world. Buzzards sail slowly above the quiet combes, throwing their shadows on the sunlit slopes below, the wild

SEA CHANGE

bubbling cry of curlews is everywhere on the moory grounds above, swallows flash in and out of ancient slate-grey courtyards: it is a timeless scene.'

Standing here now, I know what he meant. Seasons come and go; tides ebb and flow; flowers bloom and fade in a loop of time endlessly replayed. As it has been, so it always will be. A day later, 360 miles away, I stand on the northern edge of a very different county on the far side of England. Where Devon is hard-edged, sharp and obdurate, Norfolk dissolves into the North Sea like a biscuit in a saucer. In the marshes of its northern coast, there is no fixed point where land meets sea meets sky, as if nature has modelled itself on the edgeless vision of J. M. W. Turner. Both counties have had their measure of tragedy – ships driven against rock in the west, and more insidiously swallowed by the sand-banks of the east. But there is a greater difference. The wild Atlantic by and large reserves its punishments for those who dare to sail upon it. The North Sea may be shallower and slacker, but it is a more nagging and persistent aggressor.

The date everyone remembers is Saturday, 31 January 1953. A few minutes before half past seven in the evening, a steam train bound for King's Lynn came to a sudden halt at Hunstanton railway station. It had hit a bungalow. All down the east coast, from Lincolnshire to Kent, the night was full of shocks. So many things were displaced, it was like a visitation from poltergeists. In Gorleston, Norfolk, the cinema manager halted a showing of *High Noon* to warn his audience that their furniture was floating out of their houses. In Heacham, near Hunstanton, beach huts appeared half a mile inland near the station. People dreaming of goose-feather beds found themselves on gale-whipped rooftops, fighting for their lives while 9ft of seawater ripped out their parlours.

It was not like a tsunami – not a sudden knockout that came from nowhere and that no one could have expected. The North Sea has always been an edgy neighbour, best kept behind walls. The floods of 1953 are remembered as England's worst-ever

36

natural disaster. More than 300 people died, 24,000 houses were flooded and 40,000 people evacuated. But 'worst ever' is a superlative example of memory loss. There were catastrophic sea floods in 1938, 1928, 1897, 1703, 1663, 1570, 1287, 1236 and 1099. In AD 38, it was said, 10,000 people drowned along the east coast and in the Thames estuary. More recently, coastal defences were breached in 1996, and there was a near miss three years later. On Christmas Eve 1999, a hurricane was only two hours from the south coast when it veered away and killed a hundred people in France instead. But the sense of relief is only temporary, the inevitable cliché never more apt. Further inundation, with loss of life, land and property, is not a matter of if, but of when. And next time the sea may not give back what it takes.

To stand on the shingle between Cley and Salthouse, on the North Norfolk coast, is a very different experience from standing on the high bastion of Hartland Point in Devon – the difference between watching a wild beast in a cage and meeting it in the open, face to face. The wind piles in from the west, shovelling thick purple cloud over the distant coast of Lincolnshire, signified by a faint grey smudge beyond the mud-thickened waters of the Wash. In the great flood of 1953, this was ground zero. In pubs along the coast, 50-year-old photographs show telegraph poles jutting between the swells, or boats calling at bedroom windows. On walls and bridges far inland, there are markers showing how high the water rose. On the Environment Agency's new national flood map, a blue tint shows how far it might reach next time. Behind me, as it did in 1953, it will take huge bites out of the coastal villages, then roam inland to snipe at land that has been dry since the melting of the ice. In the front-line villages, sirens stand ready to sound retreat.

There is no eternal peace here; only a fragile truce in the fight for territory. Every year the sea rises by 6mm. About a quarter of this is due to the long, slow tilting of the land after the last Ice Age. All the rest is rising sea, fed by melting ice, thawing permafrost and thermal expansion as the climate warms. It might not sound a lot, but think what 6mm adds up to when spread across the entire expanse of ocean. Think what it will add up to in 50 years' time (nearly a foot). Think what such a weight of water will add to the height and power of the waves; how much further it will drive on up the valleys. In 1953 the storm surge raised sea levels in North Norfolk by 3.43 metres and at Southend by 2.74 metres. *Metres!* This was colossal. Even now, a rise of just 60cm is classified by the Met Office as a 'surge event', and the Environment Agency will send out flood warnings if it coincides with a high tide (which mercifully in 1953 it did not). At the time, the 1953 surge was a phenomenon thought likely to recur on average only once every 120 years. But times and perceptions change. The sea has risen, storms have worsened in both violence and frequency, and – though defences have been reinforced – coastal dwellers are on borrowed time, like Neapolitans under the cone of Vesuvius.

Yet Hartland on its iron promontory is the better place to contemplate the nature and scale of what we face. What you see is a textbook example of chaos. An incalculable weight of water moves in incomprehensible patterns, slanted green walls steepening, curving and bursting against the rock in asymmetric columns of foam, then flooding back to meet the next overlapping wave. Every molecule within the mass is governed by rules. It will move in and back, down and up, in utter subservience to gravity, wind and moon. Yet the mass is so complex that not a single droplet can be tracked. Waves vary in height, force and frequency. The wind rises and falls. Water expands and contracts. Currents vary in strength and direction. Kelp forests wave their fronds. Bivalves filter and suck. Fish waggle their fins. Ships plough the surface. Climate changes. Faced with all this, even the most powerful supercomputers are shy of predicting the future. Given all the unknowables – carbon emissions, natural variations in weather patterns and the theoretical nature of computer models – climate prediction is a statistical maelstrom from which answers crawl half drowned in uncertainty. How high will the water rise? How quickly, and with what effect? With one voice, scientists insist that the dangers are real and immediate; that we risk passing a tipping point beyond which there could be no return. The Greenland ice sheet, up to three kilometres thick and holding three million cubic kilometres of ice, will melt and raise seas around the world by seven metres. It will be goodbye not only to the east coast of England but to most of the world's great cities. Lowland agriculture will be drowned, we will lose the capacity to feed ourselves and our lives will end in a stinking hell of starvation and waterborne disease. We will bequeath our flooded planet to the insects.

It is all happening much more quickly then we imagined. Anyone writing about climate change now can expect his words to be out of date almost before the page comes out of the printer. Records are broken with such monotonous regularity that they have become just another kind of inflation, so lacking in surprise that a contributor to the BBC's *Thought for the Day* has just declared himself old (and implicitly wise) enough to know that 'it's always the hottest since heaven knows when, or the wettest since Noah's flood'. Leading us towards his eventual 'thought' ('Across the waters of the storms of life He comes to us, and suddenly there's a great calm'), he tells us, with biblical certitude, that extreme weather is 'simply the consequence of the way Creation works'.

Seldom can Creation have put in more overtime. The truth that the reverend gentleman has 'lived long enough to know' is precisely as he states it. Temperature records in central England go back to 1659, and nine of the 10 warmest years in that period have come in the last 18 years (the exception was fourth-placed 1949), with 2006 the hottest ever. Hottest, that is, not just by a gnat's whisker but by a margin wide enough to astonish the scientists who recorded the data. Temperature records rise normally by a tenth of a degree; in the autumn of 2006 the margin was eight times that. Globally, the 10 warmest years have *all* come in the last 12, and the prediction as I write is that records will fall again in 2007.

Unlike Creationists, politicians and green activists ('earnest souls', in the words of *Thought for the Day*), scientists have caution hard-wired into their psyches. They are interested in proof, not Old Testament prophecies or popularity with voters. Until now they have based their forecasts on fairly conservative computer models checked for accuracy by being run retrospectively (i.e. they are fed historic data and their predictions compared with known events in the past). If they get that right, the reasoning goes, then they are likely to be right about the future too. But they are beginning increasingly to look 'right' only in the sense of not being wrong.

Climate change is happening so quickly now that it has no parallel in the historical past, and the latest evidence all points to a rapid, previously unsuspected acceleration in the rate of warming. Positive feedbacks from declining albedo in the polar regions, meltwater from shrinking ice sheets and carbon release from warming soils and plants mean that computer models are being revised and the planetary clock recalibrated. We may already have committed ourselves to reaching the tipping point (two degrees of global warming) that by mid-century will flip us into an irreversible spiral – two degrees will catapult us to four, and four to six, which is where life as we recognize it will come to an end. Comparison with similar warming periods in the geological past suggests that sea-level rise could accelerate to as much as a metre every 20 years rather than the 50cm or so which the Intergovernmental Panel on Climate Change (IPCC), the global body set up in 1988 under the United Nations Environment Programme, predicts by the end of the century. This wouldn't just wipe away low-lying atoll countries like the Maldives – it would radically redraw the map of the world and send half of humanity scrabbling for higher ground, Londoners included. It may, just, be preventable, but only if governments on both sides of every ideological, racial and linguistic divide find common cause and act in concert. This means the most fundamental suppression of natural instincts in the entire history of humankind.

It means the developed and developing world coming to agreement: it means rich countries not demanding matching sacrifices from poor, and poor countries not looking to emulate Western lifestyles. This alone would set new standards in diplomacy, but – even as the permafrost melts, glaciers shrink and the Arctic turns to slush – the most powerful nation on earth continues to obstruct every initiative in which it cannot see any short-term economic advantage, or which fails to offer its citizens an even more disproportionate share of the world's resources.

The Floridian electoral fiasco of 2000 that allowed George W. Bush to beat the popular-vote winner Al Gore to the White House carries a cost we may no longer have time to pay off. Gore himself has become a kind of eco-prophet taking his message to the world, speaking wherever he can find an audience – on the Jay Leno and Oprah Winfrey television shows; at the Hay Festival and the Cannes Film Festival, where his documentary on global warming, *An Inconvenient Truth*, earned a showing alongside *Volver*, *The Wind that Shakes the Barley* and *The Da Vinci Code*. The trouble is that, given the choice, President Bush would more willingly accept the veracity of *The Da Vinci Code* than of *An Inconvenient Truth* (or the work of the IPCC or anything else that gives credence to global warming). Not even an American president, however, can go on forcing an agenda in the face of all logic and without political support.

The collapse of the Republican vote in the 2006 mid-term elections increased speculation that Bush in his 2007 State of the Union address would be forced to give ground on the environment – even that he would cap US greenhouse emissions. There were confident predictions of a 'climate-change U-turn'. In the end, all we got was a bit of lane-switching. The priority was fuel security, which in future would depend on 'a stable supply of energy that keeps America's economy running and America's environment clean'.

'For too long,' Bush said, 'our nation has been dependent on foreign oil. And this dependence leaves us more vulnerable to hostile regimes, and to terrorists – who could cause huge disruptions of oil shipments, raise the price of oil, and do great harm to our economy.' He proposed a reduction of petrol consumption in the US by 20 per cent over 10 years, 'thereby cutting our total imports by the equivalent of three-quarters of all the oil we now import from the Middle East'. But, despite the pleas of a large number of US blue-chip corporations who wanted a clear policy lead, there was to be no cap on greenhouse emissions. The president would place his faith instead on 'technological breakthroughs that will enable us to live our lives less dependent on oil'. There were no suicides in oil company boardrooms, and few Americans woke next day expecting anything other than business as usual.

Whatever happens now, no one should forget the efforts made throughout the entirety of Bush's first term of office, and at least halfway through the second, to represent global warming as 'junk science' and its proponents as enemies of the state. It was as obsessive as his subsequent 'war on terror', and a good deal more effective. Like the terrorists with their malign influence on public mood, those who believed in anthropogenic climate change had to be hunted down and blown away. The UK government's chief scientific adviser, Sir David King, thought global warming was the most serious threat facing the planet, so he was handed over to the character assassins. According to a Bush climate adviser, Myron Ebell, King was 'an alarmist with ridiculous views who knows nothing about climate change'. Given airtime on the BBC *Today* programme in November 2004, Ebell went on to argue that global warming was 'a tissue of improbabilities' cooked up by European climatologists in the pay of governments whose only interest was to 'attack America's economic superiority'.

This of course was the nub of it. Environmentalism does not sit easily with market theory and American ideas of free trade. Facing the massed ranks of the world scientific community, and prodded from behind by his backers in industry, Bush's instincts were as Texan as his embossed cowboy boots. He circled the wagons and sent for reinforcements. Hearing the call, up rode the Competitive Enterprise Institute, the American Enterprise Institute for Policy Research, the Advancement of Sound Science Center, the Fraser Institute, the Annapolis Center for Science-Based Public Policy, the Committee for a Constructive Tomorrow and many, many more. Their strategy – head-on counter-attack – was as crude, and as effective, as an old-fashioned sabre charge. The evidence for man-made climate change, they said, was flaky, flawed and unscientific. The cost of trying to stop it would harm the United States. A bit more warmth might even be a good thing (just think of all those extra fish in the sea!). Like Bush himself, they were of one mind, one vision and one master – the uniting factor throughout this 'coalition of the willing' was a common source of benefaction. They all received funding from the oil industry. In 2004 alone, the Competitive Enterprise Institute (CEI), a free-market think tank whose director is the same Myron Ebell who abused Sir David King, took $270,000 from ExxonMobil. Altogether some 40 organizations hostile to climate science had benefited financially from Exxon, and had helped speed the flow of quasi-scientific papers that warming-deniers rely upon to gloss their propaganda.

The White House itself didn't deny global warming exactly, but made it sound anything but a risk to the planet. Right-wing commentators, and those parts of the media that enjoy baiting the beardies, blew it up into headlines. Michael Crichton even puffed it into a novel, *State of Fear*, which, despite the extravagance of its fiction, was adopted by climate sceptics as a factual campaign tool. What we were supposed to conclude was that global warming was an unproven theory, so riddled with doubt and so unlikely to be harmful that there was no justification for doing anything to halt it.

One fact should not be forgotten: climate scientists throughout the world overwhelmingly concur that warming is real, that it is being caused by humans and that it poses an imminent risk to life. This is the opinion of the US National Academy of Sciences just as much as it is of the Intergovernmental Panel on Climate Change. Since its inception, the IPCC has published three major reports distilling the work of literally thousands of scientists, leading it to predict an average temperature rise during the 21st century of up to 5.8°C (though this may be about to change – see Afterword).

In June 2005, the national scientific academies of the UK, US, France, Russia, Germany, Japan, Italy and Canada issued a joint statement urging the G8 summit to 'acknowledge that the threat of climate change is clear and increasing', and to 'recognise that delayed action will increase the risk of adverse environmental effects'. These included the melting of the Greenland ice sheets, increasingly frequent and more severe storms and hurricanes, rising sea levels and disruption of the Gulf Stream.

This was the backdrop against which US obduracy had to be seen. To ignore global warming meant denying the science: you had to argue that the researchers – *all* the researchers – had made a mistake. This was the position of Myron Ebell's CEI, which complained of 'implausible scientific and economic assumptions'. Otherwise, if you hated the answer but couldn't fault the maths, you had to fall back on conspiracy theories – specifically, by accusing the scientists of collusion, and of falsifying their data in order to defraud the United States and prolong their research grants. Ebell rode this horse, too.

This is not the place to rehearse yet again the evidence for global warming. If you're not convinced by now, you probably never will be. (But if you do want to improve your understanding of why it is happening, how it might be prevented and what lies in store for us if we fail, then read George Monbiot's *Heat* or Mark Lynas's hair-raising account of the future in *Six Degrees* – or do as Lynas himself did, and spend a year reading scientific papers in the Radcliffe Science Library at Oxford.) What made Bush and his backers go on defending their parallel universe? The novelist and social campaigner Upton Sinclair (born 1878) was as wise as he was cynical: 'It is difficult to get a man to understand something when his salary depends on his not understanding it.'

Who would expect the fuel lobby or its delegate in the White House to vote for a cut in profits, or to do other than stall the enemy for as long as possible? This paragraph from the *Sunday Times* was typical of many:

> Bush last week dismayed the international green movement again when he reaffirmed his go-slow attitude towards the alleged global warming crisis. 'What we need are facts,' Bush told the White House conference. Pointing out that scientists were split about the evidence of global warming, the president called for further research on what remedial steps should be taken.

The date was 22 April 1990; the Bush in question was George W.'s father, George H. W. Bush. Sixteen years later, as temperatures climbed and Arctic ice gushed like an open tap, a Bush presidency was still calling for time. Even in June 2005, when he received Blair at the White House, Bush would not accept the link between fossil fuels and global warming. 'We want to know more about it,' he said, as if he had woken inside his father's head. 'It's easier to solve a problem when you know a lot about it.'

Even as the wrangling over Bush's election was going on, in November 2000, diplomats at The Hague were struggling to save the Kyoto protocol. For some, however, the struggle was more like a wriggle. US negotiators insisted that their country – then, as now, history's most prolific polluter, pumping out 25 per cent of the world's entire output of greenhouse gas – should not have to reduce its carbon output if it agreed to plant more trees. They suggested instead that livestock should be fed on special diets to reduce flatulence and cut the flow of methane. It was enough to raise a laugh, but not to lure East Anglians out from behind their sandbags.

In March 2001, the world finally realized what it was in for.

First the president abandoned a pledge to reduce emissions from power stations; then he withdrew from Kyoto altogether. The agnosticism implicit in the request for 'more research' was replaced by open hostility. The White House rottweilers were given a sniff of the enemy and slipped from their leash. Their first target was not some foreign anti-US conspirator but the highly respected American chairman of the IPCC, Robert Watson, who had earned displeasure by claiming that 98 or 99 per cent of qualified scientists accepted the reality of human-induced climate change. Randy Randol, 'senior environmental adviser' for ExxonMobil, had already written to John Howard, policy adviser at the White House Council on Environmental Quality. In bold type he had raised the question: 'Can Watson be replaced now at the request of the US?' To underline the need, he added a quote from a news agency in which Watson appeared to suggest that America's record on climate change was worse than China's. He might as well have fouled his mother's milk or spat on the Stars and Stripes. The oil and gas industries had paid $25.4m to help get Bush elected, and they weren't going to put up with anything so un-American as cuts in their output. It took time, but the answer to Randol's question was yes. In April 2002, after lobbying from the US State Department, the IPCC had a new chairman.

Neither Exxon nor the White House would admit that Randol's memo – cosily signed 'Randy' – had brought about Watson's demise. But the oilmen had been lobbying for years. In 1998 the *New York Times* got hold of an internal memo from the American Petroleum Institute (API) setting out a draft 'global climate science communication plan', which recommended the targeting of schools. 'Informing teachers/students about uncertainties in climate science will begin to erect a barrier against further efforts to impose Kyoto-like measures in the future,' it said.

Its strategy in opposing scientific orthodoxy was to buy in some experts of its own – it would 'identify, recruit and train a team of five independent scientists to participate in media outreach. These will be individuals who *do not* have a long history of visibility and/or participation in the climate change debate.' Victory, it said, would be achieved when 'recognition of uncertainties becomes part of the "conventional wisdom"', and 'those promoting the Kyoto treaty on the basis of extant science appear to be out of touch with reality'.

Exposure triggered the usual denials. Exxon said it did not know 'the status' of the plan, and the API said it could find no evidence that it had ever been enacted. It made no difference. Scientists could say what they liked. The only opinion that mattered was that of POTUS (government shorthand for President of the United States), and POTUS had heard all he needed. In June 2001, State Department under-secretary Paula Dobriansky was invited by the API to a meeting with the Global Climate Coalition, an industry-backed group opposed to Kyoto. Among the objectives in her State Department briefing was: 'To solicit . . . ideas on alternatives to Kyoto as part of continuing dialogue with friends and allies.' And then came this: 'POTUS rejected Kyoto, in part, based on input from you [the oil industry].' They had hit the jackpot.

To non-Americans Bush may have looked like a pariah. At home he wore his opprobrium like a medal – it was America versus the world, and America was going to win. Vice-president Cheney, too, weighed in with a sneer. 'Conservation,' he said, 'may be a sign of personal virtue, but it is not a sufficient basis for a sound, comprehensive energy policy.' On 9 May 2001, the White House press spokesman, Ari Fleischer, confirmed America's position in the post-Kyoto age: 'President Bush would not urge Americans to conserve. That's a big no. The president believes that it's an American way of life, and that it should be the goal of policy-makers to protect the American way of life. The American way of life is a blessed one.'

Not so blessed, however, that it couldn't use a bit of false witness. In February 2004, 62 of America's most eminent scientists accused the administration of systematic 'manipulation of the process through which science enters into its decisions'. A month later, the Union of Concerned Scientists published a 49-page paper whose very title, 'Scientific Integrity in Policymaking, an Investigation into the Bush Administration's Misuse of Science', reflected the extent to which a normally conservative group had been scandalized. It described a 'well-established pattern' of suppression and distortion by political appointees across a range of federal agencies covering everything from air pollution to military intelligence, and of a 'wide-ranging effort' to prevent the publication of findings inconvenient to the Bush agenda. Scientifically underqualified but politically compliant individuals were being appointed to advisory positions, and government scientists were being gagged. Research had been distorted not just on climate change but also on air quality, endangered species, mercury emissions, sex education, forest management, HIV/Aids, breast cancer, airborne bacteria and Iraq's aluminium tubes.

By July 2004 the UCS had the support of more than 4,000 scientists including 48 Nobel laureates, 62 holders of the National Medal of Science and 127 members of the National Academy of Sciences. To the catalogue of political interferences published in March, it now added more: disregarding evidence about the environmental effects of mountaintop strip mining, censoring and distorting scientific analysis to circumvent the Endangered Species Act, distorting evidence on emergency contraception, and applying political 'litmus tests' (i.e. 'Did you vote for President Bush?') to candidates for scientific advisory panels.

Bush by now had stopped expecting scientists to bend with the political wind – not even those closest to government could be persuaded to place expediency ahead of probity. Shortly after taking office, the president had instructed the National Academy of Sciences to critically examine the findings of the IPCC. Whatever he had been hoping for, he did not get it. Far from repudiating the science, the NAS emphatically endorsed it, as did the American Geophysical Union. Worse for Bush, even the State

Department accepted the reality of climate change and the danger of allowing it to continue. Bush was reduced to dismissing this heresy as 'a report put out by the bureaucracy'. In September 2002 the White House deleted a passage on climate change from the Environmental Protection Agency's annual report on air pollution, and did the same again in June 2004 when another EPA report took the 'wrong' line. Officials demanded the deletion of a 1,000-year temperature record in favour of a more limited analysis that supported White House policy; the removal of any reference to the findings of the NAS; the insertion of scientifically discredited research funded by the American Petroleum Institute; and the deletion of the scientifically uncontroversial conclusion that 'climate change has global consequences for human health and the environment'. Rather than see this travesty published in its name, the EPA withdrew the entire passage.

Anything that so much as hinted at the *possibility* of global warming was swatted like a gnat – the White House even blocked a Department of Agriculture leaflet advising farmers on ways of reducing greenhouse emissions. The full extent of the manipulation may never be known, though a little more came to light in June 2005 when leaked memos revealed the antics of Philip Cooney, chief of staff at the White House Council on Environmental Quality. Cooney, a lawyer with no scientific training, had been routinely emasculating scientific warnings in official documents – for example, by inserting the words 'significant and fundamental' before 'uncertainties', to strengthen the impression of doubt over global warming; deleting a paragraph about melting glaciers; inserting the word 'extremely' in the sentence: 'The attribution of the causes of biological and ecological changes to climate change or variability is [extremely] difficult'. In such ways does the propagandist go about his business. In this case, however, not only was Cooney caught; he was unmasked as a former lobbyist for the American Petroleum Institute. Following the revelations he suddenly discovered a backlog of untaken leave and resigned. Within days he was hired by ExxonMobil.

I have given George Bush far more space than I had intended. But this is a book about the sea, and nothing will have a bigger or more prolonged impact upon it than the climate. The mid-term elections may – just may – have signalled a shift. We are told that opinion in the US is changing; that Bush-bashing has no further purpose; that the future is in new and safer hands and the lame-duck president can be left to stew in his own oil while the world moves on without him. But there is still no US involvement in Kyoto, no emissions cap, no global leadership, no statement of faith in anything but the self-healing powers of technology. Let us not forget: the effort to arrest global warming has been set back by years, perhaps by decades, by the mendacity of George Bush and his string-pullers, and by the gullibility of those who, for whatever reason – vested interest, hatred of doom mongers, scientific illiteracy – swallowed the propaganda.

High tide sucks at the beach, tugging the shingle inexorably west-ward. Today the weather is breezy but benign. The tide is not a big one; a few brave souls are swimming, and a boy is trying to launch a message in a bottle (it will drift ashore barely fifty yards away, where it will be read by an amused angler). You don't need an expert eye to see the impermanence of it all. There is an illusion at sea level of a horizon higher than oneself, of a lurking continent of water just biding its time. And it is true: there will be winter gales and damaging storm surges (then come and stand here if you dare). A hundred yards to my left, for the umpteen hundredth time two Environment Agency bulldozers are repairing the shingle bank that keeps the sea from the freshwater marsh, the coast road and the village. Less than a fortnight later, their work will be undone by a storm.

This is not the only shingle on the move. Out at sea, dredgers take thousands of tonnes for building aggregate, creating barren, lifeless holes that coastal campaigners rightly or wrongly believe are robbing their beaches of sediment and edging their homes for-ever closer to the waves. From the same dredging grounds, sand is piped ashore to nourish beaches that have been stripped by the very defences built to protect them. You feel very small in places like this, and certainties seem far less secure. On the television screen that evening, the smirking image of America's president grates like sand between the teeth. But for a moment I wonder: can he *really* be such a fool? Despite all I know and believe, despite all I have read and written, and despite all the deviousness and dishonesty with which he has discredited his case, is it possible, is it *remotely* possible, that he could be right? Have we been blinded by distrust of a shifty politician, or gulled by eco-warriors into a neurotic, guilt-ridden state of anxiety that pointlessly denies us the rewards of our own enterprise? Is the global climate system, as a God-fearing president must believe, so immeasurably vast that it is beyond the power of humanity to perturb it? A few days earlier, watching thunderheads pile up over the Aegean, I certainly could have thought so. The storms burst over the Sporades with a violence that disturbed even those well used to climatic extremes. Hour after hour throughout the night, lightning raked the mountainsides and thunder rang at the threshold of pain. When the rain came, it turned donkey paths to rivers.

What arrogance persuades us to believe that we, who can find no answer to the common cold, could subvert the power of nature and bring on the apocalypse? Oceans throughout their existence have been literally in flux, driven by lunar and geological forces into an endless game of give-and-take with the land. Even in historical time, the shifts have been measurable in miles. Yet we imagine the changes are somehow our own creation; that we have the power to arrest them and can cement the boundaries wherever we like. Who do we think we are?

Part of the answer is that we are rationalists eager to understand as much as we can about the world we live in. We are observers of phenomena, assemblers of facts and processors of data. We like to make connections. It's how the brightest among us have been led to conclusions about gravity, evolution and the aetiology of disease. But this, too, can be dangerous, for nothing deceives like statistics. It may happen, for example (it probably does), that men who rarely change their underwear have a higher risk of lung cancer than those who wear fresh laundry every day. You see this kind of thing in health-scare headlines all the time – the literal translation of statistical association into cause and effect. Subtler analysts recognize that there is no mechanism that could link dirty undergarments to tumours of the lung, so the connection must be incidental (something to do with poverty, perhaps?) rather than causal. But the problem with the Underpants Fallacy is that it can be twisted around and manipulated. The lack of any known mechanism linking cigarettes to lung cancer enabled tobacco companies to argue for years that an addictive carcinogen was harmless. And so it has been with climate change. There is no stand-up-in-court proof that one thing will lead to another. The whole warming episode may be due to natural fluctuation and have nothing to do with humans at all. Best leave it to the Almighty.

But some things are beyond argument. The world *is* getting warmer. Arctic ice *is* melting. Sea levels *are* rising. Extreme climatic events, of the kinds that devastated East Anglia in 1953 and New Orleans in 2005, *are* more frequent. Observations by NASA suggest that permanent sea ice in the Arctic was reduced by some 250 million acres between 1979 and 2005 – far more than could be explained by natural fluctuation. The Alaskan permafrost has warmed by up to three degrees since 1980, and Inuit seal-hunters find their hunting grounds dissolving from a rock-hard pavement of sea ice to salty granita. Iceland's glaciers are in retreat. Global annual temperature records are broken with the frequency of the world pole-vault record. The European heatwave of 2003 was the hottest since instrumental records began in 1860, and probably the hottest since 1500. The 10 warmest years on record have all come since 1990, with a parallel increase in storms.

The Hadley Centre tells us that the average for the Atlantic Ocean is 10 tropical storms, six hurricanes and two 'major' hurricanes a year. In 2003 the rates went up to 16, seven and three respectively, with the bonus of three extra tropical storms outside the usual June–November season. Globally, Category 4 and 5 storms like Hurricane Katrina, with wind speeds over 56 metres per second, have doubled in frequency over 35 years – a phenomenon which the Georgia Institute of Technology has concluded must be linked to the worldwide rise in sea temperatures (hurricanes are born when the water climbs above 26 degrees). It can't be explained by naturally occurring phenomena such as El Niño or the North Atlantic Oscillation, whose effects tend to be local. The trend has been so constant, so widespread and so prolonged that the likelihood of natural causes is described by the US National Center for Atmospheric Research as 'remote'. The point to remember is that it is the *severity* of storms that has increased, not the number. Thirty-five years ago, only 20 per cent of hurricanes reached Category 4 or 5 – a force now achieved, with devastating effect, by 35 per cent. Another study, by Massachusetts Institute of Technology, has reported a 50 per cent increase in the destructive power of tropical storms since the middle of the 20th century.

Projecting all this into the future, never mind translating it into a British context, is far from easy. You can safely predict that the nasty neighbour is going to get nastier, but you can't put dates or numbers to it. With the IPCC estimate of global mean sea-level rise over the 21st century ranging between 9 and 88cm, the uncertainties make such a cacophony of statistical noise that you can't tell which tocsin is ringing loudest. The expectation is that storms around the UK will not only grow and multiply but also change track, with the result that some places (the Bristol Channel, for example) may anticipate a calmer future while others (the southern North Sea) are in for a smiting.

The Hadley Centre's expert on sea-level rise, Dr Jason Lowe, is working on what he calls a 'medium high emissions scenario' that projects weather patterns and vertical land movements into the 2080s. By then, he says, a severe surge at high tide will be much more formidable than the equivalent storm today. Even in the relatively safe haven of the Bristol Channel it could be 20cm higher. In the Channel it could be half a metre, and in the howling wastes of the southern North Sea an awesome 1.1 to 1.2 metres. It's true that storms of this severity occur on average only once every 50 years, but here too the horizons are dissolving. 'In the southern North Sea,' says Lowe, 'by the 2080s, a typical return period for what is now a 150-year event will be seven or eight years.'

But we need to pull back a bit and return to the facts. Despite what the *Daily Mail* seems to believe, the 'greenhouse effect' is not in dispute (something very like it was first proposed in the 1860s by the physicist John Tyndall). Energy from the sun passes through the atmosphere and heats up the earth's surface, whence it is reflected back into space as infra-red radiation. This is unable to pass through certain of the atmospheric gases – most importantly water vapour and carbon dioxide – and so becomes trapped like heat under glass. When the concentration of gas increases, the earth warms up. When it decreases, the earth cools down. Without it, life as we know it would not be possible. This is how Tyndall himself described it 140 years ago:

> ... this aqueous vapour is a blanket more necessary to the vegetable life of England than clothing is to man. Remove for a single summer night the aqueous vapour from the air that overspreads this country, and you would assuredly destroy every plant capable of being destroyed by a freezing temperature. The warmth of our fields and gardens would pour itself unrequited into space, and the sun would rise upon an island held fast in the iron grip of frost ... its presence would check the earth's loss; its absence without sensibly altering the transparency of the air, would open wide a door for the escape of the earth's heat into infinitude.

The average global temperature currently is around 14°C. With no greenhouse effect it would be −18°C – that's how much it matters. Since the beginning of the industrial revolution in the mid-1700s, the concentration of carbon dioxide in the atmosphere has risen from 280 parts per million by volume (ppmv) to 367 ppmv in 1999 – an increase of 30 per cent. Since 1957 the Mauna Loa observatory in Hawaii has recorded an increase in carbon dioxide of 1.2 ppmv, or 0.3 per cent a year. In 25 years worldwide carbon emissions have rocketed from five billion to seven billion tonnes a year. The synchronization of carbon emissions with global warming is paralleled by such a weight of physical evidence – ice-melt, northward migration of plants and animals – that scientists and most governments are unwilling to ascribe it to chance. If emissions continue at the current rate, says the IPCC, then the atmospheric concentration of carbon dioxide by 2050 will reach between 415 and 480 ppmv, and by 2100 to 460–560 ppmv – double what it was before the industrial revolution. If rates continue to increase, the current level itself could double within 50 years – an eventuality which, according to the Hadley Centre, would be likely to cause a global average temperature rise of around 3.5 degrees. Anything more than 2.7 degrees is likely to trigger unstoppable melting of the Greenland ice, and the drowning of much of eastern Britain. This is why I test readers' patience by dragging them through the process yet again.

It has to be understood, too, that there is no way of getting the genie back into the bottle. Not even a total cessation of carbon emissions now would bring any noticeable benefit – gas already in the atmosphere will stay there for 200 years. Worse than this: once they have been destabilized, natural systems may adopt new patterns of behaviour, simultaneously accelerating global warming and – in a classic example of the kind of contradiction that delights the sceptics – making Britain colder. Loss of ice and permafrost will have more effects than are immediately obvious. Deep in the permafrost, for example, can be found frozen vegetable remains – trees, grasses and other plants – that have been accumulating and held in cryogenic suspension for thousands of years. They amount to vast deposits of greenstuff whose disintegration after thawing will have exactly the same result as any other major release of carbon – an acceleration of global warming.

Ice-melt has further implications too. Snow-covered ice is the most efficient natural light-reflector on the planet. On average, a little under 30 per cent of the light that strikes the earth is bounced back into space, but on bright, snowy ice it is between 80 and 90 per cent. At the opposite end of the scale is seawater, which reflects only 7 per cent. The other 93 per cent is absorbed, thus warming the water, further accelerating the thaw and heating the water even faster. Sea levels then rise not only by the volume of melting glaciers but also by thermal expansion of the water. This 'positive feedback' adds to the difficulty of long-term prediction. Instead of the linear progression foreseen by most computer models, the rate of change could suddenly accelerate.

Nor is this necessarily the worst of it. Britain depends for its comfort on ocean currents bringing warm water from the tropics – part of a complex global heat-exchange system, driven by changes in ocean temperature and salinity, that scientists call 'thermohaline circulation'. It happens that in the North Atlantic, surface water cooled by Arctic winds increases in density and sinks. At depth, it then streams towards the equator at a speed and volume equivalent to 100 times the flow of the Amazon. Meanwhile it is replaced by warm surface water flowing north-ward from the Gulf of Mexico. This is what we call the Gulf Stream. It might be thought that melting ice would contribute positively to this warming trend, but it actually works the other way. The sinking of the cold seawater is inhibited when it is topped by fresh water from rain, rivers or melting ice (seawater gradually becomes fresh when frozen), which could either slow the Gulf Stream or kill it altogether. It happened before, at the end of the last Ice Age when a huge Canadian glacier melted into the Atlantic, and it could happen again.

More likely than a complete failure is a gradual slowdown. The

Hadley Centre predicts that one of the two areas of sinking, in the Labrador Sea, could be switched off by 2020, though the cooling effect on the UK should be offset by global warming. If the whole system stagnated, however, the counter-intuitive though entirely logical outcome of rising global temperatures would be plummeting thermometers in the Home Counties. Average annual temperatures in Britain would drop by as much as 5 degrees, with winter temperatures regularly below −10°C. We would face disruption of transport, drastic changes in vegetation and agriculture, and a revolution in culture and lifestyle. We would become a different people.

As always, the multiplicity of Rumsfeld-style 'known unknowns' means that the crystal ball is thickly frosted. 'Although we estimate that the chances of a switch-off in the next hundred years are low,' says the Hadley Centre, 'we do not know *how* low . . .' Meanwhile, 'some recent measurements from research ships in the Atlantic seem to indicate that changes are already taking place'. In September 2005 comes news that the Arctic ice is melting faster than ice-cream on a pavement. The source is impeccable – the National Snow and Ice Data Center (part of the University of Colorado) is aided in its research by NASA and the University of Washington in Seattle (not obvious hotbeds of anti-Americanism). Ironically, too, it comes during the same month that Hurricane Katrina devastates New Orleans. Satellite data, the scientists say, show a 'stunning reduction' in the Arctic sea ice at the end of the northern summer, leading to the suspicion that it is 'likely on an accelerating, long-term decline'.

Coming at the end of the summer melt, September is always the month when sea ice is at its minimum. On 21 September 2005, it not only reached its lowest level since satellite monitoring began in 1978 but also exceeded the previously recorded lows of the 1930s and '40s. Between 1979 and 2001, the average rate of decline in Arctic summer ice was 6.5 per cent per decade. Now it is 8 per cent and rising. The area disappearing each summer is approximately 1.3m square kilometres, or 500,000 square miles – roughly double the size of Texas. It is important to be clear about what this means. We are talking about sea ice, which can re-form in winter, not the Greenland ice sheet, the melting of which would be irreversible. Even so, the rate of 'rebound', as the scientists call it, is also declining. With the exception of May, each month between December 2004 and September 2005 set a new record low for Arctic ice at the time of year. This means the ice in winter is not returning to pre-melt levels, making it even more vulnerable to hotter summers. Arctic surface air temperatures in the first half of 2005 were between 2 and 3 degrees higher than the 50-year average, a peak on the graph that the National Snow and Ice Data Center describes as 'an exclamation point in the pattern of Arctic warming'. As a result, the melting season is beginning earlier and earlier – in 2005 it arrived 17 days ahead of the historic mean – and icebreakers are finding no ice to break. Even the North West Passage, whose frozen fangs have crushed ships and men without number, was wholly open during the summer of 2005. In the Laptev Sea, an NSIDC icebreaker found only one area of continuous ice to the east of Severniya Zemvya, one of the most northerly island chains in Arctic Russia. A year earlier, said the NSIDC's director, Roger Barry, the entire area was 'covered in thick multi-year ice'. If the trend continues, then the Arctic in summer could be entirely free of ice by the end of the 21st century.

Late August. Long skeins of inwardly migrating geese stripe the East Anglian sky, wave after wave of them heading for the mud-flats and fields – brents, pink-feet, greylags, come to escape the Arctic winter. Out on the shoreline, spindly waders flood in and out with the tide, knifing the mud. On floodbanks and beaches, birdwatchers in dun-and-olive drabs scan the sky for rarities, their massed telescopes swivelling like gun batteries. By evening their star finds will be chalked up on blackboards in the pubs, much as city restaurants show photographs of visiting celebrities.

Not every watcher has time for such frivolity. Out in the field, on mudflats and in estuaries, more methodical researchers grimly count and do their sums. It is the accountancy of despair.

Tiny changes in temperature or sea level are imperceptible to humans. What is there to notice? The tide is not lapping at our doorsteps; there is no risk of sunburn in December; our oaks and sycamores remain unbent by hurricanes; we are centrally heated and snug. In our awareness of change we are more diplodocus than dragonfly. What is immediately obvious to a bird or an insect will not be recognized by *Homo sapiens* until haddock swim up the garden path. It is wildlife that's in the front line of environmental change, and wildlife that tells us what's going on. But why should we care? So what if habitats are shrinking and populations declining? What's a guillemot more or less? In a sense, it's a bit like minding about Poland in 1939, or about Asians living in the path of novel flu viruses. They are in the vanguard. What hits them first will be coming for us next. After birds' breeding grounds come beach cafés, coast roads, railways, sewerage and drainage systems, houses. In a very real sense, those who speak for wildlife speak for us all. Like Hitler, the sea cannot be appeased.

Everyone by now will have some idea of the value of tropical rainforests. Their protection is an ecological bandwagon long favoured by pop stars and television documentary makers. Their destruction lies behind much of the antagonism towards the hamburger trade and governments in league with logging companies. We hear much less about coastal ecosystems, though they are just as important. Their necessity to wildlife is obvious, but they have a calculable value for humans too. Some of that value comes directly as income – visitors to just two North Norfolk coastal bird reserves, at Cley and Titchwell, are reckoned to be worth £4.3m a year to the local economy. But it's much more than that. Coastal habitats are necessary for the survival of commercially exploitable fish and shellfish. Saltmarshes, mudflats and shingle work as natural flood defences for towns and villages, and coastal wetlands are an important defence against agricultural pesticides and other pollutants which they trap and keep out of the wider environment.

A paper in *Nature* concluded that estuaries were the most valuable ecosystems in the world, worth £14,000 per hectare per year (1997 values). At this rate the Royal Society for the Protection of Birds (RSPB) calculates that coastal habitats in eastern England are worth more than £900m a year. For the million or more wildfowl and wading birds that live here, and for the specialized animals and plants that share their space, the future is precarious. In Essex alone, a thousand hectares of salt-marsh, a quarter of the county's total, have disappeared in 25 years. A technical report for the government-funded UK Climate Impacts Programme (UKCIP) in 1999 predicted that sea levels in eastern England would rise by between 21 and 76cm by the 2050s, which the RSPB calculated would wash away 3 per cent of the shingle, 7 per cent of the mud and sandflats and 9 per cent of the dunes, and would devastate 31 per cent of the saltmarsh and 37 per cent of the coastal lagoons.

Wildfowl are like canaries in a mineshaft. In their survival or otherwise can be read the manner of our own likely fate. We have habitats too, and they are under exactly the same kinds of pressure – pressure that is as often intensified as it is relieved by our efforts in self-defence. We are like knights riding into battle with half our armour missing, against an enemy that knows exactly where the soft bits are. The sea is pitiless. In some places the coast is hard and impregnable, either because it was made that way, like Hartland, or because we have reinforced it with concrete. The sea counters by lancing ever deeper into the weaker, unprotected parts: first the soft outer skin of tidal habitat; then the flesh and bone of human lives.

Including all its curves and inlets, the English shoreline is about 3,000km long, with some 1,900km (1,187 miles) having man-made defences. Just over half of this is to keep the water out; the rest is to prevent erosion (see Chapter 3). Without improved defences, more than a million properties with a capital value of £130bn will be at risk of coastal and tidal flooding, and another 100,000, valued at £8bn, threatened by erosion. Another 100,000 homes are at risk around Scotland. Within 70 years, unless they are reinforced, huge chunks of Norfolk, Cambridgeshire, Lincolnshire, Yorkshire, Lancashire, Newport, North Somerset, Sussex and Kent are likely to suffer damage averaging between £101,000 and £5m per hectare per year (2001 values). I can see a perfect example from Salthouse beach. The shingle bank is of natural origin but has needed regular grooming to keep it in shape. It is overtopped on average once every three years, but – thanks to a drastic change in defence strategy – this is now likely to increase to once every 12 months. An earlier plan to build an artificial floodbank behind the shingle failed on economic grounds. The criteria for coastal defences are unsentimental to the point of unfeelingness. It is like an examination in which the result is pre-ordained and cannot be affected by the examinee. To decide which places pass and which fail the qualification test, Defra applies a marking system that awards points for economic benefit (property saved must be worth at least the cost of protecting it), human suffering (how many lives or homes might be lost) and the value of the natural environment. Economically deprived areas score more highly than affluent ones that are deemed better able to look after themselves. Salthouse, with its desirable flint cottages and preponderance of weekenders, hadn't a hope. The new policy has been to lower and flatten the shingle to create a more solid barrier against surges, and to improve drainage from the marsh into the river so that floodwater returns more quickly to the sea. The underlying logic is that when the next really big one comes, nothing's going to stop it anyway.

Though the government budgeted £570m for flood and coastal defences in 2005–6, many places would have been better off buying lottery tickets. The result of the points system effectively was a competitive bidding process in which seaside villages, even those with tourist industries, were easily outgunned by inland towns on flood-prone rivers. Of the £570m, only £47m was earmarked for the coast. Factor in the cost of new defences – between £3m and £5m per kilometre, and likely to double or quadruple in the face of climate change – and you can see why people are filling sandbags.

Nobody argues that the entire coastline should be protected. That would mean walling every beach; barricading every estuary; turning the country into a concrete tank. Even if it could be done, it wouldn't be desirable. Deciding what to defend, and what to surrender to the advancing sea, is a problem of such political and technical complexity that – though many questions have been asked, consultations held and reports expensively drafted – no one has thought of an answer. You would more easily teach a kipper to tap-dance than negotiate an agreement between the competing interests. 'Irreconcilable', indeed, might be a better word than 'competing', embracing, as it does, everything from curlews to container ports. Farmers, fishermen, residential and commercial property owners, the tourist industry, port authorities and (whimpering under the weight of all the others) wildlife campaigners all believe they deserve priority, and correctly see that what is given to one must be denied to another. Nature seeks always to restore its balance but has no sense of justice. Its solutions are driven by the small print – often unreadable to the human eye – of chemistry and physics. Interfere with it and it will interfere right back. The word most often used to describe the British coastline is 'dynamic', meaning highly reactive and liable to change. Waves and tides erode sand, mud and shingle from around the shore, then dump them somewhere else. The result is the range of features – mudflats, beaches, shingle banks, marshes, dunes, cliffs – that we love and want to protect, just as we want to protect the homes behind them. The problem in the past has been that flood protection has always been looked at locally and tackled piecemeal. If you protect one place you increase the risk to another. To save a cliff is to lose a beach. To wall one village is to drown another. The sea will not be denied.

For all these reasons, the idea of a joined-up strategy for the entire coastline has lain in the file marked Impossible, buried somewhere beneath coordinated transport policy and sustainable fisheries. The government's best effort, begun in 1994, has been a programme of Shoreline Management Plans (SMPs), which are supposed to divide the coastline into manageable lengths and to reconcile all the divergent interests within them. The plans are non-statutory (i.e. they have no legal force) and have been drawn up by voluntary coastal defence groups covering 98 per cent of the English and Welsh coastlines. Altogether, 49 'first generation' SMPs have been produced by 18 coastal defence groups whose memberships include local authorities, government departments, the Environment Agency, port and harbour authorities, English Nature and various NGOs.

In recognition of nature's disdain for politics, the coast has been divided along geological rather than local authority boundaries into 11 basic units known, with a bluntness bordering on in-sensitivity, as 'sediment cells'. As far as possible they are bookended by geological features – headlands or estuaries – that restrict the movement of sand or shingle and minimize the likeli-hood of interference with the cell next door. Each cell is further divided into sub-cells, which are the subject of the SMPs, and each sub-cell divided into shorter lengths or management units. All the first-generation SMPs are supposed to be updated by 2010 and replaced by 'second-generation' studies, or SMP2s. Three pilot SMP2s are under way on the Norfolk coast between Kelling and Lowestoft, and on the south coast between South Foreland and Beachy Head, and Beachy Head and Selsey Bill.

It is hard not to be sceptical. Politically, the principal benefit of an SMP is to put a hot potato safely at arm's length from the government. Let local people fight it out among themselves, then those who lose their homes can be told, 'It's what you voted for.' For each stretch of coast, the SMP has to weigh four broad options:

- to do nothing, allowing the sea to flood or erode where it will;
- to hold the line by keeping or improving existing defences;
- to advance the existing defence line seaward;
- to retreat the defence line landward.

The aim, as explained by the coastal group in Cardigan Bay, is to achieve a 'sustainable policy' (the inverted commas, and implied irony, are its own) based on 'harmony between society's needs, the environment and the economy'. Which begs a number of questions. 'Society's needs' vary according to which bit of society you ask. They conflict with each other, with the environment (whose protectors might prefer to see a lot more 'society' surrendered to the waves), and with the economy, which understands rather more about cost than it does about value. Bizarrely in some places at first there was a reluctance to take the thing seriously, as if what was being discussed was little more than the realignment of a few groynes or the loss of some ice-cream kiosks. In the important Sheringham–Lowestoft SMP, where the coastal defences are all that stand between the Norfolk Broads and the North Sea, neither the Broads Authority nor Broadland District Council saw any need to take part in the consultation. Yet if the defences fail, the Broads – a national park in all but name – will become an arm of the sea. Neither was the threat to the fresh water supply of any apparent interest to Anglian Water. Given the importance of this coast to the gas and oil industries, one might wonder also why British Gas and the various oil companies chose to stay silent. Was it because they failed to understand the importance of what the SMP was meant to achieve, and the bitter cost of failure? Or was it because they had no faith in the process?

Whereas 'society' and 'the economy' may find some patterns of common interest, such alliances are all too likely to exclude 'the environment'. People whose homes are at risk understandably bridle at the suggestion that priority should be given to ducks, and farmers generally cannot understand why priority should be given to anyone but themselves. Yet the original briefing by the then Ministry of Agriculture, Fisheries and Food (MAFF, since subsumed into Defra) made it clear that coastal defence groups should consider natural as well as human habitats. It told them to 'identify opportunities for maintaining and enhancing the natural coastal environment, taking account of any specific targets set by legislation or any locally set targets'. Its concern extended even below the tideline, where, it said, there should be 'opportunities identified to create new inter-tidal (and sub-tidal) habitats to compensate for past and anticipated future losses'.

This is all backed up by the UK Biodiversity Action Plan, whose 'priority habitats' include grazing marshes, saltmarshes, mudflats, dunes, shingle, saline lagoons and cliffs, all of which are threatened by flooding or erosion. Analysis of 17 first-generation SMPs by the RSPB was not encouraging. If the environment was going to get a look in, then it needed to be an integral part of the process from beginning to end. Yet the RSPB found that four of the 17 briefs failed to include any environmental requirement at all, eight called for the protection of existing habitats and only two required the replacement of any that were lost. In the case of Kelling–Lowestoft, the failure to meet environmental objectives was criticized not only by the Norfolk Wildlife Trust and the RSPB, but also by the government's own wildlife watchdog, English Nature. 'Decisions in the SMP document,' it said, 'have not taken account of environmental/nature conservation objectives.' The implication was that 'all nature conservation assets are less worth defending than agricultural land and caravan parks'.

Friends of the Earth came to the same conclusion. Its SMP briefing paper, first published in 1997, identified a bias 'towards considerations of land use rather than coastal processes' – a bias that had expressed itself most obviously in a preference for the status quo, or 'holding the line'. In the SMPs for South Foreland to Beachy Head, Essex, the North Kent Coast, North Norfolk, and Beachy Head to Selsey Bill, more than 75 per cent of the management units chose this option. They ignored the likely future impacts of sea-level rise, and the effects of local protectionism on other parts of the coast. Indeed, their localism precisely replicated the piecemeal approach that the SMPs were supposed to redress, and threatened the integrity of the entire process. Norfolk County Council complained of Kelling–Lowestoft: 'The plan should still recognise concern at continued fragmentation of responsibility between various bodies in respect of coast protection, flood defence etc., and calls for a national strategy for sea defence.' Part of the madness historically has been that different bodies have been responsible for different parts of the coast. Floodplains are the responsibility of the Environment Agency. Cliffs are the local authorities'. It makes no sense. In the perpetual cycle of give and take, material from crumbling cliffs is stolen by the tide to feed the beaches that shield the floodplains. There are houses on the cliffs that will be lost to erosion; houses behind the beaches that are bound to flood. One policy may not fit all, but a plethora of competing policies, each defending its own, has been disastrous.

Whether or not SMPs can bring order to chaos is a question whose answer will be a long time coming. The deadline for SMP2s is 2010, and they will have to take account of two time 'horizons' – 2030 and 2050. So far the signs of joined-up thinking have been hard to find. In October 2005 the chief executive of the Environment Agency, Lady Young, complained to the *Guardian* that tens of thousands of lives and homes were being put at risk by local authorities allowing houses to be built in places likely to flood. Some risk fluvial flooding, but many more are coastal or in estuaries where floodplains are menaced by river and sea alike. Overall in England and Wales, taking account of both kinds of flooding, at least 5m people in 2m properties are already at risk, and the new planning consents – granted against the Environment Agency's advice – ensure that there will be many more. In 40 per cent of cases the planning authorities have simply ignored Whitehall guidance and failed to consult the agency before giving planning permission. Others have consulted the agency's flood-risk experts but then gone ahead regardless. Areas where flood warnings have been ignored included Oswestry, Worcester, South Gloucestershire, Bristol, North Somerset, Mendip, West Devon, Carrick, Caradon, Kerrier, Penwith, London, Basildon, Tendring, Waveney, Mid Suffolk, Great Yarmouth, East Northamptonshire, Norwich, Peterborough, South Holland, Rotherham, East Northamptonshire, North Lincolnshire, the East Riding and Blyth Valley.

Not all the risk is tidal, but the high-wire, no-safety-net attitudes of local authorities are starkly revealed. It may be that some of them simply fail to understand the mathematics of risk. They hear climate scientists talk of '10-year events' or '50-year return intervals', and take it to mean that a storm or surge of a particular intensity will not occur for that number of years. This is a mistake. All it means is that the average *frequency* of such events is 10 or 50 years. Statistically, it is as likely to happen to-morrow as on any other date in the millennium. Even moderate, non-life-threatening flooding is, as I put it in my book *Rubbish!*, 'the crudest and most unforgettable crushing of human dignity'. The sewers fill, flooding back up through manholes and lavatories in a foul brown surge that degrades everything it touches. No life thus defiled is ever quite the same again. Weather forecasts are fearfully awaited like sentences from a judge; nights spent fretfully alert to every small change in the force or direction of the wind, every squall of rain.

'There are a small number of local authorities,' said Lady Young, 'which are convinced they know best and are just not prepared to seek advice. As a result, 20 or so major developments get through the system each year, and about 300 minor ones, with us never hearing about them until it is too late.' It has been a game of planners' roulette which the agency, strongly backed by the House of Commons Environment Select Committee, has at last persuaded the government to stop. Since 1 October 2006, the Environment Agency has been a 'statutory consultee', which means local authorities now are legally bound to consult it before granting planning consents for developments in a flood zone. If a council then ignores the agency's advice, it will be open to legal action from any property owner who suffers damage as a result. It also makes the development effectively uninsurable.

The importance of this should not be underestimated. In the Thames estuary, for example, 85,000 new homes are planned along 40 miles of floodplain. Most of this land, most of the time, is kept dry by flood defences, but in February 2005 the Association of British Insurers (ABI) fired a maroon. Existing defences, it said, were unlikely to be adequate in a globally warmed future, and the threat in some places was so severe that houses would have to be designed like fishermen's huts with their living space upstairs. Unless its members could be reassured that the tide would be tamed, the new homes would be uninsurable, and thus unmortgageable and impossible to sell. In November 2006 the ABI struck again, with a heavy technical report, commissioned from the consultant engineers Entec UK, on the escalating flood risk along the east coast. A 40cm rise in sea level – which at the worst estimate could happen by 2040 – would put an extra 130,000 properties at risk (an increase of 48 per cent). If coastal defences are not upgraded, it says, the cost of a major flood could reach £16bn. The high proportion of retired elderly people living by the sea would ensure major loss of life, made worse by the disruption of essential services. Fifteen per cent of fire and ambulance stations in the flood zone would be lost, along with 12 per cent of the hospitals and schools. Hull alone would suffer damage to 19,000 properties, Great Yarmouth and Lowestoft 17,600, Southend and South Essex 24,000, East London 2,300. What the insurers want is exactly in tune with what local populations want from their Shoreline Management Plans – maintaining the status quo, or 'holding the line', which in practice means major spending on coastal reinforcement. Entec calculated that it would cost between £2.4bn and £4bn to upgrade the Thames Barrier and protect central London; between

£1.6bn and £2bn to protect the outer Thames estuary, and between £2.1bn and £2.6bn for the rest of the east coast from Ramsgate to Hull. What this would do to national coastal management policy, and to the coast itself, is anyone's guess (see Chapter 3), but it would be foolish to ignore the insurers' threat. The ABI's Statement of Principles on Flooding and Insurance commit it to continue 'providing insurance *for existing customers*' (my italics), so long as 'the government puts plans in place to improve flood defences and flood management'. The implications are obvious. New customers may not be welcome, and the whole east coast housing market hangs on the supply of rock armour, concrete and sand.

> The continued availability of cover for flood risk as a standard part of household and business policies [says the ABI] will inevitably come under pressure as a result of climate change. Insurers will continue to signal to government and customers where the pressures are becoming unsustainable.

One might not care too much about the risk of City suits dropping a bonus or two if the insurance and reinsurance industries take a hit, but the risk is bigger than that. A worldwide spate of Katrina-style disasters caused by climate change may be enough to bankrupt entire markets and, by the most pessimistic forecast, bring down the global economy. But insurers of course are the City's Honest Johns: they calculate the risks and declare the odds, and the one thing they don't do is stack the odds against themselves. The one safe bet, therefore, is that the ABI's threat is very far from idle. *Sauve qui peut.*

The sea meanwhile continues to snipe and tease. In the Thames estuary, for example, we see a perfect example of Neptune's perfidy. The water may be rising, but the trend is not regular. There are blips on the graph that confound prediction, of which the Thames Barrier is the most persuasive witness. Since its completion in October 1982, it has been closed against surges 88 times – a rough average of four a year. But in some years (1984, 1986, 1989, 1991, 1997) there were none at all. In the record year of 2003 there were 18. The graph shows an alpine profile of needle-sharp peaks and troughs but the overall trend is towards progressively higher peaks. The three busiest years have all been since 2000, with 13 closures coming during a single week in January 2003 – more than 16 per cent of the entire 20-year total to that date (though the picture is fogged by river floodwater as well as rising sea). At the same time, between 1999 and 2002, the mean sea level at Sheerness rose 10cm above Met Office predictions. Londoners quaked like Venetians. How long would the barrier hold? How long before the Underground flooded? How long before the sewers, water mains, power and communications systems would be knocked out? Around the water margins, straight questions float on seas of equivocation. As if to underline the uncertainty, 2004 passed with only two closures of the barrier and the water at Sheerness fell back to its predicted level. No one knows why.

And yet we are encouraged to believe that the drowning of Westminster is about as likely as the Queen getting caught in a beam trawl. No part of the UK – no part of Europe – will be more heavily defended than London. The current defences could hold out for decades, possibly even for centuries, but the risk of catastrophe becomes steadily less remote. With the government breathing down its neck, the Environment Agency is working on a long-term management plan for the estuary that will employ every kind of defence save the intercession of St Peter. The existing Thames Barrier will be upgraded or replaced when it reaches the end of its design life in 2030; riverside defences will be heightened; parks and nature reserves will be designed to double as spillways and storage lakes; drainage systems will be enlarged; new buildings will be made flood-resistant. On the outer shores of possibility, there might even be a new outer barrage incorporating a road and a tidal power plant.

The agency will take its time – the first draft of its detailed plan is not expected until 2008 – but the stakes could hardly be higher. More than 1.25m people already live or work in the floodplain, and £80bn-worth of property stands at risk of damage. The flood zone contains 68 London Underground and Docklands Light Railway stations, 30 mainline railway stations, three world heritage sites, eight power stations, 16 hospitals and 400 schools. With magnificent understatement, the Environment Agency predicts that the cost of protecting all these, as well as the thousands of new homes, will be 'substantial' – the ABI's £4bn is the current best estimate – and the question of who pays for it all (government? property owners? developers?) is not the least of the problems in search of an answer. If the agency gets its calculations right, and the sea behaves as it is supposed to, London will flood on average no more than once every 1,000 years. Given that even the IPCC's figures are in pencil and not indelibly inked, it's not easy to know who – other than Londoners 1,000 years hence – will be in a position to say whether or not they got it right. You pour your concrete; you ride your luck.

Around the rest of the coast, where farmers are pitted against their neighbours and retirement bungalows compete with wildfowl roosts, the resentments multiply and questions pile up like wrack after a tempest. Even if SMPs did allow replacement habitats for wildlife, how would they be planned and paid for? It's no use waiting until a mudflat has vanished. You have to relocate its population before it either perishes or is driven away. This will take research, planning and, very probably, the acquisition of land for which other people will have other needs. There is no scheme to finance the purchase of such land, and in the absence of any definitive coastal protection scheme the whole issue remains entirely theoretical. What will be saved and what lost? Nobody can even guess.

It is the same with houses. People who bought their homes even in the recent past did so in the expectation that existing coastal defences would be maintained, and their houses kept safe. Their

security has now been taken away from them, and they won't
know whether or not it will be restored until after the SMP2s
have been agreed and drafted into policy. It places them in exactly
the same fix as marsh grass and molluscs. There is no fund to
relocate or compensate them for losses that may shortly become
uninsurable, and local property markets are already blighted,
with values falling and sales stagnating. This would be, in any
circumstances, a bitter pill, but it is made all the harder to
swallow by the spectacle of unbuilt streets in the Thames estuary
having millions spent on their protection while existing homes
elsewhere face abandonment. If anything, as we shall see in the
next chapter, the problems and sense of injustice are even more
acute in areas threatened by coastal erosion, where homes are not
waiting to be swallowed by the sea but are simply tumbling into
it.

CHAPTER THREE

Over the Edge

It requires a certain determination – connoisseurship, almost – to fall in love with the North Sea coast. The mud and sand, the crumbly cliffs, are not the grand and tempered products of the earth's fiery core but uncooked, tide-worn geological junk bulldozed into heaps by glaciers. The sea itself lacks the deep and surfy, bottle-green grandeur of the wide Atlantic. It tends to be shallow, grey and dribbly, trapping the unwary by sneaking into tidal creeks rather than pounding honestly, head on like the ocean. Its numerous ports, from Berwick on the Scottish border to Ramsgate on the toe of Kent, are characterized by a no-bullshit, rust-streaked practicality, not brass-buttoned naval tradition or the social calendar. No admirals are piped aboard; no billionaires' gin palaces waft in on the summer breeze; no gleaming, blue-riband liners disgorge world-weary big spenders. For that kind of thing you need to look south and west. The east has no equivalent of Dover, Cowes, Southampton, Portsmouth, Dartmouth or Devonport. Its big hitters are the fishy-freighty likes of Grimsby, Hull, Immingham, Lowestoft, Harwich and the UK's biggest container terminal at Felixstowe. The resorts, too, tend to fish-and-chip earthiness rather than cocktail glamour – Southend, Clacton, Yarmouth, Cromer, Skegness, Cleethorpes . . .

. . . and Scarborough. This self-styled Queen of the Yorkshire Coast is perhaps the one convincing claimant to grandeur. Not much in the last two and a half millennia has passed it by. Its Iron Age tribesmen were ejected by the Romans, who made clever use of the defensively important headland between the town's two bays. Their signal station in turn made way for a medieval castle that survived to be pounded by Cromwell's gunners in the English Civil War and by German cruisers in 1914. It survives still as a darkly imposing crag, a nice co-production between nature and man, anchoring the harbour in the bedrock and bone of its more violent past. It takes some imagining. You wouldn't want to insult the place by calling it genteel, but it well knows the value of a boiled egg and a nice cup of tea. It was after the strafing by Cromwell in the 17th century that it reinvented itself as a spa and staked its claim as the world's (or maybe just Britain's, the hyperbole varies) first sea-bathing resort. It has all the ingredients: formal gardens, elegant clifftop hotels, a Marine Drive, esplanade and a theatre whose artistic director, Alan Ayckbourn, premiered most of his 60-odd plays here. With only a little ingenuity, you can make it sound like Biarritz. Sailors like it – or say they do – for the 'interesting' entrance to the East Harbour.

For all its singularity, however, there is one fundamental, unalterable aspect of its character that pins it not only to its own prehistory but to all the humbler towns and villages that look out upon the same ill-favoured sea. It stands upon one of the most dynamic coasts in Europe, where the freehold belongs to the water and landsmen are on borrowed time. A little further south, at Filey Bay, the landward retreat of the cliffs has been timed at 25cm a year. Though this multiplies to a galloping 25 metres a century, it is nothing like a record. In parts of Humberside the rate is 40 times faster – 10 metres a year. In June 1999, Scarborough itself was the focus of media attention when the South Cliff gave way beneath the Holbeck Hall Hotel. Lawsuits followed, with arguments centred upon issues of blame – who should have foreseen or prevented the disaster (which mercifully claimed no human life)? Landslips in Scarborough were nothing new. An earlier one that partly buried the spa building was landscaped by

Sir Joseph Paxton to become the spa gardens. Lawyers of course feed on the culpability of others, which they may divide into parcels – a bit of blame here, a bit more there. In this case, to find the criminal mastermind you would have to go right back to the Ice Age, when rock was greased with ice-borne clay, and hand the indictment to nature.

To understand what happens, try an imaginary experiment (or do it physically if you'd rather). Imagine taking a rounded stone and larding it with clay. Now wet it until the clay is soaked and slippery, then apply downward pressure. The mess you make is a microcosmic re-enactment of what happens when groundwater meets the clay inside a cliff. The lubricated land simply slides away in what geologists call 'a rotational landslip'. It's why people around the North Sea coast are now such experts in drainage. For years, however, coastal defences were designed, dangerously and erroneously, around a partial truth. We saw cliffs being pecked away by the waves, creating overhangs that became deeper and deeper, and more and more dangerous, until they collapsed on to the beach. We drew the obvious conclusion: the damage was done by the sea, and the answer was to wall it off. It's the reason why so much of the English seaside looks like the Maginot Line. Like strategists so often do, we made the mistake of ignoring the enemy within. The sea may have been sidetracked, but the groundwater kept on dripping into the clay and rotting the cliffs from the inside out. In the past this was not a problem because the tides worked faster and did their damage first, but the concrete changed all that. Instead of falling vertically, the cliffs now *slid*, avalanche-style, in angled torrents of clay, tarmac, tennis courts and brick. Worse: whereas sea damage had been visible and the collapses more or less predictable, the mischief now was out of sight. No one knew when a hotel might take a sudden lurch, or wake to find the gardens replaced by an extended sea view.

Villages along the east coast have been disappearing for as long as man has known how to put a roof over his head. Some of them are now a mile out, beyond the reach of practical archaeology and surviving only in legend (you'll be told of ghostly church bells tolling at low tide). After storms on the North Norfolk coast, skeletons climb ashore from drowned churchyards. But the problem was of little importance until a leisured Victorian and Edwardian middle class fell in love with clifftop living and had the money, time and technology to make it happen. Villas and hotels swarmed to the edge, dragging behind them an aspirant train of more modest houses, bungalows and all the bits of business and service infrastructure that went with them. Once-humble fishing villages climbed uphill to become at first elegant, then blowsy seaside resorts that grew and melded with each other into linear conurbations. They became places of architectural experiment, sexual adventure and blissful retreat. Even now, with felt-penned lines on planners' maps showing how deep the sea may bite, the process shows little sign of reversal. 'Cliff Drive' is still the most aspirational address for anyone with a decent pension.

The wealth and influence of middle-class householders, unwilling to give up their homes, meant that problems of erosion were taken seriously – hence the concrete – but it was not until the 1960s that the parallel problem of groundwater was properly understood. Left to their own devices, without human intervention, clay-and-sandstone cliffs undergo repeated shallow landslides that gradually cut back the lip and lower the gradient. They generally stabilize, with no further risk of slippage, when they get down to a limbo-dancer's angle of 1 in 7. By this time the retirees will have lost their bungalows but will at least have easier access to the sea. In some places, including some quite densely populated parts of Norfolk, this is exactly what will happen if the current Shoreline Management Plans are adopted as they stand and are interpreted literally. This is the reality of 'managed realignment'.

But it is not the only way. British engineers taught the world to transcend physical barriers by understanding natural forces and converting them to positive use (think railways, drainage systems, canals, dams), so you wouldn't expect them to be fazed by a runaway cliff. In fact they offer a number of solutions at different levels of cost, sophistication and ambition. The simplest way, closest to nature, is to pre-empt the slippage by regrading the cliff to a safer angle. The ideal of 1 in 7 is not usually achievable – roads and buildings get in the way – but there are places (on the North Kent coast, for example) where 1 in 4 is feasible. This makes a generally safe option if it is combined with a drainage scheme to collect and disperse the water. Where this is not possible, the usual alternative is to place a heavy obstacle at the toe of the cliff – usually rock armour, though a carefully maintained sand or shingle beach might also do the trick – to stop it sliding forward and to break up the waves.

Rather than treat the symptoms, however, a far better solution is to eliminate the cause. If you replay the clay-and-pebble mindgame, but now imagine that the clay is dried out and not allowed to get wet again, you can see that the whole assembly becomes more stable. There is now friction rather than lubrication between the joints and planes, and you can safely increase the weight on top. Even scaled up to the size of a sea cliff, the technology is not especially difficult. Large areas of clifftop at Herne Bay, for example, have been made safe by nothing more sophisticated than a grid of shallow drains that channel the rain away. If it can work here, you might think, it could work anywhere.

Two miles west along the North Kent coast lie the ruins of a seven-acre fort (Regulbium) at Reculver, built by the Romans to guard the Thames estuary. When it was new, around AD 210, it stood some 3km from the sea. Erosion brought the shoreline to the fort's north wall by 1780. Now it has reached the two Saxon church towers that stand at the centre. According to the local authority, Canterbury City Council, this represents an erosion rate of between 1.5 and 2.0 metres a year. But this of course is an *average*. Erosion does not track across the ground at a constant and predictable rate like the sun across the sky. The land breaks off in lumps. In the 15 weeks between November 1656 and January 1657 the coast at Reculver fell back by 30 metres. Attempts to protect the church began almost 200 years ago, in 1809, when Trinity House armed the base of the towers with ragstone and wood. Concrete sea walls followed the terrible storm and tidal surge of 31 January 1953 (when the gardens and tennis courts of the Miramar Hotel at nearby Herne Bay dropped by 14 metres). Then came a 'beach nourishment' scheme, with lorry-loads of shingle tipped on to the beach; 14 rock groynes appeared in 1995, and another 500,000 tonnes of shingle came ashore from a dredger. Four years later, the concrete sea walls were patched up and reinforced on the seaward side with thousands of tonnes of boulders. This is all typical of the kind of old-fashioned, hammer-and-nails technology with which landowners and local authorities have tried to prop up their coastlines. It works for a while but has the permanence of putty. Sooner or later (usually sooner), it needs repair, replacement or reinforcement as the sea goes about its business and the cliffs follow their instinct to crawl back and flatten.

Since 1953, engineers have learned a lot more about soil mechanics (the way the cliffs behave) and sediment transport (the way cliffs and beaches are eroded and replenished by the sea). In both cases the lessons have been hard-won, learned not from textbook or blackboard but from streets falling into the water. There has been trial-and-error fiddling with the design and position of groynes – in particular the substitution of rock barriers for metal or wood – and a multi-million-pound library of technical reports. We know now that the first generation of coastal defences created as many problems as it solved, and that our thinking in the future has to be as joined up as the coast itself. This is the reason for the Shoreline Management Plans and the root of all the bitter conflicts that lie ahead. There are two quite different categories of argument – the scientific and technological (what are the most effective methods?), and the political and economic (how and where should the techniques be applied; who should be the winners and losers?). The second set of questions grows out of the first, with each improvement in understanding bringing new agonies of indecision. How can we expiate our former sins – building in the wrong place; failing to understand that earth and water, though they can be influenced by human activity, are beyond any sort of precise or predictable control? How can we tell entire communities that they are to be abandoned? (As it turns out, the answer to this is simple: sneak it out on the internet.)

Few local authorities have had more salutary, practical experience than Canterbury City Council, whose district includes some 15km of violently friable North Kent coast between Seasalter and Reculver, including Whitstable and Herne Bay. Like every other coastal authority, it has had to learn on the hoof. In the days before anyone understood soil mechanics, most of its coastline was skimmed with concrete. This had the interesting result – Hard Lesson No. 1 – of arresting erosion by the waves while simultaneously revealing the more insidious and hitherto invisible problem of groundwater. 'Over the years,' the council said in a report on its management programme, 'there have been many earth movements, some big and some small along these cliffs. Other than tidying up after them, little could be done that was of any practical value because nobody understood what was going on below the ground.'

In the last three decades of the 20th century, however, the cliffs' inner workings became more apparent and the learning curve steepened. Thirty years ago, wherever it could do so without losing houses, the council began to cut back and reduce the angle of the cliffs to a safe 1 in 7 or manageable 1 in 4. Where this was not possible, it did the best it could but had to leave some at 1 in 3 or even steeper in order to save houses (for there would be little point in a policy that destroyed the very property it was supposed to protect). This was combined with a web of surface drains – 5.4km of them for every kilometre of slope – to catch the rain, and deep drains to remove as much as possible of what did manage to penetrate or was already there. Extra 'toe-weighting', in the form of rocks and shingle, has been stacked at the foot of vulnerable cliffs to block any future tendency to slide and brace them against collapse. Some smaller, especially dangerous areas have been reinforced with metal or plastic grids that lock the slip surfaces together. So far, the story has been a happy one – you could say a *remarkable* one given the extreme vulnerability and volatile history of the coast. The only visible failures have been in tree-planting schemes – blackthorn, elm, poplar and willow – which it was hoped would both help bind the soil and suck up excess water (the saplings evidently did not like the salt-laden air). The council is pleased enough to risk congratulating itself, though it's not risking complacency. 'Despite the extra steepness, the regrading and drainage works have been effective for about 30 years, but these steeper parts of the cliff are still at an increased risk so we need to keep an eye on them.'

The eye becomes steadily more sophisticated and beadily focused. In 30 years the technology of cliff-watching has evolved from something not much better than string and plumb-bob to remote sensing devices that flash their data straight to the engineers' computers. There are gadgets called piezometers that monitor water pressure inside the London clay; inclinometers that can detect movement even deep inside a slope; and tilt meters that do exactly what their name suggests. North Kent's problems are not over. A 30-year safety record has not so much reduced the importance of vigilance as proved the necessity of it; there is still a risk that at some time in the future the steeper cliffs will have to be regraded, with unavoidable loss of property, and the financial burden extends as far into the future as anyone can see (maintenance alone costs £15,000 a year per km of coastal defence). Yet it shows what can be done. At Tankerton, 2.3km of maintained defence will rescue 167 houses that would otherwise have been lost to erosion within 50 years. The value of property saved, including service infrastructure, is around £40m per kilometre – a figure of considerable interest to people elsewhere whose local authorities may be less considerate. It is all being done with minimal environmental intrusion, and the 'hold-the-line' policy set out in the local Shoreline Management Plan looks wholly reasonable. The SMP even won a rare plaudit from Friends of the Earth for proposing to 'identify, maintain and if possible enhance coastal habitats, natural features, landscape, amenity and the environment'.

The only downside is the perennial one – continued interference with the natural 'downdrift' of sediment along the coast. But being aware of this, as earlier generations of engineers were not, at least helps to limit the damage. At the Hampton end of Herne Bay, for example, they have allowed the old pier to be reclaimed by the sea. It had looked like a good idea when it was built as a jetty for oyster smacks in 1863, but it had the unlooked-for effect of a 'terminal groyne', blocking the downdrift of sediment and causing the shore to erode by 200 metres in 100 years (a new sea wall was needed to halt the damage). Thus does each generation pay for the errors of the last. How we break that chain, and leave to our own grandchildren a store of gratitude rather than regret, is the very essence of the problem we face.

Whatever happens, there is no corner of the conscious mind that could imagine the abandonment – now or ever – of Whitstable or Herne Bay. Their long-term protection is as near a certainty as anything in an uncertain world ever gets. For others, the wheel spins less kindly, promising only the reek of betrayal, the numbing, impossible nightmare of dreams crumbling into ruin and honest endeavour mocked. A little over 100 miles north of Herne Bay, on the high rump of Norfolk, are the north-facing resorts of Sheringham and Cromer. The first of these was so heavily armoured in 1995 that, approached from offshore, the seafront looks like a nuclear bunker. For promenaders it is like strolling the ramps of a multi-storey car park. It has £3.4m-worth of steel-reinforced impregnability (1995 values) and a degree of ugliness that would challenge an East German ball-bearing factory. Yes, you can have security but it comes at a price. Another £1.85m (1999 values) has been spent on groynes, with much of the old wood-and-steel being replaced by rock, and yet more rock piled against the sea wall. Even now there is uncertainty about the scale, design and placement of the groynes, but the beach will be monitored and any misbehaviour by sand or shingle corrected by further works in future. The 'Shannocks', as Sheringham people are known to the 'Crabs' of Cromer, can put in their earplugs and sleep soundly behind their triple-glazing. Let the wind huff and puff, and let the sea howl as it may – it can't blow their houses down.

You can't say the same for Cromer, whose seafront gains as much in charm as it loses in security from the antiquity of its defences. Viewed from the east beach, with pale winter light spilling over the pantiled roofs, and with the pier (famous for its age-defying summer variety show) striding through the combers beneath the madly ornate Hotel de Paris, the whole town looks like a single, impossibly muddled mega-building propped up by the tower of its enormous church. It's a bit run-down, a bit flaky and on-the-cheap, but you'd need a heart of North Sea flint – a hatred of England, even – not to love it just a little. A bracing swim, a tea-dance, and haddock and chips to follow. But when the clouds gather, and the storm warnings go out, Cromer looks to the sea as anxiously as a trawlerman's wife. If it is to survive (as it must), then it will have to follow its neighbour's lead and send for concrete and rock.

In 2003, a consultants' report for North Norfolk District Council warned that the existing defences – groynes, sea walls, parapets and cliff-retaining walls – were 'nearing the end of their useful life'. This was hastening the erosion of the cliffs, some of which were steep, and increasing the threat to houses, cafés, hotels and B&Bs. (To crank up the anxiety, there had been a land-slip just west of the pier in February 2002.) At several points the beach now was too low for the sand and shingle to offer any pro-tection to the sea wall, which was being undermined and in such a poor state that the waves were likely to break through within three years. Life and property then 'would be at peril' from serious landslips and the abrupt retreat of the clifftop. 'As a result,' it said, with little risk of overstating its case, 'there is considerable concern among the local community.'

If nothing were done, said the consultants HR Wallingford, property worth between £16.1m and £35.1m would go over the side in the next 50 years. If sea levels were to rise as much as the Hadley Centre said they would, the damage could be even worse. Structures at risk included not just clifftop buildings but also the esplanade and pier with its vital lifeboat station (historically one of Britain's busiest). Minimum requirements included refurbishing the sea wall; redesigning, rebuilding and extending the groyne system and replenishing the beach. This is all in line with both the original Shoreline Management Plan of 1995 and the draft SMP2 of 2005, both of which have recommended 'holding the line'. The value of the protected property far exceeds the cost of defending it, so it scores more than enough points to be confident of government aid. Cromer's outlook therefore is a bit of short-term anxiety followed by several decades of armoured security until the elements take their toll, more consultants are engaged and another generation of defences is built. It's much like treading water: if you stop, you go under.

And stop is exactly what Cromer has had to do. Having provisionally approved a £9m repair scheme, Defra suddenly pulled the plug. So much had been spent on fluvial flooding schemes inland, there was no money left for coastal defence, so – despite the severity of the consultants' warning – Cromer would have to wait . . . and wait, and wait. Not only would it not be budgeted in the current financial year, it would not be included even in 2007–8. The very earliest any new concrete could arrive was 2008–9, *six years* after Wallingford delivered its report and three years after it warned the sea wall was likely to fail. And of course there is no guarantee even of that. In the meantime North Norfolk District Council has to make do and mend, propping up groynes and parapets as best it can. As a measure of the government's commitment to coastal resorts and communities, it hardly registers as a flicker on the dial. 'Sustainability' is what it says. 'Let them eat salt' is what it means.

But while Cromer, like Sheringham, will survive its trauma and, albeit with casualties, hold like a bastion in a siege, smaller communities nearby are more like tethered goats. The unprotected cliffs that flank the two resorts are soft as cake. Scythed by storm and sea, undermined by groundwater, they crumble and slip to gritty oblivion. At Weybourne, where a row of cottages perches over the drop like a murderer awaiting the hangman, the clifftop line of Second World War pillboxes is already haunted by fish. More will follow, and the prominence of the two resort towns will become ever more extreme as the softer coasts fall back around them. Already Sheringham stands 70 metres further out than the neighbouring cliffs – a process that, in time, will maroon it on a promontory with an increasingly doleful impact on beaches to the east, whose flow of sediment it will obstruct. This is an extreme view that may be dismissed as alarmist; but it is a view which, not far away, is being pressed upon other communities with potentially lethal effect.

A word of explanation may be needed here. Some of what I write may look like special pleading for a particular stretch of coast – one near where I live, and where my parents' home is threatened by erosion. I declare an interest, but the real reason for this narrow point of focus is that it has an importance that reaches far beyond the pain of its own anticipated loss. The Kelling to Lowestoft Ness Shoreline Management Plan in north-east Norfolk is one of only three trial SMPs being taken forward to the second stage. Once completed and agreed, it will become the model for others to follow. If North Norfolk gets a bad deal, then so will everyone else. Coastal protection is a low political priority, unmentioned in party manifestos, and likely to remain so unless communities like this can make their voices heard, or until eastern England is hit by some further catastrophe with great loss of life.

Just east of Cromer, beyond the golf course, lies Overstrand, the seaside village made famous as 'Poppyland' by the *Daily Telegraph* travel writer Clement Scott in the 1880s. A one-time playground of the rich that attracted the likes of Winston Churchill and Albert Einstein, it is now a neat and popular family resort with a magnetic attraction for retirees, a classic sandy beach and clocks stuck at teatime. Ten miles further to the east stands Happisburgh, whose red-and-white-banded lighthouse, dating from 1791, is the oldest in East Anglia still working. The churchyard contains plenty of mariners who ignored its warning and failed to avoid the ship-hungry sands seven miles out. Happisburgh's flint cottages are from the more florid end of the estate agents' lexicon – charming, old-world, unspoiled, timeless. Arthur Conan Doyle is supposed to have thought up the plot for *The Adventure of the Dancing Men* while staying at the Hill House Hotel in the early 1900s. J. M. W. Turner came and sketched the sands; Ernest Shackleton entertained a packed meeting in the Church Room with stories of Antarctica; Henry Moore and Barbara Hepworth holidayed here and collected pebbles; John Betjeman and the late Queen Mother both admired St Mary's parish church; and Rolf Harris came to record a Christmas radio special in 1982. None of this, though it diverts village historians and amuses visitors, is what now places Happisburgh in the news.

Under the heading 'Key Strategic Issues', the original Shoreline Management Plan of 1996 had this to say: 'The villages of Overstrand and Mundesley are developed up to the cliff edge . . . Continued protection of these areas is a priority.' And this:

This area sees a change in the coastal area from low lying cliffs in the north to low lying flood plain to the south, with the coastline in retreat throughout. The northern end is mainly agricultural land, with the exception of the village of Happisburgh. Continued erosion will result in the loss of some assets and ultimately could pose a threat to the flood plain further south. To the south any further retreat of the coastline would result in widespread flooding of the Broads. The present seawall has prevented any natural rolling back of the natural dune system over much of this stretch. The strategy here must be to continue to prevent the occurrence of flooding in this area.

For Happisburgh and Overstrand alike, the SMP's recommendation, emphasized by capital letters, was the same: HOLD THE EXISTING LINE. It did not make news – maintaining the status quo rarely does. Those who bought homes or businesses in the villages did so with confidence – they knew the coastline was securely defended, and that it was the local authority's policy to keep it that way. There was nothing for them to worry about (or at least nothing new – despite reassurances, Happisburgh was already losing properties in Beach Road). House prices continued to rise, sucking in people's life savings like leaves into a drain.

Then came the bombshell. The revised Shoreline Management Plan, or draft SMP2, published in November 2004, was drawn up by consultants on behalf of a steering group that included representatives of North Norfolk, Great Yarmouth and Waveney councils, plus the Environment Agency, Defra and Great Yarmouth Port Authority. The consultants' brief remained unaltered – to determine how the coast should be managed in the 21st century. So did the broad parameters – to balance the needs of people, the economy and the environment. But the recommendations were shockingly, life-wrenchingly different.

It was like the judgement of a medieval court. There was to be one law for the rich and powerful, another for the poor and weak. While towns like Sheringham, Cromer, Yarmouth, Gorleston and Lowestoft would be guaranteed safety, the villages would be surrendered to the sea. Their future usefulness would be as a natural resource, to be churned into sand to feed the big boys' beaches. In the case of Overstrand:

... the preferred policy is for retreat to ensure sediment supply to ... downdrift frontages. This will deliver technical and environmental benefits, but a number of assets will be at risk. Therefore there needs to be a continuation of measures to manage losses, including erosion-slowing defences, therefore the recommended policy is **managed realignment.**

Ultimately, the shoreline should reach a point more in keeping with the natural position had it not been defended, which should enable a beach to form. At this point it is expected that erosion rates will slow and management of the shoreline will be more easily achieved, through measures such as groynes, without being detrimental to other parts of the SMP frontage.

The prose is as sluggish as an East Anglian tide, but the meaning is plain. The 'environmental benefits' are to the beaches of Great Yarmouth. The 'assets at risk' include Overstrand's sea wall, promenade, beach car park, up to 135 houses and an unspecified number of businesses, plus 'associated infrastructure services', roads and a sewage pumping station. These are cumulative losses spread over 100 years, but they show vividly the significance of the settlement (insignificant ones don't have 135 houses to lose), and the extent to which it will be harmed. Even those whose houses survive will be condemned to live with blight. The village has a permanent population of 952 (2001 census), greatly swelled by holidaymakers in summer (it receives 200,000 visitors a year, of whom 34,700 stay overnight).

At Happisburgh the plan is not even for 'managed realignment', though perhaps it is no worse for lack of a euphemism. 'No active intervention' means exactly what it says – abandonment to the sea. The cost will be 35 properties, most of them caused by the further collapse of Beach Road, plus a caravan park, the Grade Two-listed Manor House and the Grade One St Mary's Church. Overstrand stands to lose its heart; Happisburgh will surrender its soul.

So how had it come about? How did these two priorities of

1996 become the throwaways of 2004? North Norfolk District Council put up a defence of pragmatism. 'The SMP,' it said, 'takes the view that it must not commit to "unsustainable" defence options. In other words, it must be realistic about what kind of defence will be possible in decades to come and, in the words of the SMP itself, "not promise what cannot be delivered".' So we come back to the same question: what had changed? What was it that had made defending these villages suddenly an unsustainable proposition? This is how the consultants built their case against Overstrand:

> The whole length of cliffs between Cromer and Mundesley provide a vital source of beach sediment area [*sic*] for much of the SMP frontage. Therefore maintaining this sediment input and transport along the coast is a key long-term aim. However, historic defence construction at Overstrand has already formed a significant promontory, and this will have an increasing influence on the sediment drift to downcoast beaches if the present define line is maintained, preventing approximately 20% of the entire SMP beach sediment budget from moving freely along the coast. *Furthermore, there is not, at present, sufficient economic justification for new defences* [my italics].

And for Happisburgh:

> Although there are socio-economic implications, such as residential properties and amenities at risk from erosion at Happisburgh, these are not sufficient to economically justify building new defences along this frontage. Furthermore, it would not be appropriate to defend Happisburgh due to the impact this would have for the SMP shoreline as a whole, as the coastal retreat either side would result in the development of this area as a promontory making it both technically difficult to sustain and impacting significantly upon the alongshore sediment transport to downdrift areas.

But this doesn't answer the question either. If it was necessary in 2004 to allow Overstrand, Happisburgh and other parts of the Norfolk coast to crumble and feed beaches to the east and south, then it was just as necessary eight years earlier. And yet, in 1996, protecting them was 'a priority'. We must ask again: what has changed?

Part of the answer is to be found in an obscure report published in 2002. *The Southern North Sea Sediment Transport Study Phase 2* is not what you would call a page-turner, but its task was crucial: 'to provide the broad appreciation and detailed understanding of sediment transport along the eastern coastline of England between Flamborough Head in Yorkshire and North Foreland in Kent.'

It was delivered by a consortium of consultants, scientists and academics hired by a group of nine local authorities (including the three involved in Norfolk) with the Environment Agency, English Nature and the British Marine Aggregate Producers Association (BMAPA, the trade association of the dredging industry). The funding came in part from Defra. Why was such a report necessary? 'Sediment movements in the southern North Sea influence the eastern English coastline through supplying or removing beach material. It is important to understand these movements thoroughly so as to improve the data on which Shoreline Management Plans (SMPs) and the assessment of dredging licence applications are based.'

The consultants were asked to trace the sources of sediment, the pathways along which it travelled and the beaches on which it ended up. Not only this: they had also to identify 'offshore features' and work out their influence on waves and currents; provide information to help the next generation of SMPs, and (hot potato coming up) to make a 'more informed assessment' of the effects of offshore dredging. Do please forgive me for not explaining the survey methods or the processing of data. These are necessarily complex (no one would wish such a report to be simplistic), but sheer volume and weight of numbers militate against the understanding of laymen who – unfairly – can be backed against the wall and accused of ignorance. To put the thing at its simplest, the authors worked out their priorities through consultation with 'stakeholders' and by analysing the existing data. Sources included the British Geological Survey, the Admiralty, the oil and gas industry and the consultant HR Wallingford's own database.

The researchers also examined existing SMPs and reviewed maps of the seabed compiled from sonar scans. What they were looking for was evidence of movement. The wet sand-ripples you see on a beach at low tide – some straight, some serpentine – give a good idea of what happens, on a much bigger scale, in deeper water. So also do the ribbons of sand that build up around obstacles. Where sand is shifting, they tell you both the direction of movement and the type of current (counter-intuitively, steady currents produce asymmetric ripples; oscillating ones produce symmetric). Further out, under the sea, are 'megaripples' (defined as having a wavelength, or distance between crests, of between 0.6 and 10 metres, and a height of between 0.1 and 1 metre), and 'sandwaves', which can be on the scale of Saharan dunes. They may reach as high as a third of the water depth and migrate at speeds measurable in kilometres per year. Every bump and hollow tells a story. 'Comet marks' and 'wreck marks', for example, are sand structures caused by erosion or deposition that form around underwater obstacles such as wrecks. These, too, can provide evidence of flow. All this and more was fed into computers that sifted, collated and shaped it into 'models'. These were then 'validated' by field data collected at checkpoints in the Humber estuary, at Winterton near Happisburgh, and at Clacton – which emboldened the authors to declare that a 'high degree of confidence could be placed in the results'.

Only history will tell us whether or not their confidence was justified. The consequence to villagers, however, is much easier to predict – they will lose their homes. And so we have at least the beginnings of an answer – the SMP2 has to take account of the sediment study, which says that the 400,000 cubic metres of sand eroded from North Norfolk's cliffs every year are vital to other parts of the coast. But the question is still not properly resolved. 'Take account of' does not mean 'obey without question'. The political volte-face is explained only if sediment outranks every other issue. And clearly it does not. If Overstrand and Happisburgh get in the way of downdrift, then so do Sheringham and Cromer. Yet no one is talking about 'managed realignment' or 'no active intervention' here, any more than they are at Yarmouth. So what else is different?

The answer is economic. In 2003 Defra revised its points tariff so that only settlements of huge economic value could qualify for protection. If you number your neighbours in thousands, you're safe. If you number them in tens or hundreds, then it's hard cheese, your bungalow will make a useful contribution to the 'sediment budget'. At best, you can wave it goodbye without compensation. At worst, you may have to pay for its demolition if it becomes unsafe. Such is 'sustainability'.

And here is Catch-22. Local councillors on SMP steering groups insist that they share their residents' anger. But what can they do? It's Defra that sets the rules and local authorities have no choice but to comply with them. Defra meanwhile goes on insisting that SMPs are purely *local* issues, to be resolved by the steering groups. It is at its loftiest when questioned about human rights. Here is Eddie Brophy, of Defra's 'Flood Management Communications Team', replying on behalf of Elliot Morley, then Minister of State for Climate Change and the Environment, to a letter from the coordinator of the North Norfolk residents' Coastal Concern Action Group, Malcolm Kerby:

> The Human Rights Act recognises the need for a balance between public interests and private rights. Without prejudice to consideration of the circumstances of individual cases, we consider that reasoned decisions not to continue to maintain and renew existing coastal defences that are not sustainable, following consultation,

deliberation and proper pre-planning (including the provision of a reasonable period of notice to those affected), can be carried out without any infringement of human rights.

Kerby had drawn attention to Article 8 of the European Convention on Human Rights, which includes the right of respect for a person's home, and goes on:

There shall be no interference by a public authority with the exercise of this right except such as is in accordance with the law and is necessary in a democratic society in the interests of national security, public safety or the economic well-being of the country, for the prevention of disorder or crime, for the protection of health or morals, or for the protection of the rights and freedoms of others.

This of course is – as it is meant to be – loose enough for any government lawyer or civil servant to justify any interpretation that suits their purpose. 'Economic well-being of the country' and 'rights and freedoms of others' are legal plasma, able to take on an infinity of different shapes. Who is to say what they mean? In Kerby's submission, the uncompensated compulsory abandonment of homes and land would be 'disproportionate, grossly unfair and contrary to natural justice'. Few outside Defra would see it differently. In March 2005, North Norfolk's MP, the Liberal Democrat Norman Lamb, raised the issue in an adjournment debate at Westminster Hall. 'The draft Shoreline Management Plan,' he said, 'has hit coastal communities in North Norfolk like a bombshell.' Without the plan's even having been approved, there had been negative effects on the value and saleability of property, and on the availability of mortgages and insurance.

How does the Minister respond to people who have purchased property in the past few years, when the official policy was to hold the line, to defend the coastline? They are likely to have bought with the benefit of a mortgage, and could suddenly be plunged into negative equity. They will be left paying off their mortgages in the knowledge that there will be little or no capital asset left when they have finished paying.

'Just last weekend,' he said, 'I heard about a property situated a mile from the coast that had lost 25 per cent of its value.' A pub in the village was now worth only half what its owner had paid for it 14 years earlier. He went on:

> That illustrates the real and current impact of the plan. I challenge the minister to tell us whether he believes that it is socially just that a generation of people who happen to own properties in the affected villages could lose everything as a result of the government's decision that it is too expensive to defend the coastline.
>
> The Minister will be aware that I have written to him about compensation. When he wrote back to me on 16 November 2004, he confirmed that there were 'no current plans' to introduce a compensation scheme, and that there was 'nothing to discuss'.

Even without Article 8, it is not easy to make a moral argument against compensation in principle. This doesn't mean people will not try, or that the 'rights and freedoms of others' will not be invoked at the lowest imaginable threshold. 'I live in Oxfordshire,' said a senior executive from one of the marine consultants. 'Why should I, as a taxpayer, pay for someone's house in Norfolk? Where is the benefit to me?' You might as well ask: what is the benefit to a healthy person of paying for the sick, or to a working person of supporting the unemployed? All taxpayers contribute to benefits for others that they don't receive themselves; it is the plank upon which our society stands. As to benefits, the coasts are national assets for everyone to enjoy – not excluding curmudgeons from Oxfordshire. More pertinently, shifts in public policy are not acts of god: they are human interventions for which no one is responsible but the people who make them. It is only by accident of timing that the entire burden of loss will fall upon a particular generation of property owners, whose only fault was to believe – because nobody warned them otherwise – that existing policies would be maintained.

This is a crucial point because it touches upon more than just fairness to individuals. To Whitehall bean-counters, 'managed realignment' and 'no active intervention' are attractive because they cost nothing – it's homeowners who take the hit, not the Chancellor of the Exchequer. But if the victims were to be compensated for their loss – and fair compensation would have to mean the full market values of their homes and businesses as they would have been if the defensive line had held – then the economic case for abandonment could fall apart. If 'no active intervention' ceased to be the lowest cost option, then the entire policy would have to be reappraised and officials' reading of Article 8 – at least insofar as it involved 'the economic well-being of the country' – might be rather different.

Compensation is not the only thing missing from Defra's balance sheet. In an appendix, the draft SMP itself acknowledges the black hole at its heart: 'losses and benefits have been calculated only on the basis of residential and commercial property values. Other assets, such as utilities, and highways, and intangibles such as recreation, impacts on the local economy or environment, have not been valued or included.'

Politicians complain of cynicism in an electorate that no longer believes what it is told, and blames newspapers and broadcasters for the breakdown in trust. The truth is that journalists expose only a small proportion of what is actually happening. They will fasten on to lies about Iraq, or stealth taxes, or double-counting in health funding, but they seldom drill down into the appendices of shoreline management plans. This is where you find the Enron accounting, the bent analyses that weigh in the balance only those things that support the officially desired outcome, and leave out anything that doesn't. If the value to the economy of the destroyed property is not to be taken into account, then what possible credibility does the SMP have? Sometimes you have to state the obvious, and Norman Lamb did so: 'That makes non-sense of the whole plan. Surely, before taking decisions on how to progress with something so fundamental, which affects so many people's lives, we should have a clear understanding of the full cost and of the impact on the Norfolk Broads, tourism, relocation of communities and our precious heritage.'

There is no question that coastal defence is expensive, with new sea walls coming in at £10,000 per metre and groynes at £30,000 each. Overstrand's defenders say their village creates 187 jobs in the tourist industry alone, and that it contributes £5.6m annually to the regional economy. Being even-handed with my scepticism, I have no idea how accurate this figure is. Numbers rain down on one's head. As the government undervalues the property that would be lost, so might residents be tempted to do the opposite. What is self-evidently the case, however, is that no argument based on economic impacts can have credibility if it dismisses the entire local economy as 'intangible'. It is bad enough that genuine intangibles – the beauty and character of the landscape – have been assigned no value on their own merits, but what can you say about a policy that, further south and east, would hazard the Norfolk Broads?

On the question of marine aggregate dredging, which local people are convinced is the real reason beaches are starved of sand, the SMP is, if anything, even more offhand: 'Whether or not there are links between offshore dredging and coastal erosion is uncertain.' And that is all it says. To the residents' action group this alone is enough to 'render the entire SMP . . . absolutely worthless'. Their argument looks hard to rebut. The seabed is dredged for two reasons – to keep navigation channels open, and to provide sand and gravel for the construction industry. No aspect of coastal defence arouses more passion. To the residents, dredging com-panies are parasites ruthlessly enriching themselves, the Crown Estates and the Exchequer at the cost of local people's homes and livelihoods. To the defenders of dredging, the residents are unhinged zealots with bees in their bonnets and no understanding of geology. One prominent member of the industry described them to me as 'criminal'.

The residents' argument, which is supported by Friends of the Earth, goes like this: although erosion of the North Sea coast has been going on for thousands of years, there has been a rapid acceleration in the rate of loss over the last three decades. This correlates precisely with an increase in dredging activity as the country's appetite for concrete has gone on rising and an export trade has grown. Dredging is far from new. The Sediment Transport Study itself reports that the Thames was dredged for ship's ballast in the 16th century, and that by the mid-19th century 400 smacks were going out off Harwich and Walton every day to haul up Portland stone for cement. But the scale of the operation has grown exponentially, building boom by building boom, since the country was urbanized by the industrial revolution, and most especially since the 1970s. Between 1965 and 1970, between 7m and 10m tonnes of sand and gravel were removed from the seas around the UK every year. By the mid-eighties this had reached 15m tonnes; now it's 20m or 25m, of which 30 per cent is sent abroad. A large proportion of it comes from the waters off Norfolk. In 2001, 40 per cent of the national total – 9.6m out of 22m tonnes – was dredged off Yarmouth.

Technology has evolved too, enabling sand and gravel to be lifted from deeper water further out. Until the 1930s, dredging was a pontoon-and-crane business more or less confined to sheltered estuaries. Now it's all about speed and volume. In its way it is a marvel of engineering – a fleet of 35 highly sophisticated, £15m vessels now works around the clock, 365 days a year, to keep the concrete mixers permanently turning. They are of two types – anchor dredgers that remain stationary and work a limited area; and trailer dredgers that drag suction pipes at up to 1.5 knots. These leave long, shallow furrows in the seabed, usually in water at least 20 and often as much as 50 metres deep.

A big ship with powerful pumps can load 5,000 tonnes in three hours; the very largest can shift 8,000 tonnes at a time – the equivalent of 200 40-tonne lorryloads. It's big, it's efficient and, in the minds of coastal defence groups, it's very, very dangerous.

Common sense says that holes in the sea floor must be sand-traps. We know what happens when a child's beachworks are caught by the tide – the holes fill up again, and when the tide recedes not a trace remains. Exactly the same must happen at sea. For every 8,000-tonne shipload removed by a dredger, another 8,000 tonnes must be washed back into the hole – 8,000 tonnes that is no longer free to circulate and replenish the beaches. Thus it follows that if you want to pin the blame for a breakdown in 'sediment transport', the finger must point at the dredging industry and not at the groynes, revetments and sea walls of innocent seaside villages.

The MP Norman Lamb fixed on this during the adjournment debate in 2005. While welcoming the consultants' admission that the impact of dredging was at least 'uncertain', he found it 'extraordinary' that the SMP had nothing more to say. 'I become very frustrated,' he said, 'when I hear the dogmatic assertion that dredging has no effect on the rate of erosion.' A European research programme – called, inevitably, Eurosion – had concluded that dredging *could* 'increase the rate of erosion'. That 'could', however, is important, and Lamb will have chosen his words with care. There is no doubt that dredging *can* accelerate erosion. The Sediment Transport Study cites the notorious case of Hallsands village in South Devon, which had to be abandoned in the early 1900s, and several other well-documented cases from around the world. In the SMP's failure even to acknowledge this, Lamb sees the morbid influence of government policy and vested interest:

The problem is that substantial sums of money are made from dredging. In 2002 alone, the Crown Estate received £5.2m, which is 40 per cent of its total income from the whole country, from marine minerals dredging off the Norfolk coast alone. The construction industry inevitably demands ever-increasing volumes of aggregate to meet, apart from anything else, the government's own building plans.

Friends of the Earth, through its marine defence network Marinet, went even further in its indictment of the guilty:

The huge profit made from dredging by the government through royalties to the Crown Estate of 40 to 60p per tonne taken created £147,334,680 from the 137,817,564 tonnes of aggregate stripped offshore to Norfolk alone over the past 13 years. Taxation on the landed product at 17.5% (£3.50 per tonne) created £1,031,342,805 for the Exchequer from that self-same 137,817,564 tonnes of aggregate. Far more than this went to the dredging companies and their shareholders, but imparting knowledge of this profit and the turnover was refused by BMAPA. It may be estimated as some ten times more. It can thus be envisaged that this is the real reason for government controlled agencies not including the effects from offshore dredging in the SMP.

The clincher is the rate of erosion itself. In 1992, consultants used computer modelling to predict the likely line of erosion at Happisburgh in 60 years' time – i.e. by 2052. In the event, the line was reached in 12 years – 'an inaccuracy factor,' as Norman Lamb put it, 'of five'. Again FoE went further: 'This serious inaccuracy was undoubtedly because the report did not allow for the impact of offshore aggregate dredging. When that factor enters the equation, the apparent anomaly becomes fully explainable. The new SMP must consider this major cause if it is to have any credence, yet it barely has a mention in the SMP.'

The SMP's failure to engage is as much of a frustration for the proponents of dredging as it is for the opposition. No one likes a question left dangling, especially when it is of such great importance to so many people. But whereas the SMP cravenly played an ignorance card, *The Southern North Sea Sediment Transport Study* met the issue full on. Dredging, it said, might affect a coastline in one of four different ways. The most important is 'beach drawdown', where dredgers work too close inshore and sand from the beach is combed into the hole by a storm. This is what happened at Hallsands, where the workings reached right up to the low-water mark. The second possibility is that offshore dredging will alter the seabed and disrupt the pattern of waves – a process which has damaged beaches in Sydney, Australia, and Grand Isle, Louisiana. The third risk is of 'interception', where a hole traps moving sand that otherwise would have reached the coast. The fourth is the straightforward theft of material bound for the beach. Drawdown and interception are often cited as causes of erosion in East Anglia – the one stripping the beaches of sand; the other preventing their replenishment. Conclusion: stop the dredging and you stop the erosion.

The objectors are encouraged by Eurosion, which lists the Humber estuary and Sussex coast among the places it says have suffered 'sediment deficit' as a result of dredging, and which raises questions about the practice of 'beach nourishment' – heavily used on the North Sea coast – where denuded beaches are rebuilt with sand from the seabed.

> Whereas beach nourishments may have a positive effect on coastal erosion, sediment extraction for sand mining locally attributes to the erosion of the foreshore of the coast and may lead [to] erosion of the beach and dune system on the longer term. Local deepening of the seafloor can alter wave patterns and cause gradients in sediment transports, leading to local erosion.

The English may be a bit broken but the sense is clear enough. But so, throughout a lengthy document, is the authors' fondness for weasels – most especially 'may' and 'can'. These stand at a distance from 'will' and 'do', and – though they are often quoted

– tell us nothing useful about any particular case. A sagging tree branch may cause a broken head. An offshore dredging site may cause erosion. The statement is unhelpful precisely because it is unexceptionable: a possibility, not a rule. The fact is, though we wish it otherwise, the most authoritative account of the known influences on movements of material around the east coast of England is *The Southern North Sea Sediment Transfer Study*. One day perhaps it will be superseded, but for now it's all there is.

Monopolies always invite suspicion, and much is made of the fact that the principal contractor, HR Wallingford, works also for vested interests in the dredging industry, the government and the Crown Estate. But the same would be true of any company capable of fulfilling such a complex brief. They are few in number, and highly specialized – you can't just walk your fingers through the Yellow Pages. Like its competitors, Wallingford is a big company accustomed to working with local authorities. Nine such were involved in the sediment study, and none has any obvious interest in cheating its own electorate. The work also involved the Centre for Environment, Fisheries and Aquaculture Science (CEFAS), the international maritime consultants Posford Haskoning (part of the Dutch Royal Haskoning Group) and the University of East Anglia, plus a leading independent consultant of long experience, Dr Brian D'Olier. The client group also included the British Marine Aggregate Producers Association (which might be thought to favour a particular outcome) and English Nature and the Environment Agency (which would not). For reasons implicit in much of what has gone before, I find it hard to repress feelings of cynicism about many processes of government. There is no certainty that the present initiatives are going to result in a policy that is any better than the current one. But the mess is political, not scientific. The scientists are responsible for collecting and interpreting data, and for developing methodologies that will improve their forecasting. All this they are doing, it seems to me, honestly and with rigour. They are not responsible for the use to which their work is put, and –

unless we can find better, more authoritative sources of our own – theirs is the account we shall have to accept.

And so here it is. All the evidence of movement on the seabed, including the tracking of radioactive particles, seems to suggest that there is no transfer of sand to North Norfolk's beaches from offshore. This is not because supplies on the seabed have been exhausted by dredging; it is simply the way the system works. Sand and gravel, says the report, are recycled in a narrow pathway along the shoreline itself, with no exchange between inshore and deeper water. If it is true, then this alone is enough to kill any suspicion that dredging plays a part in Norfolk's problem. There could be no possibility of 'beach drawdown' (there isn't anyway, with deep-water sites so far from the shore), or of interception. But the 'if' is still justified because a computer model is involved, and we must not be seduced into believing that it's anything more than a mathematically sophisticated best guess. On the other hand, it's not just idle prediction. The model is based on observational data and can be checked.

The dredging sites themselves have been exhaustively scrutinized – even the dispersal of sand-plumes stirred by passing dredgers has been examined for ill effect. (It is important to note, however, that the environmental impacts of aggregate dredging are not limited to coastal erosion. The disruption of the seabed and its effects on marine ecosystems are also controversial and will be discussed in Chapter 8.) The most important findings are these. For all that it may resemble a scaled-up version of the beach exposed at low tide, the seabed is a very different place and it behaves in very different and often unexpected ways. For all the megaripples and sandwaves that pass through (and remember it's the waves themselves that move, not the material through which they pass), it is remarkably stable. There is very little movement of sand or gravel across the sea floor. Geologists tell us that the material being dredged is still lying where it was laid down 10,000 years ago by the glaciers – a fact borne out by what happens after the dredgers have moved on, which is . . . nothing.

The most telling piece of evidence is that, unlike the moats of sandcastles, the dredged furrows do not refill with sand or gravel. Side-scan sonar shows that the volume of water in each hole remains exactly the same as the volume of aggregate that was removed from it. 'It's like a sandpit on land,' says Wallingford's technical director, Alan Brampton. 'It just stays as it is and doesn't suck in the farmer's field.'

In developing ideas about coastal protection we are often urged to look to the Dutch, those champions of the water margin whose every dry footstep is a tribute to engineering, and for whom every millimetre gained or lost is a blow for or against survival. What is their attitude to dredging? They are so certain of its safety that they don't even bother to monitor its effects. This is not to say that coastal communities should give up the fight. Why should their villages be thought any less deserving than inland towns on the floodplains of rivers? Or than the future occupants of Thames Gateway, or their own East Anglian neighbours? Whereas it is a truism that not every inch of coast can be defended, it is equally true that we can protect anything we really want to.

We have choices in what we give and in what we take; choices between justice and travesty. As things stand, where there are enough votes to count, the line will hold. Where there are not, it won't. No one publicly will delineate the policy in quite those terms – pragmatism knows when to hold its tongue – but that is how the politics work. The best answer to it is not to argue about beach drawdown – that's not so much a hostage to fortune as a gift to the bean-counters, who would love it if that were the ground they had to fight on.

The argument has to shift to where Norman Lamb has placed it, in a cultural and economic landscape in which everything is weighed and valued, including the lives of the people who live in it. At least the current Minister of State (in 2007), Ian Pearson, is less of a dead bat than his predecessor Elliot Morley. He took the trouble to visit North Norfolk and, asked about compensation for the dispossessed, made some good-sounding remarks about the need for 'social justice'. Out, too, came the usual mantra of cornered ministers – nothing ruled in, nothing ruled out – though of course nothing ever is until the Treasury hands down its judgement. Compensation remains crucial, though the question of when and whom to pay is open to argument. Lamb suggests compensating the final owners, on the day their properties fall into the sea. But, as he also says, the effects are being felt even now, before the SMP has been adopted as policy. The very idea of it has knocked 25 per cent off property values, and it will take more than the promise of end-of-life compensation, due to some future owner, to restore the differential. A property with reduced life expectancy in a degrading environment will never be worth as much as it was before, regardless of any hand-me-down promise. What will happen is the same as always happens in blighted communities where no one wants to buy. Speculators will move in, board the houses up and wait to collect their bounty. Wherever 'no active intervention' or 'managed realignment' is applied, the principal losers will be the current owners. It is they who should be compensated. Thereafter, with no loss to anyone, the frankly blighted houses can be left to fetch what they may, and their new owners to live like nature's own, bravely and at the confluence of mighty forces.

Now that is *real* romance.

CHAPTER FOUR

The Final Harvest

My grandfather never learned to swim. He was a landsman who lived by the sea, but his seafaring neighbours, who set the tone, were no different. It was the same wherever men woke to the sound of waves. Mariners, even lifeboatmen, had little interest in swimming. If a ship went down, a man in oilskins and seaboots had no more use for the breaststroke than he had for a pipe of tobacco. What was the point? The countless numbers of drowned sailors in seaside churchyards are not there because they couldn't swim. Men who live with danger are, by definition, optimists. But there is fatalism, too; an acceptance, however grudgingly given, that the elements will have their due and luck is dealt by random chance or divine grace. It's why 'For those in peril on the sea' is the most lustily sung number in the English hymnal. It's what makes sailors superstitious, and it's part of the price of fish.

'I don't wonder, with all the men lost around the Dogger, we sometimes get human skulls, and that, in the trawl, and more 'an once I've seen a man in oily jumpers, and boots on, shot out on deck with the fish when we've opened the cod end. It made your flesh crawl, shovin' of 'em over again with a capstan bar or your shovels.' The words are attributed to a 'Great Yarmouth smacksman' of 1909, quoted in *The British Seafarer*, the book of a Radio 4 series from the late 1970s. Like all professionals who see a bit of gore, fishermen exorcize their demons by frightening others. Like the complacent consumers that computer shopping and TV dinners have turned us into, we take their bravery for granted – an untasted ingredient in the *sauce tartare*. The notion that fish-eating improves intelligence may be founded in circular logic: to catch fish, you need to be intelligent. It was one of the earliest ways in which our distant ancestors, upon diverging from apes, applied their ingenuity with tools. Small-scale inshore fishing has gone on around the coasts of Britain since prehistoric men first learned the usefulness of a hollowed log. For the first few millennia, however, until shipbuilding and navigational skills evolved to meet the challenges of the deep, the effort was concentrated sensibly on rivers and ponds. Even during the time of the Vikings, whose highways were the northern seas, most of the fish eaten were freshwater species trapped in weirs. As late as 1215, there were so many of these in the Thames and elsewhere that they impeded the free passage of the English barons and their merchandise – hence Clause 33 of Magna Carta: 'All fish-weirs shall be removed from the Thames, the Medway, and throughout the whole of England, except on the sea coast.'

From the early 11th century, there is increasing evidence of a gradual switch from river to sea-fish. Ian Friel, in his *Maritime History of Britain and Ireland*, speculates that this might have been caused by the fouling of inland waterways by urban effluents. One might suppose also that medieval tastebuds were similar to our own and, once having tasted cod, would have lost some of their enthusiasm for the mud-flavoured products of lowland rivers. For the adventurer, it was also a new and expanding opportunity for trade in which risk of drowning was balanced against the expectation of riches. While those engaged in older trades – oil, wine, cloth – could hug the coasts all the way to the Mediterranean and back, the fishermen – bravely, greedily, foolhardily – set their sails for the icy north. It was not just the North Sea that they fished. By the first decade of the 15th century, ships from England's east coast were a common sight around Iceland.

Even for a modern, steel-hulled vessel with sealed bulkheads and satellite navigation, this is far from plain sailing. In the early days, life on board was so rough that East Anglia's Icelandic fleets were reckoned to be 'the chiefest Seminarie and Nurserie' of England's navy. If a man or boy could hack it on the cod run, then he would find few terrors in naval warfare.

The ships would head out each year in March for a round trip of some 1,800 miles, after which the survivors would return with their cargos of salt cod in August or September. There were no timetables or ETAs, only destinations. In favourable conditions a ship might reach Iceland in a week. In bad, it could take a month. In the worst, the best a man could hope for was to perish swiftly. In 1419, a storm off the Icelandic coast sank 25 English boats in a day (this at a time when the entire fleet might have been no more than 30). Most feared of all was the Pentland Firth, the seething, white-water channel between the northern tip of the Scottish mainland and the Orkneys. In 1380 the Scottish priest-chronicler John of Fordun described 'a fearfully dangerous whirlpool' that 'sucks in and belches back the waters every hour'. A letter-writer of 1542 spoke for all posterity when he called it 'the most daungerouse place of all Christendom'. It remains one of the most daunting stretches of water in the world, churning the bones of entire fleets and forever hungry for more.

That shipowners were prepared to risk their vessels – some of them capable of carrying as much as 100 tons – and their captains and crews disposed to chance their lives, tells us much about the value of the trade. At first the Englishmen bought dried cod, or 'stockfish', from the Icelanders, but they soon took to catching and salting their own. There were no nets: the fish were caught either on weighted hand-lines – typically with two baited hooks on them – or, later, on long-lines that might stretch for several hundred yards, with hooks dangling every three yards or so. On shore the Icelanders dried their stockfish in the air. At sea, with limited space and weeks away from port, the English had to use salt (as they did, similarly, in the North Sea). This description of the method, from John Collins's *Salt and Fishery* of 1682, is quoted by Dr Evan Jones, of Bristol University, in a chapter on Icelandic fishing in *England's Sea Fisheries: The Commercial Fisheries of England and Wales Since 1300* (a collection of papers edited by David J. Starkey, Chris Reid and Neil Ashcroft that makes the ideal starting point for anyone who wants to study the subject in depth, and from which I have gratefully cribbed). After the cod had been headed, gutted and split, wrote Collins:

> They salt them well with refined Salt, laying them Circularly round the barrel with the Tails towards the middle, where to supply the Descent, a whole Cod is laid in; between each lay of Fish they put in a Lane of Salt, and so fill up to the Head which is well covered with Salt, where after 24 hours time they will settle and make room for more; and when the barrel is full they head them up full of Pickle.

You can see why, with a payload of between 30 and 100 tons, veterans of the Iceland run might have considered men-o'-war a softer option. A refinement later in the 17th century was to cram in yet more cargo by getting rid of the barrels and packing the fish straight into the hold. Collins's account is complete in every detail bar the smell:

> The Cod being haled on Board, they are laid upon the Decks in the Vessel, (or may be on boards or Tables;) One Man chops or wrings off the Head throwing it over-Board, and enters a Knife at the Navel, and cuts it up to the Throat and downwards, taking out the Guts, Garbidge, and Rows, to throw away; as also the Livers to reserve in barrels to make Oyle of. Another, the Splitter, takes out the back bone, and lays the Fish open to the Tail. Then they salt them, and lay them Nape and Tail in Bed on the Deck, as fast as they can dispatch. The manner of salting is, a Man hath a small salting Platter that may hold about a quart, which he disperseth chiefly on the middle or thickest part of the Fish, from whence it

SEA CHANGE

runs off on the Tail and thinnest part. And when one lay is done,
they pile them up in their Holds, and proceed to another, making
in the middle of the Hold, the course of Fish higher by two foot
than on the sides, that the Pickle descending may fall on the
sides.

In this way, says Evan Jones, a 100-ton ship might catch, load,
preserve and store between 20,000 and 25,000 cod in a single
season (a calculation he bases on the quantities of salt loaded). By
a further calculation, taking into account the weight of each ship,
he reckons that the 149 English vessels, mostly from Suffolk and
Norfolk, that sailed for Iceland in 1528 would have caught
between them some 2.5m cod – 'enough to supply one fish to
almost every person living in England at the time'. And not just
fish. An important secondary product, worth the very considerable sum of £30 a tun, was cod liver oil. These days it is taken,
usually in capsule form to protect sensitive modern palates, as a
medicine – rich in vitamins A and D and omega-3 fish oils, said
to guard against heart disease, cancer, diabetes, hypertension,
schizophrenia, multiple sclerosis, osteoporosis, rickets and much
else besides. Lucky would have been the medieval Englishman
who survived long enough to die from any of these. The oil in
those days was an industrial product used in lamps and craft
processes. It is hard to read John Collins's account of its shipboard manufacture without a clutch in the throat, if not a sudden
contraction of the stomach:

The Livers being barrell'd up, three barrels of their own nature
without any Artifice, yeild one barrel of foul Oyle, the which is
thus got, let the barrels stand 48 hours on their Heads and the
Oyle will swim at top, from whence it may be keeched with a pot,
so long as the Oyle may be taken off without Blood, which they
put in an empty barrel, let it stand six hours and then scum it off,
and there will be left about half or more in Blood and Guts. The
Remainders or Residue are called blubber-Livers, when brought

home, or to a convenience for Boyling are Boyled up, and 7 or 8
barrels of Livers may yield one barrel of Oyle.

The little-known story of the Iceland fishery is of more than
casual interest, for it introduces many of the issues – political,
logistical, economic – that have bedevilled the industry ever since.
For early shipowners the guarantee of profit – if their crews
stayed alive – was the heavy demand for fish generated by meat-
less days in the religious calendar. Others, too, waited to take
their cut. To send a 100-ton ship with 40-strong crew to sea for
six months was a costly business as well as a risky one. The
money men's calculations were as cold as the Arctic sea. Ashore,
secured loans could be had at an annual interest rate of between
8 per cent and 10 per cent. But if a shipowner wanted to raise
money for a trip to Iceland, then he would have to pay a premium
rate of 20 or 25 per cent for the six-month duration of the voyage. The investors were like gamblers hedging their bets, for they
too were risking a hit – loans were repayable only when ships
returned to port. If they didn't, it was a dead loss for all concerned. The stratospheric interest charge, says Jones, 'can itself be
taken as grim evidence of the high proportion of ships that never
made it home'.

Waiting at the dockside were bigger sharks even than the
moneylenders – agents of the Crown, claiming their toll. From
the reign of Henry VIII and throughout the 16th century, this
amounted to 200 cod or 100 ling per ship, or their cash equivalents. Then as now, lives and livelihoods were tossed, this way and
that, by international politics, bureaucracy and the greed of
governments. Seapowers in particular were jealous of their waters
and all that they contained. Though at first they were
accommodating to the English fleet – in the late 15th century,
heavily laden fishing boats returning from Iceland were levied at
just 6s 8d – Iceland's Danish rulers sent the fishery into decline
from the 1530s with steep fee increases and restrictions calculated
to favour local fishermen. In 1528, 149 ships set out from East

Anglian ports to Iceland; by 1533 they had reduced to 85, and by mid-century to just 43.

Danish protectionism was nothing compared to the damage done by the English to their own fishermen. In 1534 – apparently to stop dealers making a cartel in salt fish – an Act of Parliament banned fishermen from selling their catches to merchants ashore, or even to the shipowners themselves. This hobbled the market and blunted its appeal to investors, while local mayors retained power over prices in the markets. At the same time, the spread of Protestantism was easing the religious pressure on people to eat fish. In time, and for a while, other pressures would reverse the trend. The population of England grew rapidly during the late 16th and early 17th centuries, increasing both the demand for food and the profit to be had from trading it. By the late 1620s, East Anglia's Icelandic fishing fleet had grown again to 160-plus – rivalling, and possibly even exceeding, the enterprise of West Country fishermen in Newfoundland, which had been developing since the 1570s. (As we shall see, the competition between the east and west of the country would come to look more like armed warfare than ordinary commercial rivalry.) The Elizabethan government's maritime census of 1582 showed that – despite the success of northern ports such as Scarborough and Whitby, and of Dartmouth and Fowey in the west – 46 per cent of England's fishermen were crammed into the country's south-eastern corner, from Kent to Norfolk.

The misreading of the sea, and the unquestioning assumption of its infinitude, was a disaster that would take another three and a half centuries to become apparent. In the 1630s, King Charles I, like others before and since, could see only an ocean of money. Up went the tolls on the returning Icelandic fleet; up went the duty on salt; down went the number of ships. An upsurge in piracy and war against the Dutch added yet more to the list of disincentives, and – though the Icelandic fleet, sailing by now under naval protection, would recover to a total of 77 ships by 1659 – the decline was unstoppable. By 1668, says Evan Jones, the fleet was down to 39, and by 1675 it was 28 and falling. What really clobbered it was the tax on imported salt, which came mainly from Biscay, and without which the industry couldn't function. The import tax in the 16th century stood at 5 per cent; by the late 18th century it had reached 300 per cent, and touched a historic peak of 1,500 per cent during the Napoleonic wars, by which time the Icelandic cod-run was history. It was reported in 1702 that the number of men employed had shrunk from more than 10,000 to fewer than 1,000, and that Great Yarmouth – one of the hubs of the trade – had sent no ships to Iceland in either of the previous two years. And there was another portent of things to come. 'Although attempts were made to allow fishermen to claim tax remissions on salt used in fisheries,' writes Evan Jones, 'the State's obsession with preventing fraud meant that the regulations were so complex and stringent that, in practice, it was impossible for the cod fishermen to collect them.' Result: the East Anglians were priced out of the market, the shortfall in supply was made up by the Dutch, and the men of Suffolk and Norfolk went back to the Dogger Bank.

The Westcountrymen's transatlantic trade, too, had collapsed by the end of the 18th century, largely as a result of wars (the Seven Years War, 1756–63; the War of American Independence, 1775–83, and the French Revolutionary War, 1792–1802), and of the growth of a strong local fishing industry in Newfoundland itself. The one problem that no one had yet suffered, or even imagined, was the long-term collapse of fish stocks. Newfoundland's was the most abundant cod fishery in the world; the idea of its ever running out of fish would have been given about as much credence as the sky running out of stars. The sea was so densely packed, it was almost more fish than water. For three centuries after John Cabot landed in 1497, fishermen had no need to fiddle around with lines or nets – they could simply let down baskets. Legends of this magical pot of protein spread throughout the world. By the 19th century it was already being overstretched, with annual catches of 100,000 to 300,000 tonnes.

Local fishermen continued to dominate the industry, but by the second half of the 20th century the foreigners – and not just the English – were back in force. In the mid-1960s, Russia alone had 344 boats in the area; by 1971 it had 502, with smaller fleets from Spain, Portugal, France and West Germany all adding to the pressure. In 1968, a record – and ultimately fatal – 810,000 tonnes was landed. It could not go on, and it didn't. Between 1962 and 1977, the crucial spawning biomass declined by 94 per cent. Canada declared a 200-mile international fishing limit in 1977, but it was too late. In 1992 the breeding stock collapsed and the fishery was closed, throwing 40,000 people out of work and ruining the local economy.

It was not just cod that lured men to excess. The classic North Sea harvest, reliable as corn, was the fat shoals of herring that flashed through the sea like twists of silver light. It was one of those things by which Suffolk men identified themselves. Long after he had moved from his native county to Hertfordshire, my non-swimming grandfather would always eat a fried herring (sometimes fresh, sometimes a bloater) for his Saturday high tea, second in importance only to the Ipswich Town football result. It was like an edible football favour, or a dialect on a plate. Even his wedding date, 10 February, had an ancient Suffolkian stamp to it. In farming areas the peak season for marriages was after the corn harvest, when all had been threshed and stacked. In fishing areas it followed the catching and processing of the herring. Rural brides went to the altar in October and November; fishwives between November and early February. For centuries in places like Lowestoft and Yarmouth, the pattern of life was set not by human desires or instincts but by the spawning habits of *Clupea harengus*.

Again I must declare my debt to *England's Sea Fisheries*, which includes detailed essays on the historic and modern herring trade by David Butcher, Michael Haines and Chris Reid. By the middle of the 14th century, the herring fishery off the East Anglian coast was vast and highly competitive. Yarmouth, with its nationally important herring fair, was the market leader, though it keenly felt the threat of its Suffolk neighbour, Lowestoft. Uninterrupted free trade, then as now, was akin to anarchy in the minds of those who commanded power. This paragraph describing an early attempt at protectionism is from *Fraser's Magazine* in November 1831, where it appeared in a long article, 'The ancient commerce of England prior and to the reign of Edward III, inclusive, by John Galt Esq, FSA &c.'

But it was not until the year 1357 that the herring fishery began to obtain the attention of that great king [Edward III]. It was in that year that the act called the Statute of Herrings was made, to prohibit the people of Great Yarmouth from going out to sea to meet the herring fishers coming to Yarmouth, to forestall the market. By that statute it was enacted, that herrings should be brought freely and unsold into the haven of Yarmouth, where the fair was kept, and that none should buy any herrings in their houses by covin [conspiracy], nor in any other manner, at a higher price than forty shillings per last of ten thousand herrings (or twelve barrels modern); neither shall any pyker (a small vessel) practise the buying of fresh herrings, in the haven of Yarmouth, between Michaelmas and the feast of St Martin.

Hard as Yarmouth struggled to protect itself, the rise of Lowestoft was inexorable. By 1526 it had 20 boats and 200 fishermen – a huge proportion of the working male population in a town whose total head-count was no more than 1,300. A few fish were caught in spring, but the real focus was an eight-week season from mid-September to November (when the marrying began). The method of fishing, which persisted right up until the middle years of the 20th century, was drift netting. Boats typically were of 30 to 50 tons burden, crewed by 10 or 11 men working a chain of 100 nets, which they would set out, or 'shoot', at sunset as the shoals rose. The nets were of one-inch hempen mesh, each one approximately 20yds long and 15ft deep. These were so valuable that they were bequeathed in wills, and had their lives extended by 'tanning' like leather in solutions of oak or ash bark (the collection of which carried the economic benefits of the herring trade far inland). Suspended vertically in the water, a chain of 100 nets would make a mile-long undersea fence in which the herring would become entangled by their gills. The catches were prodigious. Drifting for herring was not as profitable as line-fishing for cod, but it was less risky, closer to port (skippers seldom ventured more than 35 miles out) and cheaper to finance. A full load, with which a boat would turn for home, was between 120,000 and 144,000 fish, which, at times of glut, might be accrued in a single night. In normal times it would take longer – two nights, sometimes three – but compared to the six-month, cold-water marathon of the cod trade it was a light-ning sprint. Investment turned to profit much more quickly, and the fish could be landed fresh, for preserving ashore, rather than being laboriously salted at sea. All the crewmen's efforts could be concentrated on catching fish.

The harvest was so fast and so heavy that there was insufficient time for it to be eaten fresh. Most of the catch was pickled or smoked, and exported in 32-gallon barrels (each holding 1,000 fish), mainly to Mediterranean countries where Catholics observ-ing their fish-days still made faithful customers. By the middle of the 18th century, 75 per cent of Lowestoft's output was going abroad. International trade, however, brings international competition. The industry took its first heavy knock in the early 17th century when the Dutch muscled into the market and sank the East Anglians into a depression from which they would not emerge until the 1670s, after the Anglo-Dutch wars. The govern-ment, as governments do, continued to fiddle with the market, but bounties offered to encourage fishermen in the middle years of the 18th century were largely offset by the hated Salt Tax (which was not lifted from the herring boats until the 1820s). The bounty system was Anglocentric – by an Act of 1756, 3s 4d was payable for every 32-gallon barrel of herring produced in

England, but only a shilling in Scotland. Yet even that was not enough to compensate for the gulf in quality. In 1808 the Scottish landed a blow on the English when the 'Act for the Further and Better Regulation of the British White Herring Fishery' imposed tough standards on the quality of fish-curing north of the border but not in England and Wales. This might have seemed unfair on the Scots, but the consequent superiority of their product meant that the Scottish herring industry in the 19th century would grow to outstrip the English and become the largest in the world.

Despite all this, the English fleet – in Yorkshire as well as East Anglia – went on growing. In the early 1830s Yorkshire would send 50 or 60 large vessels southward to join the 100 local boats off Yarmouth. Between them, including the cockleshell fleet of smaller boats that worked closer inshore, they put some 4,000 to 5,000 men at sea. In Yorkshire itself, the Whitby Herring Company was established in 1833, and by 1836 there were 400 herring boats of various sizes and origins – some from East Anglia; some from Scotland; some even from Cornwall – ploughing the waters off Yorkshire. During the herring season, the harbour at Whitby – that 'great fischar toune', as John Leland had described it in 1536 – was so heavily trafficked that people could scramble from one side to the other across the decks. Many were fishwives, paid 1s 6d a day (7.5p) for counting the fish – a process of numerical jiggery-pokery guaranteed to make landsmen's eyeballs swivel. Like all trades, fishing had its own language: herring, for example, were sold by the 'last' of 10,000 fish. But it had its own arithmetic too. Four fish made a 'warp'; 33 warps made a 'hundred'; 100 hundreds made a 'last'. Whatever the reason for this, it was not sharp practice – more a case of Buyer Rejoice than Buyer Beware. You paid for 10,000 fish. You got 13,200.

Despite the poor quality of its cured fish and the increasing pre-eminence of the Scots, English exports still went on growing. Across Britain as a whole, the 320,000 barrels shipped abroad in 1853 had more than doubled to 660,000 in 1871. By now another powerful influence was at work. The coming of the railways transformed the industry, effectively created new ports (Grimsby, Hull) and, in its hunger for cargo, accelerated the course of events that, within a century, would convert short-term bonanza into long-term catastrophe. Faster communication to Birmingham, Manchester and other inland markets coincided with improvements in the fleets. Bigger ships were able to fish further out and to chase the shoals rather than just sit and wait for them, and from the 1860s the old hempen drift nets were replaced by lighter, more flexible cotton that could be carried in greater quantity and 'shot' more quickly. By the late 1870s a single vessel might work 130 nets, stretching to two miles or more. Fish swam into them in unprecedented numbers. Even in the early 1860s, Scarborough was loading railway wagons with up to 800 tons of herring a day, and the Yarmouth fleet – by now 400 vessels – had doubled since 1819. In the 20 years to 1878, the catching power of the English and Welsh fisheries quadrupled. Wherever and whenever fish swam, irrespective of their quality, boats raced to feed the ever-open maw of the rail network – nowhere more so than at Lowestoft, where the harbour itself was owned by the Great Eastern Railway. East Anglian men had always known that the best fishing, for the best herring in the best quantity, was in the early autumn. In the new frenzy, they began to fish in summer and spring.

By 1857 the 20 or 30 boats that had traditionally fished out of season had multiplied to 300, with many of the newcomers sailing from Scotland or the south coast. Had there been any Victorian equivalent of Greenpeace, the outcry would have echoed from Ramsgate to Wick. As it is, in *England's Sea Fisheries* Michael Haines records a single Northumberland fisherman of the time complaining that spring fishing was 'ruining the coast'. In the midst of boom came the first sour smell of decay. Many of the spring herring were 'spent' fish in such miserable condition that they could be sold only as fertilizer. In 1900, however, with the first steam-powered drifters pointing the way ahead, there was room only for optimism as the industry, like a butterfly bursting from its chrysalis for a last gaudy but ephemeral fling, entered its golden age. According to parliamentary papers, herrings landed in England and Wales that year totalled 2.425m hundredweight; those in Scotland 3.520m – a total of 5.945m (743,000 tons), previously exceeded only by 1898's 6.536m. Britain continued to dominate the export market. In 1900 it shipped out 1.5m barrels, mostly from Scotland, of which the vast majority (more than 1m) went to Germany. These last few years before British seamen went to war against their most important customer was a period of uninterrupted boom. Between 1900 and 1913, herring landings in England and Wales rose by 8.2 per cent a year, with the two East Anglian giants – Yarmouth and Lowestoft – between them contributing 75 per cent of the total. In 1907 fish came ashore so fast that the industry struggled to cope with its own productivity: on one day in 1907, 90m herring were caught off Yarmouth, of which there was space ashore for only 60m. The rest had to be diverted to Grimsby. The spread of steam power was a major factor in all this. From a more or less standing start at the turn of the century, steamers by the outbreak of the First World War had taken 70 per cent of the market. Though they were no better at catching fish than the sail boats, they were bigger, much less affected by wind and tide, and so much faster that they could complete twice the number of trips and deliver fresher catches.

Landings in Scotland increased more slowly than those in England, at 1.7 per cent a year, but Scottish boats were as busy in English waters as they were in their own. The 'English' fleet was swollen each year by some 1,100 boats from north of the border, which netted at least 40 per cent of the East Anglian catch. By 1913 one in every two fish caught in British coastal waters was a herring. Significantly, in view of what was to come, only one in five British-caught herrings was eaten at home. Worse: 80 per cent of the exports were taken by Germany and Russia. The echo of Gavrilo Princip's revolver, in Sarajevo on 28 June

1914, was the echo of industrial doom. As the Archduke Franz Ferdinand and Duchess Sophie von Chotkova died, so did the livelihoods of North Sea fishermen. War killed the herring boom, and it would never come again. It was only lack of any alternative that kept the trade alive through the depression of the 1920s and '30s, when boat-owners were locked in by debt, unable to sell their vessels, and when crewmen during a national job famine could find no other work. It was of little comfort, but they were not alone:

> The herring industry was typical of many in decline between the wars [writes Chris Reid in *England's Sea Fisheries*], in that it was long-established, localised, labour-intensive and export oriented. Its main problems – the loss of export markets, international competition and the growth of protection – were commonplace among Britain's staple industries such as textiles and shipbuilding.

In the late 1930s the new Herring Industry Board did its best to separate the industry from its historic past and to set it on a more viable course for the future. Between 1935 and 1940, more than 2,000 fishermen were lent money to buy new equipment, and 42 to modernize their boats. It also ran a decommissioning scheme which, in another foretaste of things to come, and at a cost of £7,777, saw 130 boats taken out of service in 1936 and '38. But it was a measure of the industry's despair, and lack of confidence in its own future, that when the board in 1936 offered loans of up to two-thirds the cost of new drifters, it found not a single investor willing to take the risk. In 1938 the offer went up to £250,000, but even this drew only 17 successful applications and war intervened before any vessels could be built. After that, the only question was how long the industry would take to die. In the year before the outbreak of the First World War, 370,000 tonnes of herring were landed in England and Wales. By the 1940s it was down to a yearly average of 85,000, falling to 50,000 through the 1950s, and to 15,000 in the '60s. The era ended in 1967, when, says Chris Reid, 'a single drifter sailed from the port of Lowestoft'. The Scottish industry hobbled on for a little longer, but it too collapsed in 1974, and in 1977 the UK government banned all herring fishing in the North Sea.

The problem of overfishing had been apparent since the 1950s. The gradual introduction of trawling and purse-seining in place of drift-netting, and the growth of industrial fishing that wanted nothing more from the water than bulk protein, hit the sea like whales among plankton, jaws forever open, gulping whatever swam into them. Adult fish, juveniles, all went the same way, as if the fishermen's mothers had never read to them the story of the golden goose. As each herring population collapsed, so the trawlers would move on to the next and finish that one, too. Some have called it a 'salutary lesson', though nearly half a century later, with European governments and their fishermen pleading for the right to clear the seas of anything that grows fins and can be served with chips, it is a lesson that has been dropped from the curriculum. Again, Chris Reid puts his finger on it:

> The collapse of the herring fisheries was due to the collective failure of states in the region to commit themselves to solving a common problem. While the organisation for collaboratively managing the herring fisheries, the North East Atlantic Fisheries Commission (NEAFC), was empowered to set total allowable catches (TACs), they required the support of two-thirds of members and could be withdrawn on a single member's objection. This created a vacuum of responsibility: each nation had an incentive to default to increase its share of the fisheries and appease its own fishing communities.

Protective action when it came was so little and so late that it was useless. Not until 1971 did NEAFC reach agreement on a modest reduction of the fishing seasons and a ban on working the spawning grounds. We had to wait another three years, until 1974, for the first TAC to be set. Looking back now, one can recognize all the harbingers of the coming catastrophe, gathered like crows in the rigging. The TAC for 1974 was in line with scientific advice, but those for the next two years owed everything to politics and nothing to prudence (the scientific recommendation for 1976 was zero). Politicians are not stupid, but they are calculating. You see it every year in December, when European fisheries ministers meet in Brussels to agree the next year's quotas for each species under the Common Fisheries Policy. Conservation tugs them in one direction. Fight-your-corner nationalism, the clamour of their domestic fishing industries and the appetites of their electorates haul them in another. Better an empty sea, they seem to think, than a lost election.

But we need now to scroll back a bit. The east coast's love affair with herring was not shared by everyone: even during the Victorian and Edwardian boom years, the strong oily taste, lingering smell and messy preparation kept it off most British menus. The fleet fished essentially for the export trade, not for domestic kitchens. Even the great Eliza Acton, in her *Modern Cookery* of 1857, could rustle up only three recipes for herring, and two of these were for 'reds' (red herrings were an East Anglian speciality – salted whole and then smoked). The British taste is for the flaky white flesh of cod, haddock and whiting, and for meaty flatfish such as plaice and sole.

These had been pursued since medieval times, in the west of England as much as in the east. Along the rockier shores of the south-west peninsula – Somerset, Dorset, Devon and Cornwall – spotters could perch on cliffs or rock-stacks and point rowing boats straight to the shoals. They caught most of the same species as the East Anglians, including cod and herring, but took also conger, mackerel, mullet and – especially around Cornwall – pilchards and hake, neither of which was common in the North Sea. Some of the fish was line-caught, some netted, some trapped. Particularly in northern Somerset and Wales, 'sea weirs' – a bit like underwater sheep pens – were built from stone walls, brushwood and nets that trapped fish when the tide went out. (These have occasionally confused archaeologists into believing they have found the footings of prehistoric settlements invaded by the sea.)

The West Country, too, had its export trade – salted hake and conger to Gascony in the 14th and 15th centuries, and pilchards to Italy thereafter. Fishermen at the same time began to edge out beyond the headlands into deeper waters, and by the middle of the 15th century Devonians were sailing the Channel coast and rounding the North Foreland to shoot their nets for North Sea herring. On a calm day now, the quaintness of the old Cornish fishing villages projects an image of weatherbeaten contentment, rugged lives of hard-won but ample plenitude – each night's supper drawn fresh from an abundant sea, and shanties in candle-lit parlours. How we do love romantic fiction. In any kind of breeze, when the waves stiffen like garden walls, you can see from the clifftop that 'hard' was not the word for such a life. In the over-insured, risk-averse, health-and-safety-obsessed, regulated world in which we now live, it is hard enough to imagine the lives at sea of modern fishermen with their rigid hulls, fast diesel engines, eye-in-the-sky weather forecasts and powered winding gear. The very idea of physical hardship is alien to the western mind. To honestly visualize the lives of medieval sailors facing Atlantic swells in small open boats, with nothing to steady them but wind, tide and muscle power, and with no weather-warning beyond their own reading of the sky, is to realize how desperation turns to heroism. Needs must.

It was Westcountrymen, too, from Bristol, Barnstaple, Plymouth, Fowey, Poole, Bridport, Teignmouth and Dartmouth, who crisscrossed the Atlantic in the 18th century to bring back New England and Newfoundland cod. The scale of the trade was such that you have to cross-check the figures, comparing each year's to the next, to convince yourself that they are not misprints. In their peak year of 1788, a total of 2,680 English boats caught 948,970 quintals of Newfoundland cod, at a rate of 354.1

quintals per boat (a quintal is 112lb). Only about 10 per cent of the catch, salted and dried, found its way back to England – the rest of it went the same way as the herring, to Catholic southern Europe. As we have seen, a combination of factors – interruption by wars and the growth of a permanent Newfoundland fishing community, now swollen by immigrants from the West Country and Ireland – put paid to the transatlantic adventuring. In 1823 only 15 ships made the trip.

Other failures would follow. In 1834, it is claimed, 30m pilchards were landed at St Ives in a single hour (though it is not known by whom, or how, they were counted). Thirty million! The biggest customer for this linchpin of the Cornish economy was Catholic Italy, especially during the fish-hungry weeks of Lent. It had been going on in much the same way for centuries, and had been a major industry since the 1700s. The harvest was nothing if not dramatic. Spotters or 'huers' ashore would watch for the shoals and raise a cry – *Hevva!* – when they appeared. Huge seine nets weighing up to three tons were then shot around the shoals, tightened and hauled into the shallows, whence the pilchards were taken for salting. Their oil alone, being used to light the lamps of London, fetched enough to cover the fishermen's costs – all else was profit. It is alleged (though these things often turn out to be apocryphal) that, at the end of the season, the fishermen would turn in the vague direction of the Vatican and raise their glasses:

> *Here's a health to the Pope,*
> *And may he repent,*
> *And lengthen by six months*
> *The term of his Lent.*
> *It's always declared*
> *Betwixt the two poles,*
> *There's nothing like pilchards*
> *For saving of souls.*

What could not be saved was the pilchard itself. In the early 1900s, for whatever reason, the shoals simply stopped coming. In 1869, just before the decline began, the town had 286 registered seine companies. Two hundred and fifty-six of these had disappeared by the early 1900s, and the last seine was shot in 1924. Fish are like that. Possessing almost nothing that could be called 'intelligence', driven almost mechanistically by instinct, they respond to variations in sea conditions – especially temperature – which no human could detect without the aid of instrumentation. When conditions are favourable, they come. When they are not, they go. Even the Newfoundland cod fishery in its heyday knew good years and bad, as temperature affected spawning. It tells us that overfishing is not the only pressure that drives down populations; but it reminds us also that any human activity that alters the marine environment may drive away the fish.

Fishermen at sea accept risks, both physical and financial, that to City men look like madness. But they are not always so accepting of each other. When men from opposite flanks of the country sailed into each other's waters, there was always the prospect of something rather warmer than a cheery wave. In the 1830s, Westcountrymen landing fish at Scarborough aroused such fury among the locals that extra constables had to be sworn in to hold them apart. It worked the other way too. In May 1896, three naval gunboats and 300 men of the Royal Berkshire Regiment were dispatched to Cornwall's biggest fishing port, Newlyn, when, following years of irritation, local mackerel fishermen attacked a fleet of 'Yorkies' (their somewhat confusing name for boats and crews from Suffolk) and dumped their catch. The Cornishmen's fury was fanned by their religious faith. Being chapel-men, they did not go to sea on Sundays. Being looser of habit, the East Anglians had no such scruples. Unlike those in the West Country, Scillies, Ireland and the Isle of Man, their ports did not insist upon Sunday observance, and neither did they shoot their nets 'in the name of the Lord' as Cornishmen did. Sacrilege on its own might have been answered by a prayer. Sacrilege plus mackerel called for knuckles (and the praying could wait).

As it happened, fists were of no more use than appeals to the Almighty. For all its biblical echoes, fishing is an unforgiving trade – devout in a way, but deaf to pieties and not disposed to turn the other cheek. It's every fleet for itself. Cornish sailing luggers were no match for the East Anglian steam drifters that appeared off their shores in ever-increasing numbers and with ever-increasing catching power. By the turn of the century, and until its decline during the Second World War, the western mackerel fishery was dominated by men from the east. Boom time returned in the 1960s, but this time the Cornish had much more than East Anglia to contend with. Trawlers now came from eastern Europe, and the loss of North Sea herring brought boats also from Scotland and northern England, all taking vast tonnages of mackerel. Photographs from the '70s show boats at Newlyn with their glittering cargoes literally spilling over the gunwales. It ended as it was bound to, in depletion and exhaustion. By the early 1980s, glut had turned yet again to dearth.

There was nothing new in the ruthlessness of the fleets. They recognized no right of local ownership and saw no need to do other than fish the life out of every shoal they encountered. This was their duty, to themselves, to the shipowners and to the people at home waiting to be fed. Scientists and, especially, conservationists arguing for caution were dismissed as soft-skinned, book-learned meddlers who knew nothing of the sea. Every dripping netful was evidence of their ignorance. Of course there were fish in the sea! You just had to know where to look. For reasons of their own, governments sailed with the fleets. If they thought about protecting fish stocks at all, then it was to keep them for their own fishing industries and public, not to prevent over-exploitation. In the belligerent tradition of the sea, they would exercise a brand of diplomatic brinkmanship that went right to the edge – and sometimes beyond the edge – of war. The instruments of provocation were territorial exclusion zones – the girdles of sea that countries claimed as their own, and from which other nations were banned. There was nothing new in this – under the Hague Convention of 1882, most of Europe and the US had adopted a three-mile limit which, in ambition at least, set the international standard. But there were dissenters. The Scandinavians stuck to four miles; much of South America fixed on five, and Spain and Portugal went for six.

As trawling power went on increasing through the ages of steam and diesel, so smaller countries with rich fishing grounds became more and more alarmed by the multinational fleets. Iceland, which had won independence from Denmark only in 1944, was particularly edgy. Having been thwarted by Britain's refusal to cooperate over the proposed closure of cod nursery grounds in 1948, it set a course that would reach violent culmination in the so-called Icelandic cod wars. In the spring of 1952 it pushed out its coastal limit from three miles to four. Britain was one of several European countries that protested, though no action was taken beyond the banning of Icelandic fish from Hull and Grimsby. The flashpoint came in 1958 when Iceland unilaterally pushed out its limit to 12 miles – an extension that, earlier in the year, had received some support at a UN conference on the Law of the Sea but had not been adopted internationally. Again there was fury among the dispossessed, and this time the British were in no mood to surrender. The day after the limit was declared, on 2 September 1958, Icelandic gunboats arrested a British trawler working between the four- and 12-mile zones, and Britain responded in kind, with a fleet of 37 warships that vastly exceeded in firepower anything the Icelanders could put in the water. The stand-off continued until 1961, by which time many other countries had extended their limits to 12 miles, and others – including Norway and Denmark – were about to do so. Again Britain had to capitulate.

By now, more marine assets were at stake than just fish – the US in particular was interested in the prospect of oil – and there was talk of limits being stretched to as much as 200 miles. In 1972, dismayed by the catching power of foreign trawlers and the intolerable pressure on cod, Iceland acted again. Now the limit went out to 50 miles, and the second cod war began. This time it got physical. With devastating effect, the Icelanders rolled out their brilliant new short-range weapons – wire-cutters, with which they amputated the British (and some German) trawls, not only disabling the fleets (69 British and 15 German ships lost their gear) but also causing severe financial loss. The Navy came out again for a bit of heavy sparring, and RAF Nimrods flew sorties over the gunboats, but the outcome was much the same. In November 1973 the two governments reached agreement. In return for recognizing the new boundary, Britain would be given controlled access to specific areas within the 50-mile limit, from which it could take a maximum of 130,000 tons of fish in each of the two years for which the agreement ran. When it expired, on 13 November 1975, so did the period of truce. Emboldened by their success, and by the sway of world opinion, the Icelanders were ready to go even further. At another UN Law of the Sea conference in December 1973, more than 100 countries – including, ironically, Britain – had supported the idea of 200-mile exclusion zones. In July 1975, Iceland duly quadrupled its fishery limit from 50 to what had always been its ultimate ambition – 200 miles. It could not legally apply to Britain until the existing agreement expired on 13 November, but thereafter the two countries were at loggerheads again. The third cod war had begun.

Looking back more than 30 years later, it is impossible to see, in the determination of the British and others to defend their historic 'right of commons', anything other than a repeat of the purblind idiocy that had already cost the North Sea its herring, and that would wreak so much damage on those tormented waters in future. The Icelanders knew that the cod could not withstand such sustained and heavy hits from a multinational strike force whose catching power increased even as stocks declined. The fish being caught were both fewer and smaller, which meant that spawning was reduced and the entire fishery was being sucked into a spiral of decline. If it continued, there could be only one outcome – commercial extinction of the cod, and the collapse of Iceland's principal industry. During the '70s alone, stocks had shrunk by a third.

In extending its limits, Iceland acted unilaterally but hardly pre-cipitately. It had tried to arrange international conferences on conservation but had received no support from the countries whose agreement it needed. At UN conferences it had put for-ward ideas – closing nursery grounds, setting quotas and imposing temporary no-take zones – that were not only sensible but vital to the survival of the fish. Scientists were predicting that, at current rates of predation, the cod would not last beyond 1980. Having been ignored or, at best, having run into the usual block-ing manoeuvre of reference to committees, Iceland realized it would have to act alone. It would allow no other nation to fish within 200 miles, and its coastguards would board any vessel they suspected of trespass. By doing this, it said, it was merely enact-ing what would become international law anyway. Britain argued with the science and politics alike. Though it agreed that the cod were declining, it did not accept that there was any need for quotas to be set as low as the Icelanders wanted, and it insisted that Iceland had no right to act alone. For these reasons, it would go on fishing up to the margin of the 50-mile limit as the two countries had previously agreed. The gauntlet went down; once again the gunboats slipped their moorings.

And once again the forces looked unequally matched. Sixteen Icelandic protection vessels faced a British armada of 40 trawlers, 22 frigates (though not all were on patrol at the same time), seven supply vessels, nine tugs and three support ships. It was the naval equivalent of handbags at dawn: not much shooting but much bumping and jostling in which the British frigate *Andromeda* was especially prominent. Twice within 10 days she traded dents with Icelandic gunboats – first the *Tyr*, then the *Thor* – in incidents for which each side blamed the other. But there were other ways for British noses to be tweaked. For a start, the impotence of its seemingly overwhelming firepower – useless in a non-shooting war – made it look ridiculous. And the Icelanders held a trump card in the form of the US airbase at Keflavik, which it knew was essential to NATO. There was no way this could be put at risk for the sake of a few thousand tons of cod, and it was NATO itself that brokered a deal in June 1976. This was enough, just, to spare the British from humiliation, but victory was Iceland's. Britain would be allowed a maximum of 24 trawlers inside the 200-mile zone at any one time. They would be monitored and inspected by Icelandic coastguards, and would be allowed no more than 50,000 tons of fish a year – a figure made all but meaningless by the fact that the agreement ran for only six months. After that the British ships had to withdraw and 1,500 fishermen, plus 7,500 shore workers, lost their jobs.

By now the move towards 200-mile limits had gathered un-stoppable momentum. Finding itself shut out of waters off Newfoundland, the Faeroes and Norway as well as Iceland, Britain declared its own 200-mile zone in December 1976. But the rejoicing, if there was any, was short-lived. A few months later all members of the European Union followed suit, their 200-mile zones overlaying each other like scattered tiles so that no one had sole ownership of very much at all. In the corridors of Brussels, the phrase 'equal access' began to be heard, and minds were bent to the problem of converting the muddle into some kind of coherent policy. After years of what the European Commission's Fisheries and Maritime Affairs directorate describes as 'difficult negotiations', the answer they came up with was a benchmark in the history of political horse-trading and the worst news for fish since the invention of the hook. It came in 1983, and they called it the Common Fisheries Policy.

No one now pretends the CFP has been anything but a deter-mined confounder of its own ambitions. What it set out to preserve it has succeeded only in destroying. In trying to juggle politics, economics, social policy and conservation, it has dropped the lot. On one thing at least, all may agree. Unless there are radical changes in the way the EU conserves its fish, manages its fisheries and regulates its fleets, the only cod or haddock on British plates will be imported. Local herring, mackerel and shellfish will survive, but after that we'll be plumbing the ranks of 'assorted seafish' – spur-dog, scaldfish, lumpfish, sea-scorpion, weever, sandeel, horse mackerel, garfish, rat-tail, eel-pout, tadpole-fish, shad . . . Advertising agencies will be hired to dream up fancy new names for these piscatorial scrapings – rock haddock, perhaps, or Humber sole. Reconstituted and topped with mashed potato, they will appear in chill cabinets as Captain's Feast or Bosun's Bake. Enterprising food scientists will be experimenting with jellyfish, plankton and kelp.

Britain's attitude to fish has been shaped by a stultifying blend of pragmatism, anger and conservatism. Pragmatism in trimming its sails to the EU's prevailing political winds. Anger at surrendering to foreigners what the home fleet believes should be its own. Conservatism in its reluctance to interpret 'fish' as anything but cod. Like other fishing nations we tend to regard our catch as a kind of national codpiece – the bigger the better. We grant the industry the unusual distinction of a government minister all of its own (currently Ben Bradshaw), and every year spend £100m of public money on its management. And yet, as industries go, it is more minnow than whale – its 891,000-tonne haul in 1997 had a total value of £622m, no bigger than its take-away partner the potato. By 2003, the catch was down to 639,000 tonnes, and the market value to £528m. A year later it was 654,000 tonnes and £513m. In 2005 it was up again, to 708,000 tonnes and £571m, restoring its lead over the potato (£482m), but productivity in fishing is not like that of any other industry. You are not building an asset. Hitting the stock is raiding the savings.

And stock fluctuations are not exactly swings and roundabouts. The price of cod in 2005 was £1,585 per tonne of liveweight; blue whiting was £48. Since 2001, landings of cod by the UK fleet have fallen by a third. In a single year, 2004–5, the haul of blue whiting went up by 86 per cent to account for a full 40 per cent of the entire demersal catch. Forty per cent of the weight, that is, but only 3 per cent of the value. It's not the kind of business plan they teach at Harvard.

The UK government over the last two decades has been like a learner driver on an ice sheet, not knowing whether to press the brake or the accelerator. When there are fish to be caught – as in the splendidly named 'gadoid outburst' of the 1970s and '80s – it subsidizes new boats; when the trawlers have done their worst, it pays again to 'decommission' them. More than £100m has been spent on removing what it calls 'excess catching capacity', and many more boats will have to go in future. It is this very cycle of boom and bust – result of Pavlovian responses to short-term trends – that has undermined all attempts to develop a stream-lined, modern fleet whose catching power is matched to the available resources.

'Available resources', however, are the reefs on which policy founders. Oceanic chaos is well reflected in the legislative cross-currents through which the industry has to navigate. Illogicalities are everywhere. The quota system that underpins the Common Fisheries Policy is supposed to serve two objectives – protecting the stock by limiting annual catches, and ensuring that each member state gets its proper share of fish. Notoriously, it has succeeded in neither.

As a conservation tool, fish quotas, or Total Allowable Catches (TACs), are as much use as a panama hat in a monsoon. Historically they have been more concerned with how catches are apportioned than with how stocks are protected from overfishing. Cod-dependent Iceland allows its fishermen to land only 25 per cent of the calculated total amount of fish in the sea that are capable of breeding (known as the Spawning Stock Biomass, or SSB). In the EU the SSB each year takes a hit of well over 60 per cent. No prizes for guessing whose stocks are thriving and whose disappearing, and who is exporting to whom. Another problem for the EU is that 'demersal' species (bottom-dwellers that include all the family favourites such as cod, haddock and plaice) cannot be harvested cleanly, like barley or beans. They don't grow conveniently in discrete populations but gather in mixed groups. If you trawl for cod, you will also bring up haddock, whiting and flatfish. When you have filled your quota for cod but not for the others, then you face an interesting ethical conundrum. If you go on fishing for whiting and haddock, as you are entitled to, you will also catch more cod. What, then, do you do with the over-quota fish?

You can land them illegally as 'black fish', risking detection and the wrath of the law. Or you can dump them – good, wholesome, commercially valuable food – over the side as 'discards'. Either way the fish are dead, the breeding stock has taken a hit, and the CFP has failed in its purpose. The size of this 'bycatch' on its own would be a scandal. Worldwide, 26 per cent of fish caught are discarded. A survey in the North Sea in 1990 found that 26,000 tonnes of roundfish, 300,000 tonnes of flatfish, 150,000 tonnes of invertebrates and 15,000 tonnes of rays, skate and dogfish had all been thrown away. As rays and skate in particular have long lives and low reproductive rates, the consequence is potentially fatal to the breeding stock. It is in the nature of a criminal trade that nobody knows how many black fish are landed, but nobody doubts that cheating is endemic throughout the EU, including Britain. There is a persistent myth that the UK is disadvantaged by an exaggerated respect for European law. While our fishermen have to obey every regulation in a very thick book – one that lays down how much they can catch when and where, how many days they can fish and what size mesh they can use – the French and Spanish governments turn blind eyes to the institutionalized misbehaviour of their fleets. The truth is rather different. In a survey of one English region, 43.5 per cent of fishermen admitted landing up to 10 per cent more than their quotas, and 29 per cent said they had exceeded them by 25 per cent or more. Only 20 per cent claimed they landed no illegal fish at all. One reason often given for non-compliance is simple lack of respect for rules which, in mixed fisheries, make no obvious sense. Fishermen mock the use of latitude and longitude to define mobile fish populations, and fiercely resent being told to discard marketable fish (saithe, for example, for which they have no quota) which they cannot help but catch. Only 8 per cent of them think quotas are efficiently conserving fish stocks. They cite also economic necessity. If they were to adhere strictly to their diminishing quotas, then they would simply not earn enough to keep going. The government itself recognizes this, seeing the very survival of so many boats as proof of their illegality.

> This evidence is strengthened by the results of economic analysis of the various sectors of the fishing industry. In some sectors, notably whitefish, analysis suggests that if businesses were following the agreed catch limits a large number would go out of business unless their income were supplemented in some way. These visits, and responses to the Strategy Unit consultation paper, showed no high large [sic] level of bankruptcies in the industry, and so many fishermen are supplementing their legitimate fishing income with illegal fishing and/or returns from other sources of income in order to make ends meet.

So says Chapter 3 of *Net Benefits: a sustainable and profitable future for UK fishing*, a special report published by the prime minister's Strategy Unit in March 2004. It returns to the issue in Chapter 9:

> As in any industry there will always be a small number of fisher-men aiming to abuse the system to make a short-run profit, and these should be subject to tough legal penalties. However, enforce-ment is not enough and the management system must also aim to reduce levels of non-compliance by tackling structural drivers, including a lack of profitability, lack of trust in the current management system, the relatively low probability of being successfully prosecuted for illegal actions and the low level of fines.

The National Audit Office reported in 2003 that the 122 cases taken to court during 2000 and 2001 had resulted in average fines of only 1.7 times the value of the illegal landing. Also in 2003, magistrates in north-east England dismissed a case against skippers prosecuted by Defra for infringing rules designed to protect North Sea cod – the court accepted the fishermen's argument that the EU regulations were incomprehensible. The fishermen themselves are broadly forgiving of each other's behaviour and tend not to regard breaching the regulations as criminal. According to a survey quoted in *Net Benefits*, only 37 per cent of fishermen agreed that 'quotas should be complied with because they are the law'. In late 2005, 10 skippers representing nine boats and two trawler companies – most of Whitby's fishing fleet – crammed the dock in Hull crown court, charged with 55 counts of deception. Between them they had landed £475,000-worth of cod, haddock and whiting but had declared only £149,000-worth to the Fisheries Inspectorate – offences for which they were fined more than £120,000. The skippers argued that none of them was earning more than £20,000 a year and that the offences had been forced upon them by necessity. 'This is a sad reflection of the perilous state of the white fishing industry of a town,' said their lawyer. 'It is on its knees.'

A similar story emerges from Scotland. In 2004 the average net profit from a large demersal trawler – typically with an insured value of £1.4m and carrying debts of £925,000 – was just £47,991. In 2005 it fell even lower, to £46,765 (just 4.6 per cent of turnover). It's something to think about when next you enter one of the UK's 86,000 fish-and-chip shops. Fishing at sea is exactly what it appears to be – the most dangerous job in the UK. Over the last ten years, commercial fishing boats have been lost at an average of one every 12.5 days. Few people of sound mind would face such risks for £20,000 a year, and it is no surprise that skippers are finding it difficult to recruit and retain their crews.

No circle was ever more vicious. If fishermen can't earn enough from their quotas, then they are more likely to overfish. If they overfish, then the stock is depleted and profits in future are even lower. The quality of the product also declines, depressing prices and handing a yet bigger advantage to Iceland and other suppliers from abroad, while inaccurate catch statistics distort the data on which TACs are calculated and throw the entire system ever deeper into chaos. Even when they are based on accurate information, TACs are notoriously difficult to calculate. Fisheries managers cannot count their cod like shepherds count sheep. There are wide margins of error. Even with 'good' (i.e. honestly reported) data, the range of uncertainty hovers between 20 per cent and 30 per cent. The work of assessing populations and recommending sustainable catches is done by the International Council for the Exploration of the Sea (ICES), which publishes its advice in mid-October each year. Haggling then ensues between fisheries ministers at the EU Agriculture and Fisheries Council, which announces the following year's TACs in December. Almost always, the quotas are higher than the scientific advice (for cod, ICES' current advice is to completely close the fisheries in the North Sea, Irish Sea, parts of the Atlantic, Skaggerak, Kattegat and eastern Baltic).

For ministers with home fleets and consumers to placate, the choice between political suicide and ecological risk-taking is difficult but not impossible. They fight their corners, get their quotas increased and issue triumphal press releases announcing their success while scientists bury their heads in their hands. To give ministers their due, it's not a question simply of caving in to big business. Nationally, fishing is not a major industry – in Scotland, where it is strongest, it amounts to 0.2 per cent of the national workforce. In England and Wales it is 0.1 per cent. Locally, however, it is absolutely vital. Twenty per cent of UK fishermen now live in south-west England and 13 per cent in Aberdeenshire, where the local economies – especially in remote coastal communities with no other employment – are wholly dependent on the sea. In the Western Isles, 24 per cent of the local economy depends on fishing; around Fraserburgh and Dartmouth (which includes Newlyn), it is 20 per cent. Every cut in quota means economic pain, hardship in already hard-pressed families and downward pressure on the viability of the fleets. What it also means is that even worse pain and hardships lie ahead. Twenty-three per cent (by value) of the fish stocks to which UK fleets have access are classified as 'at risk', and 13 per cent 'in danger'. Most of these are the most popular demersal (whitefish) species, whose age structures have been so badly distorted that catches – and fishermen's incomes – are now highly volatile and unpredictable. Cod are at an historic low. For the population to recover, it will need a vast increase in the number of fish left in the sea to mature.

Left to die of natural causes, a cod may survive to the age of 40. Older ones are larger and more fertile, and fetch better prices. Such has been the scale of overfishing in the North Sea that 90 per cent of the survivors are less than two years old and fewer than 0.5 per cent are aged over five. For North Sea cod to reproduce itself in commercially fishable quantities, most experts suggest we need a minimum spawning population of between 70,000 and 150,000 tonnes. The actual current population is 40,000 tonnes. While fishermen, like fisheries ministers, are not blind to the obvious, they complain that they are caught in a fork. Already hard pressed, they cannot in the short term afford the deeper cuts that would ensure their long-term futures. Having seen so many dire predictions come true, their attitude to scientists has at least softened a bit. It used to make their whiskers bristle when they were told that a particular species had fallen below some critical threshold, and they would then sail out through boiling shoals of theoretically non-existent fish that they were forbidden to catch. They were professional hunters. If the fish were there, then their job, pure and simple, was to catch them – they had no notion of Spawning Stock Biomass. Even now, scarred by experience and aware that change must come, their cooperation with the scientists is at best patchy, often grudging and sometimes frankly obstructive. ICES' annual stock calculations, and the quotas based upon them, even when they exceed scientific advice, are still distrusted and challenged by the men on deck.

Few people in the history of science have taken upon themselves a more impossible task than assessing the weight of something they can neither see nor touch. Fish-counting may not be a job for rocket scientists, but it would challenge a rocket scientist's ingenuity. The UK is one of 19 members of ICES, to which it provides fisheries data via the Centre for Environment Fisheries and Aquaculture Science (CEFAS), the Lowestoft-based science and advisory centre which is an executive agency of Defra. Altogether, the international collaboration through ICES involves 1,600 scientists in an effort which, it is widely acknowledged, produces the best fisheries science in the world – no small achievement when, with the CFP, it has to cope with the world's most densely fished and complex fisheries management system. UK waters alone contain 120 commercial species, and 44,000 altogether. The EU has to fix TACs for more than 200 separate stocks. Keeping account of all this would be hard enough in calm, transparent waters fished by paragons. In murky, storm-tossed waters fished by pragmatists, it can look like the statistical equivalent of chuck-and-chance-it. By way of the various national research agencies, ICES receives its population data from three main sources – registered landings at ports, fishermen and research ships. Given the likely scale of the unregistered 'black catch', and the unrecorded volume of 'bycatch' being discarded at sea, the first two of these are, by scientific standards, grossly inaccurate. Some estimates have put unrecorded landings of cod at 10 per cent of the total, rising to 40 per cent for haddock and 60 per cent for sole, but the truth is impossible to know. So endemic is the falsification of landing records that the scientists try to allow for it in their calculations, trusting that this 'dishonesty weighting' remains a statistical constant. Putting their best guess forward, they look at the size and age of sample fish, the rate at which they were caught and the total size of the catch. From the open sea they take samples of fish eggs floating in the plankton, and juvenile fish too small for the nets. Then they juggle the numbers and calculate recommended catch limits for the politicians to argue about.

From fallible science comes worse policy. *Net Benefits*, to its credit, acknowledges this:

> The scientific work underpinning CFP decision-making is world class. However, the data that is fed into assessments is often poor and has deteriorated over time ... ICES has expressed grave concern about the quality of catch and effort data from the important fisheries in the ICES area. As an immediate consequence, ICES cannot provide reliable estimates of current stock sizes and forecasts that are used to set TACs for some species.

By 'some species', of course, it does not mean garfish, shad or eel-pout. It means the very ones that are under the heaviest pressure – cod, haddock, sole. An international fishery is not a sweetshop, but the principles of survival are the same. No shop-keeper would escape bankruptcy if he didn't keep track of his stock and replace what he sold. No fishery manager will avoid an empty sea if he fails to do the same. The lessons could not be clearer. *Newfoundland cod. North Sea herring. Cornish pilchards. Mackerel.* Yet among all the negatives there is a positive, and it affirms everything that common sense tells us. Following the closure of the fishery in the 1970s, North Sea herring have made a strong recovery and the Scottish pelagic (mackerel and herring) fleet, unlike its demersal (whitefish) cousin, is highly profitable. My grandfather, were he alive, might once again find a local bloater on his plate. But whence would come his cod?

The 2003 edition of Defra's national fishery statistics bore on its cover a photograph of weather-beaten old salts mending their nets in front of a quaint wooden boat. It's not quite an outright lie. As you potter from cove to cove, you might indeed think little had changed since some mythical Cornish heyday. Nets and lobster pots still give off their decadent reek; boats loll at low tide, and frying fish is still the defining fragrance of English town centres. As darkness falls, the shingle banks near my home in North Norfolk begin to shine like some linear suburb as anglers settle down with their lanterns, soup and unquenchable hope. Increasingly, it is an emotion they share with the deep-sea professionals.

Throughout its vast area of responsibility, from the mid-Atlantic west of southern Spain to the northern shores of Scandinavia, ICES divides the sea into fishing areas identified by Roman numerals. Those that touch the UK are IV, VI and VII. The southern North Sea, across which I stare in the vague direction of Friesland, is IVc. In 1995, 2,472 tonnes of cod were taken from it. In 2003, a dwindling UK fleet netted just 678 tonnes. In four years, total landings at East Anglia's principal fishing port, Lowestoft, crashed from 5,400 to 1,667 tonnes. In 2004 it plummeted again, to 657 tonnes, which included more sprats (272 tonnes) than the combined totals for cod (135 tonnes), soles (38 tonnes), herring (3 tonnes) and haddock (nil). From the whole of the southern North Sea, UK boats netted 402 tonnes of cod. In the following year, 2005, even that would provoke tears of nostalgia – the total cod catch by UK vessels in fishing area IVc in 2005 was 206 tonnes.

Nationally it's the same story. In 2003, 6,735 vessels landed fish and shellfish at some 280 ports, harbours and creeks around the UK. The national catch totalled 639,700 tonnes, with a market value of £528.3m, and £478m passed through the tills of the nation's 86,000 fish-and-chip shops. In 2004 the total catch was slightly up (653,000 tonnes), but the value had gone down (£513m) – a result of the widening imbalance between scarce and expensive whitefish and abundant but cheaper pelagics. *Net Benefits* in 2004 reported that 60 per cent of UK fishing turnover came from mackerel, herring and shellfish. In 2002, whitefish accounted for only 35 per cent of the volume of the national catch, but 52 per cent of the value. Pelagics supplied 51 per cent of the volume but only 24 per cent of the value. The trend can only accelerate, with income declining as the swing to mackerel and herring continues, and cod sinks forever deeper into the mire. Less than 20 per cent of the cod eaten in the UK is caught by its own fleet: the rest is air-freighted from Iceland, Russia, Denmark, Norway, the Faeroes and, in processed form, from China. Britain's own contribution to global fish production is less than 1 per cent.

The one thing the UK is unsurpassably good at is statistics. Every year Defra – or, since 2005, the Marine Fisheries Agency – publishes a detailed (and I mean *detailed*) analysis of the previous year's fishing activity and trade. The 2004 edition – the latest I have to hand – runs to more than 150 pages. Here you will find the number, size, fishing power and location of the boats; numbers of fishermen; Spawning Stock Biomass and 'recruitment' of juvenile fish; allocation and uptake of quotas; imports and exports; and registered landings analysed by species, volume, value, fishing area, port and national registration of vessels. Transcribe all this on to charts and you will see the odd blip or two, but the overall trend is downward. Catches, incomes, numbers of boats and fishermen, even TACs – all are getting smaller. Since 2000, the TAC for North Sea cod has been cut from 81,000 to 27,300 tonnes (the scientists wanted zero), North Sea plaice from 73,250 tonnes in 2003 to 59,000 in 2005, West-of-Scotland cod from 1,808 to 721, and north-east Atlantic mackerel from 591,000 to 420,000. The North Sea mackerel fishery remains closed. Other TACs increased slightly, showing the value of reduced fishing effort.

The most powerful evidence of decline comes from the fleet itself. In 1938 there were 47,824 part- and full-time fishermen in the UK. In 1994 there were still 20,703. Ten years later this had all but halved, to 11,559. It's the same with the boats. In 1995 there were 9,174 registered fishing vessels; in 2005 just 6,341. But even this rate of attrition is not enough to correct the imbalance between fishing power and available stock. The cover of the 2004 edition of *UK Fishery Statistics* shows a small fleet of trawlers, line astern. With or without conscious irony, they are unmanned and tied up. For many of them, this is the reality that the future holds.

The whitefish fleet as it currently stands is simply too big. Its appetite is beyond the capacity of the sea to satisfy, and the pressure of over-size fleets on fisheries ministers, who have to negotiate quotas for them, is like a gun pointed at its own head. *Net Benefits* does its best to sound optimistic. If the industry is well managed, it reckons, then turnover in the next 10 or 15 years could increase by between 15 and 20 per cent. Failure to modernize, however, would squeeze another 30 per cent of the economic life out of it. If the worst happened and there was a further major stock collapse – i.e. if nothing changes and the industry goes on behaving in the old same way – then turnover would be halved.

There are other pressures too. If we know one thing about the spawning behaviour of fish, it is that it's critically sensitive to water temperature. Global warming is upon us. Depending upon events far beyond the fishermen's control, it will bring either a warming of the water or an icy chill if the Gulf Stream is switched off. Either way, effects on spawning are likely to be negative. Other environmental changes are being caused by the industry itself. Beam trawlers and scallop dredgers do such damage to the seabed that they destroy whole ecosystems, threatening a myriad plants and animals including the spawn of their own target species. According to OSPAR (the Convention for the Protection of the Marine Environment of the North-East Atlantic), fishing is responsible for three of the six worst human impacts on the health of the sea. Worst of all, more damaging even than organic pollutants from ashore (which rank second), is fishing itself – unbalancing the ecosystem by removing selected species. Third worst is disturbance of the seabed. Fifth – behind pollution from nutrients and ahead of anti-fouling paint from ships – is what might be called collateral damage, the killing of non-target species. We shall return to this in Chapter 8, but for the moment it is necessary to reflect that the fishing industry currently is subject to fewer environmental controls than any other commercial user of the sea, including the gas and oil industries. This, too, is a situation that cannot continue, and which may well have a further restrictive effect on freedom to hunt. The beam trawl in particular can have no part in any sustainable policy of marine conservation.

The government's call for 'well-managed' fisheries and a 'modernized' fleet is, or should be, unanswerable. Like most pieties, however, it is easier to pronounce than it is to perform. The industry would modernize itself if it could, but ageing vessels lock it into a vicious circle. The whitefish fleet barely makes enough to keep going as it is. Where will it get the money to modernize? Who will invest? Not governments, surely. Part of the problem in the past was caused by subsidies for new vessels or technical upgrades to old ones. This is why there is so much over-capacity, and why so many fishermen now say they can break even only by fishing illegally. In 2002, the EU set what it hoped would be an example to the world by banning subsidies for new boats. Where public money was spent, it should be used only to take more boats out of commission. *Net Benefits* asks governments to consider funding the decommissioning of 13 per cent of their whitefish fleets, and recommends that another 30 per cent – at the owners' expense – should be mothballed for four years to give the fish time to recover.

Fishing as an industry is much like farming, and is impaled on the same dilemma. The long-term future of the industry can be protected only at the expense of those currently engaged in it. People whose large debts and low profitability lock them into old technologies, old attitudes and old ways of working cannot be expected to invest in new boats or new gear. Neither can they afford altruistically to surrender their livelihoods for generations of the unborn. Fishermen are rough-hewn types whose utterances lean towards bluntness. The flickering tongue of government, especially when inflected by the foreign accents of the CFP, is as unwelcome to their ear as guacamole to the tongue. In a discussion paper of December 2005, Defra set out what it perceived to be the industry's many weaknesses. High in the list was 'Failure to respond to environmental challenges (poor public image)'. Others included 'Traditional over-reliance on towed gear and on individual species', 'Lack of industry cohesion and limited co-operation with authorities', 'Poor business and management skills in some areas', 'Industry vulnerable to tighter regulatory controls and resistant to change', 'Lack of reliable data, especially from smaller vessels', 'No price incentive for quality as buyers are reluctant to pay more for quality' and 'Sub-optimal marketing'.

There were some strengths, too, but the list was a lot shorter. Even the best of them, placed right at the top, could just as well have appeared in the other column: 'Sustainable stocks of some species' – meaning unsustainable stocks of everything else. Clarion call it was not. In the end, all it did was reinforce the image of an outdated industry sagging under the weight of its own resistance to change, incapable even of recognizing a lifeline, never mind actually grasping it. An industry with a death wish. It would be fairer to see it as an industry trapped inside its old economic skin. It would love to slough it off and emerge in the vibrant new colours of tomorrow, but it just hasn't got the strength.

Quotas have been resented ever since the original CFP carve-up in 1983, and the resentment has deepened with every subsequent cut. Fisheries ministers declare their pleasure every December when the quotas are announced, but out in the real world, where the interests of fishermen collide with the interests of fish, a compromise is hardly better than no solution at all, and no one is satisfied. In December 2000, when the heaviest cuts in the entire history of the CFP were announced (North Sea cod and northern hake down by 40 per cent, other North Sea species down 10 per cent), the only countries genuinely to welcome them were Spain and Portugal, whose local waters were relatively unaffected. The UK's then fisheries minister, Elliot Morley, claimed credit for having halved the proposed 'other species' cuts in the North Sea from the recommended 20 per cent to 10 per cent. But it pleased no one. Some thought the cuts did not go far enough.

'I'm disappointed,' said a fisheries expert from the Worldwide Fund for Nature (WWF). 'They've been nibbling away at the figures instead of putting conservation at the forefront.' Others thought they went too far. 'The plans would be utterly disastrous,' said Barry Deas, chief executive of the National Federation of Fishermen's Organisations (NFFO) in the UK. 'There are so many vessels that are already barely economically viable.' In October 2001, as the next quota-round drew near, Deas issued a press release in which he appeared both to accept the need for change and to resist every proposal for bringing it about.

There is broad agreement that measures are needed to lift the level of key commercial fish stocks. But the Government's failure to address the short-term losses associated with effective conservation measures will cripple the recovery programme and bankrupt the industry.

Meetings begin on Monday in Brussels to discuss wide ranging measures to rebuild cod and hake stocks. But unless the measures are accompanied by a package of short-term financial support, the measures will fail and so will the fishing fleet. For example, a move from 100mm mesh size to 120mm mesh size will result in a loss of 24 per cent of each vessel's haddock catch and 48 per cent of its whiting catch. The fleet cannot sustain those types of losses.

A blinkered, short-term view rather than a focus on the long-term benefits of rebuilt fish stocks, has dominated government thinking for too long. Strategic investment in the recovery plans at this juncture is vital to ensure their success.

The fishing industry would be willing to consider a range of major conservation initiatives if the short-term financial support was in place. In its absence and the fleet at minimal or zero profitability, the short-term reduction in catch associated with meaningful conservation means insolvency.

This charade of falling quotas has gone on too long, it is time for the Government to grasp the nettle.

By 'grasping the nettle', he meant compensating the industry for whatever losses it would suffer as a result of further quota restrictions, limited days at sea and increases in mesh size that would allow smaller fish to escape. In the spring of the following year, the then EU fisheries commissioner, Franz Fischler, declared that it was 'make or break time'. 'Either we have the courage to make bold reforms now, or we watch the demise of our fisheries sectors in the years ahead.' The 'bold reforms' included cutting the overall size of the EU fleet by 8.5 per cent, at an estimated cost of 8,600 boats and 28,000 jobs. Many of these would be from Spain, which, as recipient of 50 per cent of the CFP's annual fisheries budget, was (like France over the Common Agricultural Policy, and for similar reasons) the most vocal opponent of radical reform. Having already sweated off 20 per cent of its whitefish fleet, and with only 16,000 fishermen against Spain's 65,000, the UK hoped the axe this time might fall on other necks, while the Spanish reiterated their fury that British boats still had exclusive rights in some parts of the North Sea. Other changes proposed by the fisheries commission included refinements to fishing gear designed to reduce the bycatch; an end to subsidies for new boat-building; money to help fishermen find new jobs; long-term catch quotas to allow stocks to recover; limits on days at sea; better protection for seabirds, dolphins and other species that were killed or forced out of their habitats; heavier penalties for rule-breakers; and new regional advisory committees that – for the first time in the history of the CFP – would involve fishermen in policy-making and management.

British fishermen liked the look of that last bit, but not the rest.

'The commission's approach,' said the NFFO in April 2002, 'appears to be to force these vessels towards insolvency by cutting their time at sea, with the ultimate aim of forcing them to decommission and surrender their fishing licences . . . This crude and brutal approach will be strongly resisted.' The threat was made good in December of the same year when 70 fishing boats with 900 crewmen blocked the mouth of the Tyne, blared their horns, tore up their logbooks, set off a barrage of flares and burned the EU and Spanish flags. Other English and Scottish boats crossed the Channel to forget their traditional rivalry and join French, Danish, Dutch and Italian colleagues in blockading Boulogne, Calais and Dunkirk. 'This should send a message to Mr Fischler,' said Alex Smith, president of the Scottish Fishermen's Federation, 'that he will have to go and think again.'

However much thinking the hooting and jostling provoked, it did not extend to any major change in the commission's proposals, which were accepted by ministers later the same year. The fishermen's bitterness was focused particularly on 'effort control', limiting the number of days they were allowed to spend at sea, which they interpreted as an assault on their livelihoods. For trawlers after 1 February 2003, this meant a monthly limit of 15 days at sea (that's 15 days out of port, not 15 days' fishing). The UK fisheries minister Elliot Morley did nothing to improve their humour when, characteristically, he returned to London trumpeting the deal as a personal triumph:

I told EU Fisheries Commissioner Franz Fischler that any deal would have to mean a realistic number of 'days' for British fishermen. We consistently said that we were prepared to face up to the serious problem of declining fish stocks but that the original proposal for a limit of 7 days per month was not acceptable. Under sustained pressure from the UK he agreed to 15, and methods of allocation that will assist the industry . . . Although painful now, in the future this could be seen as a turning point in a developing fisheries management based on sound conservation and sustainability principles.

The NFFO's Barry Deas saw it as a turning point all right, but only of the kind that occurs when somebody steps off a cliff. Sympathy for the French, too, had been dumped like an undersize whiting. On 3 February, two days after the restrictions came into force, he let fly:

> There are no signs that the new rules are being applied in other member states. The French ministry has not even bothered to provide a contact number to which our vessels are supposed to call if landing in France. On this the guidance notes are silent.
>
> Vessels limited to 15 days per month will not be viable; it's as simple as that. And yet our ministers colluded with the introduction of a days-at-sea regime, the UK will bear the brunt of the restrictions and no interim aid has been provided for the fleet south of the [Scottish] border.
>
> This malign, misguided and crippling piece of legislation must be removed from the statute books as soon as possible and in the meantime the government must support our fleet through this crisis. Without immediate support there will not be a fleet left south of the border . . .
>
> We call on the minister to re-examine his decision not to provide financial support for the vessels affected . . .

There followed the inevitable letter to *The Times*, signed not only by the NFFO's president, Sam Lambourn, and Alex Smith of the Scottish Fishermen's Federation, but also (imagine this!) by Sue Collins, policy director of English Nature, Andrew Lee of the Worldwide Fund for Nature, Professors Tim Gray of Newcastle and John Shepherd of Southampton universities, and Austin Mitchell, Labour MP for Grimsby. It was a rare meeting of minds. Fishermen, conservationists and scientists for once were all of the same opinion: whatever the reformed CFP might achieve, it would not be security of fish stocks.

Without short-term financial aid [their letter said], there is little possibility that fish stocks will be rebuilt to safe biological limits, or move towards optimal levels of harvesting. The serial failure of the CFP's conservation initiatives is reflected in the downward spiral of quotas each year. The single most important reason for this failure is that any meaningful conservation measure requires a short-term reduction in catch (and therefore earning) by fishing enterprises which are already operating on the brink of viability. Time after time, economics has defeated conservation as fishermen resist insolvency.

We believe that it is time to take a leaf out of the conservationists' handbook. No wildlife conservation initiative for developing countries would be considered sound or realistic if it did not take into account the economic circumstances of the local human populations. This lesson should be applied to fisheries. UK and EU fisheries expenditure should be redirected into fisheries recovery programmes.

The principle should be to rebuild and then apply measures to afford permanent protection of stocks against unsustainable exploitation, whilst providing financial support for the industry during the recovery period.

Recovery measures must, therefore, be underpinned by short-term government finance. This investment would be fiscally neutral in the longer term because of the increased economic activity generated by higher levels of landings in the future.

Britain holds the largest single share of the EU cod quota; it is right, therefore, that the UK should take the lead in developing this approach domestically and within the CFP.

The UK Government has committed itself to a strategy for conservation and sustainable development in its Safeguarding the Seas report. Short-term financial support will be a precondition for the practical realisation of this visionary strategy.

It made no more difference than a light breeze veering west in German Bight. The 15-day limit was still in place after the next round of ministerial haggling in December 2003, when the new UK minister, Ben Bradshaw, slipped easily into the all-for-the-best, Panglossian routine of his predecessor. 'We have successfully defended the number of days our boats are allowed to fish,' he said, 'and we have got a long-term recovery programme for cod.' This, however, did not include following ICES' advice that the only sort of 'long-term recovery plan' likely to work for cod was a total ban on fishing for it. Reduced quotas, it seemed, we could just about swallow, given a spoonful of political syrup. A total ban, however, was not something that even a fisheries minister could find a way to boast about. (The only boasting was being done by Scottish fishermen, who claimed that, for every legal cod they declared, they had been landing two illegal ones. Their purpose apparently was to confound the scientists and prove the abundance of fish.) It didn't matter which side you were on – everyone blamed the politicians, whose self-interested, national-istic haggling reduced every necessary measure to a pointless compromise. WWF complained of 'politically driven fish quotas'. Barry Deas said that the fisheries commission had exaggerated the seriousness of the cod crisis 'for their own political ends'.

It was against this background of diplomatic, scientific and economic stalemate that the prime minister's Strategy Unit published its 170-page report, *Net Benefits*, in March 2004. Its recommendations were radical, its ambition daunting – to make Britain the leader in pushing the EU further and faster down the pathway of reform. From the UK perspective, it is full of common sense – even Barry Deas hailed it as a 'good news story' for the fishing industry, though he found some parts of it 'unpalatable'. But it takes us to the heart of the European dilemma. What is good for Britain, its fishermen and their communities will not necessarily be received with applause in Spain and Portugal. The CFP, like the CAP, has been an ineffectual mechanism which has allowed national appetites to assume the force of moral absolutes. In one sense *Net Benefits* carries a less radical message than many fishermen would like to hear – it argues that the UK will gain more from staying inside the CFP than it would from cutting loose – but in European terms it is a challenge to the orthodoxy of centralized control. Ironically for such a centralizing government, it proposes that fish stocks should be managed regionally, with closer cooperation between scientists, environmentalists and fishermen in making local management decisions. It is worth summarizing the main points again:

To improve the competitiveness and profitability of the UK industry, the whitefish fleet should be cut by at least 13 per cent. More 'may be prudent'. A system of individual tradable quotas (ITQs) should be introduced, allowing fishermen to buy and sell fishing rights on the open market – normal practice in fishing nations outside the EU (New Zealand, Australia and the US, for example). One hoped-for advantage is that quotas would gravitate towards the most efficient boats and that those trusty economic policemen, 'market forces', would weed out the weak and trim the size of the fleet. Selling quota – a 'valuable property right' – would smooth the way by making it easier for the less successful skippers to quit the industry. By pooling their quotas, fishermen would also be able to reduce both bycatch and discards, with the market system working as a 'self-correcting mechanism' in which increased catches could be legitimized by the purchase or lease of extra ITQs. The overall catch doesn't increase – it just turns up in different nets so that again, in theory, there is less waste (though in theory, too, this already happens with the pooling of catches through producers' organizations). In reality, of course, quotas will go to the highest bidder, who is as likely to be from abroad as from the next boat down the quay. But again, *Net Benefits* stays upbeat. 'With a healthy UK fishing industry,' it says, 'there is no reason to expect quota to leak overseas in large net amounts.'

To encourage compliance, most offences should be decriminalized and replaced with harder-hitting administrative penalties including the withdrawal of quotas. At the moment – despite the UK's 186 land-based inspectors, 15 inspection vessels and four aircraft – only a small percentage of infringements come to light, and the conviction rate and generally low level of fines are not effective deterrents. 'Strategy Unit modelling,' says *Net Benefits*, 'suggests that the level and probability of fines routinely imposed by courts in the UK will not tend to outweigh the profits available from illegal fishing in many major UK fisheries, though these fall short of the maximum penalties which could be imposed.' So criminality, too, is a bycatch in the mesh of market forces, exerting uncontrollable and unquantifiable pressure on the stocks. ITQs might be part of the answer, giving fishermen more of an incentive to buy quota and fish legally. But surveillance, too, needs a sharper focus. It must be made more difficult for illegally landed fish to wriggle through the system.

Net Benefits struggles with its language: 'Greater transparency in recording landings and activity data and the development of capacity to track transactions through the supply chain will assist in creating a culture of compliance . . .' Put plainly, this means more port-side checks, more paperwork, every fish tracked from net to table, every mouthful of known pedigree. Serious criminal scams are seldom halted by sheaves of paper or 'forensic accounting', but they might put off some of the spur-of-the-moment, what-the-hell infringements – viewed by their perpetrators as both victimless and innocent – that go on now. For the rest, there will have to be better policing. By the end of 2006, said *Net Benefits*, every fishing vessel of more than 10m in length should be required to install a tamper-proof satellite monitoring system to make it permanently visible to an eye in the sky. It didn't entirely get its way – the rule applies only to boats over 15m – but it reinforced its argument that the EU should shift the emphasis from a quota-based system to an effort-based one, from catch control to time control. The satellite can't see what is swimming into the nets, but it *can* see how much time is spent at sea. The law-of-averages theory says that it would make no difference to the overall catch – divide the original quota by average catch-rate, and the answer is time at sea. It's exactly the same thing, just expressed in different terms. *Net Benefits* wanted vessels guilty of persistent infringements, or drawing suspicion to themselves, to be made to bear the cost of on-board official observers. This didn't happen, but it's cold comfort. Any irregularity in the satellite signal will launch a surveillance aircraft or Royal Navy protection vessel, with the certainty of prosecution if an offence has been committed.

It all adds to the fishermen's boiling sense of injustice. They view 'effort control' with the kind of contempt that a French chef might reserve for a Marmite and custard sandwich. Fishing at sea is not like a trolley-dash at Sainsbury's. You can locate the store all right. But you can't rely on the haddock being in the same aisle, on the same shelf and in the same quantity as it was last week. Effort control, say the fishermen, is a recipe for wasted time, higher costs, unfulfilled quotas and bankruptcy. To see their point is not necessarily to accept it, but a disaffected industry is a dangerous animal. Many of the problems with the CFP have arisen specifically because fishermen, for good reasons or bad, do not trust the policy-making and management systems, and think it unfair that they are expected to pay for decisions made late at night in another country by an overtired college of cardinals who do not see their profitability or welfare as top priorities. It allows them to cast themselves as seagoing Robin Hoods defying the cruel and stupid Sheriffs of Brussels.

Neither are these the only new curbs that *Net Benefits* proposes. It wants 'Strategic Environmental Assessments' on all major fisheries, to find out how they are affecting the marine environment, with the implied threat of further restrictions if the damage is severe. It wants Environmental Impact Assessments (EIAs) before new fisheries are established or new methods are applied in old ones; and it wants all major UK stocks to achieve 'sustainable fisheries certification' from the Marine Stewardship Council by 2015. Other issues are more immediate. Recognizing the need for stocks to recover, and the truism that no fish will mean no fishing, *Net Benefits* suggests that the EU should learn from the Icelanders and switch to a 'large stock' strategy, which means taking only 25 per cent of SSB each year instead of the current 60-plus per cent. In scientific terms the case is watertight. In terms of long-term economics and the survival of the industry, there is no alternative to this or some other equally stringent policy of catch control. In terms of the current fleet and the communities that depend on it – in *political* terms, that is – we're not so much talking hot potato as red hot cinder. Brave will be the fisheries minister who grasps it. The vulnerability of remote fishing communities is acknowledged, and might be helped by the introduction of 'community quotas' to ensure the viability of local fleets, but, as *Net Benefits* puts it, social objectives 'should be secondary to ensuring industry profitability and sustainability'. All right-thinking fishermen, in other words, should be prepared to sacrifice themselves to the greater good.

In December 2005 these ideas formed the backbone of a *Consultation on draft UK National Strategic Plan for Fisheries*, published jointly by Defra, the Department of Agricultural and Rural Development in Northern Ireland, the Scottish Executive and the Welsh Assembly. The future of fishing in Europe will not be like the past. If climate predictions are right, waters around the UK by the end of the century will be too warm for cod to spawn and other species will have swum into the vacuum. Already there are red mullet in the southern North Sea, squid as far north as the Moray Firth and increasing numbers of the restaurateurs' favourite, sea bass. Yet, as Barry Deas complains, cod remains the keystone of European policy. It is, he says, 'emblematic, more important than the stock itself, the criterion by which the CFP itself is judged'.

'But,' he asks, 'is that right? Shouldn't we be having a debate about it? Some people say, sod the cod, shouldn't we catch other things? Others say cod is god. Everything is geared to cod, even at the cost of reducing the fishing opportunity for other stocks.'

No one doubts the CFP will have to change. Deas himself accepts that, despite all the quota cuts, cod has shown no significant sign of recovery. He accepts the need for a further reduction in the whitefish fleet; sees, too, the wisdom of a 'large stock' strategy leaving more fish in the sea. Yet there is no agreement. The government may pay for the decommissioning of boats, but it is ideologically opposed to any kind of operational subsidy to working fishermen. The fishermen say they cannot survive any further reduction in their livelihoods without direct support from the government.

On the outcome of this long-standing impasse, the future of the sea depends. For now, as the talk goes on, so does the fishing. Against repeated scientific advice that no more cod should be fished, ministers in December 2005 voted to cut the quota for the following year by just 15 per cent. WWF responded with weary dismay. Not only had another cod quota been set, but TACs for other species sharing the same waters had actually been raised, thus increasing the bycatch of immature cod and wreaking yet more havoc on the breeding stock. 'If the EU continues this madness of setting quotas above what the species can support,' said WWF, 'other fish stocks will follow the same route to collapse as North Sea cod. Skates and rays in the North Sea, leafscale gulper sharks, spurdog, and Portuguese dogfish are also near collapse but quotas have still been set against independent scientific advice.'

We have heard it all before, and we will hear it all again, the endless repetition of the obvious, rolling down the years like an echo trapped between mountains. Unless one of the mountains shifts its ground, then dying echoes – of an industry, of a community, of an ecosystem – will be all that's left.

CHAPTER FIVE

On the Ranch

Think salmon. Think pink. Think tumbling waters with muscular fish flinging themselves up foaming weirs and waterfalls. Think grace, pace and power. Think tied flies and screaming reels. Think *sauce hollandaise*.

Think again.

The salmon on our plate is no nearer the athlete of the highland stream than a broiler chicken is to a red jungle fowl. No more naturally pink than the ink on the packet. No more likely than the checkout assistant to have hurdled a waterfall. No more an icon of freedom than any other imprisoned farm animal or man-made engine of pollution.

The true North Atlantic salmon, *Salmo salar*, is an aquatic bullet fired with lust. During the breeding season, when it heads back from the ocean to the stream of its birth, nothing will stop it from spawning or dying in the attempt. At waterfalls it leaps sometimes 10 or 11 feet into the air, like a silver ingot crashing through glass – an image of romantic heroism that bathes every pack of unheroic, farm-produced fillet in reflected glory. In the shallows of their ancestral headwaters, the hen fish and her mate will lay and fertilize a thousand eggs. Finally, with all passion spent, they float worn out, tail-first back to sea, 40 per cent lighter in weight.

In this limp state at least, they find something in common with the farmed fish whose lethal gauntlet they must run at the river-mouth. In the last few days before they meet their pre-sliced, vacuum-packed destiny, the factory fish – caged, fattened, artificially coloured and starved in preparation for slaughter – have little more animation than floating logs. The only food species treated worse than this are chickens and vegetables. Vegetables, however, do not leak into the environment to infect, genetically enfeeble and ultimately extinguish their wild progenitors.

Like vegetables, however, salmon has carried with it an aura of environmental friendliness and all-round scrubbed-up healthiness. People who call themselves 'vegetarians' still eat the stuff, and the government recommends it as part of a healthy, balanced diet.

But healthy for whom?

It is not very healthy for its neighbours. Wild salmon and sea trout are being driven inexorably towards extinction. Whole river systems live under the threat of ecological wipeout. Mussel and scallop fisheries are closed because of toxic algae.

It is not healthy for the fish themselves: they are plagued by parasites and disease.

It may not even be healthy for us. So many poisons and pollutants – not all of them legal – have been washing around in the system that it is not possible to know with absolute certainty what may end up where. Some scientists even believe that farmed salmon may cause neural damage to children.

Those words may seem familiar. They were the opening paragraphs of a piece I wrote for the *Sunday Times Magazine* in 2001, which described the environmental damage being wrought by salmon farming on the west coast of Scotland, and which at the time caused outrage. (The only time I've ever attracted more and worse abuse was when I suggested that deliberately deforming dogs for the sake of show points was a peculiar way of demonstrating affection for animals.) One of the more balanced complainants spoke of 'cynical . . . uninformed, inaccurate, mis-representation'. The fish farmers' trade body, Scottish Quality Salmon (as it was then still called), sent out a press release mis-quoting what I had said and rebutting statements I never made. An employee of the fish-farming conglomerate Marine Harvest accused me of being in thrall to 'a bunch of negative and poorly informed so-called environmentalists with hidden agendas and then spending a day cutting and pasting from their previous and outdated articles'.

In swerving around the facts like horses around a rattlesnake, the abusers confirmed what their critics already knew – that there could be no denying what everyone could see was true, and that the only issue was the strength of one lobby against another. The 'so-called environmentalists' included leading independent academic institutions and no less an authority than the Scottish Executive – an institution which, so far from being hostile to aquaculture, usually snuggles so close to it under the duvet, and is so besotted by its economic charms, that it is blind to its ugli-ness and inured to the smell. One of the three scientists who corrected my text before publication was a world expert employed by a government-funded Scottish marine institution. I repeat all this not in self-exculpation or to get my retaliation in first, but rather to give an idea of the power and fury of the Scottish farmed salmon lobby and a devolved parliament whose attitude to environmental science would not seem out of place in the White House of George W. Bush. The facts can shout as loud as they like; money will always shout louder.

In the wider context, away from the overstocked tables of Europe and North America, the case for aquaculture – or 'mariculture' as it is often known where the cages are in salt water rather than fresh – is rather different. The tribal languages of sub-Saharan Africa are unlikely to have too many words for 'profit', but many for 'hunger' and 'disease'. Overfishing is not a scourge that Europe and other parts of the developed world have kept to themselves. They have depleted other countries' waters just as ruthlessly as they have depleted their own, and with even less regard for the law. A report in 2005 by a UK-based campaign group, the Environmental Justice Foundation (EJF), had this to say about the plundering of West Africa:

> The shallow seas off the coast of West Africa are fed by nutrient rich, deep ocean currents which support one of the world's most productive marine ecosystems, upon which millions of local people are dependent for protein and employment. Countries in this region lack the resources to properly police their territorial waters, which extend 200 miles out to sea. IUU [Illegal, Unreported and Unregulated fishing] operators exploit this weakness, and in so doing steal food from some of the poorest people in the world and ruin the livelihoods of legitimate fishermen. These same fish end up on the plates of consumers in the EU, USA, Japan and other developed countries. IUU fishing operators are taking advantage of the poverty in developing countries to secure the lowest possible running costs for their operations.

Despite a resolution to stamp it out by the World Summit on Sustainable Development at Johannesburg in 2002, and further resolutions of the G8 and OECD in 2003, the illegal fleets have continued to rob the poor to feed the rich. 'Fleets' is no exaggeration. The UN Food and Agriculture Organisation (FAO) has calculated that 700 foreign-owned ships are fishing illegally in the waters off Somalia alone. According to A. J. Kulmiye, an East African journalist quoted by EJF: 'The invading ships, as they are locally known, are so crowded off some stretches of the Puntland (northeast) coast that the glow that emanates from their combined lights at night can be mistaken for a well-lit metropolitan city.'

In 2001, says EJF, an aerial survey revealed 2,313 vessels fishing off Guinea, of which 60 per cent were working illegally. Other surveys in the same year found that 29 per cent of 947 vessels fishing off Sierra Leone, and 23 per cent of 926 off Guinea Bissau, were operating outside the law. With 75 per cent of world fish stocks now fully exploited or depleted, and with the appetites of the rich and the hunger of the poor doing anything but decline in parallel to the falling stocks, the worldwide importance of fish-farming is hard to exaggerate. Yet there is something worse than irony – there is cynicism – in industrial salmon farmers in northern Europe picking up the GM industry's feed-the-world argument in defence of their rush for profit. Through binoculars from the roof of an old game lodge in central Mozambique in early 2005, I watched a criminal act being committed – two men in silhouette, ink against water, fishing like their ancestors on a lazily flowing river. Like their ancestors they worked from dugouts. Like their ancestors, too, they fished without a permit. Unlike their ancestors they practised traditional skills at the risk of punishment if they were caught. The chance of this happening was slim, but nowhere near as slim as the risk to industrial-scale poachers out at sea, packing their holds with tuna, lobster, shark and shrimp.

It was the same on land. A day earlier, in the roofless shell of what had once been a schoolroom at the headquarters of the Gorongosa National Park, bombed and burned in the civil war, I had found two men squatting by a fire. They were prisoners of the park authority, working off the fine they couldn't afford to pay for poaching warthog. The gate was open, the jungle ready to swallow them, but they had no thought of escape. Three months' forced labour was three months of food and shelter, and who would run away from that? Elsewhere across Africa, bigger game than warthog was being poached by the lorryload and sold into the bush-meat, ivory or trophy trades by the very officials who were supposed to protect it. The philosophy here is simple. When you live this close to the margins of survival, today is all that matters. Or so you might argue. Mozambique is no place for the kind of environmentalism that puts wildlife before people; still less for law-of-the-jungle nihilism that argues the opposite. The real law of the jungle is about harmony and symbiosis, not exploitation and destruction; about not taking out more than you put back in. A little over 20km from this open prison, dotted through forest clearings, is Africa as Stanley and Livingstone would have recognized it, the Africa of mud huts and smouldering fires; of tribal chiefs, ancestor-worship and witch doctors. Villagers build nothing that cannot be held together with twisted bark; eat nothing that does not come out of their own *mashambas*, or from the river or the forest. Their staple is maize porridge beefed up with fish, vegetables, baboon or cane rat. Sometimes it comes down even to mice or crickets – anything from which a dreg of nourishment might be extracted. If average health estimates for sub-Saharan Africa hold good, food deficiencies underlie a quarter of the illnesses they suffer, and malaria – still commonly diagnosed as possession by evil spirits – accounts for much of the rest. Mere survival into adulthood is a triumph over hostile odds. Nationally, average life expectancy is 46 and only 2 per cent of the population is over 65.

No one here knows anything about omega-3 fatty acids, or would care anything about them if they did. That is the privilege of first-world faddists whose greatest luxury is to fear everything they eat, and for whom the most important fact about a pre-packed fillet of farm-bred salmon is its sell-by date. But the hungry, better than anyone, know the value of a bit of fish. The FAO has calculated that 40 out of 49 African countries have at least some potential for pond (freshwater) cultivation of Nile tilapia, African catfish and common carp. Sixteen countries have the right conditions for commercial production, and 11 for small-scale aquaculture across at least 50 per cent of their national areas. At the invitation of a number of sub-Saharan countries – Côte d'Ivoire, The Gambia, Ghana, Kenya, Mauritius, Mozambique, Nigeria, Seychelles, South Africa and Tanzania – the Advisory Committee on the Protection of the Sea (ACOPS) is assessing the potential for local mariculture. If the potential advantages for malnourished people living below the WHO poverty line are obvious, then so too are the obstacles. ACOPS cites lack of investment capital and local expertise, absence of markets and infrastructure, political instability and incompetence, and lack of research into species suitable for farming. 'Many of these constraints,' it says, 'are fuelled by concerns brought on by previous attempts at establishing mariculture facilities, in Africa and elsewhere, that have either failed or have had negative ecological consequences. In many instances coastal communities are trapped within a cycle of poverty where lack of individual wealth and access to capital constrains individual development, which in turn limits available infrastructure and discourages investment from outside.'

What has all that got to do with salmon farming in Scotland? Everything and nothing. It widens the context and sharpens the perspective; tells us that 'need' means different things in different languages; reminds us that market forces have the compassion of a hyena and the wisdom of a cock crab offered bacon on a hook. The world wants Africa to be fed, or says it does, and 'let them eat fish' may be part of the answer. But Argyll is not Somalia. The only similarity is that people do not eat, and do not trade, in a physical or moral vacuum. Everything we do has an impact – environmental, physiological, economic – on someone else. If we cannot give food on a plate, then at least we must offer a good example – the 'best practice' that the various departments of UK government are always urging us to seek. The existence of a market is not proof of a need, and permanent damage is not a fair price for short-term gain. On a world scale, the health of Scottish rivers, lochs and coastal waters may not compare, say, to what global sea-level rise will do to Bangladesh, or climate change to Africa. But it pins down our attitudes like a frog on a dissection table. If we cannot make balanced decisions on issues as simple as this, then what will be our contribution to the more complex problems with which global change will increasingly confound us? How will we untie the moral and political knots?

If you were to dive beneath a salmon farm, the first thing you would notice would be the peculiar colour of the seabed. Flecks of orange float down and settle, like rose petals in a breeze. Only close examination or an inspired guess would reveal their true nature – a blizzard of excrement, whipped and stirred by the current. Wild salmon by comparison are fecal dullards. Their end product is, boringly, excrement-coloured. And yet the farmed fish's fancy cloaca is a direct consequence of its struggle to be more like them. Cooks expect salmon to be pink. To wild fish the blush comes naturally, through its regal diet of *fruits de mer*. To the captives, however, it is more problematical. On farm rations, the 'natural' tint of the unnaturally caged fish is an un-appetizing shade of grey.

To restore their eye-appeal they are fed pellets containing artificial colour, graded so that farmers can choose the exact shade their customers want. So persistent are these dyes that they tone the excrement to match. The substance of the pellets usually is compacted fish meal bound with fish oil made from industrially harvested sandeels and capelin, though in some parts of the world they may also have contained the rendered bodies of other salmon that had died in the cages before slaughter. This possi-bility was not widely advertised.

The photographer whose work accompanied my piece in the *Sunday Times Magazine* reported having seen dead fish in Norway decomposing over long periods. 'They are,' he said, 'collected in large open plastic containers standing outside, freez-ing at night and thawing for some hours in the sun, sometimes for more than a week. Imagine the smell! Then they are ground up to a brownish sauce, mixed with other ingredients and formed into pellets.'

Happily, despite persistent efforts by the industry's critics to find it, there was no evidence that this ever happened in the UK, where it has since become illegal. Until the autumn of 2003, the more usual fate of 'morts' was to be dumped in landfills – a form of pollution now outlawed by the European Union's Animal By-Product Regulations (ABPR, as described in EC Regulation 1774/2002). Others were macerated in formic acid – a process known as 'ensiling' – and exported for disposal in Norway. The new restrictions are improvements of a kind, though – as is usual with disposal problems – taking the pressure off one point simply deflects it to another one somewhere else (see below). Nor does care of the dead offer much in the way of reassurance to the welfare lobby.

There is nothing in law to compel farmers to allow their fish any more than the minimum space they need to stay alive. In Scotland they are kept at a density of up to 20kg of fish per cubic metre of water – which, according to Philip Lymbury, author of a report for Compassion in World Farming, means that each adult salmon (2.5ft long; 3.7kg in weight) has the equivalent of only a bathful to survive in. But immediately one is caught in the cross-currents of contradictory interpretation. Lymbury, having checked his figures with both the bath manufacturer Ideal Standard and the fish-farm giant Marine Harvest, backs his case with arithmetic (at 3.7kg each, 20kg of fish represents an average of 5.4 individuals; a cubic metre of water is 1,000 litres which, divided by 5.4, makes 185 litres per salmon – exactly the volume of the average domestic bath). Confusingly, Scottish Quality Salmon used the same data to prove that only 2 per cent of each sea cage is occupied by fish, leaving 98 per cent free for them to frolic in. In 2001 its then chief executive, Brian Simpson, declined an invitation to discuss the arithmetic but switched the argument to stockmanship. Only happy fish put on weight, he said, and when it comes to weight gain Scottish salmon is king.

This may or may not be true – happiness in a fish is not easily defined or confirmed – but if it is, then it's a truth that can apply only to the fish that survive to be killed. Many do not. The official tally of 'morts' varies slightly from year to year – 8.1m in 2002, 10.5m in 2003, 9.3m in 2004, 8.3m in 2005 – but it is always less than the whole story. The totals include only smolts – i.e. young fish transferred to salt water – not juveniles dying at the fresh-water stage or during transit. Lymbury acknowledged in 2001 that there had been improvement since his previous report in

1992. 'But,' he says, 'mortality in salmon is still significantly higher than it is for other farm animals. Imagine if we had such a death-rate in cattle, sheep or poultry. We would have one hell of a problem. In any case, welfare is more than just keeping an animal alive and growing.'

In 2002 the Scottish Environment Protection Agency (SEPA) reported that a total of 7,579,581 fish, weighing 4,888.48 tonnes, had died that year in marine cage fish farms, mostly on the west coast and in the islands. These were all 'routine' deaths, un-affected by one of the sporadic outbreaks of infectious disease or pollution by algal blooms. Such 'catastrophic event mortalities', as they are called, in bad years can increase the numbers exponentially (see below). In December 2004, with its landfill habit now supposedly beyond the European pale, SEPA published a report, *Developing a framework for a sustainable fish waste management infrastructure*, involving the inevitable 'stake-holders' in charting a way out of the mess. It was not going to be easy.

> The industry's production sites [it said] are widely dispersed throughout remote parts of the Highlands and Islands, presenting obvious logistical difficulties in terms of waste collection and transport to disposal outlets. These can be further complicated in the case of catastrophic event mortalities, where the source and quantity of waste material is impossible to predict. These logistical difficulties in turn made the safe storage, collection and transport of fish wastes very costly. The exception to this is export to Norway where the costs are significantly lower.

To comply with Scotland's national waste strategy, a proposed solution would be satisfactory only if it recognized the necessity of reducing waste 'at source' (i.e. in this case, presumably, by keep-ing more fish alive), and disposing of it 'as near as practicable' to its point of origin (which one must suppose should exclude Norway). Further difficulties are raised by the ABPR, which divides animal wastes into three categories according to risk. Category 1 is high risk – infected farm animals, dead pets and zoo animals. Category 2 is medium risk – waste from slaughtered animals not intended for human consumption, and food animals that die before slaughter. Category 3 is low risk – leftovers from animals fit for human consumption, including catering waste. Salmon morts are Category 2, which means they can be handled only in a small number of approved ways. SEPA lists these as follows:

> . . . direct incineration; pre-treatment (using the processes specified in the regulation) followed by incineration; heat treatment at 133C and 3 bar pressure saturated steam for 20 minutes followed by treatment in a composting or biogas plant or disposal to landfill, or use as a fertiliser; composting in accordance with rules which have yet to be established; alkaline hydrolysis at 150C for 1hr at a pressure of 4 bar in a solution of sodium or potassium hydroxide; for rendered fats, use in an oleochemical plant to produce tallow derivatives for technical use only.

You will forgive me for not explaining what all that means, but you can see that it involves what politicians like to call a 'step change' from tipping dead fish into holes in the ground.

Given the typically slow response by UK government to European environmental directives (a theme explored at some length in my previous book, *Rubbish!*), all this came years too late for there to be any hope of swift compliance. Under 'interim dispensation' from the Scottish Executive, the morts continued to go where they had always gone – to landfill, or 'ensiled' for shipment to Norway. When the landfill loophole eventually closes, as one day presumably it must, the only remaining outlet will be to Scandinavia – a route which, says SEPA, 'operates against the policy of dealing with the waste as near to the point of production [*sic*] and stifles commercial opportunities for creating a useful byproduct from aquaculture activity. It also poses a significant risk that should that disposal route become unavailable at any time in the future, there would be no alternative legal route for disposal of the waste.'

This looks a lot like a recipe for inertia. It would take much more than 5,000 tonnes of dead salmon to make a local processing plant attractive to investors (to turn a profit, shareholders would need regular outbreaks of fatal infectious disease), and it would be difficult to overturn the Scandinavians' competitive advantage. 'Although export and/or landfill disposal,' said SEPA in 2004, 'are likely to remain the only options available to the industry for the immediate (1–2yr) future, neither is thought to offer a sustainable long-term solution and alternatives need to be investigated.' In the spring of 2006 I asked the Scottish Executive how these investigations had gone, and whether the end of land-filling was in sight. Answer: there was some enthusiasm for the idea of composting the dead fish to make fertilizer but, for as far ahead as anyone could see: 'The derogation [allowing landfill] will continue to apply until such time as we decide that it shouldn't.'

Perhaps we should not get too hung up about mortality. Salmon produce vast numbers of eggs to compensate for the naturally high rates of attrition – even in the wild, very few survive – and, say the farmers, one of the reasons salmon make such good farm animals is that they are naturally resistant to stress. Survival nevertheless is a mixed blessing. The naturally voracious fish are starved for a minimum of seven days before being killed, and sometimes for as long as a fortnight. It is hard to imagine that this contributes greatly to their comfort, especially if, as Brian Simpson suggested, weight gain is the measure of their contentment. The reason, said Simpson, was customer safety – the last duty of a fish is to purge its guts of impurity and arrive spotless at the table. Biologists, however, argue that gut clearance in salmon takes only 24 to 72 hours and that anything longer is offensive to their natures and cruel.

The *Sunday Times*'s photographer described the experience of diving amid such fish in Norway as 'like crawling through vibrating yoghurt'. Not only are farmed fish flaccid. Many are malformed as a result of genetic mutation or (though this is disputed) the side-effects of medication. Common disabilities include stunted fins, distended bellies, inverted jaws, humped backs and blindness. Commoner still is infestation with sea lice, for which the imprisoned fish are as close to heaven as a brainless parasite will get. The lice feast and multiply like fleas, eating first through the skin of the salmon, then onward into flesh. Often they arrange themselves around a circular wound on the skull to form the characteristic 'death crown'. When they've done their worst, the victim becomes a springboard from which to attack passing fish of other kinds – including, most damagingly, the exhausted wild salmon returning from their spawning runs and young ones making their first trips to the sea.

Norway's Marine Research Institute has calculated that 86 per cent of young wild salmon are eaten alive, or fatally infected with viral anaemia, by sea lice. It reckons that if each farmed fish carried only a single female louse, then the damage caused to wild salmon would be 200 times worse than it was before farming began. But of course lice are not loners. The actual numbers on farmed fish vary on average between three and 100, each of which may produce 10 million eggs. Norwegian salmon may have been studied more intensively than others, but in every other way they are typical. In Scotland, too, wild fish are savagely depleted where their migratory routes take them past salmon farms, and farm-originated sea lice are blamed by rod fishermen for what they say is the probable extinction of wild salmon in a lengthening list of rivers. Extinction is another issue on which opinions tend to vary. The influential North Atlantic Salmon Conservation Organisation (see below) says salmon have already disappeared from the Avon and Water of Leith, and lists another 11 waters in which it says extinction is threatened – the Easan Biorach, Iorsa Water, North Sannox, River Catachol, South

Sannox, Abhainn Dalach, Allt Easach, River Etive, River Kinglass, River Liver and River Noe.

Bruce Sandison, chairman of the Salmon Farm Protest Group, fly-fisherman, writer and persistent antagonist of the salmon farmers, insists that wild Atlantic salmon are now extinct, or threatened with extinction, in at least another 37 mainland Scottish waters. To NASCO's list (which he characterizes as 'coy'), he adds the Polla, Grudie, Rhichonich, Laxford, Duart, Loch Roe, River Inver, Kirkaig, Garvie, Runie, Canaird, Broom, Dundonnell, Ewe, Kerry, Baddachro, Balgy, Torridon, Applecross, Kishorn, Carron, Elchaig, Shiel, Arnisdale, Inverie, Ailort, Moidart, Strontian, Aline, Euchar, Add, Ruel, Douglas, Airay, Shira and Fyne. Why such wide discrepancies? The answer may lie less in variable arithmetic than in different understandings of what the word 'extinct' actually means (we'll return to this question later). According to internationally accepted criteria laid down by the World Conservation Union and spelled out by the Worldwide Fund for Nature (WWF) in its global scientific appraisal, *The Status of Wild Atlantic Salmon*, native fish stocks in 129 Scottish rivers must now be classified as endangered.

In 2001 Dr James Butler, biologist for the Wester Ross Fisheries Trust, picked his way round the issue with typical scientific caution – 'We have fairly good evidence that rivers in areas with fish farms are more depleted than those without,' he said – but in the end the volume of evidence left room for only one conclusion. 'There is no other plausible explanation for this than the presence of fish farms. There is no question that lice populations are much higher on salmon and sea trout in areas with aquaculture.'

And it's not just salmonids that suffer. David Oakes, a local diver and scallop breeder, is disturbed by what he's seen on the seabed around the Isle of Skye. 'Lumpfish were once common in these waters,' he says, 'but now they are disappearing. In fish farming areas they are extinct. Diving in the sea, I've seen them covered in sea lice, moribund and on the point of death. You can catch them by hand, they're that weakened.' And lumpfish of course do not go about their business in an ecological vacuum, leaving others untouched by their passing. 'They are the main winter food of the otter,' says Oakes. 'When I write to SEPA about this, they say it is a matter for the Scottish Executive. When I write to the Scottish Executive, they just ignore that part of my letter. But if it's doing that to lumpfish, what else might it be doing that I'm not able to see? The lice are wiping out wild salmonids, but what other species might they be doing as well? Nobody's looking into that.' He could be right. Farmed salmon are infested by two different species of lice, one of which – *Lepeophtheirus salmonis* – is 'species specific' (i.e. it infects only salmonids). But the other – *Caligus elongatus* – is found on a wide range of species. 'It is therefore conceivable,' a SEPA official tells me, 'that *C. elongatus* larvae arising from farmed salmon may infest other species of wild fish although I have not seen any reports or evidence confirming that such a phenomenon has occurred in Scottish waters.'

Another incident on Skye, locally well known but unreported because of the victims' refusal to talk to the *Daily Mail*, illustrated the lice's undiscriminating voracity. 'A family were swimming near a fish farm,' says Oakes . . . and somehow you know what's coming next. 'The lice bit them and drew blood.'

Neither is lousiness the only curse that salmon farming brings. The densely packed sea cages, like broiler-houses, are perfect incubators for disease. In the early nineties the virulent killer furunculosis, which causes internal bleeding and death by septicaemia or kidney damage, spread from Scotland into Norwegian farms, whence it sped off to devastate wild fish in the rivers. In 1996 the UK government's official advisory body, the Farm Animal Welfare Council (FAWC), warned that high stocking densities made fish dangerously vulnerable to disease and parasites. Two years later, at an eventual cost to the industry of £38m, an outbreak of infectious salmon anaemia compelled the slaughter of 4m salmon, closed down 25 per cent of the Scottish industry and put the rest into quarantine. At the height of the crisis, 17,000 fish from a farm near Oban, suspected of harbouring the disease, vanished into the wild.

Even this may not be the worst of it. Anglers in Scotland have been scanning their waters with the same anxiety that shepherds once scanned for wolves. What they fear is proportionally worse even than foot-and-mouth disease – a microscopic parasite called *Gyrodactylus salaris* which Scotland's official Fisheries Research Services (FRS) describe in terms that would fire the imagination of a horror-movie maker:

These parasites are remarkable in that they give birth to live young. The daughter parasite is the same size as the mother, and inside this daughter there is already a developing granddaughter, in a 'Russian doll' arrangement ... They attach to the host by the attachment organ, or opisthaptor, at one end of the body and feed using glands at the other end. Attachment can cause large wounds and feeding can damage the epidermis, allowing secondary infection. *G. salaris* can build up to very high infection intensity of several thousand parasites on a single salmon parr.

It is capable of wiping out every fish in the water. Already *G. salaris* has emptied 42 rivers in Norway. In the Baltic, where it originated, it is not a risk – salmon there, having lived with it for aeons, have developed natural resistance. To salmon elsewhere, however, it brings the certainty of death – a lesson learned in the hardest possible way by Norwegian farmers who stocked up on imported Baltic fish.

The farmers themselves eventually zapped it, foot-and-mouth style, with a mass slaughter programme. In wild fish, the problem is of a different order. The only answer is to poison an entire river, using a herbicide called Rotenone that wipes out absolutely every-thing – fish, parasites, plants, insects, the lot – and then restock after the water has recovered. Chemical blitzkrieg has been tried on 20 rivers in Norway but still remains unproven and contro-versial. To sterilize a river is expensive and difficult (it works only in short rivers with few tributaries); it causes huge collateral damage; it takes years to work and even longer for the river to return to normal, if it ever does (for who will reintroduce all the other lost species?); it may not work at all, and there is a constant risk of reinfection. An import ban on salmon from infected areas has kept it at bay so far, but the barrier is far from impermeable. All *G. salaris* needs to hop from river to river, or country to country, is contact with an angler's boots, waders or equipment, or with the hull or spray-deck of a kayak or canoe. In England, the Environment Agency watches and waits:

> The parasite [it says] is now widespread in Norway, Sweden, Finland and Denmark but has also been reported from France, Germany, Spain and Portugal. So remember, if you intend to go paddling in mainland Europe, in particular Scandinavia, be aware that you might be transporting some illegal aliens back to Britain! . . . Defra recommend that prior to arrival in the UK all equipment is thoroughly cleaned, disinfected and dried.

The Association of Scottish Salmon Fishery Boards stops only just short of asking returning anglers to ring a leper's bell. All fishing equipment, it says,

> should be thoroughly cleaned and then treated to kill any parasites by either:
> Drying at minimum temperature of 20 degrees Celsius for at least two days.
> Heating for at least one hour at a temperature above 60 degrees Celsius.
> Deep freezing for at least one day, or
> Immersion in a solution suitable for killing GS for a minimum of ten minutes. Chemical solutions which have been used successfully include Virkon (1 per cent), Wescodyne (1 per cent), Sodium chloride (3 per cent), Sodium hydroxide (0.2 per cent). It is recommended that all equipment so treated should be

accompanied by a valid certificate from the relevant fish health regulatory authority in the country of origin or at the point of entry into GB.

All this it prints on its website in emphatic capital letters. In a secular age, it is the equivalent of silent prayer.

And yet in the long term the deadliest pollutant may be neither disease nor parasite but the farmed fish itself. In Scotland, where the number of farm escapes quintupled in only two years, from 95,000 fish in 1998 to 491,000 in 2000, anglers now catch four truant farm-salmon for every authentically wild one. In Norway, where at least half a million fish escape every year, farm escapes in some rivers already account for up to 90 per cent of the population. The Scottish industry and its allies in government habitually assert that the problem of escapes is vanishing towards a point of irrelevance. They were right to claim a short-term decline, but short-term is all it was. If 95,000 escaped fish were cause for alarm in 1998, then it must follow that the 67,000 lost in 2001, the 367,405 (including 200,000 in a single incident) lost in 2002, the 104,261 in 2003, the 82,646 in 2004, the 510,840 in 2005 and the 99,390 lost in the first six months of 2006 (the most recent period for which data are available) were even more worrying. And these figures almost certainly understate the true totals. Since 2002, salmon farmers leaking stock from their pens have been legally obliged to notify both the FRS (by telephone) and the Scottish Executive (in writing) of their loss. It is too much to expect that all would do so, and there is evidence that some do not. Bruce Sandison reported that twice in 2005 he was tipped off about escapes of farmed salmon into Loch Diabaig and of rainbow trout into Loch Etive. 'I asked the Scottish Executive for information,' he says. 'They said there had been no escapes in these locations. I gave them the details. Within an hour they emailed back confirming that escapes had taken place. They had telephoned the farmers concerned, who had then admitted what had happened.'

Escapes are caused sometimes by predator attack or vandalism but overwhelmingly (as in the 2005 incident) by storm damage. This means not only that the breakouts are irregular and unpredictable, but also that the cages are subject to worsening risk as global warming whips the climate into wilder, more prolonged and more frequent bouts of violence. Even if you accept official figures as accurate, the fluctuation from year to year is not evidence of a trend. If you draw a line from 1995 to 2005, you see little sign of improvement.

This is worse than alarming. Not only do the escapees compete for spawning sites but they debase the wild species by interbreeding. Farm fish may be hyper-efficient food converters – in the sea cages, a kilo of pellets yields almost a kilo of fish – but they have all the virility of lapdogs. They manage only a caponesque 16 per cent of the natives' breeding rate; and, lacking a home river, they have no instinct to return to it. Thus, instead of hurling themselves upstream, they hang about in fjords, sea lochs and estuaries with no very clear idea of what to do next. Norwegian scientists have worked out that the degree of genetic distinction between farmed and wild fish is being halved every 3.3 generations, with the unavoidable consequence that the 'wild' population eventually will be composed entirely of descendants from farmed fish. There will be fish in the water and fish on the table, but the wild North Atlantic salmon will be gone.

In Scotland the process is already well under way. The size of the catch each year is not a precise measure of the stock level (it measures also the skill, luck and persistence of the fishermen) but it does reflect underlying trends. In 1983 Scottish waters yielded 1,220 tonnes of wild salmon and 4,000 tonnes of farmed. By 1999 the industrial harvest had multiplied exponentially, to 127,000 tonnes, while the wild catch (including netted as well as rod-caught fish) had shrivelled to less than 200 tonnes. Put another way, that is approximately 70m farmed fish against only 55,000 natives – the lowest wild catch ever recorded, and a reduction of nearly 40 per cent in a single year. Some anglers have reported fishing for an entire season without seeing a single fish, and even successful anglers are denied the rewards of the table. To kill a rare wild salmon rather than return it to the water is now the quickest route to social ostracism in the Highlands. On the farm-plagued west coast, said James Butler, a mere 1 per cent of the salmon that go to sea successfully complete the return trip to spawn. On the relatively farm-free east coast, the rate is six times higher. Anglers' logs tell the same story. In the east, the wild catch in 1998–9 fell by only 8 per cent. In the west it crashed by a catastrophic 64 per cent. And so it went on. The 'wild' salmon catch for 2002 was 20 per cent down on 2001; and 2003 was 10 per cent down on 2002. The number of spring salmon rod-caught and retained (1,736 fish) was an historical low, and the grand total of 4,111, including fish returned to the water, was the second lowest on record.

More alarmingly still, much of the supposedly 'wild' catch was not wild at all but farm escapes – an imbalance that, over time, can only get worse. For every wild fish taken from the water, at least seven farmed salmon escape into it. It is possible that some west coast rivers already contain nothing but escapes. Said James Butler: 'Wild salmon populations in rivers less than five kilo-metres long flowing into sea lochs with salmon farms are likely to be extinct or approaching extinction.' It is this very conundrum – when is a salmon not a salmon? – that accounts in large part for the varying definitions of 'extinction'.

The result is that any shop or restaurant now offering 'wild Scottish salmon' is either irresponsibly exacerbating the pressure on a vanishing species or wilfully misleading its customers. And it is not only Scotland that has suffered. Norway has long com-plained that escaped farm fish from Scotland have been swimming into its rivers and diluting the wild stock there too. In April 2006, prompted by NASCO, the Scottish Executive finally sponsored an experiment in which 700 farmed fish, tagged for easy identification, were deliberately released from a farm in Wester Ross to see in which rivers they would eventually turn up (the results are still awaited).

It has been a long story, in which the reluctance of the aqua-culture industry to own up to the scale of the problem has been equalled, if not surpassed, by the wading-through-treacle slow-ness of the Executive. Governments are like diplodocuses: no matter how hard you stamp on their tails, it takes a very long time for the message to reach their brains; and then even longer for the brain to decode and evaluate it. It can be literally years before the vast, slow-moving body is persuaded to move. It was anglers who stamped first when they started hooking farm escapes and logging smaller catches of genuinely wild Atlantic salmon; then NGOs and journalists. The message reached the brain in 1998 (the year of 95,000 escapes) when the Scottish Executive Environment and Rural Affairs Department (SEERAD) set up a 'Working Group on Farmed Fish Escapes'. The word 'working' here is employed in its loosest sense. It took the group three years to produce a ten-page report that did little more than reprise well-known facts and state the obvious. Appropriate site selection, it said, was 'clearly of paramount importance'. Cage and net systems should be 'fit for purpose' and installed 'to manu-facture specification'. Farmers should have some nets handy with which to fish for the truants. 'Great care would have to be exercised to ensure that danger to native wild stocks was minimised.' Not many people's grannies would have failed to think of that, and none would have taken three years over it. Patrick Fothringham, director of the Salmon and Trout Association (Scotland), made no attempt to hide his disgust:

> It is a damning indictment of the government's fisheries policy that this whitewash of a report has taken so long to see the light of day. Sadly, in the three years that it has taken the working group to pro-duce a grand total of nine recommendations, escapes have quadrupled and farmed escapees now outnumber salmon caught in the wild. In pursuing a policy that promotes salmon farming expansion at the expense of wild fisheries, the government have sold wild salmon down the river.

Kevin Dunion, director of Friends of the Earth (Scotland), complained that the Scottish Executive was 'not showing the kind of urgency necessary to deal with the problem', and joined forces with the Salmon and Trout Association to publish nine recommendations of their own:

- mandatory recording of all escapes;
- a public register of escapes;
- fines imposed on farms guilty of allowing escapes;
- compensation for recapturing costs incurred by Fisheries Trusts;
- compulsory tagging of farmed stock;
- licences for farms in unsuitable locations to be revoked;
- salmon farms banned at sites near the mouths of salmon rivers;
- re-siting of farms in high-risk areas;
- the promotion of land-based containment.

All this, too, would have been within the scope of most grannies to scribble down between cocoa and bedtime. Clear problem; obvious solution. But publicly naming the guilty men? Fining people? Compulsory closure or re-siting of miscreants' farms? For Scottish Quality Salmon this was over-my-dead-body stuff. For the diplodocus, it was the faraway drone of an insect. One message that had reached its brain, and lodged there, was that the salmon industry made money and created jobs. Just fewer than 2,000 people are employed directly by the fish farms, with another four or five thousand in the processing and other support industries. The vast majority of these are in remote corners of the Highlands and Islands, where chances of employment otherwise are thinner than a laird's purse. 'That modern Scotland needs a thriving aquaculture industry is clear and irrefutable,' said Scotland's deputy environment minister Allan Wilson in an official policy statement in 2003. Thus it happens that when the industry stamps its foot, the message to the brain is fast-tracked. And the message from the brain back to the regulatory limb is: Slow Down. If Scottish aquaculture needed to be policed, then the job should be left to the experts – i.e. the salmon farmers themselves.

'Cooperation and collaboration is a much more effective way of dealing with these sorts of issues than improving regulations,' said an SQS spokesman, Dr John Webster, in October 2003 after yet another academic study had confirmed the risk to wild Atlantic salmon from interbreeding with farm escapes. It takes *chutzpah* to object to the improvement of something, but SQS – I suppose to its credit – has never seen any need to disguise its self-interest. On the question of escapes, its influence could be seen in the mealy-mouthed reference in the working group's report: 'Although the potential for damage to wild populations as a result of escapes from fish farms clearly exists, the degree of impact is presently not known.' Given the well-publicized research from Norway and dwindling catches of wild fish in Scotland's own salmon rivers, this did not look like a prize example of political candour.

The new findings in 2003 were no less irrefutable than Allan Wilson's need for 'a thriving aquaculture industry'. Published in the Proceedings of the Royal Society – hard to dismiss as a scandal sheet – they were the result of a 10-year study led by Professor Andrew Ferguson of Queen's University, Belfast, and Dr Philip McGinnity of the Irish Marine Institute. The researchers had monitored the results of deliberate cross-breeding between wild and farmed fish, and observed that the hybrids' ability to survive in the wild was severely compromised. 'Our experiments,' they concluded, 'uniquely carried out over two generations, demonstrate conclusively that these intrusions lower survival and recruitment rates in wild populations, and that repeated escapes produce a cumulative effect, which could lead to the extinction of endangered wild populations.' The stamping on the diplodocus's tail was becoming harder, sharper and more difficult to ignore. Independent research overwhelmingly supported the 'bunch of negative and poorly informed so-called environmentalists with hidden agendas' that my critic from Marine Harvest had complained of.

In August 2005 came news of yet another threat, when the Association of Salmon Fishery Boards complained that large numbers of 'bloated' farmed rainbow trout had also escaped into the rivers, where they were depleting the natural food supply and preying on juvenile salmon. Seven months later, in March 2006, came the intervention of an impossible-to-dismiss world heavyweight. It is worth quoting the SEEDA working group's own description of the North Atlantic Salmon Conservation Organisation (paragraph 2.1 in its report):

The North Atlantic Salmon Conversation [*sic*] Organisation (NASCO) was established in 1984 under the Convention for the Conservation of Salmon in the North Atlantic. Its objective is to contribute through consultation and co-operation to the conservation, restoration, enhancement and rational management of salmon stocks, taking into account the best scientific evidence available to it. Contracting Parties currently include Canada, Denmark (in respect of Faeroe Islands and Greenland), the European Union, Iceland, Norway, the Russian Federation and the USA.

NASCO, in short, is the world's most authoritative intergovernmental organization involved in the conservation of salmon. At its 22nd annual meeting, at Vichy in June 2005, its president Ken Whelan plainly declared his concern: 'Salmon stocks in countries across the North Atlantic remain in a serious condition. NASCO believes everyone needs to be concerned about this . . . Our organisation is fully committed to do all we can to make sure this magnificent fish can thrive again. The salmon is a symbol of high environmental quality and its plight is of great concern and importance to people around the world. We need everyone's support and involvement to achieve our ambitious conservation goals.' Evidently it could rely upon the support of SEEDA, whose report in 2001 went on to say: 'NASCO and its Contracting Parties . . . agreed to apply the

Precautionary Approach widely and consistently to the conservation and management of salmon and its habitat. Under such an approach, the absence of adequate scientific information should not be used as a reason for postponing or failing to take conservation and management measures.'

In March 2006, armed with research showing that wild Atlantic salmon faced certain extinction unless something was done to save it, NASCO called for decisive action. To preserve its genetic identity, it said, it must be protected from interbreeding with farm escapes. As escapes evidently could not be prevented, farmers should develop and breed a new sterile species that would be unable to mate. (I am not going to attempt a proper explanation of the method. Crudely put, it means harvesting all-female eggs and subjecting them to high water pressure. This alters their chromosomal make-up and renders the subsequent adults incapable of breeding.) To some people in the anti-science lobby this may look a bit too much like genetic engineering, but NASCO's Edinburgh-based secretary, Malcolm Windsor, believed consumer resistance would be minimal. 'We don't think it would be a problem as sterile fish are not genetically manipulated. Our view is that the public would accept it if they were told it would help wild salmon.' SQS by now had morphed into a new *uber* organization, SSPO (Scottish Salmon Producers' Organization), but its spokesman on scientific matters was still Dr John Webster. His response to the world authority was, in characteristic SQS style, uncompromisingly blunt. 'We cannot farm fish that way,' he told *Scotland on Sunday*. 'In a farming situation they can develop abnormal shapes and they are less resistant to certain diseases. They also do not grow as well.'

Environmental protection versus commercial interest always smacks of David and Goliath. The salmon farmers are apt to complain that theirs is the most over-regulated industry this side of Martian aerospace, but the reality is that its competitive edge is honed and cherished more than anything in Scotland since William Wallace's broadsword. The self-depictions of salmon

farms all evoke ring-of-bright-water naturalness – glittering sea
lochs, tumbling streams, the simple Highlander plying his rustic
trade. But industrial salmon farming is as far removed from the
world of lairds and ghillies as a factory ship from a fishing
umbrella. After Norway and Chile, Scotland's is the third largest
salmon industry in the world, run not by enterprising crofters
cannily exploiting their native waters but by foreign-owned
industrial giants competing in world markets. In 2001, two-thirds
of the 340 farms were owned by just two companies – Norway's
Norsk Hydro and Holland's Marine Harvest, itself part of the
giant Nutreco Aquaculture group which was also the world's
largest supplier of fish feed. Marine Harvest/Nutreco subsequently swallowed not only Norsk Hydro but also Fjord Seafish
and Stolt, then in March 2006 was itself gobbled up in a 1.325-
billion-euro deal by the Norwegian mega-giant Pan Fish, now the
largest fish farmer in the world, and apparent owner of all but a
handful of the Highlands' and Islands' 315 surviving salmon
farms.

The few remaining 'independents' have kept hope alive by
pursuing the Waitrose end of the market with certified 'organic'
fish. It would be hard to give even these a perfectly clean bill of
environmental health, but they do offer some significant improvements over their downmarket neighbours. Organic farms must be
kept away from wild salmon runs, and in water with a 'flushing
time' of not more than seven days. The fish themselves are
stocked at lower densities; are fed on fishmeal made from the leftovers – trimmings and offal that would otherwise be wasted –
from edible species caught for human consumption, and are
coloured using only natural pigmentation from shrimp shells.
Their feed has a much lower oil content (28 per cent against as
much as 40 per cent for industrial-scale feeds), so the fish are
leaner, with firmer flesh. Quality is also improved by later
harvesting – at 18–24 months instead of the more usual 12–18
months – and starvation may not be used, as it is in some
'conventional' farms, to slim the fish and improve carcass quality.

In ordinary sea conditions, the starvation period before slaughter must not exceed the 72 hours recommended by vets. Anti-lice treatments are allowed, but there has to be an extended withdrawal period before slaughter to ensure that no chemical residues remain in the steaks and fillets offered for sale. There is no such requirement for conventionally farmed fish. Even so, critics complain that the 'organic' operators are little better than their 'conventional' neighbours in terms of pollution (in 2005, just five of the 21 certified organic farms discharged between them more than 140,000kg of nitrogen, 600,000kg of organic carbon, 25,000kg of phosphorus, 141kg of zinc, and 7kg of copper). These same farms recorded more than 200,000 'morts' in 2005, with one of them producing the 12th heaviest total of prematurely dead fish among all of Scotland's salmon farms.

The industrial farms' economic domination of an area of low employment makes them a dangerous target for legislators who do not want to be seen putting jobs at risk – a difficulty made worse by the sheer remoteness and inaccessibility of the farms. You could do anything you liked in these places – feed the fish on murdered excise men; lace the seawater with DDT; skin the salmon alive – and nobody would know. Nowhere in the industrialized world would the eleventh commandment – thou shalt not get caught – be easier to observe. By any standards the Highlands and Islands are a special case. The economy is as fragile as the environment, and nowhere in the UK is the hairspring balance between exploitation and conservation more difficult to keep. To be properly sustainable, fish-farming has to be socially and environmentally compatible as well as profitable. It has to be a considerate and sympathetic neighbour whose commitment to Scottishness extends beyond made-up Highland brand names and leaping-salmon logos.

But it is not ameliorative, and does not respond well to criticism. Complainers tend to be characterized as incompetent, ignorant or biased, or driven by a malevolent urge to throw Highlanders out of work. It will denounce scientists whose findings do not serve its purpose, and just as quickly embrace those that do. In these circumstances the ferocity of its opponents is not to be wondered at. This was Friends of the Earth's opinion in 2001:

> An intensive industry which allows mass escapes of farmed fish, uses toxic chemicals illegally, discharges contaminated untreated waste directly into the sea and spreads parasites and diseases around Scotland's coast cannot be sustainable. In the final analysis, when the losses in the angling and tourist industries and in wild fisheries and shell fisheries are taken into account, intensive sea cage fish farming may make neither economic nor ecological sense.

FoE certainly falls within my Marine Harvest friend's definition of 'a bunch of negative and poorly informed so-called environmentalists'. SQS's chairman, Lord Lindsay, accused the FoE's director in Scotland, Kevin Dunion, of failing to take up invitations to talk, and of 'preferring to maintain a critical and ill informed position'. A press release accused SQS's critics of 'deriding the industry with shock tactics and unrealistic claims'.

On the face of it FoE's recommendations, which it set out in a report called *The One That Got Away*, were hardly revolutionary. The most important of them – moving sea cages away from salmon rivers – had been on the agenda for years and tops the wish-list of every Highland laird with water on his land. As long ago as 1991, the old Scottish Office issued the consultative draft of an intended advice document, *Guidance on the Location of Marine Fish Farms*. 'In view of the importance of minimising potential risk to wild salmon stocks,' it said, 'salmon cages should not be located in marine waters close to the mouths of major salmon rivers.' In the end, however, it was the Norwegian government rather than Scotland's that took the advice.

Neither was FoE wildly wrong in suggesting that sea-cage sites should lie fallow for a year to allow the environment to recover after the fish had been removed. Scotland's own world expert on the subject, Dr Kenneth Black of the Scottish Association for Marine Science, agreed that on average it took around two years for the seabed to recover from pollution, though he also argued that the area affected was too small to be worth worrying about.

This may be so, but aquaculture's handprint reaches far beyond the seabed under the cage. Conservationists are conventionally ridiculed for preachiness, technophobia and hostility to profit. They are also handicapped by the fact – clichéd but too often true – that beauty has no voice, and no bottom line. If you can't put a value on something (and what price an ecosystem?), then it won't appear on the balance sheet. (This is why, for example, government building contracts yield such hideous results.) But the wild Atlantic salmon is no mere ornament. Its financial value is not only calculable; it is vast. By some accounts, rod fees alone give *each fish* a value of between £6,000 and £8,000. If you cost it properly – including not only the rental value of fishing beats but also anglers' spending on clothing, equipment, accommodation, transport and food – then the total market value of salmon angling in Scotland is more than £400m a year, with a value to the economy of £235m. The official account, set out by the Scottish Executive in its 2004 report *Economic impact of game and coarse angling in Scotland*, pitches the figure rather lower, but it is still far from negligible:

> . . . freshwater angling in Scotland [it says] results in the Scottish economy producing over £100m worth of annual output, which supports around 2800 jobs and generates nearly £50m in wages and self-employment income to Scottish households. This is a significant contribution and it should be appreciated that salmon and sea trout angling has probably provided its annual contribution for most of the last century.

Weigh that in the balance and the economic argument no longer tilts quite so steeply in the direction of the ranchers. Nor is the sport fishing industry the only neighbour under threat. In 2000 the Association of Scottish Shellfish Growers (ASSG) refused to join a new federation with the salmon men. Why? Because the mussel men believed that pollution from salmon farms was literally killing their industry. These are men close to the water, men in total sympathy with the idea of husbanding the sea for profit. And yet in April 2001 they called for a ban on any further extension of the salmon industry. The murder weapon, they believed, was algal bloom – the sudden, exponential multiplication of plankton that occurs when light and temperature rise in spring. They accepted that algal blooms had been recorded around Scotland for centuries. But, they said, the blooms had not only increased dramatically since the salmon cages arrived, but more of the plankton were toxic. While not harming the mussels or scallops themselves, the toxins accumulate in their flesh and are a serious threat to any other creature that eats them. This includes birds, marine mammals and, more to the point, us.

Three different toxins occur in Scottish waters, all carrying potentially fatal risks. The worst is Paralytic Shellfish Poisoning (PSP), a nerve toxin that works like curare or snake venom, can kill within two hours and has no known antidote. Victims are paralysed and die of asphyxiation when their lungs fail. In 1793 it killed crew members of HMS *Discovery* after they ate mussels in British Columbia (the bay where they moored is now known as Poison Cove). Thanks to effective monitoring and closure of affected fisheries there have been no cases among humans in the UK since 1968.

The effects of Amnesic Shellfish Poisoning (ASP) strangely depend on the victim's age. In those under 40 it generally causes diarrhoea. In older people it justifies its name by causing short-term memory loss. Diuretic Shellfish Poisoning (DSP) similarly is a gastrointestinal disease likely to lock its victims in the lavatory, though it has a more sinister statistical link to cancers of the stomach and colon. All three toxins are currently present in Scottish coastal waters, and fishery closures continue.

Many scientists agree that algal blooms are likeliest when the water is over-enriched by, for example, sewage or other organic waste. Here again, critics of aquaculture have some impressive statistics with which to juggle. For example: the amount of effluent from salmon farms is now equivalent to double the sewage output of the entire 5.1m human population of Scotland. And, as the flow of water in sheltered lochs is inevitably very slow, whatever is dumped there tends to hang around for weeks. 'When waste is discharged directly into enclosed lochs and sheltered bays,' says Dr Malcolm MacGarvin, an independent environment consultant whose clients include the European Commission, European Environment Agency and WWF, 'it is rather like flushing a toilet only once a month.' The method used to calculate nutrient discharges, recommended by the international Oslo and Paris Convention (OSPAR, the body responsible for agreeing and reviewing such things), has remained unchanged despite the industry's protests.

The unavoidable results are greatly increased concentrations of nitrogen and phosphorus. In the minds of the mussel men, it is an affront to their intelligence to suggest that this would not affect the balance of life. 'Scottish aquaculture,' MacGarvin affirms, 'is responsible for one of the largest distortions of nutrient cycles of any European sea body in recent years.' He likens it to spraying fertilizer on a wildflower meadow. 'The flowers die, but the grass becomes rampant. In the sea it's very similar. If you increase the amount of nutrient in the water – the equivalent of adding fertiliser to the land – then you change the mix of plankton.'

In the summer of 1999, 10,000 square kilometres of Scotland's west and north coasts – the very heart of salmon country – were closed to shellfish harvesting because of poisoning. According to a report commissioned from consultants by SEERAD, the result was that 'the Scottish balance of payments deteriorated by about £5m'. Some of the bans, imposed in September 1999, were not lifted until the end of May 2000, and then only for two months – they were reimposed in August. The number of closures has declined slightly since then, but there has not yet been a year in which the entire fishery has remained open. Among those hardest hit was the man who, a year later, would lead the opposition to the ASSG's proposed new accord with the salmon farmers, David Oakes. His own scallop fishery on Skye – just 2km from the nearest salmon farm – was struck by ASP and closed for almost the whole of 1999.

'It's too much of a coincidence,' he says, 'that the increase in algal blooms runs parallel to the expansion of the salmon industry.' His is the gut feeling of a man whose knowledge of the sea is instinctual rather than scientific, yet white-coats across the globe have been coming to the same conclusion. Researchers in Argentina, Australia, Canada, the US, Hong Kong and Japan have all reported strong links between raised nutrient levels and toxic algal blooms.

Why, then, did Scotland's official marine watchdog, the Aberdeen-based Fisheries Research Services (FRS), not press for the inquiry that David Oakes demanded? Its aquatic environment programme manager, Dr Colin Moffat, accepted in 2001 that nutrients did play a part in the development of algae. 'But,' he said, 'we are seeing changes in environmental conditions globally, not just around Scotland, and there are probably many reasons for this. The whole business of algal blooms is extremely complicated, and the idea that one single cause is responsible is overly simplistic.' (But this was simplistic too. Nobody seriously suggested there was a single cause, only that high nutrient levels were a pre-condition.) Evidence from water sampling, Moffat said, suggested that 99 per cent of the nutrients in Scottish seawater were already present when it flowed in from the Atlantic, and that the 1 per cent attributable to aquaculture was 'unlikely to be a significant driving force' in algal blooms.

While this appears to have convinced SEPA, it did not impress MacGarvin. 'It sounds very plausible,' he said, 'but you wouldn't get far with it in a proper scientific discussion.' If the nutrients were thoroughly mixed in with some kind of gigantic electric blender, then indeed there might be no problem. The snag is that seawater is not homogeneous; not chemically identical from surface to seabed. It is stratified. Where rivers debouch into lochs, fresh or brackish water will float over the salt, and it is in this surface layer that the salmon, the nutrients and the algae are concentrated. Worse: in warm weather when algae are most likely to bloom, the stratification intensifies. 'So,' says MacGarvin, 'we get a disproportionate effect.'

The suspicion that salmon farming was, at the very least, getting the benefit of a blind eye rested on a simple, mischievous question: 'If you had a pig farm on the edge of a sea loch,' says MacGarvin, 'would SEPA be happy for you to discharge sewage from it into the water? I don't think so.'

He believes the argument could be settled one way or the other by the right kind of monitoring. 'The west coast of Scotland,' he says, 'is a stronghold of seagrass, a hugely important habitat but one which is extremely sensitive to nutrient pollution. So Scotland should be regularly reviewing the extent and health of its seagrass meadows, as other European countries such as Denmark have done for many years.'

There are other indicators too. 'The hard shells of some plankton species sink to the seabed of sheltered sites where they remain preserved for hundreds, perhaps thousands, of years. Sediment cores taken from sites such as Chesapeake Bay in the States have revealed an extraordinary, detailed and incontrovertible history of species-change related to changes in nutrient inputs. If the regulatory authorities were confident that salmon farming had no effect, they should be happy to do the same in Scottish lochs. The fact that they haven't is, I think, significant.'

In February 2006 the Scottish Executive riposted with a *Scientific Review of Literature on the Nature and Origins of Harmful Algal Blooms in Scotland*, prepared and written for it by Theodore J. Smayda, of the Graduate School of Oceanography, University of Rhode Island. The science is complex but Smayda's conclusion unequivocal. Algal blooms, he declared, were 'not dependent on nutrient wastes excreted at fish farms'. Indeed, the wastes from fish farms were not of the kind on which the harmful algae flourished, and were more likely to inhibit than to encourage its growth. This followed an earlier paper, *Review and Synthesis of the Environmental Impacts of Aquaculture*, from the Scottish Association for Marine Science and Napier University, which the Scottish Executive published in 2002. This was more equivocal than Smayda would be. 'Lack of long-term monitoring programmes over the past 30 years,' it said, 'has made it difficult to judge whether the perceived increase in Harmful Algal Blooms is real and related to expansion in the fish farming industry.'

Uncertainty, of course, is meat and drink to the spinners. 'There is no evidence to suggest that such blooms are more frequent following the development of fish farming in Scottish waters,' said SEPA when I called for an update. Absence of evidence, however, is absence of proof. By the same token, as a SEPA official concedes, there's no evidence that algal blooms are *not* more frequent. 'Monitoring programmes designed to detect such blooms were only properly developed in the early 1990s, meaning that algal blooms were less likely to be detected before this time.' Thus does 'science' drown in its own ignorance. But of course there *is* evidence – the testimony of men like Oakes who know every tug and ripple of these waters, and who know very well what they've seen.

SEPA conceded in its earlier report that there might be a cause for concern 'in a few, heavily-loaded sealochs' but – though it called for more on-site research to check the accuracy of the mathematical modelling – it still came down on the side of aquaculture. 'The supply of nutrients to the marine environment is unlikely to be the factor that limits the scale of fish farm production in the foreseeable future.' So down comes the official stamp. End of argument?

Not in the mind of David Oakes. 'Last year [2005],' he says, 'was the thickest bloom I've ever seen. It was on both sides of Skye, the east and the west. It killed vast amounts of sea urchins and starfish. I've never seen starfish killed like that before. They are indestructible. Yet there were whole bays where every one was dead.' There was worse to come. 'Now the problem I've got is *E.coli*. I'm growing my scallops in designated shellfish waters. They are supposed to be clean but the quality is falling all the time and no one does anything about it. These people are desperate to make money. Everything I've looked at says it's unlikely the salmon are producing *E.coli* spontaneously. I believe it's the feed that's contaminated, and it's passing through the fish.'

When I originally wrote about Oakes in my *Sunday Times* article of 2001, I described him, as I have done again in this chapter, as a man whose relationship with the sea was 'instinctual rather than academic'. The SQS deskmen in their response managed to turn this into a sneer. Now their successors in the Scottish Salmon Producers' Association seize upon the two Scottish Executive reports that are favourable to their cause, and flag them on their website. 'Recent research,' it says, 'has shown that salmon farming activity has little significant impact on water nutrient levels and that there is no correlation between salmon farming and the production of harmful algal blooms.' What it doesn't do is draw our attention to the two sentences from the *Review and Synthesis* paper that followed the one I quoted earlier: 'More likely to limit production are the linked issues of medicine usage and sea lice transfer to wild populations. The rate of escapes of farmed salmon is probably unsustainable and represents a major threat to wild populations.'

End of argument? It certainly should be.

There is an assumption, central to the justification of aquaculture, that farmed fish take the pressure off wild ones and are a godsend to conservation and the environment. We should bear them to the table with loud trumpets, not carp about little local difficulties with lice or make fascistic complaints about miscegenation. All sides may unite in the hope that, one day, this will be true. For the moment, however, farmed salmon are the saviours of wild fish in the same way that illegal fishing fleets are the saviours of Somalia. In taking from the poor and giving to the rich, they are King John and the Sheriff of Nottingham, not Robin Hood.

The problem is what they eat. When the allegation of enforced cannibalism was made in 2001 – the suggestion that farmed fish may have been fed their own morts – the industry reacted with fury. 'Salmon raised in Scotland,' huffed SQS, 'are fed a diet of high quality fish meal and fish oils.' Well, so they are, and that's exactly the problem. In ecological terms, at a time of extreme pressure on wild fish stocks, the economics make little sense. To create enough 'high quality fish meal and fish oils' to grow one kilo of farmed salmon, you need to catch four kilos of wild fish, driving yet more species to the brink.

Worldwide, some 30 million tonnes of fish are used annually to make fishmeal and fish oil, of which 70 per cent of the oil and 34 per cent of the meal goes to fish farms. By 2010 at the current rate of increase, this is likely to reach 100 per cent and 50 per cent respectively. By far the greatest single share – 53 per cent of the entire world output of fish oil – is eaten by salmon and trout. The wild species used in fish-feed are caught mainly in the north-east Atlantic and south-east Pacific, off the coasts of Chile and Peru. In February 2003 a closely detailed 53-page report, commissioned by WWF-Norway with the support of the Norwegian Industrial and Regional Development Fund, spelled out the problem:

In Europe, the situation for the blue whiting, a species primarily used as 'industry' fish, is depressing. A total collapse is expected if the current fishing practice continues. In 1997, FAO reported that most of the traditional fishery resources of the North-East Atlantic were fully exploited or overexploited, with several stocks in a depleted condition. The pelagic fisheries in the South East Pacific Ocean were characterised as 'fully fished' in 2001, and present catch statistics show that the fisheries are not increasing. The most important commercial species is the anchoveta. The population is highly unstable . . . At present, it is not possible to increase catches in any of the fisheries in the South East Pacific Ocean. There is also clearly no room to increase the percentage of the catch used to produce fishmeal or fish oil in this area as Peru and Chile have large human populations who can consume this healthy seafood directly. Partially due to issues over food security, both governments advocate the use of fish for human consumption instead of reducing it into meal and oil.

Nor were these necessarily the worst aspects of the feed trade (a trade in which, incidentally, the international aquaculture companies themselves are major players). The species used in oil and meal (which include also sardine, jack mackerel, horse mackerel, sprat, sandeel, pout, capelin and herring) are vital links in the marine food chain, essential to the survival of other species that eat them – not only mammals and birds but, perhaps more importantly in the narrow context of seafood, other fish. The phrase 'ecological time bomb' has lost much of its force through repetition, but its employment here by WWF looks anything but exaggerated. The industrial sandeel fishery in the North Sea did indeed collapse in 2003. 'In its current state,' said Dr Simon Cripps, director of WWF International's Endangered Seas Programme, 'aquaculture is contributing to an increased pressure on already depleting fish stocks. The ecological consequences of a decline in fish stocks used in fish feed can have devastating effects throughout the marine food chain from wild stocks of cod, haddock and other commercial species right on up to dolphins, orcas [killer whales] and marine birds . . . Governments must recognize that the best way to . . . maximize the sustainable catch of commercial fish is to ensure the health of the entire ecosystem. Aquaculture can play an important role in providing an adequate supply of fish to consumers, but it must happen in tandem with sustainable fisheries and sustainable sourcing rather than its current status as one of the primary contributors to fisheries decline.'

As it happens, this is one of the points at which, albeit for very different reasons, opposing arguments begin to converge. WWF and other conservation bodies worry that industrial fishing is destroying the ecosystem. The Scottish aquaculture industry worries that depleted stocks will mean reduced supplies and higher prices than the market will bear. 'Therefore,' said the Scottish Association for Marine Science in its *Review and Synthesis* paper, 'current and forecasted future market forces have already created a situation where fish feed suppliers are actively developing alternatives to wild fishery sources of fishmeal and fish oil.' One potential drawback here is that soya protein or other vegetable-based feeds may reduce the concentration of omega-3 fatty acids which are the industry's main selling point. The alternative would be to copy the organic producers and make the feed from the offcuts – heads, guts and so forth – of fish caught for human consumption; stuff that itself constitutes a major disposal problem when fish are brought ashore for processing. Either way, it's progress of a kind. Recognizing that overfishing is commercially self-defeating hardly counts as a moral breakthrough, but at least it acknowledges WWF's point that current practice is unsustainable. Lesson for Africa and the rest of the world: *do not farm predatory species.*

There is another, closely linked issue which, touching as it does upon the safety of farmed salmon as a regular component of the human diet, has earned more and bigger headlines than the threats to blue whiting and dolphins. In January 2004, scientists from the University at Albany, part of New York State University, announced the results of toxicological testing on seven tonnes of salmon that they had collected from around the world. As everyone now knows, the results, published in the peer-reviewed journal *Science*, made unhappy reading. Concentrations of carcinogenic chemicals in Scottish farmed fish were so high, the scientists said, that consumers should eat no more than one portion of it every four months. Among those who leaped to the

191

fish-farmers' defence was the UK government's food-and-health watchdog, the Food Standards Agency (FSA). The Americans hadn't told us anything new, it said, and its own advice on salmon (a healthy diet should include a portion of oily fish a week) was backed by the World Health Organization (WHO). So eat up and stop worrying.

Fears about the safety of farmed salmon were nothing new. They first arose in the early 1990s when Miriam Jacobs, then an independent nutritionist, later a toxicologist at the University of Surrey and the Royal Veterinary College in London, ran some tests on fish oils in health supplements and found disturbingly high concentrations of PCBs (polychlorinated biphenyls) and organochloride pesticides in a sample of salmon oil. She then extended the study to the fish itself and, helped by a friend at the US Environmental Protection Agency (EPA), analysed 10 samples of Scottish salmon, eight of which were farmed. She also collected eight samples of salmon feed and four samples of fish oil used in the manufacture of the feed, which were tested at the University of Antwerp. The results showed a classic 'bio-accumulation' pattern as the contaminants passed from the fish oil through the feed and into the salmon. The levels of PCBs in the salmon were so high that, according to some analysts, two portions a month was all it would take for a child or pregnant woman to exceed the World Health Organization's recommended safety limits for dioxins and dioxin-like PCBs.

Dr Jacobs's findings subsequently gave scientific backbone to a BBC television documentary, *The Price of Salmon*, screened on 7 January 2001. Even before it was shown, the film aroused controversy. A press officer from the FSA pulled the plug on an interview with one of the agency's officials who was being asked straightforward questions about how much salmon it was safe for people to eat. Afterwards SQS behaved as it always did when its products or practices were called into question, accusing its critics of incompetence, bias and malevolence. Miriam Jacobs, who holds a PhD in molecular toxicology, was particularly targeted for vilification and accused of being an unqualified amateur trouble-maker. The FSA went further and made a formal complaint against the programme-makers to the Broadcasting Standards Commission. It got short shrift. The complaint was thrown out, the programme went on to be judged best documentary in the British Environmental Media Awards and picked up two more awards at the International Wildlife Film Festival in the US.

The *Science* magazine bombshell dropped almost exactly three years after the BBC showed its film. The researchers reported that PCBs, dioxins, dieldrin and toxaphene, were consistently higher in farmed than in wild fish, and that the most severely contaminated of all were those which had been farmed in Scotland and the Faeroe Islands. Again SQS leaped in with both feet, insisting that the American research was 'deliberately misleading': 'In advising how much salmon should be eaten, the study ignores all the health benefits of regular farmed salmon consumption as reported in over 5000 studies . . . The health benefits of eating oil-rich fish, like salmon, are well established . . . The beneficial effects of omega-3 fatty acids on a wide range of conditions are well documented . . .'

This is true, and is the reason why the FSA continues to recommend at least one portion of oily fish a week. But it is not the whole truth. It cannot be argued, for example, that the risk of ingesting PCBs can be offset by the benefits of omega-3 fatty acids. There is, as so often, a Catch-22. Flaccid, under-exercised and overfed farmed fish are notoriously much fattier than their lithe and muscular wild cousins. This can be represented as beneficial to consumers, if not to gourmets, since it is in the fat that the omega-3 oils are found. Unfortunately it is in this very same fat that the PCBs accumulate too.

SQS was not much helped in its campaign by the supportive but bumbling efforts of the FSA, which seemed unable to open its mouth without inserting its foot. As usual, it rushed to invoke the highest authority: 'The World Health Organisation set safety levels for dioxins and PCBs in 2001 based exclusively on public health protection. These form the basis of safety levels set for consumers who eat fish sold in shops.'

This was a truth straight out of the New Labour form-book – not wrong exactly, but not the whole story either. The WHO *does* set recommended safe limits for PCBs, but it does so on the basis of total dietary intake, not on individual foods. Thus there was no specific recommendation for 'fish sold in shops'. The reassurance continued: 'The known benefits of eating oily fish outweigh any possible risks . . . For it to be a problem you would need to eat more than our recommendations every week throughout your lifetime.'

When I read this out to a WHO scientist in Geneva, he laughed aloud. 'You can't justify or deny it,' he said. 'They haven't presented data on the website to defend it. We don't like to see risk assessments presented like this. Consuming above the recommended level may not cause problems, but it might. There are a lot of uncertainties involved in picking that level.' This was not a new concern for WHO. In 2001 it became so worried by what was being said in its name that it issued a corrective: 'WHO's recommendation concerns maximum daily intake of dioxins,' it said, *'not salmon* [my italics].' The scientist's frustration was shared by the Consumers' Association. 'We think,' said its principal policy adviser Sue Davies, 'that the FSA should be clearer about whether consumers should avoid eating more than a single portion of salmon a week.'

The problem for the FSA was that, wriggle as it might, it simply could not answer the question. Its research told it only that an 'average' balanced diet, containing one portion of oily fish a week, should do more good than harm. It knew one portion was safe: beyond that it had no idea. The 'average diet' is a creature of mythology, not what anyone actually eats. We all have different preferences, different ideas of what 'balance' means, and eat a wide range of different foods in vastly differing quantities and proportions. The difference between WHO guidelines and those set by the US Environmental Protection Agency (EPA) is that the

EPA limits for toxins *do* relate to fish alone. This is why the authors of the paper in *Science* chose to apply EPA standards rather than the WHO's.

Dr Paul Johnston, principal scientist with the Greenpeace research laboratory at the University of Exeter, who appeared in the BBC film, has no doubt which data should be preferred. 'All WHO says is that you should eat a balanced diet. No regulations are attached to individual foods, and assertions that salmon, or anything else, conforms to WHO guidelines, is an untruth. Averages are very dangerous because they don't take account of individual behaviour. Some people may eat salmon three times a week, and no advice is given about that.'

The New York academic team got the usual treatment from SQS. The research published in the (peer-reviewed) *Science* magazine, it said on its (non-peer-reviewed) website, was 'deliberately misleading', and represented a 'rather obvious attempt to stir anti fish-farming headlines'. Later the same year in another peer-reviewed journal, *Environmental Science and Technology*, the Americans reported that farmed salmon had also been found to contain significantly higher levels of PBDEs (poly-brominated diphenyl ethers, used as flame retardants) in farmed salmon than in wild, and that European farmed salmon contained most of all. Again, SQS fired from the hip. 'Listening to activists could be bad for your health,' said chief executive Brian Simpson. 'The publication of a paper by Americans Ronald Hites and David Carpenter . . . is yet another example of the tactics being used by wealthy American anti-Scottish salmon farming cam-paigners to scare the public.' In its 'notes to editors' at the foot of its press release, SQS surged off on one of its long dummy-runs into deep irrelevance.

PBDEs are used as flame retardants in fabrics and soft furnishing and can be absorbed by breathing in dust from sofas, cushions, and padded mattresses. They are present in many computers, televisions, mobile phones and other electrical equipment.

Swedish research has found that PBDEs were present in the blood of office workers who use computers, and also in hospital cleaners and workers at an electronics dismantling plant. The highest levels were in the latter, demonstrating the role of electrical goods in the contamination.

There is no reason to believe any of this is untrue, but it makes a strange argument for eating contaminated fish. SQS made much of the fact that members of the same team had worked on both the *Science* and *Environmental Science and Technology* papers, and that they had received funding from 'the aggressively anti-industry US environmental group the Pew Charitable Trusts'. This objection surfaced again in late 2005, when the Albany team reported in *Journal of Nutrition*, the journal of the American Society for Nutrition, that they had downwardly revised their 'safe dose' of Scottish farmed salmon to just two portions a year, and that consumers should buy safer Chilean salmon instead. It was 'revealed' that the Pew group had also campaigned against industrial fishing in the US, and that two leading members of the Albany team, Professor David Carpenter and Jeffrey Foran, had 'a long history of involvement' in campaigns against pollution. 'Foran,' reported the *Sunday Times* in the interests of editorial balance, 'was revealed to be president of the green pressure group Citizens for a Better Environment, which conducted a crusade over PCB pollution in Wisconsin.'

The association with Pew is a constant theme of the industry's counter-attack. But it is hardly evidence of a mature argument when scientists are smeared by association with an anti-pollution campaign (would you expect them to be in *favour* of pollution?). Does this make them more or less biased than the trade organization that attacks them? And how does their supposed anti fish-farm prejudice square with their recommendation of Chilean farmed salmon? The *Sunday Times* was also fed a quote from a Washington-based think tank, the Cato Institute, which sought to dismiss Professor Carpenter as a 'health scare hyperventilator'. Think tanks, however, are not the pure intellectual equivalents of high alpine streams. Energetic they may be, but the Cato Institute's sponsors, upon whom it depends for funding, include leading companies in the oil, pharmaceutical, motor and tobacco industries, and its principal service to the environment has been to deny the reality of human-induced climate change. Its policy position – that 'Congress should vote down any legislation restricting emissions of carbon dioxide' – may have been reached quite independently of its backers at ExxonMobil, ChevronTexaco and General Motors, but you wouldn't bottle the smell, would you?

I am not a scientist. I do read scientific papers and try to understand them but, by and large, I rely as all non-scientists must on the accuracy of scientists' research, and on the honesty of those in government or learned institutions who interpret the data and make policy. On the safety of farmed salmon, the debate has been so polluted by insinuation and propaganda that it is difficult to come to any definitive conclusion about who is right. In March 2006, the wheel took another spin when the august *British Medical Journal* published the results of a study that raised doubts about the health value of omega-3 fatty acids. The research team, heavy on professors and senior research fellows, had been drawn from, among others, the Medical Research Council and various specialist units at the universities of East Anglia, Southampton, Teesside, Bristol, Manchester, Edinburgh and London. They had analysed the results of 89 recent studies of omega-3 and found no evidence to support the prevailing orthodoxy, endlessly quoted by health authorities and the salmon industry, that it helps to prevent heart disease, stroke and cancer. In a press release in January 2004, SQS had made its product sound like the best deal since snake oil (which, for all I know, also contained omega-3 fatty acids and was every bit as efficacious). This is what it said:

Scientific evidence has shown that an increase in oily fish consumption:

prevents or reduces the chances of developing coronary heart disease; reduces high blood pressure, kidney disorders, inflammatory bowel disorders and autoimmune disease; results in significant reversal in manic depression, and improves the schizophrenic patient's symptoms; may also protect against or reduce the growth of certain forms of cancer; accelerates improvement of psoriasis, used in conjunction with other recognised drug therapies, and reduces the risks of premature births and of pregnancy complications.

The *BMJ* paper did not say that all this was bunkum – merely that, in pooling the results of earlier studies, they could find no convincing evidence that consumption of omega-3 lowered the risks of heart disease, stroke or cancer. They did not report any harmful effects of omega-3 and did not recommend people to eat less salmon. Their quite unremarkable and typically cautious conclusions were that more research was needed and that the medical evidence should be kept under review. What could be more reasonable than that? Who could possibly find grounds in it for objection?

Well ... yes, no prizes for guessing. Scottish Quality Salmon (SQS) by now had morphed into the new mega-body, the Scottish Salmon Producers' Organization, but its new chief executive, Sid Patten, lost nothing in comparison with his predecessor:

Promoting this new study as contradicting over 5,000 scientific papers testifying to the positive effects on health of omega-3 consumption is misleading and potentially dangerous for the nation's health. What this paper actually seems to say is that extra research is needed in some areas to determine the specific effects of omega-3 on certain conditions.

However, what every reputable nutritional body and food advisor recommends is that we should eat at least one portion of oil-rich fish, such as Scottish farmed salmon, a week for optimum health. Although salmon consumption is increasing, as a nation we still fall a long way short of this. In short, we should eat more fish, not less, if we want our collective health to improve.

I do not say, because I do not know, who is right. But I do say that no good purpose is served when the measured language of science meets the blarney of the marketing man.

The diplodocus meanwhile had not been idle. Under the chairmanship of the deputy environment minister Allan Wilson, the Scottish Executive had set up a ministerial working group including representatives of government and various of its agencies and 'stakeholders' – the aquaculture industry, wild fishery managers, shellfish growers, the retail and banking industries, marine scientists and environmentalists. In March 2003 they published a 70-page policy document, *A Strategic Framework for Scottish Aquaculture*, which – 30 years after the birth of what it still managed to describe as a 'new' industry – at least acknowledged in plain language that all was not well. I say 'at least' because the document's title was something of a misnomer – this was not so much a strategic framework as a list of things that needed to be done before we could have one. And these things, of course, take time.

The strategic priority, however, was never in doubt. It was 'to encourage more people to benefit from Scotland's healthy, nutritious aquaculture products'. This meant not only that the salmon men would have no significant obstacle placed in their path but also that they would be encouraged to expand and diversify:

With the decline of wild stocks, the aquaculture industry is rising to the challenge of helping to fill the fish gap. (Aquaculture represents an opportunity to supplement output from a sustainable catching sector.) Demand for recognised species is increasing (farmed Scottish halibut and cod have already started to arrive in the market place, and haddock will follow soon) and, as consumer preference moves closer to added value and processed products, and retailers look for unique selling points, opportunities to include as yet untried species will arise.

'The industry,' it went on, 'will identify means of increasing production in response to market demand . . .', and would set up a 'Healthy Seafood Eating task force'. It allowed that there were problems with farm escapes, cross-infection from sea lice, water pollution from farms in 'poorly flushed or particularly sensitive areas', the disposal of morts and other fish waste, and the long-term supply of oil and meal from industrial fisheries. Various sub-groups were sent off to investigate. The Scottish Executive itself would lead a 'scoping study' on the louse infection of wild salmon and trout, and would look for ways to minimize farm escapes and, possibly, to mark farmed fish so that runaways would be easier to identify. Results and recommendations would follow over the next couple of years and, slowly and pains-takingly, the strategy would emerge. The report did ponder whether 'regulation is necessary to achieve minimum standards of cage design, equipment and maintenance, and to instigate prosecution for wilful or negligent acts (or omissions) resulting in escapes'. But the likelihood of a crackdown roughly paralleled that of barracuda swimming up the Clyde with mermaids on their backs. 'It is vital,' the report said, 'that sensitive environments and priority habitats are adequately protected, but preferably without recourse to the regulatory process, with its attendant costs for all parties, to resolve conflict.'

Instead, the industry itself, through the medium of SQS, would draw up a Code of Best Practice which the Scottish Executive would monitor. (The word 'monitor', a senior civil servant in Whitehall once explained to me, is code for 'take no action'. In this case the Executive did promise to publish 'compliance reports' by the summer of 2005, but – surprising no one – it failed to deliver.) When everyone had done their homework, the results would be incorporated in an Aquaculture and Fisheries Bill, to be introduced 'as legislative time permits'.

Consultation on the proposed new bill duly began in December 2005, but no one seemed much to like the look of it. True to its word, the Scottish Executive walked on velvet paws ('. . . a voluntary approach should deliver the required outcomes'), but then seemed to forget the script. It not only proposed the appointment of a regulator – a regulator! – but floated the idea that fish-farm operators themselves should meet the cost of inspections. Worse: it suggested that inspections might be triggered by 'intelligence' (i.e. tip-offs from the public). Where there were unresolved problems with sea lice, the regulator would have the power to order 'mandatory therapeutic treatment', and lack of cooperation from the operator would be an offence. The same applied to escapes: 'The Executive proposes the creation of a strict liability offence . . . In the event of an escape from a fish farm the operator . . . would be guilty of an offence, unless they could prove to the court that the operator had taken all reasonable steps to prevent an escape from occurring.'

Of course this was just a consultation paper, not the bill itself, inviting consultees to answer questions. (Should the regulator have both advisory and enforcement functions? Should the regulator have power to direct treatment? Should the Executive introduce a strict liability offence for escapes from fish farms?) We would have to wait and see how the Executive, and in due course the Scottish parliament, would respond to the answers. The Scottish Salmon Producers' Organization (SSPO) quickly peeled off its jacket and flashed its muscles. It was, it said, 'pleased to have the opportunity to respond . . . on behalf of Scotland's salmon farmers in mainland Scotland, Orkney, Shetland and the Western Isles and the 10,000 jobs that rely on the industry's long-term success and sustainability'. The message was clear: mess with us and you mess with the Highland economy.

The appointment of a Regulator [it said] and the consequent regulatory regime would appear to run counter to this Government's commitment to reduce 'red tape' and ease the regulatory burden on business.

If appointed, the Regulator should not have the power to recover costs for inspections.

The burden of additional bureaucracy, extra regulatory costs and duplication of inspections will adversely affect both the competitive position of companies operating in Scotland and their attractiveness to both existing and potential investors.

The industry does not fully understand the rationale of a Regulator and considers that the robust regulatory framework provided by the Code of Good Practice should be sufficient to ensure compliance.

If a Regulator is to be appointed, the industry believes that the Regulator's role should be advisory only . . .

And so on. Neither of the proposed candidates for the regulatory role – the Fisheries Research Service and the Scottish Executive Environment and Rural Affairs Department – had staff competent to carry out inspections. An obligation to provide data on sea lice was 'not acceptable'. The regulator should not be empowered to direct treatment 'unless they are prepared to underwrite any losses which will occur'. Failure to comply with such a direction should not be a criminal offence. And while the regulator should make a 'full and frank' disclosure of evidence on which any decision was based ('Transparency in decision-making is the best means of flushing out errors'), this should not extend to the publication of information obtained 'voluntarily or under compulsion' from the farms themselves. 'Premature disclosure of such information,' it said, 'may have a devastating effect on business reputation.' Indeed.

As to the regulator's having power to investigate escapes reported by third parties: 'The industry would be concerned about the potential waste of money and management time in dealing with nuisance calls.' If any farms were forced to relocate for environmental reasons, then they should receive financial support. And the public by and large should mind its own business. In answer to Question 19 – '*Do you agree that the Scottish Ministers should have powers to close fish farms where there is a clear public interest to do so and where the owners are not in a position to relocate?*' – the SSPO made clear its disdain for any values other than its own. ' "Clear public interest" would require to be more clearly defined,' it said. 'Some guidance is required. Otherwise it is liable to be meaningless, or to encompass a random collection of public concerns or interests, some of which may be irrational or irrelevant, and which in any event may conflict with the interests of the aquaculture industry itself.'

Which is as concise a statement of its position as any that could be imagined. It would be wrong, however, to suppose that proposals wringing such anguish from the aquaculture lobby would bring joy to their opponents. If anything, they were even more deeply horrified. The Centre for Human Ecology, an Edinburgh-based ecological/social think tank, complained that industrial sea-cage farming was socially, economically and environmentally unsustainable as well as scientifically unsound, and that the proposed Bill amounted to nothing more than 'fiddling while the opportunity for a sustainable aquaculture industry sinks':

The low-cost high-volume approach is being driven, not by Scottish interests but by Norwegian political and business leaders. If successful, their strategy will benefit Norway exclusively at the expense of other countries' aquaculture industries. The Scottish Executive should not support policies or spend resources which benefit the economy of another country to the detriment of Scotland and our own coastal communities.

It may be going a bit far to claim that Norwegian ownership of the Scottish salmon industry is of benefit 'exclusively' to the Scandinavians, but you don't need a degree in economics to understand that the benefit to Scotland is, at the very least, diluted by most of the industry's being foreign owned, and that the Scottish Salmon Producers' Organization is not quite what its name implies. 'In Scotland' it certainly is. But 'Scottish'? The Centre for Human Ecology's response to the consultation was written for it by Ian MacKinnon, a journalist with the *West Highland Free Press* who specializes in aquaculture. He reports that increasing centralization and concentration of ownership is achieving output efficiency only at the further cost of jobs, the economy and the environment.

> The low-cost high-volume approach is socially unsustainable as it has already cost hundreds of jobs in remote rural communities in the last five years. These losses are likely to continue.

> The merger in 2005 of two multinationals, Marine Harvest and Stolt Sea Farms, immediately led to the loss of more than 50 jobs at a recently opened processing factory on the small island of Scalpay in the Western Isles with dramatic social and economic consequences. The company say that more cuts are on the way.

> In 2002 the multinational, Pan Fish, took over Wester Ross based Highland Fish Farmers. Staff at the company report that since then the number of jobs has fallen from over 60 to around a dozen. The cuts were specifically criticised by the sheriff of a Fatal Accident Inquiry into the death of a Pan Fish employee on one of their farms in 2003.

MacKinnon questions the entire economic basis of an industry awash with debt. Overproduction has caused prices to plummet, with the companies managing to maintain solvency only by converting their debts into shareholdings by banks. Rather than return to profit by cutting production ('the method recommended by banking regulators and advisors'), the Norwegians repeated the folly of the UK agriculture industry and went for even higher production rates. The result – further financial loss – was the same, too. But Norway has bet too heavily to cash in its chips or cut its losses now. With its oil resources draining away, the big hope for its long-term economic future is aquaculture which, if it is to deliver all that's expected of it, will have to drive on towards global dominance.

> Financial assistance provided by partially state-run banks [writes MacKinnon] has played a vital role in this bid for global control. It has allowed Norwegian multinational companies to survive and actually expand their interests – including taking over companies in Scotland – at a time when the Norwegian industry was losing hundreds of millions of pounds as a result of over-production. This may have breached state-aid rules.

Add the damage to world fish stocks caused by industrial over-fishing for meal and oil and the case against the salmon farms is pretty much complete. The Norwegians have their own home-grown critics in WWF-Norway, whose report in 2003 – like so many others before and since – required it to state the obvious:

> Is fish farming a long-term answer to the fisheries crisis? No. The only cure for fisheries mismanagement is good management. Whether or not fish are produced by aquaculture will not reduce the pressure on wild stocks. An end to overfishing, reductions in fleet size, ending harmful subsidies and an ecosystem rather than single stock approach to management will contribute to ending the current fisheries crisis.

It is not so naïve as to suppose that fish farming, in Scotland or anywhere else, is going to cease. But we are all entitled to expect that the Scottish Executive's enthusiasm for 'sustainability' in aquaculture will stretch to environmental as well as commercial viability. This would mean seeing off the opposition of SSPO and the Norwegian industrial giants, not watering down its bill, and making the industry directly responsible for the consequences of its own actions. WWF-Norway set down 11 criteria which it believed were essential to safe and sustainable aquaculture world-wide, of which eight are applicable to Scotland:

[The industry should] not operate in marine protected areas and areas where the activity is likely to cause serious or irreversible effect on vulnerable species or habitats, such as the escape and interbreeding or competition of culture species with wild species or races.

Fish used for fish oil and fishmeal . . . should only come from healthy, well-managed and sustainable stocks, preferably independently certified.

Harmful quantities of waste nutrients must not be discharged to freshwater or marine ecosystems, and best available technology should be employed to ensure resource-efficient farming systems and adequate wastewater treatment.

Toxic chemicals, antibiotics or other substances that harm the environment must not be discharged.

There should be no transmission of diseases and parasites to wild species.

Exotic species and races should be farmed in closed systems where the potential for escapes can be largely eliminated.

[The industry should] cease the illegal capture or culling of fish, mammals, birds and other animals that have interactions with farming systems.

The development and spread of the aquaculture industry must be controlled and sensitive so as to avoid physical damage to coastal ecosystems and structures and negative impacts on coastal communities.

No one speaking aloud in public will disagree with any of this, though many critics argue that the only way to make salmon farming acceptable would be to remove it from the sea altogether, and switch to a land-based, closed containment system from which no marine pollution would be possible. To ensure any improvement at all, however, the Scottish Marine Aquaculture Bill will have to impose a tight, and tightly policed, regulatory regime. As I write (April 2006), the Scottish Executive has yet to reveal the strength of its backbone (see the Afterword, page 332, for a later update), but environmental NGOs in Scotland are anything but optimistic. Disturbingly, WWF Scotland and some others have stopped actively campaigning against the fish farms because (as a WWF spokesman put it to me), 'the Scottish Executive is so neatly tucked up in bed with the aquaculture industry' that there is no point expecting it to do other than oblige its mate. Greenpeace continues to urge people to boycott Scottish salmon – wild fish because they are endangered; farmed for reasons that I hope by now will be obvious. Do I eat farmed salmon myself? Not unless refusing to do so would give offence to a host, in which case I hold my breath and swallow as fast as I can (I am offput also by the fattiness). For those who do have an appetite for it, or for whom cheapness is the *sine qua non* of the family shopping list, the questions remain: how much is safe to eat, and is it actually good for you? You have already had the Albany scientists' answer (no more than two portions a year), and the *British Medical Journal*'s reservations about the health-giving properties of omega-3 fatty acids. This is what BUPA says:

Girls and women who are pregnant or breast-feeding, or who plan to get pregnant, should eat no more than two portions of oily fish a week. (One portion is considered to be 140g.) This is because there are often tiny amounts of pollutants in fish that, taken in large quantities, could be dangerous for babies. Women who don't plan to get pregnant can eat up to four portions a week – as can boys and men. Experts generally recommend that we try and eat around 100g a day of omega-3 fatty acids.

It can be difficult to monitor how much omega-3 you consume, unless you are taking it in diet-supplement form. But many foods will display the omega-3 content on an ingredients label.

All of which leads us, perhaps, too easily to drown in negatives; to forget the magnificent fish with which the story began; the way it was before the farms came, the way it ought to be. Henry Williamson was not a writer to whom omega-3 fatty acids would have meant any more than biodiversity does to a modern industry accountant. When he wrote *Salar the Salmon* in 1935, he could have had little idea how poignant his words might seem 70 years later. This is the paragraph that closes the book:

> In the gravel of the moorland stream the eggs were hatching, little fish breaking from confining skins to seek life, each one alone, save for the friend of all, the Spirit of the waters. And the star-stream of heaven flowed westward, to far beyond the ocean where salmon, moving from deep water to the shallows of the islands, leapt – eager for immortality.

Think on, as my old friend Ian Nairn used to say. Think on, cross your fingers and hope.

CHAPTER SIX

Dishing the Dirt

Many years ago, some time in the early 1980s, the then editor of the *Sunday Times* objected to my use of the word 'turd' in describing what my nose had narrowly avoided bumping into while breast-stroking in the English Channel. He relented when reminded of its impeccable Old English provenance (*tord*) and the absence from the language of any useful alternative. Only in a nurse's nightmare would anyone swim into a 'stool', though 'going through the motions' might have been as good a way as any to describe the experience of swimming near a sewage outfall.

Turds bobbing on the waves were a regular feature of the British seaside well into the second half of the 20th century. Not even the polio outbreak of the 1950s was sufficient to prove the link between polluted bathing water and disease, and the only controlling mechanisms were bathers' noses and stomachs. If the water was not so 'aesthetically revolting' as to induce vomiting, then they could paddle and splash for as long as they liked. The gradual journey to microbiological enlightenment was described at some length in *Rubbish!*, so I won't repeat the whole story here. In summary, it was not until 1976 that the EC Bathing Water Directive set limits for faecal coliforms (*Escherichia coli*, for example) in 'designated bathing waters' – of which, as late as 1979, England and Wales had only 27. Even then, it didn't strike the government as too much of a priority – there were far bigger fish in the political sea than floating faeces. It took a hostile report from the Royal Commission on Environmental Pollution in 1984 to persuade it to regard the sea as anything much more than a natural extension of the U-bend. By 1989 the number of designated bathing waters had gone up to 360, and by 2005 there were 494 (including nine inland). This doesn't mean that they are all as fresh as springtime, but it does mean that they are 'monitored'. And no, I haven't forgotten my sceptical interpretation of this usually not very meaningful word in the previous chapter, but in this case there is a modicum of action associated with it.

The waters at each beach are sampled and tested 20 times a year, at weekly intervals beginning a fortnight before the start of the officially recognized 'bathing season', which begins on May 15 and ends on September 30. What the testers look for is faecal coliforms – the bacteria carried by sewage which, when they enter a swimmer's mouth and pass through what is accurately but charmlessly known as the 'faecal-oral route', can cause anything from mild inner turbulence to acute respiratory failure. The European Commission sets a 'minimum' standard for bathing waters of no more than 10,000 total and 2,000 faecal coliforms per 100ml of water, and a 'guideline' standard of 500/100 per 100ml. For a 'minimum' pass, the water has to meet the lower standard in 19 of the 20 samples. For a 'guideline' pass, it has to reach the higher standard at least 16 times out of 20. In 2005, 85 per cent (421) of the designated waters in England and Wales satisfied the higher standard, which the Environment Agency reported was an improvement of 53 per cent over the rate achieved as recently as 1990. Almost all the rest achieved a minimum pass, with an overall failure rate of 1 per cent (the five failures were Newbiggin North, Staithes, Instow, Morecambe South and West Kirby). Defra's proud boast – 'England's bathing water quality better than ever before' – therefore is justified by the facts.

But is 'better than ever before' actually good enough? Most

people when asked how much sewage they like in their bathing water will answer 'none'. Whole turds may be less common than they used to be, but how much more welcome are their microscopic components? How many faecal coliforms is it safe to swim in? This is not an easy question to answer. While officialdom congratulates itself on what undeniably is a significant improvement, other voices are not so reassuring. In 1998 the World Health Organization's *Guidelines for Safe Recreational Water Environments* warned that illnesses could be caused by waterborne bacteria at concentrations far lower than the official standard. In particular, it said, research in the UK had demonstrated a significantly increased risk of gastro-enteritis at only 32 faecal streptococci per 100ml. On the face of it this is enough to make us clutch our throats and hang up our Speedos for ever. But then along came the UK's Medical Research Council (MRC), whose Institute for Environment and Health launched a line-by-line assault on the WHO report which, it convincingly argued, was so deeply flawed that it was not 'suitable for publication in the form in which it appeared'. It complained of mistakes in the selection of volunteers, the duration and accuracy of the monitoring and the analysis of the results – all of which, it suggested, would have tended to exaggerate the risk.

Everyone back in the water, then! But wait . . . Here comes the UK campaign group Surfers Against Sewage (SAS), not exactly with a peg on its nose but certainly with its head above water and its mouth tight shut. It's all very well counting coliforms, it says, but it's a bit like a boxer defending a left jab while ignoring the possibility of a right uppercut. The trouble with coliforms is that they do not last very long in salt water. The viruses that ride with them on the other hand survive for much longer – up to 100 days in the case of Hepatitis A – so that an absence of faecal coliforms is not itself a guarantee of safety. SAS's medical database shows that people swimming even in 'clean' seawater run a significantly higher risk of a range of illnesses and conditions – ear, nose and throat, gastrointestinal, wound, eye and skin infections, and respiratory and viral diseases. The risk is actually quantifiable. By commonly accepted criteria, the risk of contracting a gastro-intestinal illness can be calculated at 14 per cent in minimum-standard European designated bathing water, and 5 per cent in guideline-standard, *per swim*. An authoritative UK study has shown that surfers – and thus, by implication, swimmers too – are three times more likely than non-surfers/swimmers to contract Hepatitis A.

It is worth repeating that this reflects a major improvement in the general standard of sewage treatment in the UK, and that the 3.8bn litres of sewage and other liquid effluents that we produce each day is markedly less foul than it used to be. But it remains the case that not all of it is treated to the same standard – 24 per cent of it, around 912m litres, is still discharged without any treatment at all; people continue to swim from undesignated, and so untested, beaches where the number of faecal coliforms is any-one's guess, and accidents will happen.

Here again, I hope readers of *Rubbish!* will forgive me for covering old ground. In the bad old days, raw sewage was held in open tanks for just long enough – around a couple of hours – for the denser solids to sink to the bottom, where they could be drawn off, and for fats to float to the top, whence they could be skimmed. The remaining shit soup, spiked on average with a million faecal coliforms per 100ml, went straight into the sea for us to bathe in. This was called 'primary treatment' – a bit of medieval fundamentalism that continued without much hindrance right up until January 2002, when discharges from populations of 15,000 or more had to be treated to 'secondary' stage in a biological reactor, where the organic content is con-sumed by bacteria which, once they've done their job, sink harmlessly to the bottom. The resulting clear liquid when pumped into a river or the sea now carries just 10,000 faecal coliforms per 100ml. From 31 December 2005, the regulation was extended to include smaller populations of 2,000-plus. The result is – or should be – that it is only in remote areas where discharges are small and access to the water limited that outflows are still working to the old primitive standard. And of course it remains true that the concentration of coliforms at the outfall is far higher than it is in the open sea, where it is diluted and dispersed by currents. It is also the case, according to the Environment Agency, that 75 per cent of the sewage effluents discharged into rivers or the sea are treated, by filtration or exposure to ultra-violet light, to a 'tertiary' stage that cuts faecal coliforms to 35 per 100ml.

Nevertheless, nobody seriously can argue that a 14 per cent-per-swim risk of illness is an acceptable pass-mark for officially designated bathing water. The purist position, taken by Surfers Against Sewage, is that any faecal matter in the sea is too much, and who would disagree? If strawberry yoghurt was contaminated to the extent that it carried even a 5 per cent risk of diarrhoea and vomiting, it would be off the shelves before you could say 'Food Standards Agency'. Even salmon would lose friends if it had that kind of stigma pinned to its fillets.

On 24 March 2006, a long-overdue revision of the EU Bathing Water Directive came into force. 'Coming into force', however, didn't mean it was any more sensible to dive in with your mouth open than it had been 24 hours earlier. The coliforms did not hear the word of the law, swim away and bury themselves in the sand. The UK has two years (i.e. until 24 March 2008) to bring into force any new 'national laws, regulations or administrative processes' needed to comply, and until 2015 to bring the directive into full effect. Given the government's tragi-comic, foot-dragging and generally losing battle with European environmental directives (on refrigerators, toxic waste and waste electrical equipment to name but three), its blind-man-in-boxing-gloves approach to 'administrative processes', and its tendency to regard anything beyond the next general election as anyone's problem but its own, one hesitates to celebrate too wildly.

The most significant improvement will be the abolition of the old 'mandatory' and 'guideline' standards and their replacement with four new quality levels – 'poor', 'sufficient', 'good' and 'excellent' – the last two of which have the backing of the World Health Organization, which calculates that they will cut the risk of infection to 5 per cent and 3 per cent per swim respectively. The 'sufficient' standard, however, limps in at 8 per cent, or gamblers' odds of 25 to two. Given numbers like these, it's no surprise that the WHO, like the UK's Marine Conservation Society, refuses to support it, though it's no surprise either that compromise-addicted legislators, faced with rebellion over the cost of adopting 'good' as the minimum European standard, should have dreamed it up.

The Marine Conservation Society has done some more arithmetic. If the UK were to raise the standard of all its bathing beaches to 'good', it says, then it would bring a twentyfold improvement in water quality over the old 'mandatory' standard. Will it happen? Not without significant new injections of energy and willpower it won't. Defra, whose responsibility the whole thing is, reckons that only 51 per cent of English designated bathing waters currently would pass as 'excellent' and 26 per cent 'good', with 15 per cent (i.e. 61 beaches) merely 'sufficient' and 8 per cent 'poor'. It has not so far announced any decisive measures to improve the low scorers, though bathers in future should at least find it easier to recognize the danger spots (see below). Over the next several years, said Defra in early 2006, it would get together with 'stakeholders' to 'determine the most appropriate course of action to be taken at bathing waters, particularly those at risk of failing the new standards'. Translation: don't ditch the Diocalm yet. The final outcome, if there is one, will depend on wrestling matches between legislators who want cleaner bathing water, other legislators who want cheaper drinking water, and the water companies whose combined responsibility for sewage disposal and water supply seems to involve a constant conflict of priority, as if clean beaches and clean tapwater were somehow locked in eternal opposition, like cousins contesting a will.

In the meantime the best strategy is risk avoidance. The directive is keen on improving public awareness of water quality, though it's not the sort of keenness you could mistake for urgency. The European Commission has until 2010 to design a system of 'clear and simple' symbols to be used on signs at popular beaches, with a target of 2012 – *six years* after the directive was introduced – for the signs themselves to be erected. Local authorities will also be expected to get a firmer grip on short-term pollution episodes – overflows and spillages of untreated sewage and flood water after storms, for example – and to improve the speed, clarity and effectiveness of public warnings.

At her cruising speed of 17 knots, *Torrey Canyon* took 500 metres to steer through 20 degrees and five miles to stop. This means the captain on the bridge was not so much a driver as a forward route-planner. If he did not think far enough ahead, or respond to events before they happened, then the 63,000-tonne tanker would be like a gigantic, slow-motion puck sliding across ice, utterly beyond control. In 1967, *Torrey Canyon* was just eight years old. She had been built in the USA, enlarged in Japan and registered in Liberia. On 19 February, chartered to BP by her owners Union Oil, and with an Italian crew, she sailed fully laden out of Kuwait with 120,000 tonnes of oil.

Not until 23 days later, on 14 March when they reached the Canary Islands, were they given their final destination – Milford Haven. Their orders were to make all speed, and to dock there no later than 18 March – a schedule that required them to cover 2,000 miles of Atlantic Ocean in less than five days. The timing was crucial. To catch the tide they would have to be at the harbour entrance by 6pm – a small and very distant target when viewed from the Canaries. Navigation in the sixties had moved on from the time of Magellan, but not as much as you might suppose. There were no sky-borne global positioning systems to hold a vessel's course in their god-like grip – just an autopilot that would hold to the heading set for it by the captain, who worked in the old-fashioned way with charts and compass. Because crews often did not know their final destination when they left port –

owners liked to play the markets and keep their options open for as long as possible – they needed a comprehensive library of charts covering every inch of the seas they might have to navigate. For tankers heading for Milford Haven from the South Atlantic, the standard practice was to set course for Land's End by way of the Scilly Isles, 20 miles to the west.

To their inhabitants and many thousands of summer visitors, the Scillies are a distillation of several kinds of beauty. Spectacular rocky headlands that might have been lifted from their Cornish near-neighbour guard sheltered bays whose clear, sunlit waters and talc-white beaches raise echoes of Aegean islands or the Caribbean. Small boats and ferries play the parts that in most communities belong to cars and buses. The soft warm climate encourages subtropical vegetation and exotic, brilliantly coloured gardens that make the whole place look as if it has been raised in a biome. It is paradise also for divers, who like to descend upon the multiplicity of wrecks that scatter the seabed after rude introduction to its rocks and reefs. For sailors across the centuries, the arrival of the low-lying islands on the eastern horizon has been the beckoning of purgatory, leading very often to hell. For the crew of the *Torrey Canyon*, like so many before them, the Scillonian ship-trap was just one of the many hazards that life at sea required them to face. Keeping to their schedule meant there was no way they could avoid it. Big cargo; big money; big pressure. That was understood. They would have to press on even though the only chart they could find of the rock-infested waters lacked the kind of detail necessary to ensure their safety. The captain had passed this way 18 times before, and it was on his experience that the enterprise now depended.

Sea captains are easily criticized when things go wrong, but the loneliness of command, the enormity of what lies beneath their fingertips, the pressure of tight deadlines in a hostile environment, impose stresses that are beyond the comprehension of shore-dwellers. In the old, pre-satellite days, exhaustion was as much a part of the routine as Morse code and the companionship of gulls.

On the critical night of 17/18 March, as they approached the Scillies, *Torrey Canyon*'s captain, Pastrengo Rugiati, scheduled himself just two and a half hours' sleep. He went to his bunk at 3.30am and was woken according to his instructions at 6 o'clock. Finding the islands still outside the 40-mile scope of the ship's radar, he grabbed another few moments before being roused again at 6.30. The Scillies by now were in radar view, *but they were in the wrong place*. Instead of appearing on the starboard (right) side of the vessel, they lay to port.

The error left the captain with one of two options. He could veer sharply (or as sharply as he could) to port, and loop round to rejoin his intended course to the west of the islands. Or he could press ahead, aiming for the gap between the Scillies and the Seven Stones reef, where his small-scale chart indicated a deep-water passage some seven miles wide. It was not a difficult decision to make. The 40-mile loop would have added two hours to the journey and jeopardized their rendezvous at Milford Haven. They would go for the gap.

The next critical moment came at 8am when there was a change of watch. With the ship on autopilot, the helmsman stood on watch while navigation was left to an inexperienced junior overseen by the captain. By 8.15 they were abreast of the Scillies and about half an hour's steaming from the Seven Stones. The tide was running from the port side (left to right), away from the islands in the direction of the reef. The captain ordered a change of course to steer them through the gap. Probably it would have succeeded, but the junior officer, employing a fast method that used only a single landmark (rather than the more reliable three) to calculate the ship's position, made a mistake. At 8.40am, after a manoeuvre by the captain to avoid some fishing boats had carried them even further towards the starboard side of the channel, they found they were less than three miles from the reef. A further, hurried course adjustment to the north only compounded the error and brought them closer to the rocks. With just two miles of clear water remaining, the captain ordered a last-ditch emergency swing through 340 degrees. They were panicking now. The autopilot seemed not to be working, and the captain ran to check the fuses. Finding them in order, he feared a fault with the oil pumps that turned the rudder, and rang the engine room to get them checked. In his confusion he dialled the wrong number – a cook in the galley picked up the receiver and told him his breakfast was ready. Too late, he realized the autopilot control lever had been knocked accidentally into the 'Disengage' position. He hardly had time to switch to 'Manual' before the giant tanker, still cruising at 17 knots, slammed into the Seven Stones reef.

Not all oil spills are as dramatic, or as catastrophic, as this one would turn out to be. Most of the stuff we pick up on our skin and towels at the beach comes from the washing of ships' tanks or flushing of bilge or ballast water at sea (more about this later). The practice has been illegal since 1983, which has at least reduced the frequency of the fouling, but there remains a hard core of nihilistic cowboys for whom this kind of environmental crime is no more disturbing to the conscience than a flicked dog-end. In an empty sea there's no one to see you do it, and what's the harm anyway? I am reminded of a drawing by the brilliant young cartoonist Timothy Birdsall, who died at the tragically young age of 26 in 1963. It showed two industrialists looking across a northern city whose pluming chimneys blackened the sky. The older man was addressing his evidently more idealistic but less worldly companion (I quote from memory, so the words may not be exact): 'Smoke-free zone? Nay, lad, tha can't tamper wi' nature.' For some seafarers the view from the bridge remains exactly similar, oil and sea as inseparable as smoke and sky. The difference with oil, give or take the odd committed polluter, is that the spillages are mainly accidental and relatively small – 91 per cent are of less than 7 tonnes – and happen while loading or discharging in port. Every once in a while, though, there comes a disaster of such magnitude that, for years afterwards, it is hard to grasp the enormity of it. Shipwrecks around the British coast were a regular and more or less accepted side-effect of our dependence on the sea. We noted them, mourned and engaged with the drama of them, admired newspaper photographs of brave skippers refusing to abandon their upturned hulls. But we were seldom surprised.

Torrey Canyon was different. The collision with the reef impaled her on Pollard's Rock, ripped open six of her tanks and poured her cargo straight into the sea. It was the worst recorded spill in history. Even now, 40 years later, it still ranks seventh in the all-time list, 13 places higher than the more recently notorious *Exxon Valdez*, which polluted Prince William Sound in Alaska with 37,000 tonnes in 1989. The first thought, as always, was salvage. Tugs tried and failed to pull her clear; then the engine room blew up while engineers from the Dutch salvage company Wijsmuller were picnicking on the bridge. One man was killed (the only human casualty of the entire event); others had to jump into the oily sea. With salvage no longer an option, and with the oil slick lengthening and drifting towards Cornwall, the priority shifted to damage limitation.

As the ship began to break up, prime minister Harold Wilson and senior colleagues met like a war cabinet at the Royal Navy air station, Culdrose. It was like war in other ways, too, with air and sea soon swarming with military machinery. Warships formed a cordon to keep other shipping – most importantly, Russian trawlers – away from the action. (The word 'trawlers' at this time frequently wore inverted commas in honour of their role as Soviet spy ships.) The strategy was nothing if not bold. On 28 March, ten days after the tanker grounded, and with the slick now 35 miles long and 20 miles wide, eight Royal Navy Buccaneers took off from Lossiemouth with cargoes of 1000lb bombs. In all they dropped 42 of these on and around the wreck, earning derision by hitting the motionless target only three times out of four. Behind them came RAF Hunters, spraying aviation fuel to make sure the oil would blaze. It didn't end even with that. The BBC, broadcasting to a spellbound nation, was soon reporting the deployment of rockets and napalm, and sightseers crowded the Cornish clifftops to watch the attacks raining in. It was the very darkest of black comedies. The tower of oily smoke, painfully evocative for veterans of wartime convoys, could be seen for 100 miles. But for all the Navy and RAF could throw at it, the ship refused to sink. After each bombing run the smoke would drift to reveal it, blackened and broken but still welded to the rock. Worse was to come through *force majeure*. High spring tides put out the flames, leaving commanders no option but to sound the retreat, leaving the *Torrey Canyon* to go on bleeding through the night until the Buccaneers, Sea Vixens and Hunters could finish the job in the morning. Twenty thousand tons of oil was destroyed in the burning, but it was too little, too late. Thirty thousand tons had spewed into the sea when the ship hit the reef; another 20,000 escaped during the week that followed, and 50,000 surged out when the vessel broke its back. All this, 100,000 tons in all, had swelled the gigantic slick now heading for the Cornish peninsula.

The whole thing was a colossal, catastrophic, escalating misadventure in which no one passed up an opportunity to make a mistake. Weather did intervene to turn the oil aside, but not before at least 70 miles of England's most beautiful beaches (93 miles by some accounts) had been coated in brown sludge and tens of thousands of seabirds had died. The detergent used to break up the slick was itself a powerful pollutant, poisonous to wildlife. It was not just birds and Cornwall's holiday industry that were at risk. The entire marine ecosystem was subject to stress, along with fishing grounds and oyster beds in the Fal and Helford estuaries. As it happened, a range of chemicals had only recently been tested at the UK government's Warren Springs laboratory in Stevenage, where scientists assessed their effectiveness as solvents or emulsifiers to break up slicks. Testing had also been done by the Ministry of Agriculture, Fisheries and Food's (MAFF's) marine laboratory in Burnham-on-Crouch, which wanted to know how the chemicals would affect shellfish (oysters, mussels, cockles and winkles). All of them turned out to be highly toxic, and none more so than the one that would be most widely used for *Torrey Canyon*, the solvent/emulsifier BP1002. Not all the indications had been negative, however. A later report, *The Torrey Canyon Disaster and Fisheries*, published by MAFF in February 1968, set out the evidence from previous incidents where chemicals had been used:

> Between 1963 and 1967 [it said] there were a number of oil-spills in estuaries round the coasts of England and Wales, and the effects of three of the more serious of these (in Milford Haven, Poole harbour and the Medway), in all of which considerable quantities of detergent were applied, were studied by scientists from the Burnham-on-Crouch laboratory. The consistent experience was that although intertidal animals and plants [i.e. those that inhabited the zone between the low and high tide marks] were killed in the immediate vicinity of the spraying, and some intertidal winkles that had not been killed were tainted, the harm to animals below the low-water mark was negligible, due to the very rapid dilution and dispersal of the chemicals.

Torrey Canyon resembled these earlier episodes only insofar as it involved a release of oil. It was a spill of unparalleled magnitude, in open sea rather than estuary, and with an enormous slick forming. In deciding how to react, the scientists had to consider the possible effects of detergent on a wide range of very different species and habitats – free swimming fish such as mackerel and pilchards; bottom dwellers such as sole, plaice and rays; and rock-dwelling lobsters as well as crawfish, oysters and crabs. No decision was possible that would not cause damage. Whether you let the slick do its worst, or deluged the sea with detergent, there would be casualties, disfigurements and losses. The challenge was to compute and compare the costs, and to strike an acceptable balance.

In view of the immense volume of sea off Cornwall [said MAFF in its report], the great tidal mixing that occurs twice a day, and the frequency of rough seas at this time of year, it was concluded that the rate of dilution and dispersal of chemicals would be so great that even if very large quantities were used the chances of serious damage to commercial fish or shellfish would be very small compared with the advantages to the holiday industry in cleaning the beaches. It was fully appreciated that there would be substantial losses among intertidal animals, and probably some deaths locally of crabs and lobsters, but it was felt that these losses could be accepted in the circumstances.

It was therefore considered that the use of chemicals of the solvent/emulsifier type could be accepted on the sea and open coast where damage to fisheries was likely to be very small, provided that the chemicals were not used in estuaries containing shellfisheries and particularly in the Fal estuaries and the Helford River.

Given the size of the slick, the disaster that eventually struck Cornwall was only a fraction of what it might have been. The greater price was paid by the French, to whose coast an ill wind delivered 50,000 tons of oil, more than double the quantity that hit the toe of England. Spraying at sea began the day after *Torrey Canyon* went aground and continued for 17 days afterwards, during which half a million gallons of chemical was dispensed from ships sailing out of Falmouth and Newlyn. More than 90 per cent of it was in the area around and to the east of the wreck (MAFF's map of the operation showed an area measuring 35 miles from north to south, and 15 miles east to west). MAFF calculated that 50,000 tons of oil was dealt with by the sprayers, and that only 20,000 tons actually reached Cornwall in its crude state. This is how MAFF described its arrival:

Oil started to come ashore on Easter Sunday, 25 March, and by 30 March most of it was held by westerly winds in the many inaccessible coves along the rocky coastline from St Ives around

Land's End to Gwennap Head, or had been blown across Mount's Bay to come ashore at a number of points between Marazion and the Lizard. Subsequently much of the oil which had been trapped between St Ives and Land's End was blown and drifted out of the rocky coves, and was spread north-eastwards along the north Cornish coast as far as Trevose Head or brought south to contaminate again the beaches on the eastern side of Mount's Bay.

MAFF's own pollution map drew a thick black sock around the county from Trevose Head in the north to Mullion in the south, with small holes where the bare coastline still showed through on the west-facing shores of Mount's Bay and the Lizard. This was the real front line, where men fought hand to hand with muck. To arm them, another 2m gallons of detergent was issued to the army and local councils, who sprayed it directly on to beaches or just offshore from fishing boats. (It should be pointed out that the word 'detergent' in this context is linguistic convenience rather than exact lexicography: solvent/emulsifiers such as BP1002 bear very little resemblance to the stuff that goes into washing machines.) The teams worked only in daylight and usually on rising tides, pausing only in extreme storm conditions. The theory was that the incoming water would emulsify the oil, which would be flushed away overnight before the next application of detergent in the morning. The involvement of soldiers in this civil emergency, however, was not an unmixed blessing:

There is unfortunately no record of the quantities of detergents used by the Army, but service personnel applied large quantities at Porthleven, Gunwalloe Fishing Cove, around Mullion and at many points along the rocky coastline from Land's End to Hayle. In many areas the Army applied the detergents with care and according to instructions, but in others it was poured on to the rocks and seas in a way which was not only ineffective in emulsifying the oil but also caused avoidable damage to marine life.

Very soon the scientists began receiving reports that large numbers of dead fish were being washed up on beaches. When they went to check, however, they were able to verify only a single whiting, one nine-inch mullet, a plaice and a flounder (both recorded at five inches), five conger eels, a few crabs and a couple of lobsters. Test trawls by a chartered boat, the *Pioneer* from Newlyn, meanwhile had scooped a bit of good news out of the polluted sea. Working in the six areas that had received the most detergent, it had made typical mixed catches of plaice, dab, lemon sole, sole, brill, megrim, cod, whiting, haddock, pollack, saithe, pout, hake, horse mackerel, gurnard, red mullet, herring, sprat, pilchard, angler, bream, blonde ray and nurse hound. One very thin megrim was reported to have an abnormal gut; otherwise all the fish were healthy. They occurred in their normal abundance; looked and smelled normal; had clean gills and nothing unusual in the gut. Even when the trawler worked right in among the spray ships and dispersed oil patches, there was no sign in the fish of oil or detergent. At Newlyn market top prices were paid and normal commercial fishing quickly got going again, with no apparent loss of quantity or quality. MAFF conceded that there had been some damage close to shore:

Along the beaches, where detergents were applied in large quantities to oil on the sand, thousands of sandeels remaining in the sand of the beaches must have been killed. Also some conger eels and small plaice, dabs, flounder and mullet were washed up dead or seen dead by divers in the gulleys adjacent to where spraying was being done, but the total numbers of dead seen were to be counted in tens rather than hundreds and probably constituted only a very small proportion of the inshore population at the time.

Overwhelmingly the evidence appeared to support the view that relatively little damage would be suffered by animals living below the level of the oil. It was a similar story with shellfish. Four days after spraying began, scientific observers visited

Porthleven, which had been particularly hard hit by oil and was daily receiving 10,000 gallons of detergent. In the harbour they found dead lugworms, ragworms, shore crabs and a conger eel, but many other crabs, limpets and mussels were still alive. On rocks and beaches elsewhere, the only casualties seemed to be shellfish that had received direct hits from the sprays. Most intertidal life had survived. Some mussels had died near Mullion, but they were not 'of commercial quality'. Strangely, nature seemed to have thrown a cordon around the fishermen's interests, for non-commercial species living in the sands, rocks and pools were killed by the detergent in very large numbers. It was a lethal assault on children's nets and buckets. Sandeel, blenny, rockling, topknot, limpet, starfish, green shore crab, swimming crab and prawn – all perished in the chemical blitzkrieg. Divers working at varying depths brought back similar stories: dead crabs here and there; a large dead lobster in 12ft of water off Porthleven; dead starfish, swimming-crabs and sea urchins at Sennen; dead elvers at Hayle and Porth Mear; lots of dead razor clams off Newquay. Problems persisted for a while with tainted lobster flesh carrying the faint savour of paraffin, but sealife generally survived the ravages of accidental pollution far more successfully than it would stand up to the more persistent assaults of overfishing.

The one good thing that came out of *Torrey Canyon* was a rethink of maritime law. Until then, the main threat of oil pollution was thought to have been the routine flushing of oily wastes from ships at sea. As long ago as 1954, an attempt had been made to control this through the International Convention of Pollution at Sea. OILPOL, as it was known, barred captains from discharging any quantity of oil (meaning any mixture containing more than 100 parts of oil per million) within 50 miles of a coast. Further out, discharges were not to exceed either 60 litres per mile travelled, or a total during any voyage of more than one fifteen-thousandth of the ship's carrying capacity – figures that were checkable against obligatory oil record books that had to show every transfer on or off the ship. But this was at a time when, as the International Maritime Organization (IMO) now puts it, 'pollution control was still a minor concern ... and the world was only beginning to wake up to the environmental consequences of an increasingly industrialised society'.

In 1967 the world woke up with a start. Everyone had seen the terrible images of ruined beaches, oiled birds and animals, and understood as never before the need for some form of defence. It was realized, too, that Cornwall's tourist economy had been hard hit, and that there was no scheme in place that could properly compensate those who had suffered. The IMO's governing council went into emergency session and started talking about action plans. Being an agency of the United Nations, however, it could only move and turn at the speed of international diplomacy, by comparison with which a 63,000-tonne tanker is as nimble as a dodgem. Not until 1969, two years after *Torrey Canyon* hit the reef, did it agree to convene a conference 'to prepare a suitable international agreement for placing restraints on the contamination of the sea, land and air by ships'. To keep this within diplomatically navigable limits, the date for the conference was set four years hence, in 1973. The result was the International Convention for the Prevention of Pollution from Ships, known as MARPOL, which covered not just oil but also pollution by chemicals, 'harmful substances in packaged form', sewage and garbage. In the particular case of oil, however, it persisted in the view that the worse threat was from operational pollution rather than one-off *Torrey Canyon*-style spectaculars.

Where fine words collide with expediency, inertia will always defeat momentum. Member states took (a) a hard look at the practical and economic implications of abandoning their offshore dustbins and (b) no effective action. Ratification of an international convention calls for a bit more than a show of hands. For MARPOL to work, it needed the approval of at least 15 states representing between them no less than 50 per cent of the world's merchant fleets by gross tonnage. By 1976 only three countries –

Jordan, Kenya and Tunisia, representing less than 1 per cent of world shipping – had signed up. This was despite the fact that large parts of the convention – on packaged goods, sewage and garbage – were purely optional. The only mandatory parts were those relating to oil and chemicals.

Oil tankers meanwhile were behaving as if they regarded *Torrey Canyon* as a role model. In 1971 the *Wafra* spilled 65,000 tonnes off Cape Agulhas, South Africa. This was followed in 1974 by the *Metula* (53,000 tonnes in the Magellan Straits, Chile), in 1975 by the *Jakob Maersk* (80,000 tonnes, Oporto), in 1976 by the *Urquiola* (108,000 tonnes, La Coruña), and in 1977 by the *Hawaiian Patriot* (99,000 tonnes, 300 miles off Honolulu). Accidents waiting to happen included *Amoco Cadiz*, which in 1978 would spill 227,000 tonnes off Brittany, and the *Atlantic Empress*'s 280,000 tonnes off Tobago in 1979 – still the biggest spill in history.

So IMO tried again. In February 1978 it held a conference on Tanker Safety and Pollution Prevention. This produced some new regulations on the design and operation of ships, and – such is diplomacy – relaxed the anti-pollution timetable from snail's pace down to something easier for the members to keep up with. Now the only part of MARPOL that would need immediate ratification was the one that dealt with oil. The section on chemicals would not become binding until three years after the convention came into force – and it wasn't coming into force any time soon. It was in fact not until 2 October 1983, 16 years after *Torrey Canyon*, that Annex I of MARPOL, 'Prevention of pollution by oil', finally became law.

Other issues were being wrangled over too. In the late 1970s, while I was editing the environment pages of the *Sunday Times*, I was approached by a postgraduate student from King's College, London, whose PhD project was an investigation of litter on beaches. This was, believe it or not, a hot talking point. By application of common sense, everyone more or less 'knew' that the jumble of plastic bottles washing up every day must have come from ships, but intuition and common sense are not proof. And without proof of course there was no way the legislators would pick up their pens. The student's name was Trevor Dixon, and his idea was to mobilize *Sunday Times* readers in a nationwide survey. We would devise a safe survey method (i.e. no picking up unidentified metal objects or containers with chemicals in) which would prove the case once and for all. Volunteers were told to choose a point above the high tide line and walk towards the sea. On the way they would pick up all the plastic bottles – Harpic and so forth – that lay within a metre-wide transect, and write down the serial numbers they would find embossed on the base. This was better evidence even than the foreign languages on the labels. The codes would reveal their place of manufacture and show which had arrived by land and which by sea. Data flooded in to the paper's then offices in Gray's Inn Road, and the results were unequivocal. Britain's rim of plastic, unbiodegradable but slowly being abraded into plastic sand, was the special gift of the merchant marine. Dixon got his PhD, and the Department of the Environment (as it then was) got all the proof it needed to move towards ratification of MARPOL Annex V, 'Prevention of pollution by garbage from ships', which duly came into force on 31 December 1988.

Without it, the seas would have gone on stocking a perpetual and ever-expanding museum of garbage. The Hellenic Marine Environment Protection Association calculated that a plastic bottle at sea would take 450 years to biodegrade, raising the possibility that maritime theme pubs in the early twenty-sixth century would adorn their nooks with olde worlde bleach bottles. HELMEPA reckoned an aluminium can might survive in the sea for even longer – between 200 and 500 years, comfortably outlasting tin cans (100 years), painted wood (13 years), woollen cloth (1 year), rope (3–14 months), cotton cloth (1–5 months) and paper bus tickets (2–4 weeks). The damage is not just aesthetic. Animals, fish and birds become tangled in debris, causing injury, strangulation and drowning. Their efficiency as scavengers makes them their own worst enemy. More than 90 per cent of the 30,000 gannets' nests on Grassholm Island now include plastic in their building material, to the great hazard of young birds whose feet become caught. Marine animals may also mistake plastic for food, with dire results. Plastic bags swallowed by mammals, turtles and sharks block the intestinal tract, leading to starvation and injury. Globally, according to the Marine Conservation Society (MCS), a million birds and 100,000 marine mammals and turtles die every year from their encounters with plastic, which now accounts for more than half the litter on beaches and floating in the water.

'The types of plastic found at sea,' it says, 'range from raw plastic pellets (about the size of wheat grains, from which larger items are manufactured), to plastic bags and sheeting, cotton bud sticks, monofilament fishing nets and multi-pack drink-can "yokes".' The amount of plastic as a percentage of total beach litter (see below) is increasing year by year, as more and more older materials – wood, metals, glass and textiles – are replaced. By 1994, 54.8 per cent of rubbish found on beaches was plastic. By 2005 it was 59 per cent, with no chance that it would do other than go on rising.

Trevor Dixon's survey method is now used by the MCS for its annual Beachwatch survey, which has been running since 1994 and provides the most comprehensive record of the state of Britain's beaches. The 2005 survey, timed to coincide with the Ocean Conservancy's International Coastal Cleanup over two days in September, involved 3,891 volunteers on 332 beaches covering 170.7km of coastline. Only Fungus the Bogeyman would have been cheered by the results. The volunteers picked up 11,337kg of rubbish – 338,196 items in all, or 1,981 per kilometre. This was significantly more than in the previous year (1,897 per km) but an improvement on the all-time record of 2003, when the 2,075-per-km strike rate almost doubled the 1,045/km of 1994. Like all graphs it has its peaks and troughs, but the trend is all too depressingly clear. We grow fouler by the year. MCS's analysis of the finds is so meticulous, you'd think it was cataloguing a Saxon hoard. There are records for 'tyres with holes' (0.1 per cent of the total), plastic toiletry bottles (0.2 per cent), cigarette lighters (0.4 per cent), shoes and sandals (0.1 per cent), fast-food containers (1.0 per cent), balloons (0.5 per cent), aerosol cans (0.2 per cent), disposable barbecues (0.1 per cent), condoms (0.1 per cent), cotton bud sticks (5.6 per cent), tampons (0.2 per cent), sanitary towels and panty-liners (0.6 per cent), animal faeces (0.4 per cent), cigarette stubs (3.7 per cent), glass bottles (0.5 per cent), ice-lolly sticks (0.9 per cent) and on and on and on – 99 categories in all. Grossing them all up and grouping them by material type, you get the following dirty-dozen league table:

1 Plastics – 59 per cent of total litter (1,169.3 items per km)
2 Polystyrene – 8.4 per cent (165.7/km)
3 Paper – 7.3 per cent (144.8/km)
4 Sanitary items – 7.2 per cent (143.1/km)
5 Metal – 6.2 per cent (123.6/km)
6 Glass – 3.1 per cent (62.3/km)
7 Cloth – 3.0 per cent (59.9/km)
8 Wood – 2.8 per cent (55.0/km)
9 Rubber – 1.9 per cent (38/km)
10 Faeces – 0.4 per cent (7.9/km)
11 Pottery and ceramics – 0.4 per cent (7.5/km)
12 Medical items – 0.2 per cent (4.0/km)

Put another way, that's 117 pieces of plastic for every 100m of shoreline – more than one a metre. You'll meet a discarded sanitary item, flushed down a lavatory and washed through the sewers, every seven metres; a piece of glass every 16m. These are of course averages, which means that for every clean strip there must be another with a double helping. Many of these are to be found in the south-west, whose 3,936.1 items per kilometre is the worst in England. The south-east scores 1,847.0, north-west

1,579.1, and north-east 1,231.6. The English national average, 2,256.1 items per km, is markedly worse than Northern Ireland (1,877.0), Wales (1,753.0), Scotland (1,747.6) and the Channel Islands (1,207.2). There are regional differences, too, in the distribution of different kinds of litter. The northern tip of Scotland is blessed with only 26 bits of 'sewage related debris' per kilometre. In west Wales and north-east England it's 744. I must confess to exasperation when guests from London prevent their children from enjoying North Norfolk's unsurpassably beautiful beaches and creeks, but I understand well enough the reasons for their anxiety. 'Look what I've found' does here mean a crab or a razorshell, not a hypodermic syringe, but my reassurances carry little weight against the kind of headlines that Beachwatch inevitably – and mostly rightly – generates in our more excitable newspapers.

Where does all the muck come from? Of the stuff that can be traced to source, 35.4 per cent is rubbish left by visitors – people who can be bothered to pack up and cart a picnic or barbecue to the beach, or walk their dog there, but not to clean up afterwards. The fishing industry, at 14.6 per cent, is the next worst offender, followed by the ghastly 'sewage related debris' at 7.2 per cent, shipping 2.2 per cent, fly-tipping 0.2 per cent, and 'medical' 0.2 per cent. This still leaves a whopping 39.6 per cent that could have originated from almost any source and cannot be accounted for.

Theoretically, none of this should have come overboard from ships. MARPOL Annex V bans totally the dumping of plastics anywhere at sea, and severely restricts the discharge of all other kinds of food, domestic and operational waste (excluding fresh fish) into coastal waters and eight designated wider 'special areas' – the Mediterranean, Baltic, Black, Red and North Seas, the Gulfs, the Caribbean and the Antarctic – where it is illegal to dump waste of any kind within 12 nautical miles of the coast, and anything other than food waste further out. In Britain, Annex V made its way into law via the Merchant Shipping Regulations, 1988, which – as MARPOL required it to – banned all plastics and oily wastes from UK territorial waters and set out a graduated tariff of prohibitions for other kinds of garbage in the North Atlantic and Irish Sea. No rubbish of any kind may be thrown overboard within three nautical miles of the coast. Garbage not ground to a particle size of less than 25mm is prohibited to a distance of 12, and buoyant lining and packaging material to 25 nautical miles out. To make all this workable, MARPOL also requires shipowners to provide storage space for rubbish on board, and governments to ensure that there are reception facilities at ports and terminals.

The intentions look good but the flaws are obvious. Once over the horizon, ships have only the company of gulls. There is nothing to connect any particular vessel to any particular piece of garbage, and no witnesses to any offence save the perpetrators themselves, who are hardly likely to provide the kind of photographic or video evidence that courts would need to convict them. Although only 2.2 per cent of the Beachwatch litter can be proved to originate from shipping, it is likely that this is an underestimate, and that at least some of the unattributed 39.6 per cent has come over the side. The MCS cautiously agrees: 'Reports from Beachwatch organisers in certain remote locations ... suggest that some items usually categorised as "non-sourced" or "beach visitors" should be attributed to shipping debris.' Trevor Dixon himself – now a senior lecturer at Buckinghamshire Chiltern University College, where he is known as 'Dr Dioxin' – still surveys beach litter on the Kent coast and reports that 90 per cent of it comes from ships. It's the same old stuff that we were finding 30 years ago – 3-litre drinks bottles, household detergents, bleach.

It would be wrong to tar all mariners with the same brush, but, like all industries, it has an efficient, law-abiding top end, a widely varying middle and a frankly piratical lower stratum for whom the only commandment that matters is the eleventh. Undetectable offences committed against unenforceable laws are of no more concern to them than netting an undersize haddock.

Enforcement, detection and prosecution are the responsibility of the UK Maritime and Coastguard Agency (MCA), which was born in 1998 out of a merger between the former Marine Safety Agency and the Coastguard Agency. It does its best, but it's much like swatting insects in the dark. Not until March 2006 did a new MARPOL amendment (Regulation 8) even give it the power to inspect foreign vessels in British ports 'where there are clear grounds for believing that the master or crew are not familiar with essential shipboard procedures relating to the prevention of pollution by garbage'. Otherwise its only tools are the ships' own paperwork. All vessels of 400 gross tonnes or more, every vessel certified to carry 15 or more people and every exploration or drilling platform now has to keep a Garbage Record Book in which must be recorded every discharge, offload or shipboard incineration of garbage, with the date, time and position of the ship. But such records are only as good as the master's word. If he dumps rubbish over the side but records it as having been incinerated, then who is to know? The MCA's prosecution records are a hair-raising catalogue of what-the-hell negligence and wilful risk-taking – crossing or sailing the wrong way up shipping lanes, falsifying or lacking legal certification, colliding with other ships or bits of landscape, sleeping while on watch, failing to maintain safety equipment, failure to declare hazardous cargo and (endlessly) being drunk. It is impossible to believe that skippers so lightly concerned with the basics of seamanship will pay fastidious attention to the niceties of waste management and bookkeeping. And yet the number of prosecutions for MARPOL-related offences is vanishingly small, and Annex V cases all but non-existent.

In September 2003, the crew of the gas tanker *Lotta Kosan* were spotted throwing a plastic garbage bag overboard while at anchor in the Solent. Southampton magistrates fined the owners £10,000 with £5,258 costs. In September 2004, the crew of a North Sea supply vessel, *Grampian Explorer*, saw garbage including sleeping bags, polystyrene and plastic bags being dumped from a fishing boat, the *Lynden II*, near the oil production platform Ocean Princess. Peterhead Sheriff Court, noting that it was a first offence committed by a 'rogue' member of the crew, fined the owners £2,000. All other prosecutions under MARPOL since 2001 have been for oil spillages – mostly minor and caused in full public view by negligence rather than deliberate criminal acts. Intentional law-breakers take good care not to be caught.

Major spills from oil tankers around the UK did not cease with *Torrey Canyon*. In 1993 the *Braer* ran aground on the Shetlands and spilled 85,000 tonnes; three years later the Sea Empress leaked 72,000 tonnes and polluted 100km of coastline in southwest Wales, with colossal damage to birds, marine life, fishing and tourism. Ironically, *Sea Empress* happened while the government was still absorbing the lessons of 1993. An inquiry under the late Lord Donaldson had been set up after *Braer* to find ways of protecting the coast from pollution by merchant shipping. The result in 1994 was *Safer Ships, Cleaner Seas*, more commonly known as the Donaldson Report, which made 103 recommendations covering everything from ship design to emergency procedures, port control, navigation, insurance, accident investigation, routeing, surveillance and tracking. Noting that 80 per cent of incidents were caused or exacerbated by human error, Donaldson laid great stress on improvements in management, training and communication. Many of the recommendations subsequently have been implemented, and (I touch wood) at the time of writing – July 2006 – there has been no major spillage in UK waters since the *Sea Empress*. This is not quite the good news it seems, however. Although it's major accidents like *Torrey Canyon*, *Braer* and *Sea Empress* that grab the headlines, tanker incidents account for less than 10 per cent of total oil pollution in the sea. The rest is an accumulation of usually small and sometimes tiny amounts that are spilled by mistake during normal operations.

Every year on behalf of the Maritime and Coastguard Agency,

the Advisory Committee on Protection of the Sea (ACOPS) publishes a survey of discharges around the UK coast. The report for 2004, which is the latest available, runs to 89 pages and is the work of Trevor Dixon. It is a catalogue of almost maddening detail – a total of 1,354 incident reports and 'supporting information' allowed the identification of 664 separate discharges from ships and offshore oil and gas installations. Just under 90 per cent of these were of crude or other mineral oils. Most of the rest were of chemicals and 'other substances', including a tiny amount (0.3 per cent) of vegetable or animal oils. The number of incidents was 13.5 per cent higher than in the previous year (2003), though the total volume leaked was 30 per cent less. The largest single oil spill was 40 tonnes of light diesel and a tonne of hydraulic oil that escaped when a fishing boat, the *Elegance*, sank off the Orkneys in March. Twenty-three other spills arose from the sinkings of 11 other fishing vessels, 6 pleasurecraft, 2 tugs and 4 'other types'. Otherwise the spills were put down to negligence, accidental damage and botched jobs: 'bunkering spill', 'split in port side fuel valve', 'leakage from stern tube', 'faulty pump', 'failure of discharge hose', 'overflow of bilge holding tank', 'drum fell overboard' – that kind of thing. There was also the occasional 'deliberate discharge'.

The 'accidental' nature of a spill is not proof against prosecution. If a shipowner ignores safety procedures, neglects equipment, fails to train his crew or to repair known faults, then hefty fines may await. I emphasize 'may'. Given the sheer weight of Dixon's data, it is surprising that between January 2002 and the first half of 2006, the MCA records only five successful prosecutions for pollution offences involving oil, of which just four were in UK territorial waters (the fifth was in Denmark). But, as the head of its enforcement unit Jeremy Smart explains: 'This is not the full story. We only deal with incidents that occur outside harbour authority areas. Bunkering spills are prosecuted by the harbour authorities themselves.' As the vast majority of detectable spills occur in ports and harbours, this creates the unusual situation of a service provider (the harbour authority) being handed responsibility for policing and prosecuting its own customers (the shipping companies). They do this with varying degrees of reluctance, and with little publicity – the naming and shaming of clients is not usually regarded as good PR.

Discretion extends also to record-keeping. How many prosecutions? How high the fines? No one knows, for no national register is kept. To find out, you would have to contact all 761 port and harbour authorities in the UK. I tried three. Milford Haven, destination of both *Torrey Canyon* and *Sea Empress*, says that on average it prosecutes around two cases a year, almost all of them fishing boats refuelling from road tankers. Falmouth is either luckier or less litigious – its last prosecution was in September 2003, when a tanker offloading from a larger ship spilled a tonne of oil into the Fal estuary and West Cornwall magistrates fined the owners £10,000. Southampton, like Milford Haven, averages around two cases a year, and is not shy of pursuing relatively minor offenders (a roll-on roll-off car ferry was prosecuted for a spill of less than 100 litres).

But these are a bit like fishing statistics. They record the numbers netted but give no idea of the ones that got away or had the benefit of a blind eye, and there is evidence that quite serious offences may go unpunished. This is how the MCA itself recorded an incident involving the coastal tanker *Averity* at the Stanlow oil refinery on Manchester Ship Canal:

The *Averity* had arrived at White Oil Dock No.1 Berth at Stanlow in the early afternoon of Tuesday 25th September 2001 to load two cargoes of Ultra Low Sulphur Diesel (ULSD) and Kerosene. The vessel deballasted on arrival but there was a delay before loading commenced. Loading of the ULSD finally started at 0030 on Wednesday 26th September 2001. Some twenty minutes after loading commenced the Seaman on watch detected a discoloration in the water, which he traced back to the ship's side in the vicinity of the pumproom. The Seaman went down into the pumproom and found that both of the sea valves were open. After closing them the AB informed the Mate, who was in charge of loading operations. Unfortunately there was a misunderstanding between the Mate and AB and loading was not stopped. In fact shortly afterwards loading of the Kerosene commenced. Loading was eventually completed at 0320. When figures were compared it was found there was a difference of approximately 155 tonnes of ULSD. Only when the discrepancy became apparent was the alarm raised . . .

Given the size of the spill, the negligence that caused it, the failure to stop loading and the delay in raising the alarm, the expectation was that the port authority would take action. When it failed to do so, the MCA itself stepped in and prosecuted *Averity*'s owners under the Merchant Shipping Act. The outcome was a fine of £10,000 plus £7,173 costs at Chester Magistrates Court, and the ignominy of being named in an MCA press release. There are arguments on both sides. To the MCA, the spill was just too big to be ignored. The port authority on the other hand would have seen an important client – F. T. Everards – with no previous convictions, which had accepted responsibility for the incident, paid the full clean-up cost and acted to prevent a recurrence. Black and white in such cases tend to go a little grey around the margins, and the scales of justice wobble in the breeze. You could call it either way. What it does illustrate is the subjective nature of a system which – whatever the merits of the Stanlow case – is vulnerable to conflicts of interest, and which is largely closed to public view.

Oil spillages in ports and elsewhere are not generally the result of deliberate discharges but, nevertheless, the line between an unlucky accident and criminal behaviour is as thin as an underwriter's smile. Spillages at terminals are not acts of god but the foreseeable results of bad practice. The Marine Conservation Society echoes the MCA in its view that 'often, economic considerations outweigh those of ecological safety in the minds of the operators, and short cuts are taken . . .' It acknowledges, however, that shipping companies are not the only, or even the worst, offenders. As readers of *Rubbish!* will know, landlubbers are not well placed to point the finger. Sixty per cent of oil in the sea gets there by way of storm drainage systems in towns and cities, and from the illegal disposal of used sump oil and other lubricants into urban drains. Wherever there is oil there is pollution, as surely as smoke follows flame. Seepage from North Sea rigs, for example, kills or disrupts marine life out to a radius of 2km from the well-head. Approximately 60 per cent of dead seabirds washing up on UK beaches are oiled (though the oiling itself may not always be the cause of death).

One thing definitely has improved. No longer is it common practice for tankers to wash out their insides between cargoes, smearing the beaches and everyone on them with foul brown clods of crude. This was the so-called 'heavy fraction' – sludge that settled at the bottom of the tanks and had to be swilled out at sea before reloading. It doesn't happen so much now, and it never happens legally. Thanks to MARPOL, tankers have switched to a system known as 'load on top', which exploits the properties of crude oil as a solvent. It began in the 1960s when the sludge would be pumped into a separate slop tank rather than into the sea. The oily residues then would gradually float to the top during the return voyage, so that the water could be pumped off to leave only the oil in the tank. Fresh crude was then pumped on top, with the double advantage of reducing waste (as much as 800 tonnes in a big ship) by dissolving the sludge into the next cargo and converting it back into usable oil.

A MARPOL amendment in 1978 obliged all new tankers to adopt a more sophisticated but gloriously simple version of the process known as crude oil washing (COW). Instead of water, crude oil (i.e. the cargo itself) is sprayed to remove the sludge from the sides and floor of the tanks. As before, the solids dissolve back into the mass of oil and become part of the cargo. All this must be recognized as genuine improvement. By some calculations, 'load on top' every year keeps more than 8m tonnes of crude oil out of the sea. There is no process on earth, however, that is proof against error, mechanical failure or the malignity of fate, and the MCA's prosecution records bear witness to the number of ships that are only too ready to give fate a helping hand. For all the double-hulled tankers, satellite navigation and monitoring systems that require captains to account for every litre of oil pumped into or out of their tanks, and regardless of COW and MARPOL, accidents will go on happening.

One of the most important of Donaldson's conclusions in 1994 was that there existed around the UK a number of areas 'of high environmental sensitivity' that were especially at risk from shipping. These, it said, should be identified and designated as Marine Environmental High Risk Areas, or MEHRAs, which would be marked on Admiralty charts. The idea was that ships' captains would then either avoid sailing anywhere near them or at least take extra care when they did. The task of identifying likely MEHRAs fell to the Department of Transport, in partnership with Defra and aided by conservation agencies and other semi-official bodies throughout the UK. It was never going to be a question of just making a list of obviously valuable coastlines and putting up Keep Out signs. Unlike civil servants' MBEs, the MEHRA citations would be hard won and sparingly distributed. First a methodology had to be devised, of sufficient complexity to fill all the time and paper that serious government requires. The Department of Transport describes the process thus:

For the purposes of identifying the MEHRAs, the UK coast and proximate sea areas were divided up into a large number of cells on a chart. Two parallel exercises were then carried out:

(a) One exercise identified the shipping risk to which each cell was subject, taking into account ship routeing data, size and type of vessel, traffic density and analysis of past accidents resulting in pollution from ships (such as collisions, groundings and fires). A model was then created to combine this information and generate a measure of the risk per cell, taking into account the potential for an oil spill to drift from sea to shore.

(b) The second exercise identified the environmental sensitivity of each cell, taking into account a number of different criteria, predominantly of an ecological and scientific nature. In particular, the sensitivity exercise took account of the statutory designations which were in place in each cell, such as Special Areas of Conservation (SACs), Special Protected Areas (SPAs) or Sites of Special Scientific Interest (SSSIs). The environmental sensitivity of each cell was scored on the basis of the number of such sites in each cell and their sensitivity to marine pollution.

The two sets of data for each cell – shipping risk and environmental sensitivity – were then brought together to produce an overall ranking. The cells which were eventually identified as MEHRAs were those which manifested a combination of both high sensitivity and high pollution risk.

'Eventually' is right. Donaldson reported in May 1994. It was 12 years later, in February 2006, that the Transport Secretary, Alistair Darling, finally 'unveiled' (as his department put it) the 32 areas that had ticked all the boxes and emerged from their long gestation as fully fledged MEHRAs. England got 16, all on the south and east coasts – Plymouth; Berry Head; Portland; Western Solent; Hastings and Dungeness (two areas); South Foreland to Ramsgate (two areas); Harwich and Felixstowe (two areas); Spurn Bight; Flamborough Head; Tees; Farne Islands; Holy Island and Berwick (two areas). Scotland got 14 – Muckle Flugga, Unst; Fethaland, Shetland; Tor Ness, Hoy; North St Kilda; South St Kilda; Gallan Head, Isle of Lewis; West Islay, Argyll and Bute (two areas); St Abb's Head and Eyemouth; Bass Rock; Dunbar; Isle of May; Newburgh; Kinnaird Head. Northern

Ireland and Wales got one each – Islandmagee, County Antrim, and Pembrokeshire Islands. Altogether these represent approximately 9 per cent of the UK coastline. In the time it took to produce the list there had been three more serious European tanker losses – the *Sea Empress* off Milford Haven in 1996; the *Erika*, which spread 11m litres of oil along 350km of the French Atlantic coastline, killing at least 100,000 birds in late 1999; and the *Prestige*, which devastated the north-east coast of Spain with a 63,000-tonne spill in 2002.

As an exercise in bureaucratic job creation – defining terms and conditions, establishing and applying criteria, making and cross-checking lists and rendering it all down into numbered paragraphs – this was well up in the Sir Humphrey class. Twelve years! As a prophylactic against dirty seamanship, it looked more like the bastard offspring of gesture politics and wishful thinking. The Royal Society for the Protection of Birds (RSPB), the Worldwide Fund for Nature (WWF) and Marine Conservation Society were all furious. Twelve years! For this! What especially incensed them was that two crucially important and particularly vulnerable areas, the Scilly Isles and the Minches, which the Donaldson Report itself had highlighted and for which environmentalists had long campaigned, were pointedly excluded from the list – an omission made all the more bizarre by Darling's own assertion: 'MEHRAs will be an essential aid to passage planning since their primary purpose is to inform ships' masters of areas where they need to exercise even more caution than usual.'

The importance of the Scillies as an area of 'high environmental sensitivity' and their 'realistic risk of pollution from merchant shipping' would be hard to exaggerate. This is the most important seabird site in south-west Britain (20,000 nesting birds of 13 species, which makes it the most diverse in England), and a vital migratory route for birds of passage. For this reason under European law it is a Special Protection Area (SPA) for birds and a Special Area of Conservation (SAC) for reefs, sand and mud-flats. Under UK law it is a Site of Special Scientific Interest (SSSI).

If there is anything for which it is even better known than birds, it is shipwrecks, with *Torrey Canyon* merely the worst of the many scars on its own and Cornwall's memories. To define the classic MEHRA is to describe the Isles of Scilly.

So it is with the Minches – the busy straits between the west coast of Scotland and the Outer Hebrides. Thousands of ships, many of them carrying toxic cargoes, pass through every year and it is a favourite short cut for tankers. In June 2003, the German-owned MV *Jambo*, en route from Dublin to Norway, sank off the Summer Isles, spilling 1,600 tonnes of zinc oxide and prompting the Department for Transport to launch a review of safety; in December 2005 an oil tanker grounded off Skye. Dolphins, whales and basking sharks flourish in waters whose vast bird populations are covered by numerous SPAs and SACs: the Shiants alone has 200,000 seabirds, including 75,000 pairs of puffins (in the UK, only St Kilda has more). Handa, too, has an overall population of 200,000, including 75,000 pairs of guillemots – the largest colony in Britain. Priest Island has 5,000 pairs of storm petrel. The island of Rum is a National Nature Reserve and an SPA for birds that include the biggest population of Manx shear-waters in the world – 60,000 pairs. Loch nam Madah and Obain Loch Euphoirt are designated SACs for their coastal lagoons. Ascrib, Isay and Dunvegan are an SAC for the common seal. The UK's only inshore cold-water corals are at the Minches' southern end, near Mingulay . . .

And so it goes on. Here is a busy marine thoroughfare with a history of accidents, internationally important wildlife and coast-lines of famous beauty. Yet somehow the architects of MEHRA in their 12-year deliberation contrived to produce definitions of 'environmental sensitivity' and 'risk of pollution' that excluded the two most obvious candidates. It prompted the Labour peer Lord MacKenzie of Culkein, who spoke of local 'disbelief', to raise the question in the House of Lords. Why had the Minches not been declared a MEHRA? He got his answer from a government whip, Baroness Crawley, who produced the classic bureaucrat's defence – the rule-book. The criteria for identifying MEHRAs, she said, 'were set out in the late Lord Donaldson's report ... Although they are environmentally sensitive, the Minches did not meet those criteria because of the volume and type of shipping in the area and the protective measures that are already in place.' This is true as far as it goes, but overlooks the fact that the Scillies and parts of the Minches were precisely the examples Donaldson gave of areas most likely to qualify. Would he have drawn up criteria that confounded his own purpose? Without the services of a medium one cannot ask, but the idea swims with the mermaids in the outer reaches of theoretical possibility. Be that as it may, it is the government that makes the rules and, as the noble lady made clear, no matter how much disbelief they provoked in the hairier districts of western Scotland, rules were rules and may not be gainsaid.

It is not, quite, as daft as it sounds. The Department for Transport argues that the Scillies and Minches are well enough fortified by existing legal and voluntary defences, including MARPOL, and so don't need reinforcement. This is paragraph 5.5 of its report, *Establishment of Marine Environmental High Risk Areas (MEHRAs)*:

> During the process of identifying MEHRAs, it was recognised that a number of particularly sensitive areas around the UK coastline already benefit from protective measures. One such example is around the Scilly Isles where there is an extensive pattern of Traffic Separation Schemes with associated Inshore Traffic Zones around the Isles and between Seven Stones and Longships a voluntary reporting requirement which applies to laden vessels. There is also an IMO [International Maritime Organization] recommended deep water route to the west of the Hebrides for laden tankers over 10,000 gross tonnage which greatly reduces the volume of traffic through the Minches and, consequently, the risks to the environment.

The 'voluntary reporting requirements' ask captains to notify coastguards an hour before they enter certain specified waters. As well as the Scillies, these include laden vessels in the Fair Isle Channel, Pentland Firth and Kyle of Lochalsh, and all vessels in the Minches. 'Voluntary', however, means 'not compulsory', and the DfT concedes that compliance has been 'varied'. The trouble with this is that the good guys who cooperate were never the problem – it's the non-compliant corner-cutters who are the danger. As the MCA's records show, the worst of them have little enough regard for the law, never mind voluntary reporting schemes. Despite the reassurances it gave when it announced its list, and despite the omission of the Minches, the government evidently did conclude that the area needed better protection. Weirdly, Alistair Darling's announcement of this became part of his justification for non-designation:

We have a continuing programme of vessel traffic surveys around the UK coast. As part of this programme, traffic surveys of the Minches and the waters to the west of the Hebrides were carried out, and on the basis of these surveys, we are going to propose new protective routeing measures for the Minches to the International Maritime Organization in July [2006]. The measures which we will propose are the introduction of a new traffic separation scheme off Neist Point and the upgrading of the existing recommended tracks (through the narrows south of the Shiant Islands) to IMO-adopted status as recommended routes. It is worth noting that the Minches already benefit from improved vessel traffic monitoring because of the increased number of ships carrying Automatic Identification Systems, and that this too has the effect of enhancing safety of navigation and providing additional protection for the waters and the coasts of the Minches.

The Automatic Identification Systems he talks about are shipboard transponders which automatically transmit information about a vessel's identity, course, speed and position to the coastguard and other ships and aircraft. Like the proposed refinements to recommended routes, this is obviously a good thing. But, again, it does not ensure compliance and does not add up to a cogent argument against classifying the Scillies and Minches as MEHRAs. As Lord MacKenzie put it in the Lords: 'It would have been a sensible belt-and-braces policy for the government to designate the Minches as a MEHRA in addition to the protective measures already in place. There are huge environmental sensitivities in that area. Thousands of ships transit it with pretty awful cargoes, including the MV *Jambo*, which sank a couple of years ago, spilling huge amounts of zinc oxide . . . If the current environmental measures, which are almost all voluntary, do not prove to be effective, will the government consider imposing further restrictive management measures, including giving the Minches an area-to-be-avoided status?'

The only answer he got from Lady Crawley was a reiteration of the new routeing proposals that the government had put to the IMO, and an assurance that 'we do not plan to identify further MEHRAs'. Noting that the IMO was 'not known for its lightning speed of reaction and response', the Tory peer Lord Geddes wondered what scope the UK government had for independent action. It brought him no joy, for out again came Lady Crawley's straight-bat defence. 'The setting up of the 32 MEHRAs,' she said, accurately but irrelevantly, 'is a matter for the British government. We also are within a protection zone of the IMO, but the setting up of these sensitive areas is a matter for us.' And that was that.

Whether any of this is worth a row of kelp is a question that still awaits answer. The IMO was not expected to respond to the routeing proposals until late in 2006, and the earliest they could come into force was mid-2007. Even then, it would be some considerable time before any improvements in safety would become apparent. MEHRAs too, of course, are an unknown quantity of uncertain benefit. There will be no patrolling gunboats to ensure compliance. Indeed, as the DfT made clear, there is nothing legally to enforce:

Classification of a location as a MEHRA will not result in a new statutory designation; there is no basis in United Kingdom law for such a designation. MEHRAs will be advisory as proposed by *Safer Ships, Cleaner Seas*. If specific protective measures apply in the vicinity of a MEHRA it will be because they are already in place or because their introduction can be justified and approved, if necessary by the IMO.

What kind of sense does it make when 'specific protective measures' already in place are used as an excuse *not* to designate a MEHRA? Is this good value for 12 years' work? Where MEHRAs do exist, what can they be expected to achieve? Alistair Darling, or whoever wrote his press release, put it like this: 'MEHRAS will now be notified by a Marine Guidance Note to mariners who will be expected to exercise an even higher degree of care than usual when passing through them. They will also be marked on Admiralty charts.'

What might this mean in practice? Here is the DfT again:

As Lord Donaldson indicated in paragraph 14.120 of *Safer Ships, Cleaner Seas*, it will normally make sense for a ship to '. . . keep well clear . . .' of a MEHRA. But sometimes, and most especially when a MEHRA is close to the approaches to port, ships will not be able to keep well clear; in such cases, they will instead have to [here comes that phrase again] exercise an even higher degree of care than usual.

Then again, the circumstances of MEHRAs will differ, so that in some cases it will be necessary for ships to stay further away from the coast (e.g. because of marine wildlife) than in others, and in these cases we can achieve a targeted effect through specific routeing measures – e.g. by directing passing traffic further offshore. These routeing measures will, of course, be marked on charts. The combination of the MEHRA along the coast, and the routeing measures shown on the chart in the relevant part of the sea, will mean that the Master has all he needs to know in order to decide how to conduct his ship in the vicinity of a MEHRA.

In 2003, as the wait for MEHRAs entered its tenth year, WWF did a bit of totting up. It calculated that there had been 104 tanker-related oil pollution incidents in UK waters in the four years between 1998 and 2002, and that one in ten ships between 2000 and 2002 had been involved in accidents. In 2003, the MCA monitored or investigated 585 separate spillages of oil or chemicals. In the face of all this, WWF was not inclined to be impressed by the government's obsession with methodology:

Limitations and assumptions [it said] have been acknowledged. For example, operational pollution was not considered and the traffic database used does not include non-routine traffic such as naval vessels, fishing vessels, pleasure craft or offshore traffic transiting to mobile drilling units. The comprehensiveness of environmental sensitivity criteria has also been questioned. Furthermore, where measures were already in place they were taken into account and the risk assessment carried out on top of existing measures without analysing whether these measures were working . . . Almost a decade after the Donaldson Report DfT are due to announce the list of MEHRAs. During this period stake-holders have only been engaged in consultation once (on the original methodology). Consequently there has been a lack of opportunity for seeking additional expertise . . .

In common with the Wildlife Trusts, WWF viewed with scepticism the neo-Panglossian, motherhood-and-apple-pie con-viction of the policy's authors that good-sounding encouragement of unimpeachable behaviour would be all they needed to bring the cowboys into line. The RSPB, too, was 'disappointed' by the omission of the Scillies and Minches but doubted that the designated areas would see much benefit either.

The management measures utilised to protect the MEHRAs from future oil spills are too weak at present. In our opinion, if the proposed protection and management measures are inadequate then the listing of MEHRAs will have been a waste of time. We are continuing our campaign for more effective management and comprehensive monitoring and enforcement programmes for MEHRAs.

The shipping industry also let it be known that it was less than impressed. Here is John Dempster, chief executive of the UK Major Ports Group, in a letter to Defra in May 2004:

We have had a number of discussions with the Department for Transport about this proposal. While it is comparatively straight-forward to identify those places which would qualify as MEHRAs, we have always failed to establish what the practical implications of the creation of a MEHRA would be. If the intention is that commercial shipping should be encouraged to avoid the area, the process becomes circular (because the presence of commercial shipping is a factor in determining a MEHRA). If shipping is not to be discouraged from using MEHRAs what are [sic] their purpose? There are already a number of possible designations of sensitive sea areas, such as ATBAs [Areas To Be Avoided] or PSSAs [Particularly Sensitive Sea Areas], and it is not clear what advantages another designation would bring. We suspect that it is problems of this kind which have prevented the DfT from proceeding with a recommendation which was made some 10 years ago. In our view the idea should be dropped.

Fat chance. Once the pheromonal reek of an 'initiative' has reached its nostrils, the diplodocus is even harder to stop than it is to start. The pace may be slow but the momentum is irresistible. Maybe it will work. Maybe drunken skippers will programme themselves to sober up and double the watch as a MEHRA approaches, and make sure they have accidents only in undesignated waters. Then again, maybe this marriage of opposites – grafting vague appeals to goodwill on to 12 years' worth of punctilious map-making – is an implicit acceptance of an absolute truth. Accidents will happen. What matters is how we prepare for them.

One thing we're not short of is law, and all the apparatus that goes into the making of it. If you could legislate pollution out of existence, even the diplodocus would have done it years ago. As well as MARPOL we have the International Convention for the Safety of Life at Sea (SOLAS), which sets standards for the construction and safety of ships; the International Convention on Standards of Training, Certification and Watchkeeping for Seafarers (STCW), which does what its name suggests; the Convention on the International Regulations for Preventing Collisions at Sea (COLREG), which sets standards for navigation and signalling; the Loadline Convention, which prohibits overloading; the International Convention on Oil Pollution Preparedness, Response and Co-operation (OPRC), which requires countries to make contingency plans for coping with spills; the International Convention Relating to Intervention on the High Seas in Cases of Oil Pollution Casualties (International Convention), which authorizes states to take action after casualties have occurred; the International Convention on Salvage (Salvage Convention), which promises additional rewards for salvors who prevent or minimize environmental damage after a spill; the International Conventions on Civil Liability for Oil Pollution Damage (CLC), which require shipowners to pay compensation for damage; and the International Conventions on the Establishment of an International Fund for Compensation for Oil Pollution Damage (FUND Conventions), which allow for top-up funding when the limited liability of a shipowner is inadequate.

The UK's own last line of defence is the National Contingency Plan for Marine Pollution from Shipping and Offshore Installations, which would be triggered by a Tier Three emergency (see below). This is controlled by the MCA, whose

Counter Pollution and Response (CPR) branch grew directly out of the old Coastguard Agency's Marine Pollution Control Unit, set up in 1967 as a response to *Torrey Canyon*. Its job is to 'provide a command and control structure for decision making and response following a shipping incident that causes, or threatens to cause, pollution in UK waters'. Spills are placed in one of three internationally recognized categories. Tier One is a small operational spill that can be dealt with locally. Tier Two is a medium-sized spill – usually from an operational discharge or minor accident – that may need regional resources to clear it up. Tier Three is a major spill requiring the involvement of one or more governments. It is the degree of environmental risk, not the volume of oil, that decides the category, and the responsibility for dealing with it depends on both the source of the spill and the destination of the slick. The MCA itself takes the lead when the pollution is from ships at sea. Port authorities and oil terminals bear responsibility for cleaning up after Tier One and Tier Two spills within their jurisdictions. Offshore installations are responsible right up to Tier Three. Local authorities have to clean up whatever washes on to their shorelines, and the Environment Agency deals with pollution that reaches the sea from land.

The national contingency plan should at least prevent the kind of panic reaction that ordered the bombing of the *Torrey Canyon* and saw untrained soldiers firing at will with their chemical sprays. As with all government procedures, you need a knowledge of jargon and a head for initials. The first thing that should happen after a spill is that someone – ship's captain, aircraft pilot, member of the public – will report it to the local coastguard, who will then warn MCA's duty Counter Pollution and Salvage Officer (CPSO) if there is a risk of pollution. The CPSO will then decide the appropriate response. If the risk is serious, he will alert the Secretary of State's Representative for Marine Salvage and Intervention (SOSREP) and the MCA's Marine Emergency Information Room (MEIR) at Southampton. SOSREP may then set up a Salvage Control Unit (SCU) to approve and oversee salvage; the MCA will run a Marine Response Centre (MRC) to coordinate counter-pollution and clean-up operations at sea, and local authorities will coordinate coastal clean-ups through a Shoreline Response Centre (SRC). All these will have the benefit of advice from an Environment Group, whose members will include representatives from statutory nature conservation bodies, the Environment Agency and the Defra fisheries directorate. Priorities are identified, tasks assigned, manpower and equipment strategically deployed.

The hardware is kept by CPR (Counter Pollution and Response branch – remember?) at various sites around the UK. Shoreline clean-up equipment, booms and gear for fighting pollution at sea are held at Milford Haven, Huddersfield and Perth; booms are kept also at Oban, Llanelli, Truro, Ely, Darlington and Belfast; and chemical dispersants at 11 locations across the country. There are eyes in the sky – regular surveillance flights and a satellite shared with European partners – both to spot new pollution incidents and to monitor their progress afterwards. The aircraft themselves carry spraying equipment; there are four tugs on permanent standby – in the Northern Isles, the Minches, the south-west approaches and the Dover Straits – to take damaged or stranded vessels in hand, and the likely behaviour of oil slicks or chemical spills (rate of dispersal, direction of drift) can be predicted by computer. The whole caboodle is tested several times a year by exercises at sea.

In the storm-tossed and barnacled world of practical seafaring, this is probably as good as it's going to get. By improved design, navigational aids and traffic management we can reduce but not eliminate the risk of accident. We can reduce but not eliminate environmental damage when accidents happen. And we must not forget that, though tanker accidents are the glamour end of the pollution market that grab the biggest headlines and cause the most spectacular damage, they account for only a small percentage of oil and chemicals in the sea. Figures from the International

Tanker Owners Pollution Federation (ITOPF) show a steep reduction since *Torrey Canyon* and MARPOL in both the number and volume of oil spills worldwide. In 1970 there were six spills of between seven and 700 tonnes, and 29 of 700 tonnes and over. Some bad years followed. In 1974 there were 89 in the 7–700 range and 28 majors. In 1975 there were 95 and 22. But by 1985 it was down to 31/8, and by 1995 to 20/3 – the approximate level at which it has since remained (19/4 in 2000, 16/3 in 2001, 12/3 – the best yet – in 2002, 15/4 in 2003, 16/5 in 2004 and 21/3 in 2005).

Total volumes fall into a similar pattern – 330,000 tonnes of oil in 1970, reaching a peak of 640,000 in 1979 and then gradually declining to an all-time low of 8,000 in 2001. The graph is far from smooth, however. There are some very big spikes in it, showing just how much damage a single rogue can do. The 174,000 tonnes lost in 1989, for example, were mostly from the *Khark 5* (80,000 tonnes, off Morocco) and *Exxon Valdez* (37,000 tonnes, Alaska). The *ABT Summer* (260,000 tonnes, off Angola) and *Haven* (144,000 tonnes, Genoa) pushed 1991 up to 430,000 tonnes – the second highest on record. The following year saw the *Aegean Sea* (74,000 tonnes, La Coruña) and *Katina P* (72,000 tonnes, off Mozambique) swell the global total to 172,000 tonnes. Next year came *Braer*, off Shetland, spilling 85,000 of the 139,000-tonne world total; and in 1996 the *Sea Empress*, off Milford Haven, boosted that year's loss from eight to 80,000 tonnes. Tellingly, the best year on record (8,000 tonnes, 2001) was followed by another bad one – 67,000 tonnes, of which 63,000 came from the *Prestige* off north-east Spain, causing that country's worst-ever environmental disaster. Experts predicted it would take at least ten years for the environment to recover, during which time we'll be more than lucky if nothing worse happens.

Prestige offered a pretty good illustration of what might be floating towards us, and why the voluntary, be-a-good-captain-and-avoid-the-MEHRA code might not always impress the man at the wheel. A report in the *New Scientist* succinctly outlined the problem: 'The Greek-operated, single-hulled tanker was flying a Bahamas flag, had a Liberian owner and had been chartered by a Swiss-based Russian oil company.' This last had originated in Gibraltar and had a number of British directors but was ultimately owned by a Russian conglomerate called the Alpha Group Consortium with interests in oil, banking, insurance, a supermarket chain, food processing and telecommunications. According to Friends of the Earth, its projects also included 'ownership of 40% of all Mongolian meat exports and a venture to launch communications satellites in Iraq, Iran and Syria'. The chairman of its supervisory board was Mikhail Fridman, who made so much money from the privatization of Soviet state assets that *Fortune* magazine listed him as the world's ninth richest man under the age of forty, worth more than two billion dollars (other sources have put it as high as 4.3 billion, not far behind the more famously *uber*-rich Roman Abramovich, owner of Chelsea Football Club). One of the Alpha Consortium's most important profit engines is Tyumen Oil, whose main assets, including the huge Samotlor oilfield, lie in the environmental disaster zone of the Nizhnevartovsk region of Western Siberia. The *Observer* in October 2003 described it thus:

There are lakes of oil on the surface of the tundra. The air is poor. So is health. There are high incidences of disease related to poor environment, and high death rates. According to independent consultancy IWACO, which published a survey two years ago, up to 840,000 hectares of land has been polluted by oil in Western Siberia. At least 6,500 falls within the Nizhnevartovsk region – 2 per cent of the land surface – caused largely by spillage from pipelines and wells, from drilling and chemical waste and leaking storage facilities throughout the Soviet era in which 100m tonnes a year of oil was sucked out of Somotlor at its peak.

Now rivers and underground aquifers are polluted at up to 50 times Russian safety standards. Samples of drinking water taken from one river in the region over five years showed 97 per cent polluted with oil. Fish, animals and plants are affected. Greenpeace, which commissioned the IWACO report, maintains the damage continues – pipelines are leaking 500 litres of oil every second.

The Russian oligarchs get a bad press even in their own country, and (whatever might be meant or implied by it) you seldom have to wait long for the word 'mafia' to appear. The oil in the *Prestige* may or may not have come from Tyumen, but the ethos of the trade with its rust-bucket charters and flags of convenience is as clear as a Siberian dawn. According to WWF, doubts about the ship's seaworthiness had been raised even before it got to Spain. Typically its ownership and registration were not of the same nationality, and even the latter was playing away. The Bahamas Maritime Authority, with whom the *Prestige* was registered and whose flag it flew, had its origins and principal office not, as you might expect, in Nassau, but in Minories, near the Tower of London. The complex, multinational weave of ownership, chartering and registration drew comment from the United Nations Environment Programme (UNEP) magazine the *Environment Times*:

It is believed that a Greek shipping dynasty is behind the registered owner of the *Prestige* in Liberia, the Mare Shipping Incorporation, which only operates this tanker. It bought it in 2000. The transport itself was chartered by a Russian-owned Swiss company. Such situations, covering 'hidden' interests under the flag and registration of some convenient administration, have become typical during the last few decades. Experts from the US Bureau of Shipping had ordered dock work after finding cracks in the ship's hull. Welding was carried out in China, and the ship was subsequently inspected three times in two years in China, Dubai and Saint Petersburg respectively. European ship-owners control 34% of the world's fleet, but the majority of their ships are registered under flags of convenience, offering lower fees, less restrictive laws and access to low-wage crews [in this case they were Lebanese]. Although corporate globalisation is not a risk in itself, tanker law cannot be effectively enforced under such conditions . . .

The wreck of the *Prestige* and its aftermath highlight the anarchic character of the shipping industry. This situation suits major corporations as it helps them avoid regulations and taxes. It is a further example of the conflict between basic safety and pollution concerns and a system based on profit and national considerations.

That says it all. The architects of Britain's MEHRAs might as well have spent 12 years embroidering mottos on samplers for all the effect they will have on the buccaneers. Is it really to be expected that they'll cut their speed, or make a detour, out of respect for puffins or seals? Yo ho ho and a bottle of rum! There are precious few encouragements to be taken from the *Prestige*, other than perhaps the fact that mismanagement on such a scale is unlikely to be repeated in the North Atlantic. When the 25-year-old tanker sustained hull damage in heavy weather off Cape Finisterre, the Spanish authorities could have towed it into port, kept it afloat and contained the damage. Instead they ordered it to be towed out into deep water beyond the 120-mile limit, trailing a lengthening slick as it went. This excited the interest of their Portuguese neighbours, who responded by sending a warship to keep it out of their own territorial waters. After five days, with Pyrrhic spite, the *Prestige* paid back the Spanish by breaking in half and sinking 130 miles out. Sixty-three thousand tonnes of oil slimed its way across 3,000km of Galician coast, bringing all the familiar images of wrecked beaches, blackened harbours and oiled wildlife. Three hundred thousand seabirds were killed; 30,000 people in the fishing and shellfish industries suffered damage to their livelihoods, and the clean-up cost ran to billions of euros. A new chapter had been written into the pollution-control handbook: How Not To Do It.

Single-hulled tankers, in which the cargo is separated from the sea only by the ship's bottom or side plate, still account for approximately half the world's oil fleet. *Braer* and *Sea Empress* were both of this design. The Americans unilaterally in 1990 (following *Exxon Valdez* the previous year), and the IMO through an amendment to MARPOL in 1992, have acted to phase such vessels out. All tankers of over 600 tonnes deadweight built since 1996 have had to be double-hulled (i.e. with tanks protected by a second, internal plate to reduce the risk of penetration in impact). But, like everything to do with international law and the sea, it will take time, and in some places the risks will get worse before they get better. The Americans' head start over the IMO has meant that vessel age limits in US territorial waters since 2005 have pushed more and more old ships out into the rest of the world, where the last surviving single-hull will not reach the breaker's yard until 2015.

Until then, the rising price of oil and the bounty to be had from it will drive the captains of an ageing fleet into an ever more desperate race against time. The irony is that the British especially, and seafaring nations generally, have always found their greatest heroes among the racier kind of seadog. Put Nelson at the helm of a 200,000-tonne supertanker instead of a 2,000-ton wooden man-o'-war, and imagine which way the blind eye would turn. Half-speed ahead, MEHRA on the port bow?

Not until the sea cows come home.

CHAPTER SEVEN

Blocked Exits

One day in the 1970s a friend took me for what he called 'a spot of fishing' off the Essex coast. It involved a weight of gear – boxes, bags, rods, flasks, oars, outboard, lifejackets, proper wooden dinghy – which our Edwardian forebears would have wanted a train of porters, sailors and a dog-cart to carry to the water. Simon's Volvo stood in for the dog-cart but everything else had to be shifted with our own soft, ripe-for-blistering hands. We thought that in some atavistic, Baden-Powellish sort of way this would be good for us. In caps and guernseys, doing our best to look like the old salts we weren't, we cast off from the beach with nothing worse than wet trousers and a flooded Wellington. Close inshore the sea lay calm, its ribs rising and falling in contented sleep. A wetted finger found not a breath of wind; a thin curtain of cloud parted to reveal a benevolent sun; we made up a sea shanty and toasted the day in orange juice (it was too early for the Chablis).

Looking back all these years later, I cannot be certain exactly where we were – Frinton, Walton on the Naze – somewhere round there. We rowed a little way out, then fired up the outboard and burbled off towards Denmark. For me, the greatest pleasure of being at sea has always been the sight of land. Better than from any other vantage point you see how it was put together – how geology, time and weather have done their stuff, and how settlements have wormed into the sheltering planes and folds. So it appeared this morning, as Essex unravelled astern and showed us what it was made of: towns, villages, harbours, islands, estuaries. Somewhere to the north lay Orford Ness, textbook example of longshore drift; beyond it Benjamin Britten's Aldeburgh. Round the curve to the south lay Clacton and the Blackwater estuary. Suddenly, absurdly, the sea shanty wanted to become an ode.

Another thing I cannot remember is how long it took for heaven to decline through purgatory (a ripening breeze and low swell plucking at my breakfast) into hell (vomiting, loss of balance and white knuckles on the gunwale) as the boat began to roll and pitch. On the Beaufort scale such a wind would hardly have registered. On the shipping forecast there would have been no hint of inclemency; on seamen's brows not a furrow. Even Simon, who spent perhaps three days a year with salt under his keel, presented an altogether convincing impression of a man in his element. For a solid-ground man like me, it was like being swung on a bungee across the Styx.

It got worse when Simon killed the engine. At first it sounded like silence, but then came the hard, arrhythmic slap of water against planks. Long fingers of sea flicked us around like a spin-bowler testing a ball. I heard Simon's voice ('wine . . . sandwiches . . . pork pie'), then my own wordless retching. And then something else – the incredibly low, incredibly loud and incredibly adjacent boom of an incredibly large ship. I didn't know what it was. Tanker, freighter, ferry . . . It was the first of many heading for Harwich or Felixstowe, each one bulldozing the water into hills and valleys that were deeper than our boat. The view flipped like a semaphore shutter, up and down, in and out from bare blue sky to glassy depths; my limbs so rigidly braced that the unabsorbed shocks climbed right up into my skull, detonating a blinding headache. In the chaos my reel went over the side so I could not have fished even if I'd wanted to. For the rest of the several aeons that we were out there, I could do no more than lie unconvincingly ('No, I'm all right, really'), truthfully insist I wasn't hungry and hope that each measly codling or whiting that Simon or his cousin hauled aboard would satisfy their idea of 'enough'.

Of course the danger was illusory. We were no great distance from land, the boat was comfortably in its element and, though close to a shipping lane, we were not actually in it. Any captain trying to run us down would have ploughed into a sandbank first. And yet the juxtaposition of not entirely complementary interests was a hard lesson in the facts of maritime life – a demonstration of the obvious, perhaps, but one that we struggle to grasp. Like no other wild place or playground, the sea is also a commercial highway. More than 95 per cent by volume, and 75 per cent by value, of all Britain's imports and exports enter and leave by ship. It is our lifeline, our national feeding tube, but it is also the most powerful evidence for the incoherence of our thinking. More eloquently than the traffic jams on the M25 and M6 that it helps to create, it confirms the absence of integration from our 'integrated transport policy', and our failure to realize the true commercial, social and logistical value of our greatest national asset.

Not the least of our oddities is that we can't seem to agree even on what qualifies a place to call itself a port, or on how many of them there are. The Maritime and Coastguard Agency lists 761. Others say 600, though some of these may handle little more than a few day trippers or a bucket of whelks. Sea and Water, the government-funded agency responsible for promoting coastal and inland water transport, counts 300. If you limit the definition to places with regular trade in cargo or passengers, then the total reduces dramatically. The British Ports Association (BPA) has a membership of 124, reaching from Sullom Voe in the Shetlands to St Helier in Jersey, and from Londonderry in Northern Ireland to Lowestoft on the outer rim of East Anglia. The Maritime Statistics Directive, whose figures are published by the Department for Transport (DfT), bases its data on ports that handle a minimum 1m tonnes a year, which cuts the total to 52 but still includes 97 per cent of the trade. Provisional estimates suggest that in 2005 they unloaded between them 342.53m and loaded 223.27m tonnes of cargo (though these are not quite the same as 'imports' and 'exports', as they include transfers between UK ports) – a grand total of 565.8m tonnes, which the addition of 15.8m from 'minor ports' raises to 581.6m. Written out in full, that is 581,600,000 tonnes. Which is 66,348.8 tonnes an hour, 24 hours a day, seven days a week, 52 weeks a year. Or 18.43 tonnes a second. The vast majority of this leaves or enters the ports by road.

The top ten hubs in 2005 were Grimsby and Immingham (58.06m tonnes), Tees and Hartlepool (55.79m), London (53.84m), Southampton (39.95m), Milford Haven (37.41m), Forth (34.22m), Liverpool (33.78m), Felixstowe (23.14m), Dover (21.15m) and Sullom Voe (20.54m). Those may sound like anoraks' statistics of no interest to anyone but traffic managers and investors, yet – as we shall see – they have a more direct impact on our lives than many of us might think. Much of the stuff heading in and out is basic raw materials – oil, chemicals, petroleum, coal, ores, liquefied gases, timber, grains and feed-stuffs – that are the building blocks of the national economy. In 2004, the most recent year for which itemized figures are available, the total value of cargo shipped through UK ports was £330 billion. 'Finished' goods adding to the volume included vehicles, food, timber, iron and steel, building materials, machinery, shoes, clothing, computers, 'white goods', televisions, furniture, books, carpets, you name it . . . Pretty much anything you can think of, or lay a hand on, is shipped in or out in some form or other, including people. More than 67,000 passengers passed through UK ports in 2004. Ports are also home to the fishing industry (including, often, their own fish markets, as at Grimsby, Hull, Lowestoft, Brixham and Newlyn). They provide ferry links to the islands, supply terminals for the oil and gas industries, landing stages for dredged sand and gravel, and yacht marinas to bring in the blazered pound as well as the oilskin euro. Seventy thousand people work in UK ports which, as employers, are of prime importance to local economies – especially where, as in my far-away encounter with the North Sea shipping lanes, leisure is combined with commerce.

To describe the international shipping industry as competitive is a bit like noticing the wetness of water. Ports and shipping lines are locked in a battle for local, continental and global dominance, flexing their deadweights and ready to take on all-comers like grogged-up sailors at closing time. *Reckon you've got container capacity, do you?* Container ships are getting bigger and bigger, no longer constrained by the old 'Panamax' limit dictated by the dimensions of the Panama Canal; and bigger ships need bigger ports, deeper water, faster and more capacious landward links. It's not just a question of importing in bulk for consumption in the UK: the serious business is in 'trans-shipment' ports – huge transit hubs where incoming containers are reloaded for shipment to other ports, often in other countries. The UK up to now has been rather good at this. It handles more goods through its ports than any other European country, and carries nearly double the container traffic of its nearest rival, the Netherlands. In January 2005 Felixstowe claimed a new record for the most containers ever moved on and off a single ship, 4,077 on the 334-metre-long Chinese-owned mega-ship *CSCL Europe*. Each container, let us not forget, is the size of an intercontinental lorry or railway wagon – a fact that, as any regular traveller on the A14 will know, brings particular problems of its own. In July 2006 the port received an even bigger ship, the 106,700-tonne *Xin Los Angeles*, also Chinese-owned, which stretches 337 metres from end to end and delivers 9,560 TEUs. (Quick jargon-break: TEU stands for 'twenty-foot equivalent unit' and is the container industry's standard unit of measurement. Containers are metal boxes of regular size: usually 20ft or 40ft long, 8ft wide and 8ft 6in or 9ft 6in tall. A 20ft-long container is one TEU; a 40ft container is two.

Single or double TEUs are the standard-size units you see on the roads.)

Vast ships like this, far beyond the ken of anyone who thinks aircraft carriers are big, are the dominant force in world trade. Of the ten vessels that docked at Felixstowe's nine container berths on a randomly chosen day in August 2006, eight were bigger than the Royal Navy's flagship, the aircraft carrier *Invincible*. Not long ago a ship would have been thought big if it could handle 6,000 TEUs. Modern giants like *Xin Los Angeles* are pushing up towards 10,000, and the industry expects the next generation to reach 12,500. It means that the port companies are like dunnocks with cuckoos in their nests. There is a worsening imbalance between the size of ships, the size and depth of docks and the span of dockside cranes. An imbalance, too, between the speed at which marine engineers can increase the size of vessels – why should they stop even at 12,500 TEUs? – and the speed at which ports can expand to service them. It is this, more than anything, that drives international competition and puts UK transport policy through the mincer.

Owners of such colossi are never going to run them at less than maximum efficiency. They want full cargoes, direct routes between international hubs and no hanging about for tides or berths. Nor do they care to make diversions into remote back-waters like the North Sea. Felixstowe and Southampton are handy stop-offs on routes to Antwerp, Rotterdam or Hamburg, but in any language (and especially Chinese) a 250-mile detour to the Tees makes no sense. If there is no available berth in the south, then they'll steam on to Rotterdam and the UK can fetch what it needs from there. (The do-it-yourself chain B&Q already does this as policy.) Hence the concentration of deepwater container berths in what planners call the GSE – the Greater South East – and the scramble to build a whole lot more.

The race-against-time cliché is not misplaced. The continent is not sitting on its hands while the likes of Felixstowe and Southampton tie up the international supply lines. Hamburg,

Bremerhaven, Rotterdam, Antwerp and Le Havre all have ambitions of their own in which they are enthusiastically supported by their governments. Their chance will come when the UK hits maximum capacity and the world's biggest ships have to go elsewhere to set their records. Shipping giants like Maersk Sealand, the world's largest container line, have already fired warning shots across the industry's bows. In evidence to the House of Commons Transport Select Committee in 2003, Maersk complained of a shortage of deep sea container berths, and warned of delays and 'inefficiencies to the supply chain'. This was worrying but not surprising. In late 2000 the government itself had recognized the need for expansion and issued a stark warning on the consequence of failure:

> If the port industry fails to meet demand . . . shipping lines may divert primary services to overseas ports . . . The primary services would no longer collect and deliver UK trade to UK ports, adding the cost of trans-shipment in a foreign port to UK trade. A higher proportion would arrive in or depart from the country on road trailers. There would be a significant effect on the cost of UK trade, and thus on the competitiveness, as well as on the volume and pattern of road traffic.

Given the Chinese disdain for any part of the UK outside the GSE, the prescribed remedy was not difficult to foresee. Though the government claims a 'hands-off' attitude to ports, which are privately owned and market-driven, in reality it retains control through the planning system, and the market won't get what it wants without ministerial backing. Ministers, however, were backing plenty, and the transport committee in 2003 was encouraged by what it described as 'significant proposals already in the system'. The importance of these was emphasized by the minister for shipping, David Jamieson. 'Had these proposals not come forward,' he said, 'then we would have had to have a different view.'

Indeed they might. The mixed fortunes of those 'significant proposals' were such that, in July 2006, only three years after its previous examination of the ports industry, the transport committee announced a further inquiry in which it would 'revisit some issues of particular concern'. These included questions of ownership, ability to meet demand, and inland transport links – each of them not so much a hot potato as a white-hot ingot of contention. At the same time, the government itself launched a long-awaited Ports Policy Review covering many of the same issues – demand versus capacity, market forces versus 'sustainable development', 'regional development objectives' and, from the apple pie and motherhood end of the political rainbow, encouragement for smaller ports 'to realise their potential as businesses and for the benefit of their wider communities'. The period for consultation closed on 1 September 2006, and the review itself was expected 'in the first half of 2007'. The one crucial question touched upon by the committee but excluded from the policy review was that of ownership, which should damp down the expectation of anything too radical.

Unlike their continental rivals, UK container ports are privately and not publicly owned, and thus not integral to any supposed integrated transport system. The result often is that nothing goes anywhere fast. The ports have underused, inadequate and inefficient rail links, the great majority of which have insufficient headroom for the new 9ft 6in 'high cube' containers favoured by the shipping lines. New tracks and upgrades are needed, but railways are not a 'free good' like the roads. The arguments and uncertainties about who should pay for them have had the predictable outcome that every road user knows. Eighty-four per cent of freight in the UK now travels by road, with 40 per cent of the mileage on motorways. Lorries swarm out of the ports in elephantine herds (2m a year through Dover alone). Heading north from the south and east, where most of the containers arrive, there is reliable congestion on the M1, A1, A12, A14, M4, A27, A21, M20, M3, M40, M20, M25 and M6. The M25 at peak periods is more like an orbital car park than a motorway, and the Freight Transport Association estimates the cost of road congestion to UK industry at £20 billion a year and rising. The solution it calls for is a nationwide programme of road widening, which may well be what its haulage-trade members want to hear. But it's the same old malarkey. Wider roads bring more traffic, more greenhouse emissions, more global warming and accelerated land-loss. The one thing they do not bring is an end to congestion and delay. As hard experience repeatedly has shown, bigger roads like bigger hamburgers simply invite their own consumption. Traffic grows to swallow all space available to it, with no advantage gained.

To those who drive transport policy in the south-east, none of this registers as important. The curses of gridlocked motorists may be Anglo-Saxon but they drown in a babble of tongues. Decisions crucial to our quality of life are being dictated not in the mutant, stakeholder English of the UK government but in unfamiliar languages from foreign boardrooms. Roads are choked by container lorries because this is what makes sense to foreign shipowners. The price of a competitive ports industry is to wait upon the convenience of others. And the price is going up.

The most important of the 'significant proposals already in the system' in 2003 was a new container terminal for Associated British Ports (ABP) on an area of marsh and mudflat at Dibden Bay on Southampton Water, opposite ABP's own port of Southampton. It would be of a size to receive 9,500-TEU Chinese giants six at a time. Thirty per cent of the containers would be reloaded for trans-shipment to other ports, 21 per cent would switch to rail and 49 per cent squeeze on to the M27 and M3. This would involve 3,700 container lorries a day, plus 1,800 employee and 600 support vehicles.

Objections poured in not just from local groups but also from the RSPB, Friends of the Earth and English Nature. Dibden might be undeveloped, but it was not unoccupied. The government's own conservation watchdog, English Nature, argued that the port would harm internationally important wildlife sites, including two Special Areas of Conservation, a Special Protection Area and eight Sites of Special Scientific Interest. Among the birds at risk were Brent goose, oystercatcher, ringed and grey plover, dunlin, curlew and redshank. Other objectors feared round-the-clock noise, light pollution, dredging and fuel spills. But all the same . . . Port expansion was government policy, and even the usually hyper-critical transport committee was onside. Birds versus the economy: it looked an easy win for ABP. A public inquiry listened to the evidence; the inspector made his recommendation and, in April 2004, the DfT pronounced.

The birds had won. The Freight Transport Association, hardly able to believe what it was hearing, declared itself 'shocked and disappointed', and predicted rejoicing in Rotterdam and Hamburg.

> We are concerned that such a vital economic project should be rejected on environmental grounds. Government should consider the benefits to the economy and thus the environment as a consequence of making planning decisions which further local, regional and national economic development.
>
> Industry must now look to the prospect of developing the Shell Haven and Harwich ports, but once again road and rail links would need to be improved considerably for the ports to be successful.

As we shall see, that phrase 'road and rail' – and particularly the absence from it of 'coastal shipping' – is a dark hint of what we might be in for. Shell Haven is a former oil refinery at Stanford-le-Hope, Essex, on the north shore of the estuary in the Thames Gateway redevelopment area, which P&O wanted to turn into a deep-water superport. The plan was for 2.3km of quayside – enough to handle 3.5m TEUs a year. At Harwich, Hutchison Ports wanted to develop Bathside Bay in the Stour estuary as the second largest container port in the UK after its near neighbour Felixstowe, which it also owned and where it proposed simultaneously to build another deep-water terminal and a 1km quay extension.

Once again the opposition was ferocious. Feelings ran so deep that a whole new network, Portswatch, was set up to link the efforts of the Campaign to Protect Rural England (CPRE), Friends of the Earth, the Marine Conservation Society, the RSPB, Transport 2000, the Whale and Dolphin Conservation Society, the Wildfowl and Wetlands Trust and the Wildlife Trusts. English Nature also weighed in against Shell Haven, predicting that it would seriously harm species and habitats 'at local, national and international levels', and would breach conservation law. The RSPB worried particularly about Mucking Flats, part of a designated Special Protection Area which in winter contained 16,000 wildfowl and waders, including 1,200 avocets. Dredging and construction, it argued, would cause sedimentation, which in turn would convert the mudflats into marsh and destroy an exceptional breeding resource. Altogether, said Portswatch, the development – which included a commercial and business park – would damage 60 hectares of intertidal mudflats and displace 33,000 wintering wildfowl. A local opposition group, Shell Haven Project Environmental Action Committee (SPEAC), said that half the local community were opposed to the development, and that another 30 per cent were 'seriously concerned'. They were unimpressed by the promise of new jobs, which would go to commuters or incomers rather than long-term local residents, and no one liked the idea of 12,000 extra vehicle movements and 60 freight trains a day.

It was the same at Harwich, where NGOs, residents' groups, fishermen and statutory bodies complained of damage to habitats, loss of tranquillity, traffic nuisance and pollution. (Friends of the Earth claimed that lorries to and from the port, which was designed to handle 1.7m TEUs a year, would hit the A120 at the rate of one every 25 seconds, day and night.) And same again at Felixstowe, though opposition here was muted by the fact that the extension would be on a brownfield site rather than imposed on pristine wilderness. The new terminal nevertheless would add another 1.5m TEUs to Felixstowe's current throughput of 2.7m a year, piling yet more pressure on the roads. Portswatch feared also that 'increased dredging could affect subtidal habitats which support marine ecosystems and wildfowl'. As a call to arms it was hardly a spine-tingler – rather more like a pawn sacrifice, or tactical feint in a longer game. It's not likely that anyone thought they could hold the line at all three sites, a fact tacitly admitted by the RSPB when the DfT announced that it was 'minded to approve' Shell Haven.

> The conditional government go-ahead for a deep-sea container port at London Gateway ... should mean that Bathside Bay is reprieved ... The Gateway development ... and the extension of port facilities at Felixstowe South ... will satisfy the need for more capacity and minimise environmental damage ... If the London Gateway proposal goes ahead, ministers should turn the Bathside Bay plan down. The sacrifice of so much of the wildlife for which the UK has an international responsibility, to make way for more ports is totally unnecessary.

The gambit failed. If Dibden had been an unexpected victory for the birds, then the provisional green light for Shell Haven and full approvals for Felixstowe and Bathside more than levelled the score. Birds 1, containers 3. It is hard to understand what all this might mean to what economists like to call 'UK plc'; harder still to find anyone on either side of the ideological fence who is happy with the way things are going. Andrew Traill, head of rail, maritime and air cargo policy at the Freight Transport Association, acknowledges the uneasy relationship of seaports with the rest of the transport system. To the most basic question – does Britain have enough container capacity? – he gives the expected answer: 'No!'

Sometimes the transport lobby gives the impression that it will not be satisfied until the entire landscape has been reconfigured to sweep from its path everything capable of slowing it down. The only thing that matters more than size is speed, which somehow has ascended to the plane of heavenly virtues as if more and wider motorways were the expression of divine will. The argument is not wholly wrong. Where goods are perishable or urgently needed, then the case for speed is obvious. Where they are imperishable, part of a continuous supply chain or otherwise non-time-sensitive, then the case is non-existent. We'll consider the implications of that in a moment. But first let us examine Traill's argument that, in seeking to increase public benefit, the transport industry is being ruthlessly blackmailed by an exploitative and greedy government. The word 'blackmail' is mine, not his, but it exactly conveys his meaning.

One way or another, docks have always spelled trouble. The postwar Labour government of Clement Attlee sent soldiers to London, Liverpool and Avonmouth during strikes in 1948 and '49. Harold Wilson's Labour government declared a state of emergency during the seamen's strike of 1966; and dockers were prominent among the unions whose strikes provoked the Tory government of Edward Heath to declare no fewer than five national emergencies between July 1970 and October 1973. Like almost anything to do with transport, docks policy is a swamp in which no footprint holds its shape for long. The privatization of the British Transport Docks Board (BTDB) by the Thatcher government in the early '80s and the abolition of the National Dock Labour Scheme in 1989 had the desired effects of improving efficiency and snuffing out a hotbed of industrial unrest, but it surrendered power over the ports to the even more uncontrollable monsters of market forces and globalization. Out of the ashes of the BTDB arose Britain's biggest port company, Associated British Ports (ABP), owner of 21 ports including Fleetwood, Grimsby, Hull, Southampton and the biggest of them all, Immingham on Humberside. It is not just a question of owning and operating the quaysides. Port companies also wield statutory power as harbour authorities, controlling navigation, setting harbour dues and prosecuting offenders under maritime law. You could say that they service three levels of 'need' – the need of the British public to be regularly and reliably provisioned; the need of the national economy for growth; and the need of the companies and their shareholders for profit. As the DfT puts it: 'Shipping drives global development. Ports are our gateways to the global distribution network. Trade accounts for nearly 30% of our GDP. With an open economy, the UK's economic fortunes depend more than ever on our access to efficient, reliable and resilient worldwide connections.'

Which means in effect that the UK's 'open economy' depends more and more on foreign gatekeepers. Both Felixstowe and Bathside Bay are owned by the Hong Kong conglomerate Hutchison Whampoa. In the summer of 2006, ABP was taken over by a consortium headed by the American bankers Goldman Sachs with Borealis Infrastructure Management of Canada and GIC Special Investments of Singapore. At around the same time P&O Ports, would-be developers of Shell Haven, was bought by Dubai Ports World (DPW), which outbid PSA International of Singapore – a contest inspired less by the value of P&O's business in the UK than by its container terminals in the US and China. Earlier the same year an Australian company, Babcock & Brown, took over PD Ports, owner of Teesport – which, in terms of volume, is second only to ABP's Immingham. All this co-incidentally came at the same time as BAA, owner of Heathrow, Gatwick, Stansted, Glasgow, Edinburgh, Aberdeen and Southampton airports, was falling to a group led by the Spanish construction giant Ferrovial, which successfully fought off a rival bid by none other than Goldman Sachs.

In an age of multinationalism, foreign ownership of British infrastructure is not necessarily a thing to be feared. Investment is investment no matter where it comes from. Spanish ownership of English runways won't keep airliners out of British skies any more than French ownership of UK water companies kept water from the taps. The same goes for ports. As John Ford, operations director of the Felixstowe-based shipping agent Johnson Stevens, puts it: 'We are not terribly interested in the nationality of port ownership, provided they are port people.' He was unworried by Dubai Ports' takeover of P&O 'because they are ports people interested in port business'. Others, however, 'the commercial people', could be more troubling. 'I would be worried if ports fell into the hands of people who weren't interested in port development. You have to ask – is their motive port development, or property development?' While this is no threat to the likes of Immingham, some of the smaller ports could be vulnerable to the kind of apartment-plus-yacht-marina transformations that have added a row of noughts to dockside land values in London, Bristol and Liverpool. The country, we are all agreed, needs docks, not Docklands.

And it needs them, crucially, as part of the integrated transport system we are always being promised but never seem to get. The interface between privately owned ports, publicly owned roads and a regulated railway network will never be an easy fit. In 2004, 82 per cent of goods moved within the UK went by road, leaving just 6 per cent for water (mostly by coastal shipping), 5 per cent for rail and 7 per cent for pipeline. Converting the figures into tonne-kilometres (i.e. multiplying cargo tonnage by distance travelled) shifts the balance more in water's favour – 24 per cent against 64 per cent for road – but the story is essentially the same. As things stand, the Freight Transport Association's support for port expansion in the south-east is a campaign to put more freight on the roads and railways. But what nags at Andrew Traill is what nags at the DfT and everyone else who attends this uneasy, public–private marriage. Who picks up the bill? If a road has to be widened, or a railway line upgraded for container traffic, is that a commercial benefit for which the ports themselves must pay, or a public benefit that should be charged to the public purse?

The planning consents for Bathside and, potentially, Shell Haven are both conditional – expensively so. Felixstowe's owners, Hutchison, will have to fund the upgrading not only of the local branch line (which will also serve Bathside Bay) but also of the east coast main line from Peterborough to four freight terminals in Yorkshire – Selby, Doncaster, Wakefield and Leeds Stourton. The purpose of these 'remote works' is to enable the line to carry the modern 9ft 6in high containers, which means improving it to what rail engineers call 'W10 gauge standard'. This involves track-lowering, bridgeworks and modifications to overhead power lines and station awnings. Given the way costs and specifications tend to creep forever upward, it's not possible to put a figure on all this, but the Strategic Rail Authority's initial estimate was 'in excess of £75m'. At the time of writing (August 2006), the DfT was still 'minded to' approve Shell Haven but had not finally done so, and the haggling over contractual detail was such that some outside observers – perhaps wishfully – were beginning to speculate that it might bring the whole thing down. As the DfT put it, the 'minded position' required P&O to upgrade the Thames Haven branch line and pay for improvements to local access and trunk roads, leaving open the question of further rail improvement. 'The opportunity remains for the promoters or others to invest in upgrading more remote rail lines.'

It is this that eats at Andrew Traill. The Freight Transport Association, he says, has no objection to corporate funding at the point of public/private interface. 'We would accept local enhancement of road layouts and sidings.' But remote works on faraway sections of a public rail network are a different matter. If the government or Network Rail wants to attract more freight on to the railways, then – like any other business – it should upgrade its own infrastructure to meet customers' needs. That's the way markets work. In the case of Felixstowe, Traill says: 'We are talking about millions of pounds of private investment in an open-access, nationally strategic part of the rail network. It sets a precedent.' More surprisingly, he bridles at the idea of a national ports strategy. 'We need a national *freight* strategy, of which ports are a part. The market should decide where freight wants to move, not the government.'

You might not agree with him, but – bearing in mind that his job is to protect his members' interests – you can see his point. Look at it another way, however, and what's harder to understand is why the conditions should apply to road and rail but completely ignore water. We need perhaps to backtrack a little here, to turn away from the coast and think about inland waterways. The canals in their heyday were one of the most brilliantly engineered trading networks in the history of commerce, but the love affair with wheeled transport has left them leaking, purposeless and stranded. On a budget of sticks and shoestrings (which the government is cutting still further, even as I type), the best they could do was to struggle back to life as a linear holiday resort trading on nostalgia. It's different in Europe, where waterways have never been swallowed by 'heritage'. You would not hear a German say – as an official of British Waterways said to me – that advocates of waterborne freight were 'romantics'. Nor would you stand on a bridge over the Rhine, as I did above the Thames at Westminster, and see nothing but tour boats (though if I'd waited longer I might have spotted one of the waste-carriers exporting London's garbage to Essex). In Germany 64.3 per cent of freight goes by waterway; in the UK less than 1 per cent does.

The last commodity to be moved in any volume by inland waterway was coal, which accounted for the bulk of the 3.7m tonnes of freight carried as recently as 1995/6. With coal out of the picture, tonnage slumped to 1.6m by 2004/5, though it would creep up again to 1.8m in 2005/6. This was due largely to the aggregate company Cemex, which began using barges to shift sand and gravel on the River Severn. All you need to make sense of this is basic numeracy. Each barge carries the equivalent of more than 20 lorryloads but uses only a fiftieth of the fuel needed by a single lorry. Cemex's barges on the Severn will save 34,000 road journeys a year. Whichever way you look at it – company balance sheet, greenhouse emissions, damage to the environment – it makes luminous good sense.

But the Severn is a very different proposition from, say, the Kennet and Avon Canal. British Waterways' enthusiasm for the project is real but muted. Restoring the freight-carrying potential of a river or canal, it says, is hugely expensive, and its pockets far from deep. A spokesman slams down the figures like a Position Closed shutter at the bank. 'To effectively carry freight, waterways often need substantial additional investment, and we need the same upfront investment whether we move one freight vessel or one hundred. This is high risk to BW, and while we welcome the public benefits of freight by water we must weigh up the financial risk. In 2005/6 we received an income of £500,000 compared to £600,000 in the previous year. When you consider that last year we invested £107m in maintaining the waterways – repairing structures, dredging the channels, managing vegetation – the earned income is minuscule by comparison. BW is willing, but it can't do everything.'

What it *was* doing at the time this conversation took place was striving to rescue east London from the corner-cutting negligence of planners who, pressured by an overexcited, almost hyper-ventilating government, had given permission for the 2012 Olympic complex at Stratford to be built on the basis of road transport alone. There was, providentially, a better way, and on a rainy afternoon in mid-August 2006, BW offered to show me what it was. From Wood Wharf, just beneath the looming towers of Canary Wharf, its high-speed rigid inflatable skimmed across the Thames past the Millennium Dome into Bow Creek. Beyond a derelict food factory and a burned-out furniture store, melted on its steel frame as if modelled by Salvador Dali, we picked our way into a forgotten web of backwaters, the Bow Back Rivers, following the course of the River Lea north of its confluence with the Thames. It is possible, just about, to believe that this was once east London's main commercial artery. Never pretty, it drew to its banks the kind of bad-neighbour industries – scrap metal, garbage, chemical works, breakers' yards, sewerage – that were unwelcome anywhere else (though it also had three handsome mills and a gin distillery). Waterside features marked on the map tell their own story: *Depot, Industrial Estate, Gas Works, Warehouse*. So do the names given to the various stretches of water: Bow Creek slides past Bow Locks to become, first, Prescott Channel (no, it's nothing to do with *him*), and then Waterworks River before transmuting at Stratford into the Old River Lea. Neighbouring tributaries and channels are eloquent too – Three Mills Wall, Channelsea, City Mill and Pudding Mill Rivers. Its birth as a trading waterway probably dates to the Vikings, though its antiquity now is obscured by an altogether more modern kind of decay.

The concrete banks were last reinforced in the 1930s and barge traffic mostly had petered out by the 1950s. For all but four hours of the day, when the water is high, it's now all but unnavigable. When the tide turns it drains right down to the mud (sometimes houseboats get so firmly stuck in it that they fail to rise on the flood and are overwhelmed). On this particular day the tide perversely rises 28cm above its predicted height so that even the low-slung inflatable can't get back under a bridge and we have to hang about for an hour until it subsides (which it does in a turbulent rush). Wherever you look, there is something abandoned, swinging on its hinges or patched with corrugated iron. The result is a kind of stark subtopian chic that might look good in black and white but which in life could hardly seem more dead. Even the buddleia and Japanese knotweed bursting through the banks appear to extinguish life rather than enhance it.

And yet, in a multiplicity of ways, these are rivers of hope. In Waterworks River the helmsman stops to rescue a half-drowned baby coot that has been washed out of the reeds. Its first, involuntary outing on open water has taken place right next to the site designated for the Olympic aquatic centre. Waterworks River and the Old River Lea will be the design focus of the Olympic Park, wellspring of a reinvented, self-confident East End. The banks will be terraced; riverbed cleared; old bridges removed or realigned; new ones built. In all but grid reference it will become an entirely new place, delivered from another planet. But that is not why British Waterways wants to show it off. The revival of Waterworks River need not be just a landscaper's dream. There is real work for it to do. Building the Olympic site – stadium, velodrome, aquatic centre, basketball and hockey venues, athletes' village, food halls, roads and vehicle parks – will take a small mountain of aggregates, asphalt, cement, steel, glass, wood and concrete, thousands upon thousands of lorryloads which, in the Blackwall Tunnel and on east London's already log-jammed streets, would ensure permanent gridlock. The salving balm, green as you like, is the river.

What the Bow Backs were in the past, they can be again. All it needs is a £15m lock on Prescott Channel, and for the first time in forty years the level above Three Mills Island can be controlled and the navigation reopened. This is the plan which, as I write, now waits only upon a funding package which British Waterways hopes to wrap up before the end of the year (2006). The lock would enable the passage, two at a time, of 30-metre-long, 350-tonne barges, each the equivalent of fourteen 25-tonne lorries. Richard Rutter, BW's regeneration manager, calculates that the overall saving would be at least 100,000 road journeys at greatly reduced cost and with minimal noise and pollution. The materials suppliers are on side; so are the London Thames Gateway Development Corporation, the Olympic Delivery Authority, Transport for London and the Environment Agency. After the Olympics, the river will make an ideal exit path for east London's garbage and recyclates – another 250,000 tonnes a year taken off the roads. It is, as Rutter puts it, 'a no-brainer', and the only puzzle is why water transport was not made a planning condition in the first place.

It might also be wondered why a book about the sea has made such a long detour inland. The answer is that (though there are some in the waterways industry who might prefer to ignore it), the Bow Backs have set a precedent. They tell us that, yes, derelict waterways can be returned to economic use. Yes, heavy freight can be shifted by barge and, yes, it follows that there is potential for cargo to be trans-shipped inland from the ports. Turning potential into action, however, is not something that can happen without reversing the flow of official thinking. For all its protestations to the contrary – and, as we shall see, there have been plenty of those – the government is simply not water-minded. In August 2006, only a few other bits and pieces were in prospect – a new wharf for handling waste at a recycling centre on the Grand Union Canal at Willesden, west London; a contract to move incinerator ash on the River Ouse; a government grant to refurbish a couple of barges to carry aggregates on the Aire and Calder navigation and the Trent. Worthy, yes. But an exciting glimpse into a dynamic new future for water transport? Yawn.

Government policy not untypically is Janus-faced. If lip service did any good, then inland and coastal waters would be churning with freight and the motorways would have reverted to their primary purpose as high-speed thoroughfares rather than 24-hour lorry parks. In 1994 the Royal Commission on Environmental Pollution lent its imprimatur to a weighty statement of the obvious. There was an urgent need, it said, to switch traffic away from the roads and on to less environmentally damaging modes of transport. It recommended specific increases in the volume of freight carried by rail and water, and wanted grants to be made available for ports to promote coastal shipping.

The message was endorsed four years later by a government White Paper, *A New Deal for Transport*; again in 2000 by a follow-up paper, *Waterways for Tomorrow*, and in 2001 by the House of Commons Transport Committee, whose report on inland waterways acknowledged that the narrowness of most canals would make it impossible for UK water-freight to rival Germany's, but reported 'significant opportunities' for freight on larger waterways. The MPs called upon the government to 'offer more encouragement and investment', and in particular to help freight operators modernize their fleets; to abolish waterway freight tolls; and to encourage industrial development on water-side land that could be served by water. In 2002 the DfT even launched a 'water-preferred policy' for Abnormal Indivisible Loads, or AILs – the giant turbines, transformers and other lumps of industrial plant that straddle two lanes and can reduce entire motorways to the pace of a pensioner with a shopping trolley.

For a while it looked promising. An £8.5m government grant helped the transport engineers Wynns to develop the *Terra Marique*, a huge multi-purpose pontoon (MPP) capable of carrying AILs of up to 1,200 tonnes around the coast and into rivermouths. This was launched in 2004 with a 400-tonne daughter vessel, the *Inland Navigator*, which it could carry inside like a floating dry-dock. By releasing *Navigator* in estuaries it could extend its range as far inland as Leeds, Maidenhead, Nottingham, Rotherham, Worcester and York. It seemed the freight industry at last had received into its sclerotic heart a life-saving shot of ice-cold rationality. But then what is rationality when set against faith in the great god MacAdam?

In July 2006 the Transport Committee issued a stinging rebuke to that faith's high priesthood in the Highways Agency:

> The 'water preferred' policy [it said] does not appear to be en-couraging more freight onto the inland waterways as intended. Since the Highways Agency assumed responsibility for the policy in 2003 they have not published a single significant piece of research or guidance on it. Little real effort has been made to divert freight off the roads and onto the water, particularly 'abnormal indivisible loads'. Indeed, we have received evidence that the Agency's own policies are working in the other direction.

The blockades to progress are self-interest and inertia. The Highways Agency, which has to authorize each AIL to travel by road, is supposed to lean towards water, but there is a hurdle over which it seems rarely able to lift a leg – the issue of cost. On the one hand, the freight industry complains that water transport is more expensive than road. On the other, the water lobby argues that the real cost of road transport far exceeds what hauliers pay in tax. Taking into account congestion, pollution and accidents, the DfT's own figures suggest that every road-mile of freight costs an average 51p to the public purse (up to £1.74 in cities), which adds up to very big numbers indeed. In 2005 alone, the 430,000 HGVs on Great Britain's roads clocked up 13.9bn miles (22.23bn kilometres), swallowing £7bn-worth of invisible public subsidy. This cuts no ice with company accountants or transport managers. They may 'look at' the water option but they seldom take it. In two years, *Terra Marique* and *Inland Navigator* never once worked as they were designed to do, as mother and daughter. Operating independently, by August 2006 *Navigator* had made just three paid-for trips, carrying electricity transformers from Goole to Newark. *Terra Marique* had done rather better – ferrying a complete Concorde from the Thames to Scotland for the Scottish Museum of Flight, and 19 other coastal trips carrying electricity generating equipment for National Grid. Even so, it was running at only 66 per cent capacity and had been unable to exploit its unique selling point.

Historically the problem for water has been lack of a Big Voice to match the road lobby's. In 2003 the DfT itself tried to correct the balance by funding Sea and Water, a new campaign organization based in London. But don't expect water transport to be the subject of any nationwide media blitz. S and W's income – £120,000 a year from government and £60,000 from sponsors – won't stretch much further than running the office and paying its three full-time staff. A measure of the scandal (for scandal it is) is that it's hard pressed even to crystallize its own vision. Defining any kind of transport policy is like navigating in a fog with the radar switched off. Somewhere over the horizon, utopia lurks. But you don't know where. You are starved of facts. So devout is the faith in MacAdam that, despite the self-evident truth that road transport in the long term will throttle itself to death, the government has made little effort to push the alternative.

The bigger the question, the unlikelier it is to be answered. What proportion of freight potentially could be switched to water? How many lorries would this take off the roads? How long would it take? How much might the government be prepared to invest to make it happen? Who knows? The DfT certainly doesn't, and there is no one else with the will or the resources to find out. 'Nobody is putting up the money to get that knowledge,' says Sea and Water's director, Heather Leggate, who is left having to speak in general terms about 'a lot of potential'. (Ironically, DfT assures me at the same time that it is 'funding Sea and Water to . . . identify all existing research on the potential for water freight . . . and identify knowledge gaps . . .')

Where, then, is the vision? Britain's coastal waters are variously described as a 'conveyor belt' or 'ring road' – zero maintenance, uncloggable, environmentally friendly (60 per cent less carbon emissions per tonne/kilometre than road transport) and *free*. From rivers like the Thames, Severn, Mersey, Ouse, Humber, Tees and Clyde it has access to a network through which modern vessels can reach inland towns and cities. Yet it's one of the emptiest ring roads on the planet. In 2004, 120.5m tonnes of freight was hauled from southern to northern England by road or rail, and just 8.2m tonnes, or 6 per cent, by sea. 'It concerns us,' says Heather Leggate, 'that two-thirds of the containers coming into Southampton will be delivered by road north of Birmingham. To us that seems absolutely ridiculous. We are trying to encourage more trans-shipment around the coast to ports which at the moment are under-used. There are 300 commercial ports in the UK, so that's a lot of potential.'

To her the solution is obvious – a 'feedering' service of smaller ships ferrying containers from southern hubs to the north, whence they could finish their journeys by road. David Cheslin, chairman of Coastlink Network, a campaigning body for shipping professionals, is promoting the idea of a daily service up the North Sea coast from the Thames or Felixstowe, and up the west coast from Southampton. One small ship alone would carry 300 standard-size containers, so two on each route would take 1,200 off the road every day, plus 1,200 return journeys no longer needed. Suitable vessels are available for charter, and the need for infrastructure would be minimal. Unlike the mega-ships, which draw up to 15 metres of water, coasters need no more depth than an old-fashioned collier. All it takes is a bit of vacant quayside and a mobile crane.

Cheslin concedes that such a service at the beginning would be underutilized and unprofitable. 'It would need some government subsidy but it wouldn't be enormous, certainly not compared with the cost of building a mile of motorway. It would build up volume to make it viable, and could be self-sustaining in six or 12 months.' Thereafter it could expand to three, five, maybe even ten ships a day. 'We could run as many services as you like.'

I put this to the Freight Transport Association's Andrew Traill, but he is not enthusiastic. The problem, he says, is 'a lack of companies willing to invest. They won't do it without a long-term guarantee of volume.' As switching from road to sea currently would result in a 20 per cent increase in freight bills, this could mean a long wait. Turkeys don't vote for Christmas. Businesses don't vote for bigger bills. End of story.

But the added costs are not the will of god. John Ford explains how the system is slanted towards road. 'The ports charge a fixed handling cost of £75 or £80 per container. This includes lifting it from ship to quay, and lifting it again on to a lorry. But it does *not* include lifting on to a railway wagon or other ship, which carries an extra charge of £40–£50. With a further charge at the destination port, it puts up the cost by £100 a container.' All this would be solved by switching to the continental system, whereby a basic charge is made for delivery to the quay, and a supplementary charge made for lifting on to any other vehicle – lorry, train, other ship, whatever – so that sea and rail users don't pay over the top for a road service they don't use. 'That would level the playing field.'

The practicality of feeder servicing has been shown over the past three years by the do-it-yourself chain B&Q. Previously it trucked imports for its northern distribution centres all the way up to Warrington, Scunthorpe, Doncaster and Worksop from Southampton. Now, in the absence of any regular coastal feeder service from the south, it trans-ships from Rotterdam into Immingham. Result: an annual saving of 6m road miles. It *works*.

The slow pace of a ship is not an issue. Very little of the stuff heading in and out of the UK is perishable (and even perishables can ride in refrigerated containers). Once the conveyor is running, journey times are irrelevant. A daily delivery is a daily delivery, never mind how long the load has been in transit. And what makes sense for imports equally must make sense for deliveries within the UK. Heading south on the M1, you'll see trucks driving from Aberdeen to London. Aberdeen! A seaport! Where is the sense in spending two days clogging the roads with expensive lorries when you could load the stuff straight on to a ship?

But Ford is under no illusion that transport is a forum in which the best argument wins. 'People get set in their ways,' he says. 'Nothing will be done until the system gridlocks. The government doesn't have the will.' For all these reasons, Sea and Water has some heavy weather ahead. The Freight Transport Association has joined up as a member, but it looks more like infiltration than committed support. 'They will say to you,' says Heather Leggate, 'that we are anti-road.' (She's dead right – that's exactly what they do say, and with the implication that it disqualifies S and W from grown-up debate.) British Waterways has also signed up, but – Bow Backs apart – it is more likely to sell wharves for redevelopment than it is to reopen them for trade. In the words of one industry insider, this is 'like running a railway without stations'.

No one, and certainly not Leggate, believes the ocean giants can disgorge their contents straight on to the old narrowboat system. You might as well expect an airbus to land on a grass aerodrome in the Weald, or the Arctic Monkeys to take up the shawm. There may be an increased role for canals in moving aggregates and waste, but the real, pragmatic thrust is towards the sea. Leggate's discipline is economics, not romance. By day she is director of the Centre for International Transport Management at London Metropolitan University, and she is an adviser on ports policy to the House of Commons Transport Committee. This means she is uniquely placed to recognize the disconnection in policy. 'DfT don't seem to talk to Defra,' she says, 'and they don't seem to talk to the Department for Communities and Local Government. We've been fighting quite hard to achieve an integrated approach and we feel strongly that there should be some sort of water freight or transport group that crosses government departments. Transport is not just an issue for DfT. It's an environmental issue, and it's an issue for the regions. We really need to achieve joined-up thinking but we're finding that very, very difficult.'

Neither is her voice always heard by company managements. Tesco, for example, likes to advertise its commitment to the environment. Burrowing deep into its website, I found this: 'Tesco remains committed to exploring all possible alternatives to road haulage, and we are testing the viability of rail distribution in two projects at Edinburgh and Inverness . . .'

Rail distribution! All very welcome, but how radical is that? Leggate wrote to them in the spring of 2006, suggesting that water might play a part in the transfer of non-time-sensitive products and waste, but by the end of August she had received not a word in reply – not even a *pro forma* acknowledgement.

Before gridlock finally forces the government's hand, the best shot in sanity's locker is road pricing. There is no argument about whether or not it will happen. The DfT is committed to it, and both road and sea lobbies have pledged their support. Their reasons for doing so, however, are very different. Sea and Water is pushing for hauliers to pay the full cost of their impact on the roads. 'Certain [sea] routes,' says Heather Leggate, 'aren't competitive because road users don't pay the full cost. And when road pricing comes in, I think water will become more competitive. We're trying to get the DfT to look at this and level the playing field. There are grants available for start-up operations, but really in the long term they're only sustainable if road users pay the full cost.'

It's this kind of talk that makes the transport industry gag on its Yorkie bar. 'We support road pricing,' says Andrew Traill, 'so long as it's cost neutral.' In other words they don't object to a change in the way road use is taxed, provided it doesn't cost any more. In their opinion the main benefit would be to catch foreign drivers who currently use British roads for free. 'What we have a problem with,' says Traill, 'is that there are too many people around that organization [Sea and Water] who see road freight as a whipping boy. They want to put up road freight costs so that everyone goes to them. By all means find alternatives, but don't punish road freight and drive it out of business. If that happened, all the prices in the shops would go up. Economic growth would stop and you'd drive business down the drain. What's the point of that?'

This is an old, old tune, played whenever hauliers perceive a threat to their interests. They play it despite the fact that road congestion, which the new port developments will surely make worse, already costs UK industry £20 billion a year, and that pouring more and more money into roads is not the answer. I ask Traill about recent hold-ups on one of the routes to Felixstowe, and the answer rings like a knell.

'The A14 gets very congested at times,' he agrees. 'The solution is to increase the number of lanes and upgrade it to a motorway.'

Not even golden-hearted whores have had an easier ride in English fiction than pirates, buccaneers and bootleggers. They enjoy a tradition of lovable roguery, saucy scallywags whose victories over the excise men – unloved traffic wardens of their day – have been celebrated in parlour and snug from Cornwall to the Orkneys. Smuggling historically is perceived to have been not merely victimless but, in its thwarting of the hated tax officials and redistribution of benefits, a positive public good. Other than those infected by low-church sanctimony, who would ever complain about cut-price alcohol, tobacco, silk or tea? It would have been a crime to say no. A few ounces of smuggled shag or a pint of rum would oil the local economy just as well as the poachers' rabbits, and a good deal better than the parson's prayers.

Much of the old, traditional trade still goes on, though literal 'bootlegging' – the stuffing of contraband down sailors' boots – has gone the way of peg-legged hearties with parrots on their shoulders, and HM Revenue and Customs (HMRC) these days can literally see through a smuggler's cover. There are X-ray scanners the size of car-washes that can peer through entire trucks and their contents. There are sniffer dogs, night-vision goggles, fibre-optic cameras and, from a longer tradition, the dreaded 'cutter', which in its latest incarnation can either screech in high-speed pursuit or stalk soundlessly through the water to capture by stealth. It enables the HMRC to shed the clod-hopping, village-idiot reputation of its 17th-century predecessors and all but challenge the brigands to bring it on: 'Smuggling by sea is still a route that smugglers prefer. With so many ships and travellers arriving in UK ports, smugglers think they can slip through unnoticed. However, our highly trained officers know what to look for and when.'

Combined with all the 21st-century technology at its disposal, this hawk-eyed vigilance makes it 'very difficult to smuggle with success'. Well, it does and it doesn't. Being an agency of government, HMRC is apt to contradict itself. 'Modern day smuggling is not the same as it was 200 years ago,' says one page on its website. 'Little has really changed over the centuries,' says another. It may boast of the obstacles now placed in the smugglers' way, but at the same time: 'Today the smuggling of alcohol and tobacco is a huge problem all over the country, not just at the UK's major ports. It is a problem we take very seriously as the government can lose hundreds of millions of pounds every year through this crime alone.'

The scale of cigarette smuggling is astonishing. We can't know what proportion of smokers' pleasure in earlier centuries was delivered under the counter or fell off the back of a haycart, but it can't greatly have exceeded the rate recorded in 1999, when, according to official figures, more than one in five cigarettes smoked in the UK was smuggled. Just as in earlier times, the cut-price tobacco, alcohol and other booty was impudently exchanged, right under the excisemen's noses. If it was 'difficult to smuggle with success', then it was a difficulty which a very large number of people had learned to surmount. The HMRC's tone becomes almost desperate:

> More often than not you can find these items sold at markets, car boot sales, factory floors and pop festivals. It is also known that some pubs and shops sell these products to their customers.
>
> For many people, buying smuggled goods can be seen as a good way to buy at low prices. However, people often do not know that by not paying the duty means [sic] that essential services like education and health care lose out and, even more worrying, the profits from some tobacco smuggling could end up funding organised crime and terrorist gangs.

In March 2000, the Treasury and HM Customs (as it then still was) published a joint strategy paper, *Tackling Tobacco Smuggling*. This spoke with the usual forked tongue, simultaneously condemning smoking as 'the single greatest cause of premature death and preventable illness in Britain' while bemoaning the loss of an annual £2.5bn-worth of tax revenue. 'So smoking is leading to less money for schools and hospitals, and forces other taxes to be higher.' Message: for the sake of the NHS, your children's A-levels and keeping down inheritance tax, please go on puffing as much as you like, but mind where you buy, and make sure you pay the full price. The Treasury looked with particular horror at Canada, and especially at Quebec, where smuggling accounted for 60 per cent of all the tobacco smoked.

Without a crackdown, the UK surely would go the same way. Already, the market share for smuggled hand-rolling tobacco in the UK was close to 80 per cent, and the share for cigarettes would top 35 per cent by 2003–4 if nothing was done to stop it. The cost of tighter policing at the ports being only a fraction of the cost to the exchequer of increased smuggling (£209m against an annual £2.7bn), there would be reinforcement of the defensive line (scanners to detect high-volume contraband in freight containers), clearer identification of duty-paid cigarettes and hand-rolling tobacco (from April 2001, legitimate packs would have to be labelled 'UK DUTY PAID'), heavier penalties for offenders (fines, imprisonment, seizure of assets and confiscation of vehicles), extra manpower (1,000 more frontline customs officers and investigators) and a publicity campaign to 'increase public awareness'. The target was, first, to halt the increase in smuggling, and then actually to reduce it.

It was like dipping into a criminal brantub. In the first six months of 2000–1, the scanners found 80m illegal cigarettes and 4.5 tonnes of hand-rolling tobacco. By the end of the year HMRC had broken up 43 organized crime gangs, intercepted 2.8bn cigarettes and 'seized' (their word) more than 10,219 cars, vans and lorries. Along the way they also cut cross-Channel beer-smuggling to near zero, halved the influx of illegal wines and spirits, and happened across 1.6 tonnes of cannabis and 46kg of heroin. In all this, however, the proudest achievement – which HMRC was not shy of trumpeting – was not actually to *reduce* the market share of smuggled tobacco in the UK, but only to hold it steady at 21 per cent.

And not everyone was applauding. Cries of pain came from the road transport industry, whose trade body, the Road Haulage Association (RHA), raised a great tumult about delays and disruptions at the ports. One shipping line at Southampton, it said, had suffered a 300 per cent rise in the number of containers being singled out for inspection, though 'singled out' might overstate the level of discrimination. 'The current selection process,' it said in March 2002, 'appears at best random, at worst faulty. Transshipment and empty containers and even export consignments are being scanned, although none of these bring smuggled cigarettes or tobacco (or indeed any goods) into the UK.' Worse: some ports were organized so that containers marked for scanning could not all be available at the same time. Sometimes a mobile scanner would be switched to another site before it had finished, and not return for several days, thus leaving containers effectively impounded. The RHA pointed out that this was happening despite HMRC's assurance that the new system would speed up frontier checks and thus save money by eliminating expensive delays. 'Clearly,' it said, 'these situations identify a lack of proper coordination between selection and operation procedures.' It wanted proof that the rate of detection and seizure had gone up since the scanners were introduced so that the trade could 'assess the effectiveness of the initiative'.

It had another problem too. Innocent firms acting in good faith, it argued, might be tricked into hauling trailers for dishonest clients. Or it might happen that, unknown to the operator, a truck's load or bodywork would be tampered with by a third party; or the firm might innocently hire a dishonest or corruptible driver who would try a bit of freelance business of his own. When that happened, the legal sledgehammer would fall quite unfairly on the vehicle's owner, who might find his lorry seized and legally held to ransom. This was continuing to rankle in late 2006, when I spoke to the RHA's head of international affairs, Peter Cullum. Complaints about delays at the ports seemed to have dried up, he said, but not so the sense of injustice over seizures.

It was hard on drivers. 'They could be towing loads they've never seen. It's difficult especially when it's tobacco and it's put in the bodywork so the driver would have no idea the vehicle had been tampered with.' It was even harder on owners. Although the cab might be owned by the haulier himself, the trailer might belong to a client company whose staff were outside his control. Even when the rig was wholly owned, companies could come unstuck. They could, for example, take all reasonable precautions when hiring drivers; could set down rules and dismiss them when they transgressed; and yet could still face seizures and financial penalties when offences were committed without their knowledge.

Even then, some drivers are guiltier than others. Some are chancers habitually on the make; others are bribed or coerced. Beneath it all, there is always that centuries-old, Cornish-cove feeling that it's somehow only a game. Brave buccaneers versus doughty duty men, same as it's always been. But as always, too, it's a game of high risk and uncertain outcome. If a smuggler scores a win, he earns a handy slice of the down-payment on his Spanish villa. If customs win, they earn the right to play judge, jury and jailer. As a seized truck is legally crown property, subject only to internal constraints (HMRC itself adjudicates on appeals against its own decisions), it can pretty much fix whatever charge it likes.

'The penalty,' says Cullum, 'is at customs' discretion.' He complains that one (in his view, entirely innocent) operator, who had made it quite clear to his driver that smuggling was a sacking offence, was still hit with a £3,000 fine. On the other hand, it grates on him that some small-scale offenders are simply let off, being allowed to keep the goods they have tried to smuggle in return for nothing more than the duty payable on them. 'It's here are the goods, pay us the duty and that's the end of it.' Thus the guilty amateur goes free while the innocent professional faces the loss of his livelihood.

HMRC, no surprise, puts a different spin on it. Minnows, it allows, do escape with paying nothing more than the going rate. But if officials suspect that the trafficking is not for personal or friends' consumption, then the penalties climb pretty steeply towards the threshold of pain. 'Next stage up,' says a spokesman, 'we would restore goods at twice the revenue owed.' Given that it includes import duty and VAT as well as excise duty, this tots up to the far from negligible sum of around £35 for 200 cigarettes.

Anyone who can't or won't pay will forfeit their vehicle: simple as that.

The truth is, of course, that HMRC didn't install expensive scanners for the sake of stopping the odd bit of schoolboy naughtiness. It's after the bad guys who operate on a commercial scale – the kind of scale, let's not forget, that not only pushed the smugglers' market share to more than one in five cigarettes smoked but held it there throughout a whole year of a determined, high-priority crackdown. Consignments can be vast. 'In a hard-sided vehicle,' says the spokesman, 'you would find the cigarette pallets pushed right to the front of the trailer, the cab end, hidden behind a load of pottery or lettuces or whatever. In a soft-sided vehicle they are arranged like the filling of a sandwich down the middle.' There could be three, four, maybe even five million cigarettes in there.

In cases like this there is no question of either contraband or vehicle being handed back to the smugglers. These are not the kinds of enterprise that can happen under the noses of unknowing drivers or hauliers. This is authentic, premier division, organized crime. Gangs buy second-hand lorries specifically for smuggling and will write them off if a job goes wrong. The duty (i.e. smugglers' profit) on five million cigarettes is £875,000. You don't need to slip many of those through the net to cover the cost of a second-hand truck, or to convince a biddable driver that it's a risk worth taking. By 2004–5, the number of cigarettes seized since 2000 had reached 11bn. In 2004–5 alone HMRC hauled in 2bn, broke up another 68 gangs and confiscated £2m-worth of vehicles and assets. It was a victory of sorts, though only in the sense that the margin of defeat had been narrowed. Detailed analysis of that year's figures is not yet available, but in the previous year, 2003–4, the gangs still managed to bring in 12bn illegal cigarettes at a cost (to them) of 1.8bn seized. The sop for HMRC was that it had cut the illegal market share to 16 per cent, well ahead of its 20 per cent target, and it was emboldened to announce an extended target for 2007–8 of 13 per cent.

The most popular smuggled brand, amounting to 8 per cent of the total, is Sovereign, followed by Superkings and Dorchester at 7 per cent and 5 per cent respectively. But there is a statistical glitch here that HMRC would like everyone to know about. These are 'genuine' branded goods that, with others, account for only 31 per cent of the smugglers' haul. A further 20 per cent is of uncertain origin, and 48 per cent are known to be counterfeit. That is to say that anyone in the UK buying a cut-price smoke has an almost 50:50 chance of buying and lighting up a fake. The cigarettes are produced mainly in the Far East and eastern Europe, but the real craftsmanship goes into the expertly forged packaging which, in HMRC's own words, 'makes it . . . difficult to differentiate between genuine and counterfeit products on appearance alone'.

Hence its understandable fondness for the 'gang' word. It doesn't want anyone to run away with the idea that these are ash-tray Robin Hoods, fearlessly running the gauntlet for the benefit of ordinary people oppressed by tax-obsessed overlords; or to imagine that violence plays no part in the management of the trade, or that the crime is in any other sense victimless. You buy this stuff, you (a) surrender what little control you otherwise might have had over the carcinogens entering your lungs, and (b) get taken for a mug. In any black-market business plan, ripping off the public is as important as monkeying the Revenue.

The designer clothing trade does not stand as a towering symbol of moral rectitude. Less than heartwarming, one might think, is its utilization of the developing world as a universal sweatshop paying slave wages for garments of unremarkable quality whose 'value' (i.e. selling price) is superficially jacked up by a stuck-on label. One struggles to weep for the losses some manufacturers suffer through counterfeiting. Against that, however, it is hardly to be expected that workers in pirate factories churning out cut-price replicas are going to be treated any more generously than their 'legitimate' counterparts. Almost anything with a famous brand name attached to it is a temptation to fakery. In the very week that I was writing this, in September 2006, customs officers at Harwich intercepted 11,000 pairs of counterfeit trainers, newly arrived from Austria with a retail value of £1.5m. Much of the stuff originates in China, a country whose unsentimental, ultra-pragmatic view of the business world takes full account of greed and gullibility (which I do not suggest are exclusively weaknesses of the West). Jeans are commonly faked. So are handbags, shoes, belts, pharmaceuticals (including Viagra), geographically labelled foods, DVDs, CDs, cameras, watches, personal stereo players, jewellery, perfume, sportswear and all kinds of clothing. Even razor blades, car parts and batteries sail in under false colours.

To be swindled in this way might look like divine judgement on our obsessions with image and conspicuous consumption – trial by temptation in a price-slashed Garden of Eden. It also offends HMRC, to whom such piracy represents not so much lost innocence as lost import duty and VAT. In 2004–5, it recorded 2,863 seizures of 'goods breaching intellectual property rights', involving 8,483,675 separate items. If we assume that the ratio of goods smuggled to goods apprehended is similar to that for tobacco, then you can reckon on 56.5m fake items hitting the streets. In reality – free from the dockside scanners and heightened vigilance employed against cigarettes – the general goods trade is likely to be very much higher. By recent estimates, counterfeit goods account for between 5 and 9 per cent of world trade. *Caveat emptor*, you might say, though, like worshippers at false shrines everywhere, the victims' urge to believe may be beyond the reach of doubt or rational inquiry. 'Look! Genuine Rolex! Got it direct from the importer for fifty quid!'

It can't all be passed off with a Del Boy chuckle, though. A pair of phoney trainers may be as comfortable as the originals (they may even have come from the same Asian factory), and the wearer may stay happily duped. Phoney medicines, brake pads or exotic drinks on the other hand may have less happy outcomes. Nostalgia fuels the public's generally lenient view of the old-time bootleggers' staple, alcohol. Compared with the modern drug trade it looks like a red-nosed hangover from a merry age of innocence (never mind that the Black Jacks of treasured myth would have smuggled narcotics if they'd known or had a market for them), but it's hard to imagine any future generation looking back with similar wistfulness on the hard-core contraband of the early 21st century. In 2004–5, customs made 128 seizures of heroin, totalling 1,613kg, plus 2.7m Ecstasy tablets, 8.6 tonnes of cocaine, 57.5 tonnes of cannabis and 33.5 tonnes of 'other synthetic drugs'. I'll leave aside the arguments about legality and morality with all their pitfalls, for an habitual wine-drinker, of hypocrisy and sanctimony. And we must remember that the ports are not a one-way valve, with nastiness oozing in but only goodness flowing out. This, in précis, is how I described one highly specialized traffic stream in *Rubbish!*:

In the UK there is an imbalance between recycling targets, the infrastructure needed to meet them, and available markets for recycled materials. This is why we have kept up a steady flow of end-of-life exports – fridges, electronic equipment, batteries – to our better-organized European partners. But the export trade is a wide and stretchy carpet beneath which all manner of horrors can be swept. The classic way for a rich industrial nation to solve a problem is to export it to a poorer country on the other side of the globe. In a kind of grossed-up parody of the Victorian dust-yard, the world's poor sift through the leavings of the wealthy in search of marketable salvage. It is, or can be, a double benefit. Where the trade is legitimate (plastic bottles, for example), the exporting country can claim success towards its recycling targets while the host country, which does the actual recycling, profits from the sale of the recycled material. Where it is illegitimate (toxic waste), the exporters prey on the desperation of people whose poverty drives them to risk their health, their lives and their environment. It is a sophisticated modern adaptation of the cave-man's proto-Nimbyism: don't do on your own doorstep what you could do on someone else's.

This was written in 2004. In April 2006 the Royal Geographical Society warned that the problem was bound to get worse. The only way the UK could hope to meet its recycling targets, it said, would be by doubling its waste exports. Professor Adam Read, head of waste management at Hyder Consulting, spelled out the implications:

> Unless we invest heavily and quickly in the development of new paper mills and other reprocessing facilities [he said at an RGS conference], we will be faced by a glut of recyclables collected from the kerbside and nowhere to treat and process it. Without overseas markets, both in the EU and wider afield in the rapidly developing economies of Latin America, China and India, we may sink under the weight of our unprocessed recyclables.

As the RGS itself points out, this is even less savoury than it sounds:

> The potential for increasing waste exports raises concerns about the quality of waste sent abroad. Approximately 5% of exported waste is contaminated with other forms of unsorted waste, and is in contravention of EU shipment regulations.
>
> Contaminated, unsorted waste is of limited value to the overseas market and is dumped in landfill, simply transferring the problem from the UK to abroad. Increased mixed recycling to attain government targets could increase levels of contamination due to the expense in hand-sorting and lack of current infrastructure.

If anything, the dilemma is more acute even than this dire prediction implies. If ports can be read as a kind of economic and moral barometer, then we may diagnose an advanced and possibly irreversible case of infection. Spot checks by Environment Agency inspectors in 2005 revealed that 75 per cent of waste export containers at UK ports contained illegal material. 'When inspected,' said the EA, 'the suspect containers which were described as having paper for recycling were found to contain mixed rubbish including plastics, textiles and rotting food infested with maggots.' This is a deeply unpleasant insult – you might say even a racial slur – as well as a criminal fraud on the foreign purchasers. But it is not the worst of it. In 2003 the Industry Council for Electronic Equipment Recycling (ICER) estimated that between 10 per cent and 15 per cent of discarded electrical and electronic equipment in the UK – about 160,000 tonnes a year – was being exported for disposal elsewhere. The great majority of this – 133,000 tonnes – was IT or telecoms equipment, of which some 110,000 tonnes was legally 'declared exports, properly documented on shipping forms and going to permitted destinations'. The guessed-at 23,000-tonne remainder was undeclared and untraceable, though the principal destinations are likely to have been China, the Indian subcontinent and West Africa. Almost half this highly dangerous, toxic junk was used PC monitors; much of the rest was mobile phones. I apologize for returning again to *Rubbish!*, but what I wrote there is as relevant now as it was in 2005.

> The problem is that much of the junk masquerades as legal trade in workable second-hand equipment and either passes undetected or is given the benefit of the doubt by port inspectors who can't tell the difference between reusable equipment and scrap. Sometimes the deceptions involve long and complicated paper trails designed to confuse, often with re-routings via other ports (Rotterdam, Gibraltar and the Middle East, especially Dubai, are popular). Sometimes they are almost mockingly crude. A container of 'plastic' awaiting shipment from Felixstowe to Lahore on inspection turned out to be a rubble of computer monitors and other electronic waste on its way to Pakistan from South Wales. As legal disposal in the UK becomes both more difficult and more expensive – it can cost £5 to recycle a single computer monitor here – so yet again the cowboys are saddling up and the pirates putting on their eyepatches.

Also in *Rubbish!*, I quoted the observations of Jim Puckett, project coordinator of the Seattle-based Basel Action Network, which had fronted an investigation by an international coalition of NGOs. The trail they followed was of exports from the US, but there is no reason to assume that stuff from Britain finds its way to any happier or healthier homes. At Guiyu, on the Lianjing River in the Guangdong Province of China, the investigators found a colony of 100,000 migrant workers – men, women and children – living in what Puckett described as a 'cyber-age nightmare'. Back, for one last time, to *Rubbish!*:

> There are no health or environmental controls. Plastics and wires are burned in the open; soldered circuit boards are melted and burned; lead-contaminated cathode ray tubes are dumped. Observers reported seeing women and girls heating lead solder in woks over open fires, then using the molten solder to loosen memory chips from computer circuit boards. Afterwards the used lead, universally recognized as a neurological toxin, is tipped like kitchen-slops on to the ground. The residue of material – metal, plastic, chemical – that has no value is dumped in fields and irrigation canals, with the result that local well water is polluted and fresh water has to be trucked in from elsewhere.

Moral philosophers are fond of experiments designed to reveal how much pain we would be prepared to inflict, for our own benefit, on faraway victims whose suffering we would never see. Here is our answer: we do it without thinking. And here, too, is the truth about piracy. It wasn't nice in the era of rum and yo-ho-ho. It's even nastier now.

CHAPTER EIGHT

'Inadequate Stakeholder Consensus'

Sometimes, by which I mean often, I start to hate the sound of my own voice. It comes back off the page at me like a distorted image in a hall of mirrors. Am I really so disagreeable? Do I really find so much to complain about and so little to admire? Gloom is the elephant trap that lies in the path of all who call themselves 'conservationists' or 'environmentalists'. As it happens I lay claim to neither of these rather grandiose labels – 'interested observer' is the best I'm entitled to – but it doesn't save me from the elephant trap. Not a single whinge or moan do I wish to retract, but I do want to add a grain or two to the other side of the balance.

One of the abiding problems of environmentalism is the fervour of those on the fundamentalist wing, in whom the fire burns as brightly as any religion. No demagogue of the Victorian pulpit ever preached hellfire with greater certainty, or with finger pointed more fixedly at Armageddon. I can't say they're wrong, but I can see why they're not everyone's idea of a good time. Subtler protagonists invite us to marvel. To want to protect the world, we first need to love it – easier for some than for others, obviously, but nowhere easier than in a country as diverse, beautiful and well-provided as our own. It is a few days before Christmas. The refrigerator is stuffed; the wine-rack full; the logs stacked. Outside my window, an early fog yields to a frosty sunshine in which bluetits and goldfinches dart through lavender and bay, then dash to the top of the beech. A bluetit hangs upside down from a windowsill, cocking its head like a hyperactive bat; a dove cleans its feathers. If I climbed to the top of the neighbouring church tower I would be able to see medieval field patterns, seven more church towers and a steely apron of sea. Literally as I write, a magazine editor emails to counsel my views on national identity. Who are we? What do we value?

These are questions to which most of us respond with feelings rather than words – only in poverty can people list all the things that make them what they are. In *The Selfish Gene*, Richard Dawkins coined the term 'meme' for the fragments of cultural inheritance – 'self-replicating elements of culture, passed on by imitation,' as the *Oxford Dictionary* subsequently would put it – that are copied from generation to generation, seeding themselves in our brains in much the same way that genes seed themselves in the cells of our bodies, surviving, evolving or disappearing according to their usefulness. Dawkins suggested, as examples among millions, 'tunes, ideas, catch-phrases, clothes fashions, ways of making pots or of building arches'. In his later book, *The God Delusion*, he adds religious faith. You could argue – philosophers *do* argue – that memes are the atomic particles of the mind itself, each one like a page in a book in a library. One of these pages, handed down unaltered since the first sapient beings dipped their toes in the water, is love of the sea. We are born with it. It is part of the state of being human.

I have not seen every part of the British shoreline. I have not even seen every part of the East Anglian coast in the region where I live, and it will take a major breakthrough in gene therapy or cloning if I am to see more than half of what I'd like to before my genes and memes journey on without me. For the whole of my adult life I have had an ambition to walk, in a single, prolonged act of pilgrimage, the entire coastline of Devon and Cornwall. I know now that I'll never do it, but if I keep patching in the missing bits I might at least manage it piecemeal over time.

Everyone has a favourite bit of coast; a favourite memory of the sea. We all carry in our heads the sound and the smell of it, and are sensitive to its traditions. Memes to me seem to unlock the secret of what we call 'folk memory', when a strange place evokes a sense of homecoming that is more than just déjà vu. As will have been made obvious by what has gone before, I am not a seafaring man and I do not come from a seafaring family; and yet the sea always does that for me. I am *of* it.

In November 2006, government ministers were talking yet again of a 'right to roam', dismissing landowners' objections and creating an 11,000-mile coastal footpath all the way round mainland Britain. The cynic in me says I'll believe it when I see it. The optimist is buoyed with hope. This government badly needs to find something it can leave in better shape than it was in before it took office. A joined-up coastline would be one decent memorial. So would a well-drafted Marine Bill. This long-awaited, urgently needed piece of legislative business has yet to find a place on the parliamentary agenda, though there is a long-standing ministerial undertaking, recently repeated, to introduce it 'in this Parliament'. Defra will not admit to a timetable, but the best guess of well-informed outsiders is that we might see it in the Queen's Speech of 2007.

In a policy paper of 2002, *Safeguarding Our Seas*, the government declared its ambition to establish and protect 'clean, healthy, safe, productive and biologically diverse seas'. This was a neat, brief expression of a messy agglomeration of conflicts in which the corridors of judgement are roamed by the ghost of Solomon. Where interests collide not everyone wins, and there are collisions wherever you look. A drainage engineer sees coastal water as a convenient flushing mechanism for (usually) treated sewage and waste water, and measures his success against numerical standards set by law-makers. Anglers, sailors, swimmers and walkers see a leisure facility and measure their success by how much enjoyment it provides. Access, for them, is a 'right'. But so it is also for jet-ski riders, water-skiers and others whose pursuit of pleasure is not easily reconciled with other people's thirst for tranquillity.

Trawlermen see a tribal hunting ground with ancestral 'rights' attached. Marine scientists see a degraded environment from which, during the lives of our children, most life will become extinct. The shipping industry sees a global superhighway needing more and more deep-water ports for bigger and bigger ships. Environmentalists see wrecked salt marshes, polluted estuaries and roads clogged with container lorries. Energy companies see, variously, wind farms, gas rigs, oil pipelines and nuclear power stations. Fishermen and conservationists see disturbed and displaced wildlife, and pollution. Seaside romantics see an Edwardian playground of piers, promenades and white-painted villas serving kippers for breakfast. Planners see poverty, degradation and chronic unemployment. Climate scientists see the end of it all.

Law-makers in the past have skirted a maelstrom of irreconcilables and judged their success against criteria they invented for themselves. Hence the churning embarrassment of European fisheries ministers returning from each year's quota-round to the sound of their own applause. Some scientists are now saying that sea change is exceeded on the scale of impending disaster only by climate change itself. To turn aside from catastrophe, they say, law-makers will have to sail their ships of state straight across the maelstrom and back again. It will take courage on the bridge, and a quality of leadership unseen since the *Iliad*. This is how Defra's consultation paper explains the need for a Marine Bill:

The arrangements in place for managing marine activities and protecting marine wildlife and the marine environment are complex and can be confusing and costly for all involved. New activities, changes in technology and a deeper understanding of the seas around us and the way we affect them have also exposed some gaps and limitations in this system. Recent reports and reviews suggest that as the pressures on our seas increase and change we do not have all the tools we need to reconcile and integrate conservation goals with the full range of demands that we place on the marine area to help meet our economic and social needs.

During the spring and early summer of 2006, Defra received more than 1,200 replies to its consultation paper – a weight of evidence sufficient in itself to slow the process of digestion. The terms in which the proposed bill has been welcomed, however, serve only to underline the difficulties that lie ahead, for the geese and the ganders want very different sauces. Subjects under review included the planning and licensing of marine developments and industries, nature conservation and a possible new Marine Management Organization (MMO). Small wonder, then, that the responses, though generally positive in tone, concealed some wickedly sharp edges. It's like juggling with razor blades on the deck of a trawler caught broadside in a force 10. Blood on the planking, you'd think, is only a matter of time. The consultation document itself is a fitting adversary for Captain Ahab – any reader swallowed by it will not emerge for a very long time. The Royal Institution of Chartered Surveyors spoke for many when it complained of its vast length (309 pages), repetitiveness and overcomplication, which it feared would 'dilute the overall impact of the key proposals'.

The language slides without friction across the consciousness, traceable only by the leaden weight left hanging from the eyelids. 'The Government's objective,' said Defra in answer to the House of Commons Environmental Audit Committee, 'is to bring forward holistic legislative proposals that take account of all activities wherever they occur in the marine area.' And: 'An holistic ecosystem approach already lies at the heart of our strategy to integrate conservation objectives with sustainable social and economic development goals.' It speaks of 'using marine resources in a sustainable and environmentally sensitive manner in order to conserve ecosystems and achieve optimum environmental, social and economic benefit for the marine environment'. And of 'obtaining best value from different uses of our valuable marine resources whilst maintaining and protecting the ecosystems on which they depend'. On the other hand: 'We do not propose to introduce inappropriate restrictions on development without understanding the impact of activities on marine ecosystems and biodiversity. However, there may be cases where we would wish to take a more precautionary approach.'

Read in one way (if you're still awake), this is a recipe for motherhood and apple pie in which everyone gets a slice with clotted cream and custard. Read another way, it's a guarantee of bellyache. It's like reading the list on a food packet, where the largest ingredient is put first and the smallest last – not subtle enough to be called 'nuanced', but it matters. This is why concerned readers look not just for phrases like 'ecosystem approach', 'sustainable development'or 'best value', but for their relative seniority in the sentences in which they occur. They also scan the consultation document for some mention of fisheries, but they scan in vain – an omission which the Institute of Marine Engineering, Science and Technology (in common with everyone intellectually upstream of haddock) found 'nonsensical' and 'incoherent'.

'Fisheries using towed gear,' it said, 'represent a major threat to the marine environment and must be included/addressed if marine management is to be even-handed.' The Royal Society, in its more headmasterly way, advised the government that 'taking an eco-system based approach to managing the marine environment requires that fisheries be managed within this framework. The Royal Society considers the impacts associated with fishing (including discards, bycatch and illegal fishing) to be the most important threat to the marine environment.' The Environment Agency, too, weighed in heavily: 'We are disappointed that the consultation did not invite comment on marine fisheries. It is essential that future decisions on marine fisheries reform are not made in isolation from other elements of a Marine Bill . . .' Even the Institution of Civil Engineers had no doubt which activity at sea most threatened the ecosystem: 'Fisheries using towed gear.'

As if fate has ears, before I can begin the next paragraph an international team of scientists publishes in *Science* magazine the results of a four-year study warning that, at current rates of attrition, world fish stocks will be exhausted by 2048. 'Unless we fundamentally change the way we manage all the ocean species together, then this century is the last century of wild food,' says Steve Palumbi of Stanford University, one of the report's authors. This may be why the government repeats so often the phrase 'ecosystem approach'.

'Nature first,' it seems to imply. But the Royal Society smells a rat. 'The marine conservation theme,' it says, 'asks stakeholders which marine management regimes should include consideration of marine ecosystem objectives. This is confusing and suggests some regimes may not be subject to application of the ecosystem approach.' Wildlife and Countryside Link, an alliance of environmental voluntary organizations including the Marine Conservation Society, RSPB, WWF and the Wildlife Trusts, also sees a threat:

> We support sustainable development, but strong nature conservation measures are essential to achieving it – 'balance' and trade-offs will not always be possible. Nature conservation should not be seen as the Bill's secondary goal, to be delivered as long as it does not affect development and resource use. Equally, there should not be an assumption that negative impacts on the environment can be balanced against economic and social benefits.

Marinet, the marine arm of Friends of the Earth which is campaigning not just for a Marine Bill but for a new Ministry of the Sea with a Secretary of State in the Cabinet, put it bluntly (and simultaneously spelled out the marine industries' abiding, wake-at-night fear):

The precautionary approach should be founded on the principle that no activity is allowed to occur until it can be shown that no damage will result from that activity. It should not be founded on the reverse – i.e. any activity may occur until there is reason to believe that it may be causing damage, although proof remains unavailable.

Management should recognise that it is not possible to manage the marine environment. Our knowledge and understanding of this environment and its processes is simply too limited. Rather, the purpose of management is to manage human activities and their effects on the ecosystem, not to manage the ecosystem itself.

The management of human activities must always be based on protecting the resources in the long term, and not on protecting the economic gain in the short term.

And there you have the fault line. The government can go on as much as it likes about 'balance', in the hope perhaps that by repetition it will persuade us that it's real. But of course it isn't. There is no scientific method, of multiplying this by that and dividing by the square of x, that could satisfy a peer-reviewed journal. Balance in this case is all about perception, and perception is all about attitude and values, including commercial self-interest. It is, in short, a matter of opinion. The Institute of Marine Engineering, Science and Technology, for example, believes that nature is all right in its place, but its place is not to get in the way of enterprise. Because 'the level of science available for ecosystem management is not comparable to our awareness of economics', it follows that 'marine ecosystem objectives ... should not have primacy over other social, economic and environmental objectives'. The British Ports Association agreed; so did the Institution of Civil Engineers, which seemed indignant at the very idea of nature getting the vote: 'A statutory duty to consider ecosystem objectives (outside designated special areas) may be perceived as giving primacy to nature conservation, as lacking even-handedness, or as being unjustified – and may therefore prove to be counter-productive.'

What can one say? Has not the story of fishing told us all we need to know about the folly of commercial short-termism? Nature is not like some loved but unruly pet. We can't ghettoize it or shut it away in marine parks and hope the result will be a healthy and productive sea. The Marine Conservation Society puts it well: 'Only by providing adequate and effective protection for marine ecosystems, habitats and species will we ensure that the marine environment is able to not only support a high level of biological diversity, but also continue to provide the many resources and services on which society depends . . .' And it chides the government for misunderstanding its own mantra:

> Reference to the ecosystem approach as a means 'to reconcile and integrate conservation goals with the full range of demands that we place on the marine environment to help meet our economic and social needs' is to confuse the ecosystem approach with a sustainable development approach. The ecosystem approach according to internationally agreed definitions such as ICES is a means to 'achieve sustainable use of ecosystem goods and services, and maintenance of ecosystem integrity'.
>
> The consultation presently implies that conservation will happen as long as it does not affect development in other sectors. This would be a dangerous precedent, and would compromise not only the future of the marine environment per se, but future economic and social benefits as well.

No wonder the Bill slipped down the legislative agenda, or that the government planned another round of consultations 'as early as possible' in 2007. The complexity of the legislative weave was underlined by the Royal Society's bewildering assertion that 'there may be situations of over-riding public interest that compromise the specific environmental, social or economic objectives of the legislation'. It is as well that the Royal Society includes such a high proportion of geniuses, for it takes a genius to understand how it could be in the public interest for every single objective of the Bill to be overridden. However, with 'stakeholders' not able to find common cause even in basic priorities, and with little evidence of consensus in any of the main areas of contention, the jaw-time needed to achieve all the necessary compromises is not going to be measurable in hours or days. How will we manage the interface between land and sea (i.e. how ensure that land-based development does not cause damage offshore)? What kind of agency (or, more likely, agencies) do we need to control planning and licensing? How will sea fisheries be brought into line? How will 'marine protected areas' be set up, managed and policed? Most importantly, what kind of Marine Management Organization would be appropriate, and to whom should it answer? The Institution of Civil Engineers' answer to this – 'We would not support the use of the Environment Agency as a model. We further believe that an MMO should not be answerable to Defra' – shows the gulf between the opposing theologies. Defra after all is the lead department drafting the Bill, and opposition to it presumably hangs on the fact that the 'e' in its name stands for 'environment'. What would its opponents prefer? A new Ministry of the Sea, as suggested by Marinet? One hardly imagines so. More likely, they have an eye on the Department of Trade and Industry, whose record on environmental issues (see *Rubbish!*) would score full marks with Cheney and Bush. Fine if you want an Anti Marine Bill; hopeless if you want a living sea. The Marine Conservation Society identifies a number of 'emerging trends' which it wants the Bill to control, and in which the 'T' and the 'I' in DTI would be in direct opposition to Defra's 'e'. These include major new port developments going ahead without proper assess-ment of existing capacity; the mushrooming growth of 'ocean villages' and hard coastal defences; the increasing number of pontoons and moorings, and the harbour dredging that goes with them; offshore wind farms; extraction of sand and gravel, and bio-prospecting (e.g. for new medicinal cures).

If the Marine Bill can build a framework of management for all that lot and still put the ecosystem first, then a decisive blow will have been struck against the dark legions of cynics and dis-believers. Again as I write, news comes of a proposal by the energy company Centrica to develop on Teesside the first coal-fired power station to be built in the UK since 1974. It may or may not happen – the Marine Bill will or ought to be a factor – but if it does, it will be as remote from the old-time smoke-belching monsters as nicotine gum from a Havana cigar. The coal would be gasified before burning, and carbon emissions harm-lessly piped off into depleted North Sea oilfields. As the worsening energy crisis will have to be balanced against the even faster-growing crisis of climate change, it could become every-one's favourite oxymoron: 'clean coal'.

Energy policy on its own would make a long, if not exactly racy book (George Monbiot's *Heat* is a pretty good primer; so is Jeremy Leggett's *Half Gone*), and I don't intend to go into it here. It's enough to say that the generation of energy by tidal or (especially) wind power, and the disposal of the products of com-bustion will be a thorny problem for whichever body inherits responsibility for marine planning and management. The Institution of Civil Engineers, for example, sees 'no serious technical barriers' to 'carbon capture and storage' (CCS), so is all for it, while the Environment Agency and Marine Conservation Society worry about 'environmental risks and uncertainties', and so are against. Parked in the middle, the Royal Society thinks CCS is 'a potentially useful tool for reducing carbon dioxide emissions in future', provided we can achieve a watertight agreement on who is responsible for the permanent safety of an indefinite storage system. It's the same question that nuclear waste throws up. Who will manage infinity?

Few things give more pleasure to the anti-environment lobby than the sight of angry green activists stamping on each other's sandals. Righteous dissent! It's like a form of bear-baiting: you could sell tickets. When it comes to firing up the gladiators, nothing works better than 'renewable resources', which at sea means wave, tidal and wind power. The basic premise is incontestable. Aside from the few scientific illiterates who think climate change isn't happening, nobody thinks the UK's declared target – 10 per cent of energy to be generated from renewable sources by 2010 – is excessive. In policy terms, this is basic greenstuff. But no development of any kind is possible at zero environmental cost, and environmental cost means, inevitably, opposition from environmentalists. This is especially true of tidal power. Superficially it looks like a no-brainer. We don't need Cnut to remind us of the gravitational effects of moon and sun on the oceans. In and out flow the tides with remorseless punctuality, only to dissipate their huge energy uselessly on the beach. Put up a barrage, install some turbines, and – shazam! – the energy crisis is solved. For as long as the planets keep turning, we will have free electricity on tap. But of course it's not as easy as that.

I've no idea how the maths works, but the experts tell me that the energy available from a tidal power station is proportionate to the square of the tidal range (i.e. the average rise and fall between high and low tides). This means that it is a practical proposition only where the tides are big, and where there is a suitable site for a barrage – a combination of factors which (again I rely on the experts) occurs only very rarely. So rarely, indeed, that Europe has only a single working example, built in the 1960s across the estuary of the River Rance in Brittany; so rarely that the World Energy Council (WEC) can name only 26 potential new sites worldwide. Two countries top the international list with five sites each – Argentina and the UK. The one British example everyone knows about – *cause célèbre* or *bête noire* depending on your particular shade of green – is the Severn estuary. Along with the Mersey, this was intensively studied and evaluated in the eighties, and it is widely believed that it was environmental objectors, warning of damage to the ecosystem (in particular, disturbances to wading birds and fish), who turned the tide against it. The truth is both less glorious and less reassuring (this was, after all, the Thatcherite eighties, when sentimentality was barred by *fiat*). The fact is, tidal power failed on economic grounds: it simply did not compare well with other forms of renewable energy – i.e. wind farms – which is why we heard so little about the other nominated sites in the Duddon, Wyre and Conwy estuaries, and why the DTI generally has been dismissive of tidal technology. It has not ruled it out exactly. Needs may change; technology may improve; the economic argument may develop reverse thrust. For all these reasons, in its Energy Review of July 2006 the government claims a continuing interest in 'improving our understanding of how to make best use of the potential tidal resource in UK waters'.

But it's a bit like the sound of one hand clapping. One day it may happen (and well done for trying), but not now. Now is all about wind. There have been arguments about capacity; arguments about economics (these come usually from the same people who say man-made climate change isn't happening); arguments about dangers to aircraft; arguments about noise and un-sightliness; arguments about disturbances to birds and fish; arguments about diverting resources and attention from the real business (as industry hard men see it) of driving forward a new and extended nuclear programme. Whatever. But wind power will have its day. Offshore, the gun was fired in December 2000 when the Crown Estate assigned the first sites for wind farms in UK waters. 'Round One', as it was called, was a 'demonstration round' allowing developers to test their designs but limiting the size of each installation to a maximum of 30 turbines. As I write, five of these are up and running – at Blyth, off Northumberland; Barrow, off south Cumbria; North Hoyle, off North Wales; Scroby Sands, off Great Yarmouth; and Kentish Flats in the Thames estuary. Another, at Burbo Bank, off Crosby, Merseyside, is under construction. Eight more have planning consent and three await decision.

Compared with old-fashioned windmills, the wind turbine is a pared-down masterpiece of modern industrial design with a classic form-follows-function aesthetic. You could say it was graceful, and few would argue. But concrete flyovers are graceful too, with their subtle curves and economy of line, and I respond to them in much the same way. I wish I could like them, but I can't. The nearest to shore are those in the 30-turbine Scroby Sands wind farm, 2.5km off Great Yarmouth (only 1km off Caister) and hogging the seaward view from pier and promenade. The DTI, which invested £107m in the Round One developments, is commendably unafraid to state the obvious: 'Wind turbines near to shore can have a visual impact, although opinion on the impact is usually divided. The further offshore a wind farm is located, the less effect it will have when viewed from the shore.'

My own view is that Scroby looks out of scale, out of character, out of place – a cruel setback to Great Yarmouth's almost heart-breakingly courageous attempt to re-establish its credentials as a resort. But I may be out of step. Though I find no mention of the wind farm on Yarmouth's official tourism website, I know that the Scroby Sands Information Centre on the Esplanade received 35,000 visitors in its first year of opening, and that boat trips to the site are popular. I welcome the implied rebuke to my techno-phobia and salute the better sense of those who take a more positive view of change. But I welcome more enthusiastically the British Wind Energy Association's recommendation that future projects should be at least 5km offshore, and that an 'exclusion zone' of 8km has been set for the major Round Two developments in the 'Greater Wash' (i.e. the North Sea at the mouth of the Wash), the Thames estuary and Liverpool Bay. In places of 'particular environmental sensitivity', this will stretch to 13km, and the huge 'London Array' station in the outer Thames estuary will be 20km (12 miles) out. 'Huge' is right. With a proposed maximum of 271 turbines, it is nine times the size of Scroby Sands. Whereas Scroby was supposed to provide power for the equivalent of 41,000 homes (in the event, technical problems in its first year limited this to 12,000), the consortium behind

London Array say they will generate enough to serve 750,000 homes – equivalent to the whole of Kent and East Sussex, or 25 per cent of Greater London. According to the Crown Estate, which is leasing the sites, the 15 Round Two schemes between them will power more than four million households – quite enough to stifle the aesthetic carping of people like me, if not the pro-nuclear, anti-warming ideologues who still seem to think that 'green energy' is a contradiction in terms.

What they are right about is that wind alone will not fill the energy gap. In the long term, even the world's longest undersea gas supply line, the 1,200km (746-mile) Langeled pipeline from Nyhamn in Norway to Easington in Yorkshire, opened by the two countries' prime ministers in October 2006, won't be enough to keep Britain lit up and humming. With a capacity of 20bn cubic metres a year, the Langeled is capable theoretically of supplying 20 per cent of the UK's peak winter gas demand for the next 40 years. The trouble is that the existence of a pipeline does not guarantee a supply of gas to send through it, and even at full capacity it still leaves 80 per cent of the UK market to be served from other sources. So it's not just pipes and cables that the sea may have to swallow: Defra raises the question of 'sub-seabed geological structures' being used to store not only waste carbon dioxide but also natural gas brought by ship from abroad (the UK has been a net importer of natural gas since 2004). Some kind of storage will certainly be necessary. As the government explains:

> Storage within the UK would help ensure security of energy supply as North Sea supplies inevitably decline, providing greater resilience to seasonal changes in European and global demand and greater market stability.

> To date the UK has only one major offshore sub-seabed storage facility, the Rough Field, which uses primarily indigenous gas and has been operational since 1983. Significant opportunities for such storage exist in depleted oil and gas reservoirs as well as in a number of suitable salt structures (saline aquifers) and commercial

interest is growing. The technology for importing commercial natural gas by ship is developing, and there is commercial interest in constructing offshore unloading facilities.

Oddly, it's an issue that many of the respondents seemed either not to notice or to think undeserving of comment. Among those who did take the trouble, the Institution of Civil Engineers said only that it would 'have no objection' provided the techniques and infrastructure were up to the job. But the Marine Conservation Society, and Wildlife and Countryside Link, reared up in alarm. Here was yet another threat to the stability and integrity of seabed habitats, a Trojan seahorse that would disgorge a further rash of port developments and block the progress of renewables. The Environment Agency, too, was worried that brine pumped out from the salt deposits (necessary to create storage space) would damage water quality.

And those are just the broad objections at policy level. Locally when a specific scheme is brought forward, the outcry will be furious. Disruption of wildlife, damage to the ecosystem, pollution, danger of leakage, risk of explosion, unsightly development both offshore and on . . . These are not the kinds of neighbour that anyone is going to vote for. Yet the gas will have to go somewhere, and storage ashore will be even less popular than burial at sea. The Buncefield explosion at Hemel Hempstead in 2005 was in an oil depot, not gas, but it cast a pall over public opinion that will take a very long time to lift. And this, really, is the nub of the problem. The health and welfare of the sea is a pressing issue, but it cannot be considered in isolation from the land, as if the point of interface were an impermeable membrane through which could pass only fish in one direction and effluent in the other. We can't have a policy for the sea without it being also a policy for the land, and vice versa. There is no virtuous circle. Even to replenish more beaches and build more ports, marinas and coastal defences, never mind roads and Olympic stadia, will be to plough more and more of the eastern Channel for aggregates.

This is the likely weakness of the Marine Bill, and the Achilles heel of a marine management organization that will not be entrusted with the key of its own door. Fisheries policy, energy policy, ports policy – all these and more will be pushed through its letterbox from outside, leaving it to answer only the 'how' question rather than the 'what'. The 'ecosystem first' sticker may stay in the window, but it will not deter the Treasury, DTI and Department for Transport from taking what they want. Like the Green Cross Code it may reduce the number of casualties in a blighted environment, but it will not remove the blight. Attitudes are warped by the perception – at the root of every stress we have ever placed on the sea – that land is private property and the sea is a public resource.

This is why the engineers, developers and shipping companies may be closer to the 21st-century *realpolitik* than the NGOs. The Marine Conservation Society is right: what the Marine Bill promises is not the enclosing rigour of 'ecosystem first' but the soft elasticity of 'sustainable development'. The government promises only 'close links' between the 'marine spatial planning system' [i.e. exploitation of the sea], the designation of marine protected areas and 'the application of ecosystem objectives'. The most important thing it can achieve is the one thing its consultation ignored – the integration of the fishing industry into a system of management that can see further than tomorrow morning at Grimsby Fish Dock. For marine conservation in general, it identified five 'strategic goals'. It wants to:

halt the deterioration in the state of the UK's marine biodiversity and to promote recovery where practicable;

support healthy, functioning and resilient marine ecosystems and further the conservation of marine species, habitats, physical features and natural processes which play a key role in sustaining the variety of marine life and the benefits derived from it;

improve and maintain the water quality of the marine environment and mitigate the effect of human activities on its physical and oceanographic processes in order to provide an environment where biodiversity can thrive;

integrate marine nature conservation into human activities and plans affecting the marine environment to deliver an ecosystem approach consistent with the wider sustainable development goals for the wider marine environment;

increase and broaden understanding and the application of knowledge about marine ecosystems to provide the best available information for policy development and decision making processes, and to promote understanding among stakeholders.

A number of things are evident from the way these are phrased. First and most obviously, none of the first four is achievable without the involvement of the fishing industry. Second, the entire edifice has more escape hatches than a Cabinet war bunker. Note, for example, the weasely 'where practicable' in the first objective. Not 'possible', but 'practicable' – and who will decide exactly what *that* means in a regime that has to 'leave room for all three pillars of sustainable development (social, economic and environmental) and seek to look for genuine win-win situations with benefits to all three, or at the very least, strike a balance between them'? Just in case we haven't understood, point four drills it home with a careful elision of irreconcilable opposites, 'ecosystem approach' and 'sustainable development'. Translation: the ecosystem is important, but not as important as economic development. Which is pretty much the kind of thinking that brought the sea to the very state of calamity from which the Marine Bill is supposed to rescue it. In theory, marine wildlife and habitats already enjoy the benefit of protective legislation. The Common Fisheries Policy is perhaps the most notoriously counter-productive example, in which all three 'pillars of sustainable development' have collapsed under the weight of legislative jerry-building and boathook diplomacy. Most of the rest is at least better-intentioned. As Defra points out, Section 9 of the Wildlife and Countryside Act, 1981

> prohibits the intentional killing, injury, taking possession or sale of listed species of wild animals. It prohibits the intentional or reckless damage or destruction of structures or places that they use for shelter or protection and their disturbance whilst doing so. It also prohibits the deliberate or reckless disturbance of dolphins, whales and basking sharks ... Section 14 prohibits the release of alien species of wild animals and restricts the introduction into the wild of non-native plants.

Section 36 of the same Act empowers 'nature conservation agencies' to identify potential marine reserves out to a distance of three nautical miles. Sections 1–8 make it illegal to kill, injure or capture wild birds, or to damage their nests or eggs, or to disturb protected species at the nest. (These include, for example, avocet, black-tailed godwit, greenshank, green and purple sandpipers, little gull, shorelark, and black, little and roseate terns.) It is the means by which European conservation directives have been transposed into local law. The most important of these is the Conservation (Natural Habitats &c) Regulations 1994 – more commonly known as 'the Habitats Directive' – which obliges the Secretary of State to nominate sites of particular importance to protected species. Once these have been agreed by the European Commission, the government has six years to designate them as Sites of Community Importance (SCIs) and Special Areas of Conservation (SACs). All these, together with Special Protection Areas (SPAs) designated under the Council Directive on the Conservation of Wild Birds – 'the Birds Directive' – come together in a network known as Natura 2000.

It sounds like good news for gannets, but it's not that easy. Even if you could rely on the willing support of every marine 'stakeholder' from RSPB to beam-trawler, wildlife protection at sea would remain hellishly difficult to guarantee. It's easy enough to protect a nesting site. But birds need also to feed, and how do you protect their right – if indeed it *is* a right – to forage undisturbed in the open sea? Seabirds are not like terrestrial species with regular hunting grounds. They are more like big cats on the plains of Africa, tracking highly mobile and wide-ranging prey. Manx shearwaters, for example, may fly for several days and hundreds of miles in search of fish. It is a search which, without wider and more radical legislative controls, can only get longer and harder. One of the biggest abuses of the sea is industrial fishing, whereby millions of tonnes of small shoaling fish – sandeels and sprats, for example – are sucked up to make feed for fish farms and livestock. You could quite accurately describe this approach as 'ecosystem last'. Small fish are the base of a marine food chain that includes bigger fish, birds, mammals and man. To hit any part of the chain is to hit the whole, and the lower you aim the worse it gets. Small species, big impact.

One of the worst obstacles to reform is simple ignorance. For obvious reasons, science knows far less about marine ecosystems than it does about terrestrial ones. As was evident from the Marine Bill consultation, it is a shortcoming that commercial interests are not shy of exploiting. If no one knows the effects, they argue, then there is no case for standing in our way. Let us fish/drill/dredge on regardless. In 2004, despite the fact that sandeel fishing had been banned in the North Sea since 2000, seabirds on Shetland and Orkney suffered terribly from lack of food. Arctic terns, kittiwakes and, especially, guillemots were hit hard. For the second year running, reported the RSPB, 'guillemots have been devastatingly affected. [They] can fly tens of kilometres from their breeding colonies . . . to find shoals of sandeels and can dive to more than 100 metres below the surface to catch them. Now they are returning with empty beaks and stomachs.'

The result was the worst breeding season ever recorded in Scotland. In the same year, the British Ecological Society reported that kittiwakes in the North Sea had reduced by more than half since 1990, a decline that it attributed to a combination of sandeel fishing and – the biggest 'known unknown' in an entire ocean of uncertainties – climate change. Rising water temperatures and changed currents are thought to affect the plankton on which the sandeels feed, driving them away from the birds' feeding range. The purpose of this digression is to give weight to the rather obvious point that the issues are complex, and that single manifestations of environmental damage can have multiple causes and be symptomatic of a deeper malaise. As I write, the North Sea sandeel fishery remains closed, but the fishing lobby and its ministerial champions are still the biggest single obstacle to ecological prudence.

It had long been expected that the Marine Bill would be in the 2006 Queen's Speech. Not only was it missing, but – earlier the same week – a 'leaked document' aroused suspicion of yet another government retreat. Central to the concept of marine nature reserves is the 'no-take zone' from which all fishing would be banned. This is the *sine qua non* of the scientists' case. Common sense – *any* kind of sense – says that threatened species need places of refuge from the hunter, and that damaged habitats and depleted ecosystems cannot recover unless they are given time and space. As it is for forest, moor or mountain, so it is for seabed. This has been proved on the Great Barrier Reef in Australia, around the islands of Hawaii in the US and at Goat Island, north of Auckland in New Zealand, where the world's first no-take zone was declared in 1975. Previously the seabed there had been scraped down to bare rock spiked with sea urchins. Now it's a flourishing kelp forest so dense with fish that some species are nearly 30 times more numerous inside the reserve than out. More importantly, it gives scientists a rare opportunity to watch and understand how a marine ecosystem works – essential if we are ever to understand how the sea might be 'managed', and how some real meaning might be injected into that flip-chart favourite, 'sustainability'.

It was always understood by the Marine Conservation Society and others that the government's avowed commitment to 'a network of highly protected reserves' meant no-take zones. What else could 'highly protected' mean? Yet on 13 November, two days before the Queen's Speech, the *Daily Telegraph*'s respected environment editor, Charles Clover, reported that Defra had changed tack and was now 'drawing up plans for a network of reserves that will not have any no-take' element.

Instead, [a] leaked presentation given to conservationists by Defra staff shows that marine protected areas will be designed to protect only certain designated species or habitats.

They will be put in place by local sea fisheries committees, which conservationists say are institutionally biased towards commercial fishing interests.

Leaked documents are not always the best evidence. The leaker always has a motive, and the document itself may reflect only one option among several. In this case, however, there's little room for doubt. The 'leak' turns out to have been a Powerpoint presentation given to 'biodiversity stakeholders' by Defra at a meeting on 5 October 2006, which gives a clear and precise indication of the government's thinking. If not quite a U-turn, there had been a significant policy swerve. This is what Defra said publicly in its consultation paper of March 2006: 'The UK Government is proposing the introduction of a flexible mechanism for the designation and management of marine protected areas, where existing provisions do not suffice, from areas of minimal restriction through to highly protected marine reserves.' And this is what it said semi-privately eight months later: 'We are proposing that the existing MNR [Marine Nature Reserve] regime is replaced by the new Marine Protected Area mechanism.'

It looks unexceptionable, but the wording – or, rather, the

omission of wording – is crucial. 'Highly protected marine reserves' mean what they say. No fishing would be allowed in them; nor would dredging, oil and gas extraction, construction or any other kind of exploitation. In the very fullest sense, and in every possible way, they would be 'no-take zones'. Their inclusion in the consultation, and explicit support by the fisheries minister Ben Bradshaw, had convinced the Marine Conservation Society that Defra finally had understood the need to protect whole ecosystems rather than individual species. At the MCS's annual conference in 2005, Bradshaw insisted he was 'confident that [in respect of highly protected marine reserves], government will be able to meet what the Marine Conservation Society wants'.

Elsewhere he declared the UK's only existing no-take zone, a tiny (3.3 square-kilometre) area off Lundy, established in 2003, to have been 'a resounding success' for crabs and lobsters, and said the government would 'continue to explore the environment and fish stock benefits of creating a network of similar areas'. Officials still insist that no-take zones have not been ruled out, but the definition they put forward ('area of the sea closed to some or all types of fishing activity on a permanent or temporal basis') is typically non-committal. To a conservationist, a no-take zone is a place of recovery for a damaged ecosystem, in which the ecosystem itself is a thing of value. To the fishing industry, a no-take zone is just a fished-out desert where nothing marketable is left to take, its purpose to let the target species, not the ecosystem, recover until it is worth hitting again. The two interpretations are as remote from each other as an ancient forest from a Christmas tree plantation, but both fit the Defra blueprint. Suspicion is further aroused, if not confirmed, by Defra's spokesman: 'We're not running away from any commitments. There will be flexible marine protected areas which take account of the marine life they are designed to protect. They will be "no take" where species have dwindled to the extent that they have to be built up.'

Ecosystem first? Pull the other one. 'Flexible' is another of those cult terms taken up by the stakeholder generation without which no official document is complete. It's not included in Defra's glossary of terms but might be taken to mean 'negotiable, open to compromise; won't hurt if you bump into it'. This is pretty much the way things have gone for marine conservation in the past. The hope now is that the 'spatial planning' and licensing systems envisaged by the Marine Bill will enable existing legislation to work more effectively. It certainly needs to. The legislative and regulatory network under which marine protected areas of various kinds are designated and managed is mind-bendingly complicated. Neither Defra nor its statutory adviser the Joint Nature Conservation Committee (JNCC) succeeds in explaining it clearly, and no one invests much effort in trying to defend it. A 'Review of Marine Nature Conservation', ordered by the former Department of Environment, Transport and the Regions in 1999 and delivered to Defra in 2004, declared it to be 'not fit for purpose'. Wildlife and Countryside Link in its *Marine Bill Bulletin* No. 7, of May 2006, complained:

> Only three MNRs [Marine Nature Reserves] have been designated in the last 25 years, and the Natura 2000 network of sites, whilst important, even when complete will have significant limitations. In particular, the legislation applies only to a handful of marine habitats and species, and only sites deemed to be of international importance will be designated, leaving the majority of the UK's marine biodiversity ineligible for protection.

This is why scientists have been pressing so hard for Highly Protected Marine Reserves (HPMR – now invariably capitalized, and fully established in the thickening shoal of initials that cluster around the information outfall). It explains also the anger of conservationists who see Defra wilting before the economic and industrial broadsides and preparing to abandon ship. In its summary of responses to the Marine Bill, Defra with sublime *chutzpah* now claims the role of lexical sole arbiter and accuses conservationists of misunderstanding their own terminology:

> Some respondents raised concerns about the focus on the environ-
> ment that [the ecosystem approach] seemed to advocate. However
> some of these concerns seemed to arise from misinterpretations of
> the terminology 'ecosystem approach' as encompassing environ-
> mental issues only, rather than being a means to aid a holistic
> approach to the management of human activities . . .

One would have thought that nothing could be more 'holistic'
than an ecosystem, but language in Spin City is nothing if not
flexible. It also explains the Marine Conservation Society's
'dismay' at the seemingly bland wording of Defra's October briefing, and the furious response of its biodiversity policy officer,
Jean-Luc Solandt:

> Instead [of considering HPMRs], government is intent on setting
> up another set of Marine Protected Areas based on the same failed
> management structures as European Special Areas of
> Conservation, i.e. where progress to achieve protection takes place
> after damage has occurred, and decisions on fishing activities that
> affect biodiversity are made by sea fisheries committees.

The UK has only three Marine Nature Reserves designated
under the Wildlife and Countryside Act – Lundy Island in
England, Skomer Island in Wales and Strangford Lough
in Northern Ireland. Together they add up to around 209 square
kilometres, or less than 0.12 per cent of UK territorial waters
within the 12-mile limit. Nothing illustrates the weakness of the
system better than Strangford Lough. One of the most important
reasons for its designation (as a Marine Nature Reserve in 1995
and Special Area of Conservation in 1996) were the huge horse
mussel reefs that covered the bottom and provided a home for
hundreds of other species including anemones, tube worms, sea
urchins, brittle stars, sea squirts and soft corals. When divers
from Queen's University, Belfast, surveyed the loch in 2003 they
found that only one small area of reef still survived. Reason?

321

Scallop boats, with or without a 'holistic approach to the management of human activities', had simply smashed the beds with their dredging gear and given conservation a two-fingered salute. Only after lobbying by the Ulster Wildlife Trust and Friends of the Earth had brought the threat of fines from the European Commission did the Northern Ireland Department of Agriculture and Rural Development announce a permanent ban on scallop fishing in 2004. A horse mussel bed is not something you can put back overnight or even necessarily at all, and WWF fears the Lough may never recover. You may or may not care much about horse mussels and their dependent colonies of invertebrates, but – unless you own shares in a scallop dredger or a beam trawler – you must feel, at the very least, some unease at the evident lack of protection the law provides, and will continue to provide unless government policy, with all its 'balances', 'sustainabilities' and 'three-pillared approaches', is purged of get-outs and ambiguity.

Defra in its consultation also raised the question of 'voluntary' protected areas, and asked 'stakeholders' how they thought marine industries would respond to 'voluntary site protection measures'. Incredibly, only 17 respondents thought this worth answering. Eight of them thought it unlikely that businesses would change their behaviour for the sake of the environment. Four predicted a 'high level' of take-up; five said the response would depend on 'other unspecified factors'. Defra itself summed up candidly: 'The degree of activity, modification and level of take-up of measures may be vulnerable to the presence of short-term financial impacts and changing circumstances.'

In fact history had already delivered its verdict. For more than a decade, the Devon and Dorset Wildlife Trusts, working with English Nature and local fishermen's organizations, had tried to prevent excessive damage by scallop dredgers in Lyme Bay, which contained, among other things, large densities of pink sea fans – a species protected under Schedule 5 of the Wildlife and Countryside Act and included in the UK Biodiversity Action Plan.

Turkey was talked, reasonableness prevailed and, in 2001, two voluntary no-trawl zones were declared. Outcome: the number of boats doubled, with increased damage to reef species throughout the bay, including the voluntary no-trawl zone at Saw Tooth Ledges. Defra reported 'widespread destruction of the sea floor'. A similar no-take zone agreed among crab and lobster fishermen at St Agnes, Cornwall, was undermined, according to Defra, 'by the refusal of one commercial fisherman to adhere to the arrangement'. The lesson is as clear as the Eddystone Light.

No-take zones are essential to the survival of undamaged ecosystems. An incomplete or unenforced no-take zone is not a no-take zone at all but just another driver of competition. The only answer is statutory, not voluntary, control – a fact that the fishing industry understands just as well as the conservation bodies do, but which leads it to a very different conclusion. No-take zones could affect fishermen's livelihoods; therefore they are a bad thing. Marine scientists think no-take zones are essential; therefore marine scientists are a bad thing too.

In addition to the three Marine Nature Reserves, the UK has 63 marine Special Areas of Conservation (SACs), more than half of them in Scotland, which are the approximate equivalents of Sites of Special Scientific Interest on land. The Habitats and Species Directive is very specific about the kinds of habitat that may be designated – 'submerged or partly submerged sea caves; sandbanks which are slightly covered by seawater all the time; mudflats and sandflats not covered by seawater at low tide; reefs; submarine structures made by leaking gas'. It is prescriptive also about species – grey and common seals, harbour porpoise, bottlenose dolphin, otter, loggerhead turtle, lamprey, sea lamprey and shad. Like SSSIs on land, SACs are better than nothing but only just. They should prevent the total destruction of sites but do not altogether proscribe activities liable to damage them, and they are blind to the value of species not on the European list.

The problem is exemplified by the Overfalls, a range of sand-covered gravelly banks covering an area of six square miles in the outer Solent east of the Isle of Wight. I owe my account of them to Wildlife and Countryside Link's *Marine Bill Bulletin No. 6*, published in February 2006. Like all important wildlife sites, the Overfalls benefit from a particular combination of circumstances – in this case a 30-metre depth of sea and strong tidal currents. This causes water to cascade over them and creates the ideal environment for a wide range of sea life, including most importantly sandeels, which attract bass and other predators. 'According to local anglers,' says Link, 'bass wait in the slacks between the banks, picking off the sandeels and other prey as they spill over the top.' The area is also important for several species of shark and ray, including the blonde ray (or blonde skate), *Raja brachyura*, which is in such a state of decline in the UK that it is a candidate for the Red Data Book. Its favoured habitat is precisely what the Overfalls provide – sandbanks and strong currents. 'The unusual geology and hydrodynamics,' says Link, 'thus contribute to its particular wildlife community.'

They also account for its popularity with humans. At the last count, four commercial fishing boats and 30 charter vessels were regularly fishing there with rod and line, earning an estimated £50,000 annually from the catch and £150,000 from recreational anglers (who return much of their catch to the sea). More worryingly, the site is open also to British and French trawlers. More worryingly still, what's inviting to a blonde ray is inviting also to the construction industry. In 1999, Hanson Aggregates Marine Ltd applied for a licence to dredge sand and gravel from an area of seabed that included half the Overfalls. Inevitably, and rightly, this caused an outcry among local anglers, supported by the local Wildlife Trust, who feared the site would be irreparably damaged and the habitat destroyed. Hanson's response in the circumstances was perfectly reasonable. It sought, and found, an alternative site that would allow it to leave the Overfalls undisturbed. What it wanted in return, however, was an assurance from government that it would not be an empty or self-harming gesture – i.e. that commercial competitors would not be allowed to move in and take advantage of its scruple. Again this seemed a reasonable position for the company to take – a perfect example of the 'balance' which the government continually insists it is eager to promote. Snag is, the Overfalls are not a legally protected site and so there is no legal basis on which such a deal could be struck. Worse, says Link:

> The local English Nature team advised the Action Group that there is no statutory ecological or geological conservation mechanism suitable for the site. 'Sandbanks which are slightly covered by sea water at all times' are eligible to be designated as Special Areas of Conservation under the EU Habitats Directive. However, this is currently only applied to sites in water depths of less than 20 metres.

Which of course rules out the Overfalls. Nature is messy and untidy, at its best when it brings together unusual combinations of factors that defy the tidy-mindedness of official definitions. In a tick-box regime, it's the sites most in need of protection that are least likely to get it. At the moment the future of the Overfalls remains uncertain. There has been a government-funded research project by the University of Portsmouth, accompanied by optimistic talk of 'voluntary codes of conduct', but it is not an optimism which the government itself seems to share. In its summary of responses to the Marine Bill consultation, it says:

> A further example [of costs to industry working against ecological objectives] is provided from the Overfalls Project, initiated to control the impacts of aggregate extraction and fishing in an area of the Eastern English Channel. As of March 2006 the voluntary scheme has cost £107,969 with limited success due to inadequate stakeholder consensus.

Inadequate stakeholder consensus. A brutally unpoetic phrase that you wouldn't want to set to music. (If you did, it would be all sharps and discords on quivering strings, the aural signature of Danger.) *Inadequate stakeholder consensus.* Much of the language of government is spun to imply meaning that isn't there: weasel-packed sentences that collapse into meaninglessness as soon as you put any weight on them. But here we have reverse spin – a bit of dull jargonizing that conceals a wounding truth, like a potato with a needle in it. *Inadequate stakeholder consensus.* Translation: the 'three pillars of sustainable development' do not support a unified philosophical structure. When lateral force is applied, it's the environmental pillar that crumbles first and the economic pillar that is most resistant to movement. This is the lesson that history teaches. It is the root of environmentalists' anxiety about the Bill, and why 'ecosystem first' and 'sustainable development' are foes in logic, not partners in virtue. Economic gain is impossible to achieve without environmental loss: in each particular case, to be *for* one is to be *against* the other. Will the Marine Bill provide the alchemical apparatus that will turn discord into consensus? Doubt and hope fight like crabs in a bucket.

The Worldwide Fund for Nature (WWF) talks of seas in crisis. Its latest Marine Health Check (2005) offered a sketch of what things ought to be like: the waters around the UK hold half the country's biodiversity and a wider variety of sea life than any other country in Europe. Some 7,300 animal species have been recorded here, including 33 mammals and 333 fish, plus thousands of plants and algae, and 187 species of bird. The lists go on for page after page, but they are much like the old salts mending their nets: dying breeds. WWF looked in detail at 16 key species and habitats, and found all but three in a desperate state. No one can be unaware that fishing and aquaculture have put the skids under cod and wild Atlantic salmon. Less well known is the plight of the common skate, *Dipturus batis*, which has suffered so grievously that researchers' attempts to count the surviving population found not a single fish. There is no terrestrial equivalent to the bottom trawl. It is not just a question of driving to extinction the thing you want to eat: you destroy entire ecosystems from top predator to maerl bed. Dragging heavy nets along the seabed wipes out corals, sponges and the deep-sea nursery grounds of the very species the fishermen are trying to catch. On a typical 15-day trip, a trawler will sweep approximately 33 sq km of seabed, crashing through everything in its path. In conservation terms it's like harvesting rabbits by bombing the Chilterns. Given that even such pragmatists as the Royal Society and the Institution of Civil Engineers (whom you can certainly acquit of any misplaced sentimentalism about the primacy of nature) agree that towed fishing gear is the biggest threat to the marine ecosystem, the measure of the Bill, or of any other legislation designed to 'deliver' a healthy sea, will be its success in diverting the fishing industry from its self-selected course to disaster. If there is no stakeholder consensus, then there will have to be stakeholder coercion.

The species monitored by the WWF are important less for their own sake than as ambassadors for their habitats. What is bad for one is bad for all. The harbour porpoise, for example, represents the cetaceans (dolphins, porpoises and whales), of which 28 species have been recorded in British and Irish waters. Between August 1992 and March 1994, some 2,200 of them died in fishermen's nets in the Celtic Sea. Science puts a figure of 1.7 per cent on the maximum amount a population can lose this way and still hope to survive. On the evidence of the Celtic Sea, the actual losses are running nearly four times higher than this, at 6.4 per cent.

For leatherback turtles, the lethal hazard is hooks on long-lines. For basking sharks, whose fins go into the famous soup, it is overfishing. For the long-snouted seahorse, *Hippocampus guttulatus*, it is habitat destruction by trawling, dredging and marine pollution, exacerbated by the seahorse's fatal attraction to Asian medicine makers, curio dealers and the aquarium trade. And so it is wherever you look. The beautiful, fragile fan mussel is another species sacrificed to bottom-fishers. The native oyster is being hit by overfishing, pollution and competition from slipper limpets that arrived on the backs of imported American oysters. Maerl beds, made of calcified seaweed, are vital to a vast range of sea life (including, unfortunately, scallops). Individual nodules grow at 1mm a year so that the beds take many centuries to develop. Left to themselves, they have a life expectancy of 6,000 years. Under the assaults of scallop dredgers, fish farmers and those who extract them for soil improvers or filter media, this can shrink to nothing. Other habitats, and the life that depends on them, are swirling around the same plughole – saltmarshes, eelgrass beds, deep-water mud (ploughed for scampi), and reefs.

It's not just life underwater that is in danger. As we have seen, birds too suffer when their food is hit, and the protection afforded by the Birds Directive is more balsa-clad than iron. The Medway estuary, for example, once contained an area of mudflat called the Lappel Bank, which hosted large populations of shelducks, ringed plovers, grey plovers, dunlins and redshanks. In 1989 Medway Ports Authority won planning permission to develop the bank as a car and cargo park, though it did not immediately go ahead and build. Four years later the Medway estuary and marshes were declared a Special Protection Area (SPA) under the Birds Directive, but the still-undeveloped Lappel Bank was not included. In the view of the (Conservative) Secretary of State for the Environment, John Selwyn Gummer, the value of the site for port expansion exceeded its value for ducks and waders. The RSPB protested that the Birds Directive allowed no such discretion and applied for a judicial review which, by way of the House of Lords, came eventually to the European Court of Justice. The court ruled that the RSPB was right – economic arguments cannot be used to justify exclusion from an SPA, and the UK government had acted illegally. By this time, however, the Ports Authority had exercised its planning consent and Lappel Bank no longer existed.

The RSPB's victory was not entirely hollow. The verdict at least served to clarify a point of law – one that may yet come in handy as discussion of the Marine Bill proceeds – and it forced the government to find other sites to compensate for the losses in the Medway and at a similar site, Fagbury Flats, in the Stour/Orwell estuary. The fact remains, however, that, for all the thunder and fury of the tides, the marine ecosystem lives in a house of straw. In the Marine Bill consultation (Question 67), Defra asked: 'Are there threats to the conservation of marine species in the offshore area that are not addressed by existing measures and controls?' Of the 54 respondents who answered, 91 per cent said protection was inadequate. Defra reported, encouragingly, that the responses were from 'a wide range of sectors' (i.e. not all from conservation bodies), but added bizarrely that 9 per cent 'could not identify any threats to marine species'. You wonder where they could have found a depth of sand sufficient to bury all their heads in. In a sense, arguing about the Marine Bill is a bit like swatting mosquitoes while being charged by a rhinoceros. No weight or quantity of numbered clauses, no three-pillared alliances, no degree of stakeholder consensus, adequate or otherwise, can stand against the malevolent onrush of global warming. It's not just rising sea levels that we have to fear – it's the changing nature of the sea itself. In June 2005 the Royal Society published a 60-page report, *Ocean Acidification due to Increasing Atmospheric Carbon Dioxide*, which articulated the fears and convictions of scientists worldwide. To keep it simple:

Carbon dioxide in the atmosphere is absorbed by the oceans. It follows therefore that the more carbon there is in the atmosphere, the more there is in the sea. The result is a chemical change which makes the water more acidic – or, to put it another way, reduces its pH.

> In the past 200 years [says the Royal Society] the oceans have absorbed approximately half the CO_2 produced by fossil fuel burning and cement production. Calculations based on measurements of the surface oceans and our knowledge of ocean chemistry indicate that this uptake of CO_2 has led to a reduction of the pH

of surface seawater of 0.1 units, equivalent to a 30 per cent increase in the concentration of hydrogen ions.

Not even the most distorted vision of the three-pillared ocean economy could absorb damage on that scale. It is 'ecosystem first' only in terms of its impact. If the trend continues, the pH of seawater could fall by another 0.5 units – 'equivalent to a threefold increase in the concentration of hydrogen ions', says the Royal Society – by 2100. This would be the lowest level for hundreds of millennia, and the rate of change 'one hundred times greater than at any time over this period'. Why does it matter? Scientific knowledge is incomplete, but the doubt is all in the detail. Acidification of the ocean is now certain and unavoidable. Damage to marine ecosystems is certain and unavoidable too, though some species will suffer more than others. The report goes on:

Predicting the direction and magnitude of changes in a complex and poorly studied system such as the oceans is very difficult. However, there is convincing evidence to suggest that acidification will affect the process of calcification, by which animals such as corals and molluscs make shells and plates from calcium carbonate ... Other calcifying organisms that may be affected are components of the phytoplankton and zooplankton, and are a major food source for fish and other animals.

Abandoning the measured language of the Royal Society, we find ourselves once again gasping at the magnitude of our own stupidity. While we argue about cod quotas, the size and location of offshore wind farms, the abiding nuisance of jet-skis, the vandalism of Brighton pier, we imperil the sea by the very fact of our existence. No-take zones in the long term may have no more meaning than fertility dances. Unless – as the Royal Society and everyone else with a GCSE in science now insists – we drastically cut our carbon emissions, we face not only the well-publicized erosion in survivability of the land but also permanent destruction of life in the sea. Yes, 'permanent' is an exaggeration, but not in the context of human timescales. Ocean acidification, says the Royal Society, is 'essentially irreversible during our lifetimes'. 'It will take tens of thousands of years for ocean chemistry to return to a condition similar to that occurring in pre-industrial times.'

We humans are good at many things. One of the greatest ironies is that the catastrophes now threatening us are the products not of complacency or indolence but of genius. Yet the genius that gave us wings and wheels is nothing to set against the genius we now need to save ourselves from their consequence. We are, as a species, conspicuously bad at accepting responsibility for our own actions. Witness, for example, Scottish fishermen's preferred prescription for the shortage of fish in their nets – shooting seals.

Right now I'm going for a long walk along the northern shore of my home county, Norfolk, where climate change may bite more savagely and more suddenly than anywhere else in Britain. The immense skies and infinities of marsh and sand have settled into travel-writers' clichés, but clichés are T-shirts worn by truth. I love these places of milky horizon, just as I love their craggy, vertical antitheses in the far granitic west. Who doesn't, or couldn't? But love never kept anyone from the grave, nor anything from history's midden. I am back in the elephant trap. The ocean of words, earnestly exchanged and debated ad infinitum, drowns all but the most stubborn fragments of hope.

Inadequate stakeholder consensus.

As a requiem for the age, it's unimprovable.

Afterword

Writing a topical book – particularly on an environmental subject – can be a dismaying experience. Not only are the facts depressing in themselves, but they keep on changing: the target will not stand still. When the deadline comes, the text has to be abandoned rather than 'finished'. Many times during *Sea Change* I have had to go back, revise and bring earlier chapters up to date. Even this Afterword, added after the rest of the book has gone to press and updated again for this paperback edition, cannot be the last word but only the latest. What does not, and will not, change is the basic proposition – we are not efficient, caring, forward-looking managers of the sea, and we cannot afford to go on abusing it.

This has been given especial emphasis by the latest report of the Intergovernmental Panel on Climate Change (IPCC). Its message is sombre, depressing and unarguably right. Against such a weight of evidence, the is-it/isn't-it-happening 'debate' is over. The unreasoning abuse ladled out by the sceptics is exposed for what it is, and not even Washington has the neck to pretend otherwise. You don't have to be a 'tree-hugger' to realize what the loss of Arctic ice or of cultivable land in Africa and southern Europe will mean, or an 'eco-nutter' to fear the consequences.

But IPCC reports, too, are topical – detailed scientific snapshots, not definitive accounts that will remain true for all time (which is why they go on producing new ones). Being the work of scientists, the reports also lean towards caution. More recent work suggests the influence of positive feedbacks from melting ice and warming soil will precipitate 'tipping points' that will accelerate warming and sea-level rise beyond even the frightening rates that the IPCC predicts.

There are a few places in the world – Bangladesh, the Maldives, the Netherlands – where the consequences of a rising sea will be more acutely felt than along the east coast of England, but not many. The issues of flooding and erosion, explored in Chapters 2 and 3, remain acute. In the area to which I gave most attention, North Norfolk, the district council has now rejected the local Shoreline Management Plan (SMP), which recommends abandoning villages to the sea. In a letter to residents, it reported that it had received more than 2,400 responses to the public consultation, of which only ten had been in favour. This meant the SMP 'could not be accepted and adopted by the clients [i.e. the local authorities which had commissioned it]', and it would continue to patch up its existing coastal defences as well as it was able. What is politically impossible locally, however, may have a different spin nationally. The Anglian Coastal Authorities Group, of which North Norfolk is a member, continues to insist that the SMP is 'based not only on the latest available scientific knowledge of the effects that the North Sea will have upon our coastline, but also upon the current legislative and funding arrangements for coastal defence construction'.

These political and economic constraints will remain obstacles to justice and common sense until the government changes its mind. But will it? In October 2006, Ian Pearson, Defra's then minister of state for climate change (since replaced by Phil Woolas), told a meeting of the all-party Parliamentary Group on Coastal and Marine Issues that 'social justice' should have a voice, and – specifically – that the question of compensation for losses caused by changes in coastal policy should be 'addressed'. No one yet seems to know how or when this might happen, but at least it was an improvement on the insensitivity of Pearson's predecessors.

In December 2007, his successor, Woolas, announced a 'blueprint to help to deliver improved protection for people and property from coastal flooding and erosion . . .' This was the Environment Agency's *Strategic Overview Implementation Plan*, which is supposed to smooth the links between local authorities and other agencies and to 'improve the prioritization and management of all work on the [English] coast'. It followed Defra's earlier announcement that the EA would oversee all coastal 'risk management' from 1 April 2008. What this means, among other things, is that the agency will be responsible for the 'strategic oversight' of Shoreline Management Plans. The hope is that this will produce more consistent policy and a 'sustainable result'. In the longer term, EA will be responsible for funding as well as 'identifying, prioritizing . . . and delivering' coastal erosion and flooding defence works, and will publish 'coastal responsibility maps' to make clear who is responsible for what.

These are all worthwhile improvements. The co-ordination of erosion and flood risk makes sense; so does a joined-up approach to SMPs. But without commitment to a far higher level of funding, shuffling responsibilities between Defra and the EA will do little more than shift the blame. The power of life and death over coastal communities still lies where it always has done, at Westminster. 'Government will still set the criteria that projects will need to meet in order to receive funding,' said Woolas in a caveat that will hardly persuade East Anglia to sleep more easily in its beds.

There has been a change of fisheries minister too, from Ben Bradshaw to Jonathan Shaw. In December 2006, Bradshaw returned from the European ministers' pre-Christmas haggle making all the usual noises. British fishermen, he said, could 'look forward to healthy incomes for the third year in a row', and he was pleased to announce quota increases for mackerel, hake and monkfish in the south-west, prawns in the Irish Sea, monkfish in the North Sea and west of Scotland, and Rockall haddock. The bad news was that the North Sea cod quota had been cut by 14 per cent, and days at sea by between 7 and 10 per cent depending on the size of the trawler.

The worse news was that there was to be any cod quota at all. As usual, the deal pleased no one – not even Bradshaw himself, who had wanted a 15 per cent cut in days at sea for cod but predictably was thwarted by the politicking. As usual, too, howls of protest came from the fishermen. In the opinion of Bertie Armstrong, chief executive of the Scottish Fishermen's Federation, the days-at-sea cut was 'wholly unsatisfactory'. Careful negotiations had been ignored, he said, and the commission had adopted 'a totally unacceptable starting position ... Such decisions affect the livelihoods of fishermen and should not be taken in a highly charged political atmosphere where little account is taken of the huge efforts made by the Scottish fleet to fish sustainably and responsibly.'

Alex Salmond, leader of the Scottish National Party, knew a populist cause when he saw one, and hammered another little wedge between the governments. 'The Scottish fleet,' he complained, 'are represented by a Whitehall minister who doesn't care, and a Scottish minister who's not there when it counts ... This annual pantomime has turned into farce.' But Salmond of course is a politician, not a scientist, and what he's fishing for is votes. 'The one glimmer on the horizon is that next year Scotland has the opportunity to elect the first pro-fishing government in Scottish history. The future of our coastal communities will depend largely on the outcome of the election.' Translation: vote SNP.

A year later, Jonathan Shaw returned from Brussels to announce an 11 per cent quota increase for cod in the North Sea, with increases also for Irish Sea and Rockall haddock, and North Sea megrim. It is the kind of thing that makes scientists bury their heads in their hands. Professor David Read, Biological Secretary and Vice President of the Royal Society, deplored the outbreak of national breast-beating in a process that ought to be driven more rationally. 'Yet again,' he said in 2006, 'we have seen scientific advice on cod quotas being compromised by political decisions. Given the already alarming condition of stocks, European fisheries ministers should be clear that they may be presiding over the total collapse of cod in the Atlantic. And if this does happen, we can't be sure that there is any possibility of recovery.'

Environmentalists, too, felt anger and disbelief. 'The scientists must wonder why they bother with their surveys,' said Tom Pickerell, Fisheries Officer of WWF-UK. 'It amazes me that world-class survey results are treated with such disdain, while anecdotal views from those with vested interests in maintaining quotas are often given credence. We will now need a miracle to save cod.' This was echoed in 2007 by the Greenpeace oceans campaigner, Willie Mackenzie. 'It's clear that these quota decisions need to be taken out of the hands of fisheries ministers if there is to be any chance of real recovery for Europe's decimated fish stocks.'

Given all this, the consultation paper launched by Defra in February 2007 – *Fisheries 2027 – towards a contract for the future of marine fisheries* – appears to set a course for cloud cuckoo land. The department's 'vision of the fisheries sector in 20 years' time' is a utopian vista of brimful seas, bulging nets, plates piled high and nary a cross word 'twixt contented European neighbours. By 2027, it reckons, 'EU fisheries and environment policy will be coherent', and fisheries management 'will be informed by good data and understanding of fish . . .' Overfishing will be a thing of the past, and 'processors, retailers and others will invest only in those fisheries operations in the UK or overseas that are environmentally responsible'.

It was as if someone had copied the slogans from a flipchart at a weekend seminar – there was just time between coffee and lunch to write up the wishlist, but not to work out how to achieve it. Before that can happen, Defra will need a show of hands. 'In this consultation paper,' it tells its 'stakeholders', 'we have not set out how we want to achieve the vision because we want to agree the vision with you first.' All those in favour of brotherhood and fish pie, please show.

And it's not just from the deep sea that conflict is supposed to disappear. Twenty years hence, healthy salmon and sea trout will be passing in and out of rivermouths uncontaminated with lice; waters around fish farms will be clean and pollution-free; there will be no fear of communicable disease or damage to shellfish; salmon will be fed from sustainable sources. 'Those working in aquaculture,' Defra believes, 'will make sure that the environmental impacts are acceptable.' If by 'acceptable' it means agreeable to environmentalists and not just to the industry itself, then – as Chapter 5 made clear – a lot of polar opposites will need to be conjoined. Hardly a week passes without further bulletins on farm escapes, chemical inputs, infectious diseases, fish mortalities, organochlorines, breaches of 'organic' certification conditions, misleading advertising, falsification of records, algal blooms, untreated sewage discharges, overstocking, worker safety violations – so much, and in such detail, that I can't keep up. Maybe Defra can't either.

In 2005, 877,883 fish escaped from Scottish fish farms, followed by another 240,076 in the first 11 months of 2006. This brought to nearly 3m the number lost since 1997. In December 2007, another 24,000 were lost in a single outbreak from Marine Harvest's operation at Loch Ewe. According to the Pure Salmon Campaign (PSC), between 2000 and 2006 at least 10.2m farmed salmon and trout leaked into the wild worldwide. In Scottish rivers, escapes now outnumber rod-caught wild fish by roughly ten to one, and you don't need to be a geneticist to imagine what this must be doing to the wild breeding stock. The PSC has also calculated that, between 2000 and 2005, more than 1.18m farmed fish escaped from sites hit by the infectious viral disease IPN (infectious pancreatic necrosis). Even healthy escapees will have been treated with sea-lice chemicals and may not be safe to eat. 'If anglers are catching fish they believe have come from an escape,' says the Scottish Executive, 'our precautionary advice is they should not eat them because we cannot be sure that the fish will have come from a pen that the farmer would consider suitable for putting on the market.'

Scotland's Aquaculture and Fisheries Bill did finally become an Act, coming into force on 1 August 2007. As expected, one of its sharpest teeth – the appointment of an industry regulator – was knocked out, but other measures unpopular with the industry have survived. These include compulsory submission of data, mandatory inspections of fish farms for parasites or escapes, enforcement notices and fines for offenders. If it is stringently enforced – which, I concede, is another question entirely – then the biggest regret may be that it didn't happen a decade or more ago when there would still have been time to avert disaster. So far (I write in January 2008) there have been no prosecutions.

In January 2007, the House of Commons Transport Committee published its report on the ports industry of England and Wales. It drew attention to many of the same nonsenses described in Chapter 7, and was 'adamant that the [Department for Transport] should not accept unquestioningly the views of vested interests'. It saw the danger of increasing foreign ownership, especially by companies with no experience of the ports industry which may be tempted to sell off the land, and wanted the government to intervene when the national interest was threatened. 'Our ports are too valuable to be exposed to the unregulated whims of international capital,' it said.

True to form, it complained that the evidence it had taken on the need to divert cargo to ports outside the Greater South East was contradictory. 'Each vested interest insisted that theirs was the only possible approach.' The committee itself recognized the need for 'a more even distribution of port traffic across the country', and urged the government to use its planning and fiscal powers to nudge the market in the right direction. It wanted an 'integrated freight plan', and reminded the government that 'the commercial inland waterways are part of the country's strategic transport network and they deserve better'.

What the waterways actually have been getting, of course, is worse, with a hopelessly overspent Defra seeing them as a soft target for funding cuts. The Transport Committee quoted approvingly the words of John Dodwell, managing director of Water and Sea Freight Advisory Services, who complained that 'Defra have no interest in transport at all, so the commercial waterways are withering away for lack of attention.' The Transport Committee's recommendation – switching responsibility for waterways from Defra to the Department for Transport – sounds like good sense, though the implied disconnect between 'environment' and 'transport' is one of the reasons this country does not have a cogent transport policy. No one would quarrel with the committee's truism that the 'right balance' needs to be found between port development and environmental protection, but its own conception of what is right – expressed in the very next sentence – will chill as many hearts as it gladdens: 'Environmental concerns should not be allowed to trump economic considerations when port planning decisions are taken.' Substitute 'fish quota' for 'port planning', and you can see exactly where that kind of thinking takes us.

More encouragingly, British Waterways did, eventually, manage to put together the funding package it needed to open up the River Lea to construction traffic for the Olympic site. It came very late (February 2007), and the hope now must be that the race against time – to get the new lock built and in use – will be run at gold medal speed.

On 15 March 2007, Defra published its Marine Bill White Paper, *A Sea Change*. As my own book with its disconcertingly similar title was already heading for the printers, I had no time to read line by line through all 168 pages, but I did quickly search and find what I was looking for – confirmation that, yes, the government was still proposing a network of Marine Conservation Zones to protect endangered species and habitats, and to give damaged ecosystems time to recover. Most importantly, the level of protection in each zone would vary according to need, and could include 'highly protected marine reserves' from which 'all damaging or potentially damaging activity' would be excluded.

There were questions to be resolved about how many such zones should be designated, where and how big they should be, how long they should remain in force, the precise level of constraint in each case and what would happen when 'the ecosystem approach' conflicted with socio-economic objectives. Questions, in particular, about the great sea-elephant in the room – the fishing industry, whose rampage the White Paper did not directly confront, and whose activity is most damaging of all. Questions, too, about the strength of the government's own commitment. The campaign to get a Marine Bill into the legislative programme has been going on for at least eight years. Consultation followed consultation but it was finally expected – indeed Defra said as much – that it would happen in 2006–7. In its small print, the Queen's Speech of 2007 did include a commitment to proceed, but only as far as a draft (to be published by Easter 2008) rather than a full Marine Bill – in effect, yet another round of consultation. The best hope now is that this can be concluded in time for the bill – at last – to be drafted and laid before Parliament by the end of 2008, and that Labour will honour its manifesto commitment for a Marine Act before the next General Election. The fight goes on.

Index

Birds Directive, 315, 328, 328
Birdsall, Timothy, 218
Black, Kenneth, 182
Black Sea, 6–7
Blackpool, 27, 31, 32
blue whiting, 129–30, 189, 191
BMAPA, *see* British Marine
  Aggregate Producers Association
BMJ, see British Medical Journal
boats, *see* ships
Bournemouth, 25
Bow Backs, 274–7, 282
BP, 215
BPA, *see* British Ports Association
Bradshaw, Ben, 129, 148, 319
Braer, 234, 252, 256
Brighton, 18, 22, 23, 24, 28, 31
Bristol Channel, 53, 54
Britain: eastern, 36–9, 53, 75–6;
  human population, 9–11;
  separation from Europe, 7–8;
  shipbuilding, 12–16; temperatures,
  56–7
British Association for the
  Advancement of Science, 10
British Ecological Society, 316–17
British Marine Aggregate Producers
  Association (BMAPA), 89, 98, 100
British Medical Journal (BMJ),
  197–8, 207
British Ports Association (BPA), 259,
  304
British Resorts Association, 25, 28
British Seafarer, The, 104
British Transport Docks Board
  (BTDB), 269
British Waterways, 273, 274–6, 282
British Wind Energy Association, 310
Broads Authority, 64
Broomhead, Steven, 28
Brophy, Eddie, 91
BTDB, *see* British Transport Docks
  Board
BUPA, 207

Bush, George, Sr, 45
Bush, George W., 41–2, 43, 44,
  45–50, 51
Butler, James, 167, 173
bycatch, 131, 144, 153

Campaign to Protect Rural England
  (CPRE), 267
canals, 273, 274–7
Canterbury City Council, 77, 79
carbon capture and storage (CCS),
  307
carbon emissions, 329–31
Carpenter, David, 196–7
Casino Advisory Panel, 27
Cato Institute, 196–7
CCS, *see* carbon capture and storage
CEFAS, *see* Centre for Environment,
  Fisheries and Aquaculture
  Science
CEI, *see* Competitive Enterprise
  Institute
Cemex, 273
Centre for Environment, Fisheries
  and Aquaculture Science (CEFAS),
  100, 136
Centre for Human Ecology, 203, 204
Centrica, 307
CFP, *see* Common Fisheries Policy
Charles I, King, 110
Cheney, Dick, 47
Cheslin, David, 280–1
Citizens for a Better Environment,
  196
CLC, *see* International Conventions
  on Civil Liability for Oil Pollution
  Damage
Clover, Charles, 318
coastal: defences, 61–2, 71–2, 78–84,
  95; ecosystems, 59–60; strategy,
  62–9, 75
Coastal Concern Action Group, 91
coastline change, 4–5
Coastlink Network, 280

dredging, 89–91, 95–102
drugs, 293
DSP, *see* Diuretic Shellfish Poisoning
DTI, *see* Trade and Industry,
Department of
Dubai Ports World (DPW), 270, 271
Dunion, Kevin, 175, 181

Ebell, Myron, 42, 43, 44
EIAs, *see* Environmental Impact
Assessments
EJF, *see* Environmental Justice
Foundation
El Niño, 53
England's Sea Fisheries, 107, 112,
116, 118
English Heritage, 31, 32
English Nature: on CFP, 146; Dibden
Bay objections, 265–6; Lyme Bay
concern, 322; Overfalls position,
325; sediment transport study, 89,
100; Shell Haven objections, 267;
on SMPs, 65
English Tourist Board, 24
Environment, Department of the, 228
Environment, Food and Rural
Affairs, Department of, *see* Defra
Environment Agency: on bathing
water standards, 210; Bow Backs
plan, 276; coastal defences, 50;
energy policy, 307, 312; flood
map, 37; flood warnings, 38;
flood zone building concerns,
66–8; Marine Bill, 302, 306;
pollution role, 250; sediment
transport study, 89, 100; on
sewage treatment, 213; SMPs, 86;
Thames strategy, 70; waste
inspections, 294
Environment Times, 254
Environmental Impact Assessments
(EIAs), 151
Environmental Justice Foundation
(EJF), 157

Environmental Protection Agency
(EPA), 192, 194–5
*Environmental Science and
Technology*, 195, 196
EPA, *see* Environmental Protection
Agency
erosion: dredging effects, 97–102;
North Kent coast, 77–8, 79–81;
North Norfolk, 81–4, 101;
tackling, 78–9
Escherichia coli, 188, 209
European Commission, 128, 210,
215, 315
European Convention on Human
Rights, 92
Eurosion, 97
Exxon Valdez, 219, 252, 256
ExxonMobil, 43, 46, 47, 49, 197

faecal coliforms, 209–12
Falmouth, 222, 236
Farm Animal Welfare Council
(FAWC), 168
FAWC, *see* Farm Animal Welfare
Council
Felixstowe: cargo tonnage, 260;
containers, 261–2; development
proposal, 267–8; ownership, 267,
270, 272; road links, 284
Ferrovial, 270
Fischler, Franz, 144, 145
fish farming: case for, 156, 159–60;
density, 162; economics, 204–5;
effects on wild fish, 166–8, 172–3,
176–8; escapes, 171–2, 173–4,
176–7, 200; excrement, 160–1;
farmers' views, 178–9; fish food,
189–91; FoE recommendations,
181–2; government policy, 174–5,
199–203, 205–7; health of farmed
fish, 165–6, 168–71, 200; human
diet concerns, 191–9, 207–8;
morts, 161–5, 180, 189; organic,
179–80; ownership, 203–4;

Marine Management Organization
(MMO), 301, 306
Marine Nature Reserves, 321, 323
Marine Pollution Control Unit, 250
Marine Research Institute, 166
Marine Response Centre (MRC), 251
Marine Stewardship Council, 151
Marinet, 98, 303, 306
Maritime and Coastguard Agency
(MCA): list of ports, 259; role,
233, 249–51; survey of discharges,
234–5, 236–7, 247
Maritime Statistics Directive, 259–60
Market and Coastal Towns
Association, 30
Marmara, Sea of, 6–7
MARPOL, *see* International
Convention for the Prevention of
Pollution from Ships
Massachusetts Institute of
Technology, 53
MCA, *see* Maritime and Coastguard
Agency
MCS, *see* Marine Conservation
Society
Medical Research Council (MRC),
211
Medway Ports Authority, 328
MEHRAs, *see* Marine Environmental
High Risk Areas
MEIR, *see* Marine Emergency
Information Room
Merchant Shipping Act, 237
Milford Haven, 215–16, 217, 236,
241, 251, 260
Minches, the, 242–5, 247, 251
MMO, *see* Marine Management
Organization
Moffat, Colin, 185
Monbiot, George, 44, 307
Morley, Elliot, 91, 102, 143, 145
MRC, *see* Marine Response Centre
MRC, *see* Medical Research Council
Mucking Flats, 267

NAS, *see* National Academy of
Sciences
NASA, 52, 57
NASCO, *see* North Atlantic Salmon
Conservation Organisation
National Academy of Sciences (NAS),
48–9
National Center for Atmospheric
Research, 53
National Contingency Plan for
Marine Pollution from Shipping
and Offshore Installations, 249–50
National Federation of Fishermen's
Organisations (NFFO), 143,
145–6
National Piers Society, 22
National Snow and Ice Data Center,
57, 58
NATO, 128
Natura 2000, 315
NEAFC, *see* North East Atlantic
Fisheries Commission
Net Benefits: on fishing data, 137; on
quota enforcement, 132, 133;
recommendations, 141, 148,
149–52; on UK fishing turnover,
138, 140
Network Rail, 272
New Deal for Transport, A, 277
New York Times, 46
Newfoundland, 110, 111, 121–2,
123
Newlyn, 123–4, 135, 222, 224, 260
News of the World, 18, 24
NFFO *see* National Federation of
Fishermen's Organisations
no-take zones, 317–19, 323, 330
Noah's Flood, 5–6, 7
Norfolk Broads, 64, 95
Norsk Hydro, 179
North Atlantic Oscillation, 53
North Atlantic Salmon Conservation
Organisation (NASCO), 166–7,
173, 177–8

United Nations (UN): Environment
Programme (UNEP), 40, 254;
Food and Agriculture
Organisation (FAO), 157, 159;
Law of the Sea conferences, 125,
126, 127

Waddell, L. A., 11
Wallingford, HR, 83, 90, 100, 102
waste exports, 293–6
Waterways for Tomorrow, 277
Waterworks River, 275–6
Watson, Robert, 46
Webster, John, 176, 178
WEC, *see* World Energy Council
Wester Ross Fisheries Trust, 167
Whale and Dolphin Conservation
Society, 267
Whateley, Bishop, 10
Whelan, Ken, 177
Whitby, 115, 133
whitefish, 132–3, 135, 138–9, 141
WHO, *see* World Health
Organization
Wildfowl and Wetlands Trust, 267
Wildlife and Countryside Act, 315,
321, 322
Wildlife and Countryside Link, 303,
312, 320, 324–5

Wildlife Trusts, 65, 267, 303, 322,
324
Williamson, Henry, 208
Wilson, Allan, 175, 176, 199
Wilson, Harold, 219, 269
wind farms, 309–11
Windsor, Malcolm, 178
World Conservation Union, 167
World Energy Council (WEC), 308
World Health Organization (WHO),
192, 193–5, 211, 214
World Summit on Sustainable
Development (2002), 157
Worldwide Fund for Nature (WWF):
on CFP, 146; on fish farming,
205–6, 207; on fish-feed, 189–90;
on fish quotas, 143, 148, 153;
fishery concerns, 191; Marine
Health Check, 326–7; on
MEHRAs, 241, 247; on *Prestige*
disaster, 254; salmon report, 167;
Strangford Lough concern, 322;
Wildlife and Countryside Link,
303
WWF, *see* Worldwide Fund for
Nature

Young, Lady, 66, 67

ALSO FROM EDEN PROJECT BOOKS

RUBBISH!
Dirt on Our Hands and the Crisis Ahead
by Richard Girling
ISBN 9781903919446, £7.99, paperback

We can no longer cope with our waste. Every hour in the UK we throw away enough rubbish to fill the Albert Hall – a statistic quoted so often that perhaps we've stopped imagining what it means. And every year the flow accelerates.

The story of our rubbish – from the first human bowel movement to the littering of outer space – is at the heart of Girling's book. But it is also, unmistakably, a call to arms – not simply for us to remember the three 'R's – Reduce, Re-use, Recycle – but for us to fight for investment in new ideas and put brave initiative ahead of reliance on ancient systems now crumbling before our eyes. Hard-hitting, passionate, provocative, Girling is also persuasive, often funny and always entertaining.

'Compulsively readable and often hilarious, as well as important.' John Carey, *Sunday Times*

CONFESSIONS OF AN ECO SINNER
Travels to Find Where My Stuff Comes From
by Fred Pearce
ISBN 9781905811106, £12.99, trade paperback

In search of the source of the cotton in his shirt, the prawns in his curry and the people who grew, mined or made all his stuff, Pearce travels from rainforest to desert, up mountains and down mines from oil field to shanty town to brothel. And tracking his personal 'footprint' he finds himself questioning an extraordinary number of accepted green truths. Should Kenyan green beans go back on his shopping list? Should he stop campaigning for a clean coastline and start shouting 'Save wildlife, sh** on the beach'? While he's at it, should he be cheering for Bangladeshi sweatshops too?

Challenging a series of green assumptions, Pearce moves green thinking on to a new more sophisticated plane.

'Fred Pearce goes out and sees the world as well as thinking and writing about it; he is one of the few that understand the Earth as it really is and we must listen to him.'   James Lovelock, author of *The Revenge of Gaia*

WHEN THE RIVERS RUN DRY
What Happens When Our Water Runs Out?
by Fred Pearce
ISBN 9781903919583, £8.99, paperback

The world is running out of water. Some of the world's largest rivers now trickle into sand miles from the ocean, exhausted by human need. We are emptying ancient reserves of underground water and most will never naturally refill. Even England faces crisis. With less water per capita than Ethiopia or Sudan, the demand for water is accelerating but it is raining less.

As landscapes shrivel, conflicts over water grow. So is there hope? Yes – but only if we revolutionize the way we treat water. Terrifying about the consequences if governments fail to act, Pearce is also truly empowering in his advocacy of the ways we all need to change.

'If ever a book has been written that demands to be read it is this one. This is that rare thing – a journey through a hugely important and complex subject in the company of a natural storyteller who makes you feel intelligent.'   Tim Smit

THE LAST GENERATION
How Nature Will Take Her Revenge for Climate Change
by Fred Pearce
ISBN 9781903919880, £8.99, paperback

Since the last ice age we have prospered in a stable, predictable climate. But our generation is the last to be so blessed. Pearce lays bare the terrifying prognosis for our planet. Climate change from now on will not be gradual. We are reaching tipping points. Man-made global warming is on the verge of unleashing unstoppable planetary forces; Planet Earth is primed for chaos.

Forget what environmentalists have told you about Mother Nature being a helpless victim of human excess. The truth is the opposite. She is a wild and resourceful beast given to fits of rage. And now that we are provoking her beyond endurance, she is starting to seek her revenge.

'The most frightening book that I have ever read.'
John Gribbin, *Independent*

A GOOD LIFE
The Guide to Ethical Living
edited by Leo Hickman
ISBN 9781903919897, £16.99, trade paperback

Ethical living is about more than environmental concerns. It is also about achieving positive change by improving our relationships with those around us, and also those we never meet but who make the products we buy.

This guide to the ethics of everyday life, with its invaluable directory, has already established itself as a bestselling resource for the twenty-first century. Now updated and expanded it is a must-have book for all.

'The ideal book for anyone who wants guidance on making choices that will benefit them, their family and the planet.'
Country Living

THE FINAL CALL
Investigating Who Really Pays for Our Holidays
by Leo Hickman
ISBN 9781905811069, £7.99, paperback

The Alps . . . the Caribbean . . . Thailand . . . We are all keen tourists. But behind tourism's façade of stunning sights and smiling locals is an ugly reality, and it is spreading unchecked across the globe.

Travelling around the world, from sunlounger to ecolodge, theme park to golf course, Hickman speaks to all the key protagonists to discover who is really paying for our trips away, and how to make sure we have a 'good' holiday.

Here is what is NOT in the glossy brochures.

'Excellent. One of the clearest and most sobering analyses I've ever seen on the environmental, social and economic damage done by tourism.' Philip Pullman

THE MEANING OF THE 21ST CENTURY
A Vital Blueprint for Ensuring Our Future
by James Martin
ISBN 9781903919866, £8.99, paperback

We live at a turning point in human history. Ahead is a century of massive change. Either we learn to manage this change, or we allow it to control us and face devastating consequences. James Martin explains with clarity and precision the nature of the challenges we face, from global warming to famine, religious extremism and technological advance, and then defines the thinking that will provide us with solutions for the future. Far from doom-mongering, his book is an extraordinarily optimistic and empowering argument for transition on a global scale: a ringing call to arms and a pragmatic blueprint for action. It is essential reading for everyone.

'On rare occasions a special book introduces a vital new idea into the public consciousness. This is one of those books.'
Susan Greenfield, Director of the Royal Institution